Black Powder
GUN DIGEST

Edited By Toby Bridges

with R. O. Ackerman

Dan Cotterman

Bob Furst

Dean A. Grennell

Turner Kirkland

Jack Lewis

Skeeter Skelton

Chuck Tyler

Bob Zwirz

DIGEST BOOKS INC., NORTHFIELD, ILLINOIS

ABOUT THE COVERS

Our covers, front and back, illustrate the wide variety of black powder guns and accessories available to today's shooters. The front cover pictures replicas of a percussion squirrel rifle, a flintlock Kentucky pistol and a flintlock Pennsylvania rifle, along with powder horns, coonskin cap and hunting pouch. Featured on the back cover are replicas of an 1860 Army revolver, a Civil War canteen and an 1860 U.S. Cavalry saber. The Sharps carbine is an original. All items are from Dixie Gun Works, Union City, Tennessee. Photo of the Minuteman on the inside front cover was taken at Knott's Berry Farm, Buena Park, California, as was the photo of the Thomas Jefferson bust on the inside back cover.

Editorial Director
JACK LEWIS

Technical Editor
DEAN A. GRENNELL

Research Editor
MARK THIFFAULT

Art Director
ANDREW J. GRENNELL

Staff Artists
RAYMOND H. BISHOP
CATHERINE A. READE

Production Supervisor
JUDY K. RADER

Produced by
Charger Productions

ISBN 0-695-80360-3   Library of Congress Card Number 72-86645

CONTENTS

INTRODUCTION

I'D LIKE TO think that Davy Crockett, Daniel Boone and Fess Parker all had something to do with the returned interest in the black powder shooting sports. There is no way, of course, of determining precisely what really has affected this interest, but I do know that, after I portrayed Davy Crockett in the Disney series, I began to receive a great number of letters from black powder buffs. Even then — well over a decade ago — there were more individuals interested in this form of recreation than one would have suspected.

Then, about the time that I started the Daniel Boone series, I found the mail from those interested in muzzleloaders reaching a new high. And I suppose that puts me in something of a chicken-and-the-egg situation, wondering whether the TV series helped spark interest in black powder shooting or whether it might have been the other way around.

Whatever the reasons, both Daniel Boone and, although not in true historic sequence, Davy Crockett did much to develop my own interest in target shooting and even hunting with muzzleloaders.

As a boy on my grandfather's ranch in Comanche County, Texas, I started with a BB gun, graduating in turn to a .22, then a .410 shotgun. In those Depression days, rabbit stew was a frequent part of the family diet.

But I didn't handle a black powder firearm until cast as Davy Crockett, when I had to learn to load and fire with enough authority not to arouse the black powder brotherhood. After that, I was asked to ride on the National Rifle Association float in the Rose Bowl Parade. From that, I began to learn just how much interest there really was in caplock and flintlock shooting.

My son, Eli, is almost 12 at this writing and I enjoy taking him into the mountain country to introduce him to the way in which his ancestors hunted and protected themselves.

In helping him to load and fire the replica muzzleloaders of today, I cannot help but feel he is gaining a slight taste of what it took to build this country...and perhaps I'm re-experiencing some of those feelings, too. I've never tried to analyze the feeling of comradeship during those periods when we're shooting together, but I know they're good. And I want to keep them that way!

Fess Parker

Santa Barbara, California

Fess Parker

CHAPTER 1

IN THE BEGINNING...

As With Creation,
There Is Some Doubt
Among Doubters As
To The Origination
Of Black Powder!

It IS WITH CERTAIN dismay that we must regard the manner in which the beginnings of explosive mixtures have been obscured. We can, with little effort, trace modern smokeless propellants back to their cradle, but woe be unto the person who hopes to suffuse the mists that forever dim the origin of black powder.

He is confronted at once with a bewilderment of contradictions, even within the texts of responsible historians. If the scope of his efforts would take the reader to the very roots of discovery he is obliged to deal in cautious generalities. In the opposite case he may, without risk, follow a path already worn to boredom by a few literary buffoons and thereby color his own picture of what happened in those distant centuries. There is doubtless some comfort within such undisciplined intellectual vacuums, enjoyed by those who write without conscience and those who read without concern. A certain British author implies, frankly and without embarrassment, that gunpowder was "invented" by a child early in the Fourteenth Century!

It is appropriate to acknowledge from the outset that no one can state with certainty where, when or by whose hand gunpowder first was made. Countless hours spent reading and re-reading dozens of texts, library references and historical chronologies will only add to one's confusion and generate strong feelings of disillusionment. If, of course, you are willing to read one book and thereby settle for one author's version of what happened, you probably will find no cause for discontent. Just remember that, if he makes positive statements with respect to dates, geography or cultural origin, he is inviting you onto thin ice.

We will come to more positive statements later. Right now, we are groping around in the first couple of hundred years after the birth of Christ. It is not without reason that we may assume that gunpowder was the independent discovery of several cultures. There is a weight of evidence

The heavy armor worn by this warrior might have saved him from the arrow's deadly tip or the lance's sharpened edge, but it was little comfort against the wheel-mounted cannon sitting in the background.

Crude as the methods might have been, the early uses of incendiary substances were helpful to both attackers and defenders alike; for one it was a means of capturing a well armed fortress, for the other a means of protecting it.

which tips the scales in favor of experimenters of the Later Han Dynasty in China. However, Hindu and Arab alchemists also were said to have known of the combustion properties of niter, charcoal and sulphur.

The fact that each could have worked without the benefit of knowing what the other was doing can be blamed on the poor communications of the time. Paper, for example, was expensive and preciously scarce, its use customarily reserved for the recording of religious text. Far to the west, Hellenic alchemists, like their Han, Hindu and Arab contemporaries, pursued in vain such fancies as magical elixirs of life and a way to counterfeit gold.

Disregarding an animistic belief in magic and demons, even the practice of geomancy, we must acknowledge the accumulation of a large body of experience as a direct result of the painstaking and methodical work of the alchemist. Magicians, sorcerers — whatever they may be named — these practicioners ultimately managed to elevate their quasi-science to a level worthy of respect. The essential ingredient of gunpowder, niter (potassium nitrate), could not have been produced by them had they never undertaken a careful study of the separation and purification of salts. Even at this level of development alchemy faced several centuries of involvement with mystical spirits, astrology and other diversive beliefs before its liberation as a science of rationality.

Because of the presence of niter in gunpowder, an ambient source of oxygen was not necessary. In other words, since the niter contained oxygen, this black, mealy concoction would continue to burn even though "smothered" in close confinement. The phenomenon was to tax medieval physicists and chemists to the utmost. Could the influence of a fire drug's power have ended with this curiosity? Obviously not.

The elbow cannon was of Venetian origin and, like today's modern mortar, depended upon a very high angle of trajectory. Illustration was taken from a 1535 Paris book.

This early illustration depicts Marcus Graecus and his invention, the fire tubes. This was an early combination of rifle and cannon. Note the complexity of its design.

Fascination with its special properties piqued Taoist alchemists of the T'ang Dynasty into pouring the black mixture into segments of bamboo to create what was probably the first firecracker. At about the same time, it is written, the Hindus also were going bang and ducking splinters. And, speaking of occupational hazards, a Taoist bulletin is reported to have cautioned alchemists that attempts to further stimulate the action of the fire drug with arsenic could result in singed beards.

Conditions that stimulated the advancement of gunpowder's use are necessarily left to surmise. It is, however, reasonable that someone derived the intelligence to employ the stuff as rocket fuel from observing the effect of leaving one end of a bamboo cracker open. By the time the years of our calendar reached a thousand there had been such innovations as rocket arrows, grenades, simple bombs and other pyrotechnic delights. Nonetheless, gunpowder's white cloud was not destined to mushroom into serious military use for another two or three centuries. Those Chinese bombs and grenades of the Liao Dynasty did not contain charges of sufficient brisance to produce anything more serious than a distracting whoosh!

Gunpowder was moving west where its influence served to change the life-style and destiny of every human for all time to come. In the meanwhile, it serves our purpose to pause for a moment to consider Greek fire. This burning liquid seems to have made its first appearance in warfare in the latter half of the Seventh Century as an invention of Callinicus, a Syrian architect who had become a citizen of Constantinople.

Greek fire, wild fire, sea fire or whatever, its composition appears to have varied as much as its name: Pitch, naphtha, sulphur, phosphide of calcium — even quicklime. Whatever its ingredients, Greek fire succeeded in engulfing

Appearing to have been made of heavy wooden planks, this version of a Sixteenth Century 'tank' is evidence of the increased development in the use of firearms at that time.

Although not very practical, this pistol from the Renaissance period could be used as a hand-to-hand weapon once it had been fired. It was most likely used as an ornamental weapon only.

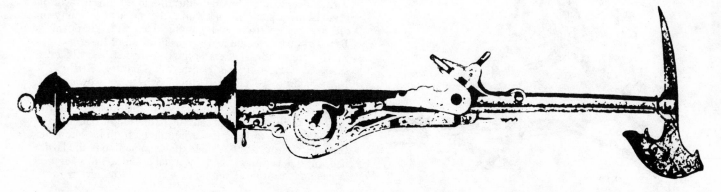

more than one marauding armada in a horror of flame. Notable among these events was an attempt to take Constantinople in A.D. 673, when Saracen ships were burned. Again, in A.D. 941, Russia's Prince Igor brought 10,000 ships to conquer that same well defended city only to have them thoroughly incinerated. Squirted from large tubes, this fearsome liquid burned when it came into contact with water. In addition to being indifferent to snuffing by water, Greek fire is said to have possessed the uneasy capability of exploding when attempts were made to move it overland. That last characteristic would have hampered its widespread use in those bumpy times. It is significant in closing to remember the use of flamethrowers in Twentieth Century warfare; a distant relationship seems to exist.

At this point, the justification of assuming any relationship between Greek fire and gunpowder is left to the reader. The important consideration here is gunpowder's refinement as a constituent of war as it moved westward. A Greek monk, Marcus Graecus, produced a manuscript in A.D. 846 that is said to have contained thirty-five recipes for making gunpowder. However, W.H.B. and Joseph Smith, in their book, Small Arms of the World, observe that some of the intelligence relating to gunpowder could have been an investation of Thirteenth Century translators. Another author, Raymond Dawson, in The Legacy of China, illustrates a "first" formula for gunpowder as extracted from a series of columnar characters discovered in a manuscript of the year A.D. 1044.

At about the same time there is evidence of a Saracen awareness of the ignition factor of niter. From these manifestations we are inclined to favor a more widespread credit for the development of gunpowder than is allowed by the presumptive ex parte of some historians.

Whether, prior to the Thirteenth Century, the advent of those crude, explosive improvisations was a matter of simultaneous creation or a discovery specifically attributable to an individual or culture, must forever remain meat for the contention of those who care to argue. It is more important for us to move ahead to A.D. 1248 when, upon being impugned by certain of the clergy for the practice of black art, Roger Bacon wrote at length as if to glorify the many wonders of nature and thereby divorce his experiments from any manner of magic.

His paper includes this significant observation: "Thus we may imitate thunder and lightning; for sulphur, nitre and charcoal, which by themselves produce no sensible effect, explode with great noise when closely confined and set on fire."

Those who credit the "invention" of gunpowder to Roger Bacon may have failed to note that Bacon, himself, laid no claim to its creation. Furthermore, while Bacon was capable of scientific rationality and did, in fact, conduct experiments on a level worthy of our respect, our picture of contributors holds better perspective for us, if we remember that his time and endeavor was probably more taken with concern over Christian educational reform in favor of establishing a pan-Catholic world, the moral philosophy of religious comparison and so on, than with gunpowder. Bacon's papers contain little or no mention of firearms.

The amorphous backgatherings described begin to take shape as we enter the Fourteenth Century. Bartholdus Niger, later to be called Berthold Schwarz, (Schwarz was intended to be descriptive of his reputed involvement with black magic) was interested in what this novel explosive mixture might do as a means of exorcising a ball from a tube. Pursuant to his interest he moved from his abode in Frieburg, Germany, to Venice, Italy, sometime in the latter half of the century where he established a shop for the design and making of a cannon. Passing acknowledgement of

One of the earliest uses of flame throwing devices appeared in the fifteenth century edition of De machinis Bellicis. The syphon was based on the bellows.

From the same edition is another rendition of an early flame throwing device. This second type of thrower used a piston.

Designed by Leonardo de Vinci, this was one of the more advanced designs during the early sixteenth century. The field piece displayed the ability to be aimed both vertically and horizontally. Note the spearlike projectile.

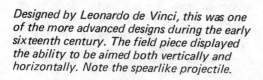

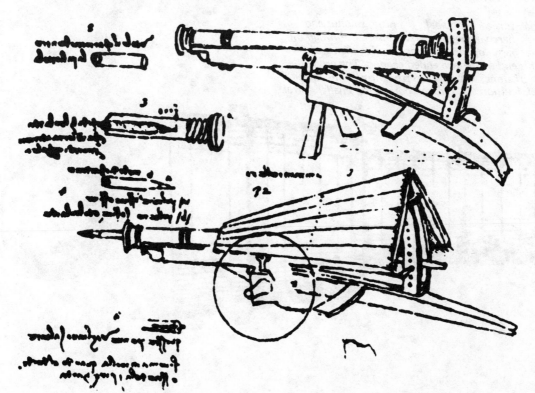

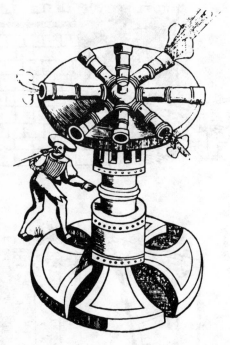

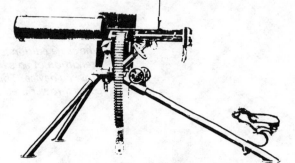

This repeating, rotating cannon was nice in theory, but in most probability turned into a real disaster if ever really built. It was one of the first repeating designs.

Having a design all its own, the weird looking armament at the top was another early, nearly practical, repeating concept. It used several barrels assembled in a fan like configuration. The belt-fed .30 caliber machine gun was later based on this design and proved successful.

To load this early odd-ball, the nitre, sulphur and willow charcoal gunpowder was inserted through the smaller barrel opening. A wooden plug then sealed off this end of the two ended cannon. The projectile, made of stone, was then inserted through the larger barrel. Ignition was through port in the smaller barrel.

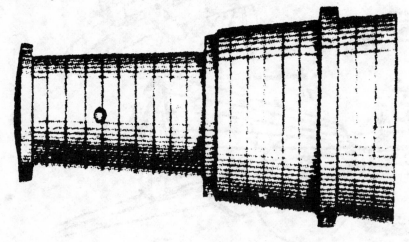

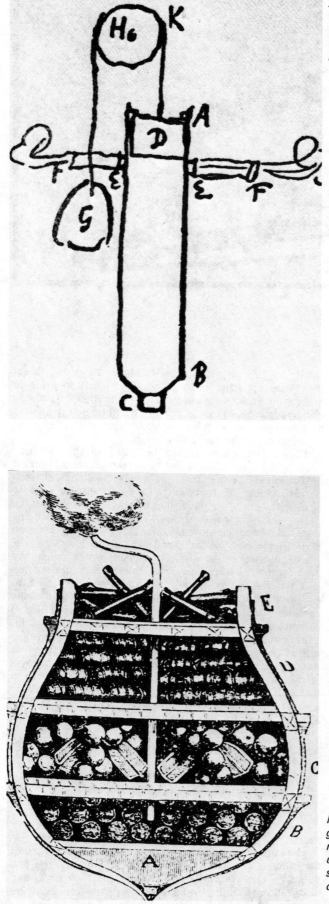

Although early cannons fired, they rarely shot where they were supposed to. Plans show the use of quadrants to aid in getting right elevation.

this Franciscan monk's contributions to the advancement of gunpowder and cannon tersely mentions that in 1384 he was sentenced to death by the Senate of Venice, ostensibly for becoming too vocal in complaining of not being paid for his work.

Berthold Schwarz and his work with propellant forces is no more than mentioned when, as if to throw us back into controversy, a voice is heard proclaiming that, early in the Twelfth Century, the Chinese made a transition from the rocket to the barrel gun.

The Sung people were supposed to have used a fire lance against the Chin Tartars at that time. Then, circa 1280, there is the hazy claim for an appearance of a metal barreled gun somewhere in the Old World. However, the fire lance is described as a small tube full of rocket powder that was secured to the end of a long pole to be held by soldiers and used in close fighting. There is no justification for regarding this device as a "barrel gun" and references to metal barreled firearms "somewhere in the Old World" seem to usurp one's intellectual self-respect. Indeed, the fire tubes employed for the hurling of Greek fire in the Seventh Century seem to deserve classification as metal barreled guns if we are to use definitions freely.

Just as we have come to realize the foolishness of favoring any individual or culture with the invention or discovery of gunpowder, we must now see that a similar attitude could easily be assumed as regards the beginning of the gun. Of greater consequence to the objective of this discussion is the realization that gunpowder, for all its use in primitive rocketry and fireworks, achieved no status until it was first used in the cannon. From that time forward its impact on social balance and the entire military, economic and political system of ideas was to be felt by all the world.

The cannon with its awesome power, and ultimately smallarms with their superior range, fostered a technical revolution in the art of war. Those who were forced into battle without cannon and gunpowder suffered from an impossible disadvantage while those fortunate enough to possess them achieved an invincibility never before known.

The indignity with which an aristocracy of lords and nobles was to receive gunpowder in Europe is understandable. Realize for a moment that the booming of cannon foretold an end to the bastions of a system of determining social and economic superiority that was based on the holding of large areas of land.

This "evil brew concocted in the dark vaults of the devil's kitchen" was changing warfare from a pastime of kings and nobles to the serious business of killing and destruction. Through the use of gunpowder the commoner began to assume a stature that imperiled that of the ruling aristocracy and, with equal significance, put an end to the threat imposed by droves of roving barbarians. At last, the Occidental world had its own fire-breathing dragon.

Resembling an oversized hand grenade, this early infernal machine was designed to hurl unusable cannons, iron and stone cannon balls in every direction as powder ignited.

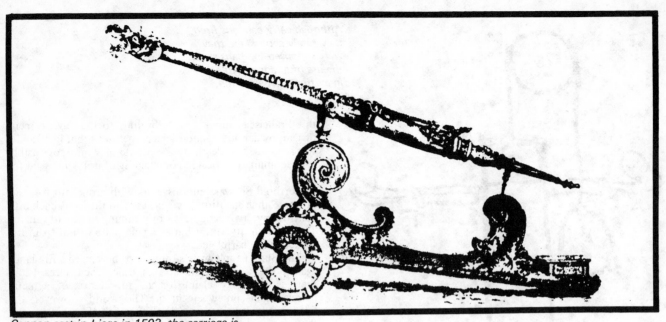

Cannon cast in Liege in 1503, the carriage is made of carved oak, the barrel is made of chased bronze. This is not merely an ornamental piece of work, but it is really an excellent example of a very early breech-loading black powder cannon.

Although historians share a broad tendency to disagree with regard to gunpowder's time and place of origination, none of them lack accord or conviction in appraising its significance. If asked to name the one most important discovery since pre-historic times, one could, with every scholarly confidence, name gunpowder. The development of the compass and the introduction of block printing usually are named along with gunpowder, but no authority assumes priority for either. Gunpowder, in fact, is usually the principle of such analyses as would establish logical reasons for crediting it as a sort of foundation for all modern science and technology. The flash it made and its pungent smoke attracted the attention of everyone.

To the alchemist there was the prompting of additional curiosity toward the wonders of solution and crystallization, as in the production of one of its essentials, niter. It was known that neither sulphur nor charcoal would burn if smothered, therefore the assumption that the niter somehow furnished air for combustion. Additional deduction led to speculation that air must, in some way, contain niter or, at least, some spirit thereof. Furthermore, it had long since become common knowledge that animals, like fire, could not endure in the absence of air. Centuries of experimentation and controversy, thus based on such simple assumptions and curiosity prompted by the performance of this rudimentary mixture, ultimately led to the discovery of oxygen and finally to the basis of modern chemistry.

The influence of gunpowder on technology was perhaps even more powerful. The casting of bronze had scarcely begun to shift from church bells to cannon when there arose a need for more sophisticated implements to be employed in providing a smooth, straight bore within the rough casting. That is, after the introduction of iron balls. The first objects to be propelled by gunpowder were stones sometimes said to measure as much as twenty inches across! These brutish missiles were devastatingly effective against fortress walls, but as can be imagined, were dangerously unpredictable in the matter of accuracy.

The cry for shot that could be put on target with greater confidence, followed by the ball and the machines to bore

for its use, apparently was the foretoken of greater things than were apparent at the time. J.D. Bernal, writing in Science in History, states with certainty that "...the machinery developed for the boring of cannon was to be used in making accurate cylinders which gave the early steam engines a chance to prove their efficiency."

Further influences are to be noted in the increased interest in ballistics that must have been generated because of the greater range that was made possible with gunpowder. Subsequent considerations of ballistics were to deal with problems involving objects in rapid motion, violently discharged by the powerful action of expanding gases. Mathematics moved forward by reason of renewed curiosities in physical and chemical sciences.

For all its dynamic implications, gunpowder's biography is not without its droll moments. There was an understandable tendency among nobleman and commoner alike to regard an invasion of noise, flame and smoke with suspicious indignation. Late in the Fourteenth Century, Froissart chronicled this account of Philip van Artevelde and his army laying siege to Oudenarde: The cannoneers "made a marveylous great bombarde shotying stone of marveylous weyght and when this bombarde shot is made suche a noyse in the goynge as though all the dyvels of hell had been in the way." In A.D. 1346, Edward III had at least twenty guns at the siege of Calais, according to Carmon in Firearms. A poem of the time glimpses the action:

> Gonners to schew ther arte
> In to the town in many a parte
> Schote many a fulle gret stone.
> Thankyd be God and Mary myld
> The hurt nothir man, woman ne child.
> To the housis thow they did harm
> Sent Barbara! then was the cry
> When the stone in the stone did fly.

Here are some other excerpts from literary comment of the time: "The reik, smeuk, and the stink of the gun puldir." "The women have their arms..and their necks and faces, adorned with..various sorts of figures impressed by

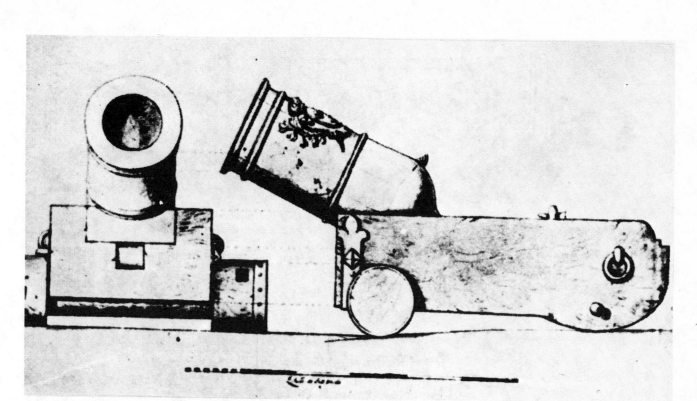

Designed in 1660 by the Chevalier de Ressous, this early mortar was designed for use aboard warships. Ship builders had to completely re-design ships to handle placement and tonnage.

Galileo looked at the cannon with physics in mind. Later, Benjamin Robins established the first ballistics table.

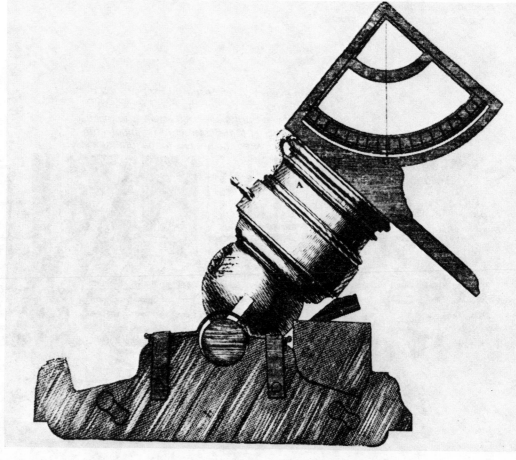

About the time that this seventeenth century German cast cannon was made, such weapons were designated in caliber by the size and weight of the round they fired; this was an eight pounder.

Drilling the cavities became known as boring. The use of mechanized equipment to bore cannon barrels marked a very important technical development.

Cannon makers were constantly trying to discover better methods of casting the iron for cannon barrels. It was during one such attempt to make a stronger barrel that Bessemer in the nineteenth century discovered the process to manufacture steel.

gunpowder." "Dievlish practises, of poysons, of pistoles, of stabbing knives, and of gunnepouder traynes." "Such Gunne-powder Oathes they were, that I wonder how the Seeling held together." "If he founde a corner of his neighbour's house burning, he wold of great love and polycye lay on fagottes and gunpowder to put out the fyre."

The alchemist thought of niter as the very essence of combustibility. However, before we examine its indispensable contribution to the combustion of gunpowder, a closer look at the nature of niter — or saltpeter as it is popularly named — is worth our time. It is, as has been noted, capable of evolving oxygen. In form it appears as long, six-sided, prismatic crystals. It produces an immediate cooling sensation when taken into the mouth and, as might be expected, tastes salty. Although used medicinally, a dose of as little as thirty grams has been said to be capable of causing death.

It is appropriate here to note that a similar reference reports the possibility of recovery from a dose of as much as sixty grams. In fairly recent times jealous wives are said to have slipped a measure of saltpeter into their husband's food or drink in the belief that they were thereby suppressing the latter's amorous inclinations. The husband thus suspected might better have allowed his wife to continue in the belief that the stuff was working. Saltpeter is in no way an anaphrodisiac. She may as well have hidden his boots in agreement with Aristotle's belief that going barefoot helped to hold the oversexed in control.

This most interesting of black powder's triunity bursts asunder when heated, because of intra-crystal pressure developed from the excitation of vapor occluded at the time of crystallization. It is said to ignite at relatively low temperatures and will melt at between 335 and 340 degrees Centigrade. Its oxygen is released continuously during the burning of the sulphur, which ignites at between 360 and 365 degrees Centigrade, and the charcoal. The process results in the changing of potassium nitrate to potassium nitrite, while the sulphur becomes sulphur dioxide and the carbon leaves carbon dioxide. One gram of powder normally will yield from 250 to 300 millimeters of gas, accounting for the violent explusion of projectiles.

Like sulphur, saltpeter can be mined from caves or fissures in rocks. Dried at 105 degrees Fahrenheit for four hours, it contains not less than ninety-nine percent potassium nitrate. The old way to make saltpeter involved the building of sheds for protection from rain and the drying effects of the sun. Animal refuse and vegetable remains were used with ashes and calcareous earth, all of which were mixed with loose soil. The mixture was turned frequently with a spade and liberally sprinkled with urine, which contains a large amount of nitrogen.

After a couple of years this nitrogen converts to nitric acid which gets together with the potassium carbonate in the ashes and refuse and vegetable remains to form niter. The potassium nitrate was then separated through lixiviation. A newer method manufactures potassium nitrate from native potassium chloride and native sodium nitrate. Both of these crude materials are cheap and abundant and the so-called "conversion saltpeter" thus produced results in 99.9 percent pure potassium nitrate.

Van Nostrand's Scientific Encyclopedia says that "Black powder consists of an intimate mixture of finely divided solids, seventy-five percent potassium nitrate, fifteen percent carbon, ten percent sulphur. Powders for sporting guns contain a slightly larger percentage of potassium nitrate (seventy-five to seventy-eight percent), smaller percentage of carbon (fifteen to twelve percent), and a variation of sulphur from nine to twelve percent. Mining or blasting powders, where large volumes of gas are desired, may have

fourteen to twenty-one percent carbon and thirteen to eighteen percent sulphur. The heat evolved per gram is 500 to 700 calories, and the temperature of the explosion is estimated at 2700 degrees Centigrade."

The formula copied in the foregoing paragraph, as well as any others that appear in this discussion are not intended as instructions for the mixing of black powder. Weighty volumes dedicated to pharmaceutical dispensing invariably caution the druggist not to sell saltpeter to "young experimenters." Adults, too, are well cautioned regarding the dangers of experimenting with making black powder. Our intent is to discuss, not instruct, with the idea of taking an informative look at black powder to find out what it actually is and at the same time review its somewhat apocryphal history.

With sulphur igniting at just over 360 degrees Centigrade and black powder igniting at just under 290 degrees on the same scale, we have a strong suggestion of the potency of saltpeter as a part of the mixture. Formulation appears to vary greatly with proportions of each ingredient being regulated in order to achieve some special effect. Roger Bacon, for all his diversified activities, took time to state a formula calling for roughly forty percent saltpeter, thirty percent sulphur and thirty percent charcoal (he preferred hazelwood). Compare that with the Van Nostrand formula. In so doing you will have a fair comparison between what might be thought of as "early" and "late" concepts.

As if to add to the haze of variety, there was the adoption of brown powder or "cocoa powder" in Germany, circa 1880. Initially, it consisted of large grains — about an inch long and one-and-one-third inches in diameter — each having a single canal. Brown powder differed from ordinary black powder in that its making utilized either underburned charcoal or a so-called "red" charcoal made from burning rye straw. The composition of brown powder reportedly called for a higher proportion of saltpeter with a reduced amount of charcoal and sulphur. The rye-straw variety saw some sporting use in the United States in the 1890s, principally as a product of the old California Powder Works.

The dizzying array of components and proportions continues as we borrow the following from Philip B. Sharpe's Complete Guide to Handloading: "Chlorate gunpowders of various compositions have been proposed and patented ever since the Civil War, and even before it. Besides potassium chlorate, they contain almost anything that might be found around the house or laboratory, patents revealing that such materials as charcoal, coal dust, sawdust, coffee grounds, sugar, alum, corn oil, linseed oil, ground bark, charcoal from seaweed, etc., have been incorporated in the various formulas."

Sugar was used in the manufacture of "white gunpowder" of Civil War prominence. This was another powder which made use of potassium chlorate, along with a measure of yellow prussiate of potash and twenty-three parts of sulphur.

Sharpe relates, "While it lacked many of the excellent propelling qualities of ordinary black gunpowder and was extremely corrosive on the soft iron and mild steel barrels, it simplified the process of cleaning the gun and therein lies its sole virtue."

By now we may well be thinking that, as long as saltpeter or something similar is present to supply the oxygen needed to sustain combustion in the absence of air, most anything will burn and thus produce the expanding gas necessary to classification as a propellant. The assumption is essentially correct. However, to achieve any acceptable degree of efficiency, careful control must be exercised. With this acknowledgement we come to the commercial

This illustration of the Eighteenth Century
cannon clearly shows the advancement of the cannon in
less than three centuries, from the odd ball designs
of the Renaissance to the rise in armored sea power.

manufacture of black powder.

Primitive gunpowder making is said to have employed the crudest of techniques. The resulting product was equally rudimentary, a fact that rendered it more useful as a fuel for pyrotechnic displays than as a propellant. At first the niter, sulphur and charcoal were pulverized and blended in stone mortars. Mills were used later in the interests of increased production, but the product remained imperfect and the action of the mills imposed the danger of explosion. In powdered form the mixture burned too rapidly with the result that even the most careful artistry of the cannoneer in preparing his charge was often not sufficient to avoid disaster. To the reverse, too cautious a load would fail to expel the projectile with the needed velocity.

With a need for predictability, powder makers began to use a simple process of graining in addition to the practice of varying ingredient proportions. This newer approach to a controlled burning rate, an advent of the Fifteenth Century, represented a major advance in technology. The powdery blend was wetted while being pounded in a pestle. The wetting agent best for this purpose is said to have been alcohol or, possibly in favor of economy and availability, the mother liquor would be urine.

The patty cake that could be formed as a result of the process just described was then pulverized through the action of balls of metal being churned about. A method of progressive "screening" followed with grains of different sizes being roughly separated. The granules so classified were then labeled and assigned a burning rate, however broad the limit may have been.

In more modern manufacturing the amount and kind of impurities within the various ingredients are objects of meticulous control because certain impurities can affect both the manufacture and the performance of the finished product. The early pestle-and-mortar or mill stamping operation has been supplanted by a cylindrical tumbler.

The cylinder contains metal balls that act on sulphur and charcoal with a continuous dropping and pulverizing movement as the drum rotates. This "intimate" mixture then is dampened slightly with water, just plain water, as a safety precaution taken before the potassium nitrate is added. Knowing, as we do, the treacherous nature of niter, further explanation of the need for moisture seems unnecessary! The amount of moisture, however, must not be too great for fear of leaching out any of the valuable potassium nitrate.

The trio of ingredients brought to proximity by this blending is compacted into closer contact by huge mill wheels weighing several tons, an operation that takes from three to six hours, depending to some extent upon how much mixture is involved. Throughout the foregoing stage, moisture is kept at a carefully controlled level. The stuff then is made into cakes with the use of powerful hydraulic presses.

After moisture has evaporated from the powder cakes they are broken up in what is called a "corning mill." This is by far the most dangerous of all steps used in gunpowder manufacture. The building in which this mill is housed is separated by barricade from others in the factory complex with operation taking place by means of remote control. Regulated granulation is accomplished through the use of corrugated rollers which crush the dry chunks into a variety of smaller particles. These are then separated by a graduation of screens; the smallest, the next larger and so on until division is complete. As a touch of refinement, a glaze of lubricating graphite usually is added to make loading and handling easier.

With every care being exercised in the several steps necessary to a realization of the completed product, gunpowder is not ready for use as a propellant in small arms until it undergoes practical testing. The "trial by firing" serves to reveal within the limits of reasonable safety the pressure factor of each powder "lot." This factory service offers the additional benefit of improved accuracy through more uniform pressures as the result of using a particular grade of powder. The mixing of powders to achieve uniformity is generally referred to as "blending" and can be regarded as highly important to the shooter.

We've mentioned "white" and "brown" powders. It's time now to say that, if your "black" powder is black, something is wrong, like too much charcoal (carbon) if quite black.

Black powder that is "right" is perhaps best described as having a slate gray complexion. If it is bluish, it may contain too much moisture, while the appearance of bright points or blue-white spots may indicate that the saltpeter has effloresced. If it marks a sheet of paper or your hand when allowed to run across, it has too much moisture or "meal powder."

The pinch test, as between fingertips, should not result in decomposition into dust. Instead, such pressure and gentleness of grinding should result in smaller, angular fragments. The grain size and density of powder granules is highly important as related to burning rate. The loss through deterioration of factory-controlled granular density suggests a need that it be disposed through the porcelain convenience.

Black powder is said to be stable chemically, its ingredients being practically nonreactive with one another to temperatures of as high as 120 degrees Centigrade. That is, in the absence of moisture. Stability departs when moisture infiltrates as both the saltpeter and the charcoal are somewhat hygroscopic in air. Moisture causes black powder to react with some metals such as steel and brass. "Keep your powder dry" has even greater meaning when you come to know that water can leach out the saltpeter, destroy the structural integrity of the grains and remove sufficient niter to virtually render it a non-combustible.

The birth of the elongated projectile and the rifled barrels needed to keep it from tumbling downrange created a need for slower burning propellants. "Slower" in this sense means progressive. Attempts of early experimenters to create a progressive-burning powder had encountered difficulties of complicated manufacture. For example, one type of early Fossano (progressive) powder was "formed by pressing mill cake to a density of 1.79, then breaking this press cake into one-eighth to one-quarter-inch grains, mixing these grains with a prescribed quantity of fine grain powder, pressing this mixture to a mean density of 1.76 and breaking this press cake into grains about two and one-half inches square by one and three-quarter inches thick."

A New York professor, R. Ogden Doremus, introduced the preceding methods which are said to have resulted in grains of varying density which burned progressively.

Meanwhile, U.S. Army Captain (later Brigadier General) Thomas Rodman had been busy experimenting with fifteen and twenty-inch smoothbore guns which he had invented. Rodman found that he could reduce initial breech pressures in these guns, without a loss of velocity, by using perforated discs of compressed powder which were of a

The armament on this early battleship was kept below deck for several reasons; to protect the cannoneers from rifle fire and so as to keep the gunpowder from being subjected to the ravages of the battle.

During the nineteenth century, cannon making had been perfected to the point that bigger and longer range weapons came into existence. Although still crude compared to modern day weaponry, the basic design of this cannon was the same as artillery pieces of WW I.

diameter equal to the caliber of the gun (!) and between one and two inches thick. He called this enormous "grain" of powder a "perforated cake cartridge."

In a work published in 1861, he demonstrated mathematically that upon the beginning of combustion, such discs presented a minimum of free surface for burning. But — and here's the idea still being used in much of today's manufacture of modern, smokeless, progressive-burning propellants — as the powder continued to ignite, there was a constant enlargement of the perforations, whereby the area of surface exposed to the flame was increased constantly with the result that the volume of evolved gases grew in direct relation with the increasing volume of the chamber as caused by the movement of the projectile along the length of the barrel. The pressure exerted upon the base of the projectile and throughout the bore was more uniform during the entire discharge cycle than had been possible with granulated powders previously used.

Development of Rodman's innovation of marvelous simplicity was halted by the Civil War. However, a Russian military commission visiting this country at the time was so impressed by the accomplishment that, following its recommendation, manufacture was taken up in Russia and carried on extensively. The idea quickly spread to other countries and ultimately back to the United States.

Gradation of black powders is commonly denoted in series of the letter F, for "fine." The more Fs, the finer. As many as five Fs have appeared in the past, indicating the mealiest of granulations. As the Fs decrease, the grain size increases with Fg representing the larger size. More descriptive references are sometimes seen, to wit: mealed powder, superfine, large grain (LG), large grain for rifles (RLG), mammoth, pebble, pellet, cubical, hexagonal, sphere-hexagonal, waffle, and so on. Practically speaking, nothing

past RLG is worth considering for sporting use; some of them wouldn't fit through your trigger guard, one grain at a time!

One notable attempt to replace or improve upon black powder was known as Lesmok or semi-smokeless. The attempt was relatively short-lived and of particularly dismal outcome. The "improvement" turned out to be dangerous to manufacture and deadly to possess and handle. Much of the unfavorable reputation from which gunpowder has suffered over the years can be traced to mishaps involving the handling of Lesmok by persons unfamiliar with its dangerous nature.

Even upon looking back through the many centuries of black powder's dramatic saga and being fully aware of its nostalgic appeal, it is difficult to forget its faults. The gaudy puffing of white smoke was disliked by the military, if not the sportsman, and its tendency to deposit corrosive salts in prized bores is favored by no man. If these are of insufficient severity then add the spotted upholstery, the blotched curtains and wallpaper and the stained clothing that may certainly be the result of unfouling a gun after a session with black powder. The stuff is hard on brass cases and hard to get off. But for all its shortcomings it has a quality in performance that will sustain its existence indefinitely.

The production of black powder bids fair to continue for many years to come. Its use in older guns is practically indispensable by reason of the fact that it does not produce the pressures of modern smokeless propellants. Because of its readiness to ignite from a spit of flame it is, in this appraisal, superior to smokeless as a primer. It is, of course, basic diet for countless antique and replica firearms in the hands of enthusiasts. – *Dan Cotterman*

The traditional canister at left still was being used for DuPont black powder until just a few years ago. The can of Bullseye – an early type of smokeless, still made – has to date from a time between its introduction in 1898 to 1902, the year Laflin & Rand was taken over by Hercules. Powder makers of olden days would be amazed at the progress made since then in both arms and propellants!

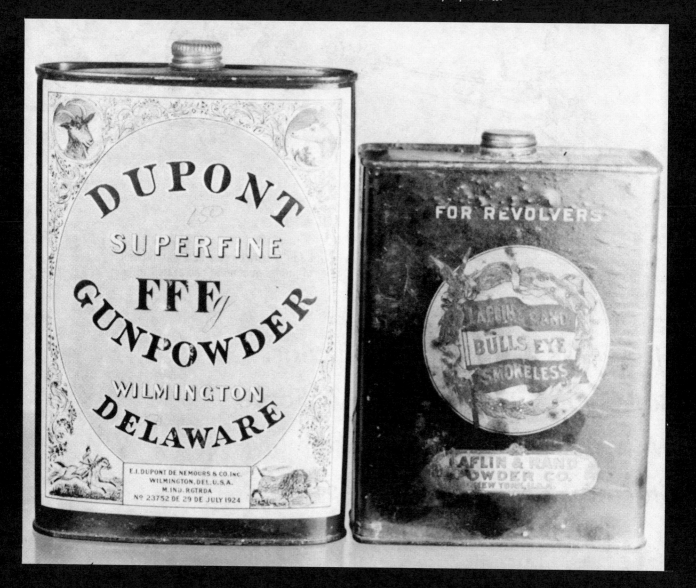

HARNESSING THE POWDER DEMON

CHAPTER 2

"From a puff of white smoke came a hell-based missile that would doubtlessly be steered by an unseen demon into the breast of some hapless knight. Armor, long the amulet of nobles in combat had ceased to be effective."

Fireworks May Be Spectacular, But Gunpowder Became A Force With Which To Reckon After It Started Hurling Projectiles!

THE FIRE LANCE and whoosh bomb of the Chinese were articles of defense, perhaps employed as much for their value in terrifying an enemy as for their capability to inflict injury. That the fire drug evolved to use as a means of defense is reasonable, as the Chinese had been bothered by the intrusions of barbarian raiders through the dynasties of Han and before the years of P'an Ku.

Whatever parallel may have existed between Chinese and European feudal systems, there appears to have been no equality between the happy, content philosophy of the Orient and the grumbling discontent of the European vassal who, with growing unwillingness, pledged loyalty to a band of overlords. This striking difference takes much from the logic of those who exalt the Chinese for using black powder

primarily as fuel for fireworks in public celebrations.

The development of firearms cannot, however, be laid so conveniently upon a comparison of philosophies. An objective appraisal of centuries past shows alternate patterns of progress and stagnation. Of contradictory significance is the fact that the Thirteenth Century, whose crest lifted our Roger Bacon to pinnacles of achievement, gave way to virtual regressiveness that was to last for nearly two hundred years. However, it was during that period, represented by the Fourteenth and Fifteenth Centuries that, beginning with the cannon, the gun was subject to one of its most significant eras of advancement.

Somewhere between sanity and the outer reaches of chaos we will find proof, with all scientific authority, that acknowledge the first type of gun which could be carried, pointed and fired by one man: the matchlock.

The multitude of weapons throughout the Fourteenth and Fifteenth Centuries were found in the hands of armies not yet equipped to progress from the use of longbows and catapults, the hand cannon among them. The matchlock, though at first little more than a meager refinement of the hand cannon, represented an advancement in design and usefulness, but did not make itself known to any marked extent until about the middle of the Fifteenth Century.

The name, "matchlock" contradicts our image of a match by present definition. In its broader extremes, the word, "match" referred to a thick length of cotton string set on fire at one end. The string was held by a C-shaped device which was attached to the right side of the stock just aft of the rearmost extension of the barrel. The "C" could be tipped so as to bring the lighted end of the string in contact with a tiny priming charge which was cupped around the ignition hole or "touch" hole. Later the "C"

A Soldier of the time of K. James I. armed with a caliver.

This soldier of the mid 1500s is most likely armed with an "une arquebuse du calibre de Monsieur le Prince," French for an arquebus of calibre of the prince as it was known then.

the first gun was a mortar in which black powder was being mixed with the first projectile being the pestle. We will, with greater satisfaction, surmise that the first gun was a tube which, in one crude manner or another, had been fashioned with the specific intent of containing a powder charge capable of firing a projectile. The method of ignition is determined by the necessity of setting fire to the charge behind the projectile. There is no point in speculating on the degree of success attained through these elementary experiments — guessing at the number of overloads, blow-ups or misfires — since any importance is overshadowed by the greater significance of realizing what it meant.

Whether by accidental discovery or invention, man had progressed, through trial and success, to a point where he was ready to shoot something of potentially greater accuracy than the arrow or quarrel. The longbow was on the threshold of being replaced as a weapon of war, though it was destined to endure in coexistence with the gun for many centuries. The catapult, the nightmare of countless medieval sieges, would yield during competition with the cannon.

Granting full credit to the use of field artillery and the indispensable role it played in the eventual death of feudalism, we move into the birth and development of smaller, more portable firearms. The natural transition from field cannon to hand cannon probably began taking place sometime during the latter part of the Fourteenth Century. Without getting stuck in a mire of definitions, we will

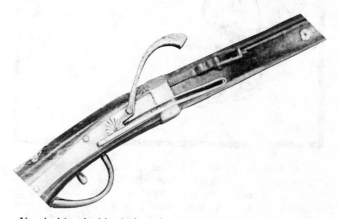

Nearly identical in design, these two Japanese matchlocks from the 1600s feature S-shaped serpentines. The match was held in place by a U-shaped ferrule and struck forward, not back towards the shooter as had C-shaped matchlocks.

configuration was replaced by an "S" or serpentine string holder whose fulcrum point was located to have a heavier amount of the "S" on the down side. This intentional unbalance was doubtless in favor of helping to prevent unintentional discharge as a result of having the serpentine accidentally tip forward. This development may be regarded as a blackboard diagram for a kindergarten project. However, any system that kept kindling and gun together was better than grasping the gun with both hands while trying to touch off the charge by means of a burning straw held between clenched teeth!

To achieve a longer lasting, more uniform glow, the cotton string used for the matchlock was soaked in a saltpeter solution and allowed to dry before lighting. Whether this process lessened the tendency of the string to drop unwelcome sparks into the powder charge is not known.

The design of this soldier's hand cannon is advanced for its time. Note how the match is levered to the touchhole. Earlier models were designed so that the cannoneer touched the match to the touchhole with his free hand, which was then quickly withdrawn to save fingers from flash.

Probably nothing short of squeamish concern on the part of the shooter ever avoided such accidents. Add to spark dropping the uneasy tendency of those first free-swinging serpentines to tip forward when brushed by a twig or an excess of clothing and you will appreciate the need for some means of greater mechanical control!

It is appropriate to note some of the other drawbacks of the first serious attempt at solo shooting before we can fully enjoy the improvements that will come later. The wind, then as now, existed as a deterrent to accuracy and, in larger proportions, as an outright prohibition to shooting. The first stout puff would blow away that precious pinch of priming that surrounded the touch hole. If not lost in the wind or scattered by an ill-timed sneeze, a priming charge could be tipped away by the slightest cant of the gun. Finally, as if all this weren't enough to justify a factory call-back of everything in production, those early models were cursed for blowing a cascade of sparks into the shooter's face. The absence of shooting glasses in those medieval times should have been cause for protest, even among the most stout-hearted men.

By the beginning of the Sixteenth Century, gunmakers had brought forward a number of matchlock ignition mechanisms, each with some most welcome safety features. Quite possibly as an inheritance from the crossbow, the gun now had a trigger. It also had become heir to the power of spring tension, used to conspicuous advantage in gaining further control over the movement of the serpentine. In one form or another, both the trigger and the spring are in widespread use today. Still another component, the sear, which releases the strength of the spring when the trigger is squeezed, is well known to modern gunnery.

The expansion of thought and innovation also brought about a more satisfactory method of holding the priming powder. The touch hole was now drilled in the side of the breech where the primer could be contained in a small, covered pan which had a lid to shield it from wind and at least a minor amount of rain. Still another shield to the rear of the flash pan protected the shooter's face from sparks.

And, instead of being hand-held at arm's length or, for the bravest, against the chest, this newer matchlock had wood that looked like a real gun stock!

While the breech end of the earliest hand cannons had been simply welded shut, the latter part of the Fifteenth Century witnessed the blessing of a threaded breech plug. To the breech plug there was attached a flat piece of metal which extended from the rear of the barrel back over the stock. This metal extension, better called a tang, helped provide a more solid mating of barrel and stock when the tang was firmly secured to the stock by a large screw. To say that the coming of the tang meant an improvement in accuracy would be a modest understatement.

The matchlock, as it reached maturity, emerged as a monument to the determination and skill of the gunmaker's art. Craftsmen throughout Europe had worked to bring their best efforts to a firearm that represented the greatest advancements of their time. Not merely a tool of defense, the matchlock posed proudly with its precisely machined exterior, mirrored bore and glistening finish. Stocks, too, were selected from the most beautifully grained woods and extravagantly carved and inlaid with silver, ivory and gold. This was treatment man traditionally reserved for his most favored treasures. Had he at last accomplished perfection in a personal weapon? Could this basically simple firearm, with its serpentine, match and flashpan, be the best of design and craftsmanship?

As one might expect, the improvements brought into the design and making of guns were, in a sense, paralleled by a continuing improvement in the manufacture of black powder. In the century that followed Roger Bacon's declaration of a formula, there was a growing tendency to increase the amount of saltpeter in proportion to the amounts of sulphur and charcoal. Bacon was aware of the importance of purity of the three ingredients, but perhaps not as keenly as later experimenters. The purification of saltpeter, for example, was a subject that involved repeated processes of crystallization. As discussed in Chapter One, the dry method of powder making was replaced by

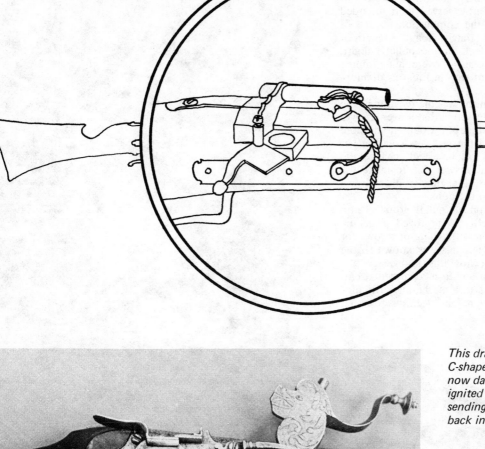

This drawing of an early C-shaped matchlock shows now dangerously the match ignited the primed flash pan, sending a shower of sparks back into the shooter's eyes.

This wheellock, although appearing rather crude in design, was expensive and hard to produce during the 1600s. This is the reason that matchlocks were used.

advanced techniques involving the use of damp cakes which were then sieved into granules which could be sorted according to size and combustion rate.

It can be observed that neither gun nor powder were actually ready for each other when they got together. Ideally, the propellant would have burned completely to shoot a projectile at maximum speed while leaving no residue in a gun that was capable of standing up to any pressures generated in the process. It didn't happen that way. Even the most casually interested firearms enthusiast is aware of the gobs of fouling that accumulate as a result of burning black powder and the complete destruction of guns because of overladen powder chambers is not unknown to historians.

The problems of improper loading had reached at least partial solution by the middle of the Sixteenth Century when musketeers are said to have benefitted from the use of prepared charges. A small, elongated paper or cloth sack would contain a measured powder charge — presumably classified for use in the firearm for which it was prepared — and, at one end, a ball. The "cartridge" was tied at each end to prevent spillage and a third length of string encircled the sack and was driven tight to keep ball and powder separated. This, truly, was the first belted cartridge.

Fouling of gun bores must have been known — if not so much a problem — even to the shooters of stones. However, the tighter bore-to-projectile seal made possible with the introduction of the metal ball, along with an increasing dissatisfaction with woefully inaccurate shooting, strengthened the need to minimize the effects of fouling. Adding emphasis to the need for a gun and powder combination that would remain reasonably clean through the ordeal of sustained shooting was the military significance of firepower: The more frequently a shooter was forced to stop loading and firing in order to clean a hopelessly fouled gun, the less effective he was in battle.

It is speculated that some unknown gunmaker, probably during the Fifteenth Century, hurried to his shop and tooled a number of equally spaced grooves into the bore of a gun. These grooves subsequently served their intended purpose by trapping some of the combustion residue of black powder. The grooves were straight along the length of the bore and so had little effect on the bullet's flight. Regardless, there was at last a means of overcoming fouling and this contributed a significant step in firearms development.

The next important development was the twisting of the grooves. In addition, someone reasoned that longer grooves of about the same width and depth would hold more fouling. Deepening or widening the grooves would either weaken the wall of the barrel or, in effect, change the caliber of the piece. The logical answer was to make the grooves longer by cutting them so that they would follow a spiraling path down the length of the bore.

Whether, with the introduction of fouling grooves, anyone expected the added benefit of improved projectile accuracy is not known. The helical fletching of arrows for the betterment of flight characteristics was known to the ancient Egyptians. Whether or not this knowledge was generally widespread, it is important to recognize that cutting straight grooves presented less machining difficulty than would have been encountered in attempts to spiral

At one time guns were only owned by the wealthy. This is reflected in the ornately finished butt stock at left and the gun held by its owner Turner Kirkland above.

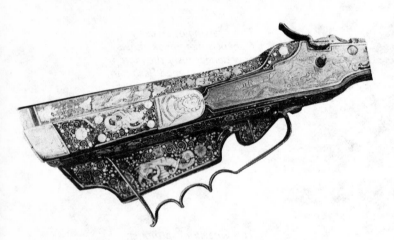

them. It is supposed that several decades elapsed between the cutting of straight and spiraled grooves in gun bores. Whether the interval was necessary to allow for the improvement of machining techniques and tooling or an expanded awareness of the nature of projectiles in motion is another matter for speculation.

As if to stand in defiance of the demonstrated superiority of the matchlock's range and penetrating power, longbow shooters were persistent in their allegiance. This weapon, whose prowess had been established by kings and noblemen throughout the centuries, could let fly a dozen arrows while the gunner prepared and discharged a single ball. In a social sense, archers were gentlemen while shooting was something within the capability of the commonest peasant. As a general rule, the rank and file serfs were too busy working to afford the time necessary to achieve proficiency with bow and arrow.

The sustenance of the longbow and its kin, the crossbow, as significant influences in battle were destined to yield to the gun, regardless of noble sentiment. The soldier could be trained to a satisfactory level of proficiency with a gun in a fraction of the time necessary to make a good archer. The importance of whether the trainee could intentionally hit anything was offset by the gun's equal value in frightening an adversary. Invader and defender

alike respected and feared the mere presence of a gun in battle. The dull "thunk" of the bowstring had been replaced by the roar and flame of an even more impressive weapon. From a puff of white smoke came a hell-based missile that would doubtlessly be steered by an unseen demon into the breast of some hapless knight. Armor, long the defense of nobles in combat, ceased to be effective.

Medieval physicians and surgeons were not unaware of the necessity for quick treatment of bullet wounds. The danger of infection were such as to nearly equal the effects of the ball itself. According to Boothroyd, one favorite recipe for treating gunshot wounds called for mixing equal parts of oil and wine and injecting them into a live dog which was then boiled. Finally, a poultice of the boiled dog meat was applied. None of the benefits of the foregoing treatment seem to have been recorded. We may, however, reflect upon the humane aspects of allowing the dog to get smashed before the moment of his execution.

The penetration of armor breastplates an acknowledged capability of the swift projectile, its tendency to err in flight was still in question. That is, prior to the boon and revelation of the spiraling grooves already discussed. This significant innovation, along with the fixing of some means of sighting to the weapon, settled the contest that had been raging between whether projectiles were guided by the gods or individual's accuracy. The rifle balls now flew with predictability and at last the shooter could call his shots. The gunner who previously had been proud to shoot a hole through a wine barrel at a hundred paces could now send a ball whistling into a tankard at the same distance.

Regardless of his improved accuracy with barrels that would spin the projectile, the smoothbore was to continue in favor. Man had begun to hunt with his solo gun and the small birdshot used in hunting could not be effective when

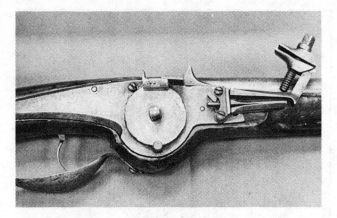

Not all wheellocks were elaborately finished with ivory and mother of pearl inlays, but were rather drab and only functional in their design. These were mainly military arms.

discharged through a bore with twisted grooves. Experiments show that the shallow rifling impressions in today's barrels will spin shot into a doughnut-shaped pattern. Imagine the spraying effect that must have resulted from shooting an ounce or two of tiny pellets through barrels with much deeper grooves.

Reviewing the saga of weaponry brings about a distinct awareness of type overlapping. Like shingles on a roof, each representation of the technology of its time continues for a while, coexisting with its replacement. After competitive tests it is either abandoned to the archives or sustained for sentimental reasons. The bow, for example, remains in use today, having endeared itself to many as an object of romantic background whose mastery demands the best abilities of the archer. To another extreme, catapult and cannon might represent two shingles that overlapped only briefly. Who could get sentimental over a catapult?

The development of the matchlock was still in a state of progress when, during the first quarter of the Fifteenth Century, the wheellock appeared. As the name suggests, this newer idea incorporated the use of a wheel with a rasp-like edge. The wheel was wound a little less than one turn by use of a small wrench, something like a rollerskate key. At this point, the wheel was held in readiness by a sear whose tip had been automatically indexed into a hole on the inside of the wheel.

The squeezing of the trigger animated a conglomerate of components into the following mystery of actions and reactions: Wheel, a small segment of which protrudes into flashpan, begins rapid rotation when pulled by a tiny chain which is held taut by the tension of a spring; cover over flashpan moves aside allowing fool's gold (iron pyrites) which is clamped in jaws of pivoting "doghead" to move into union with wheel; the resulting sparks set fire to the priming mix in the flashpan. Consequently, the powder charge was ignited and the shot was on its way.

Marvelously, the muddled mechanics of the wheellock took only a split second; trigger pull and shot were nearly simultaneous. Quickness of locking time was insignificant among the wheellock's advantages when compared to its readiness. The pyrite ignition meant that the arm no longer had to be carried about with the hazard of a glowing wick hanging uncomfortably close to the priming charge. The wheellock could be loaded and stored or carried afield where it would be ready to shoot as quickly as the need arose.

Possibly for the first time, the hunter was ready to carry

All types of devices were used, or at least thought about, that would give armed forces an advantage over one another. Here soldiers use an elevated platform to expose the enemy.

the gun into forest and meadow in search of game, probably in the company of one or two humorously skeptical archers. In the case of the wheellock, the nimrod provided an embarrassing share of laughs as his fool's gold crumbled uselessly into the grass or, worse yet, he stood drenched in a shower of sparks. Or the blush of humiliation that must have come upon being left sprawling on the ground by a horse frightened into sudden acceleration by the boom of black powder. The bow and arrow lads were justly amused.

Distrust of the wheellock system was exemplified by shooters having an auxiliary serpentine and match built on their guns. Thus, if the complex parts in the wheellock's mechanism became inoperable as a result of the inevitable accumulation of powder residue, the old dependable "match" was available. The cost of the wheellock, to say nothing of the added expense of a second ignition system, rendered guns with double ignition the exclusive property of the wealthy. The best of both was not good enough. Something better had to come.

Progress in design suffered from the diversity of several attempts to improve on the old spinning wheel concept before it was abandoned. Such examples of the wheellock as may have endured were preserved for the value of precious metal inlays and artful carvings, rather than for their actual efficiency as working firearms. Perhaps by reason of simplicity, better ways to create the spark continued to elude discovery.

Flint had first been tried with the wheellock, but due to

On opposite page, musketeer stands at rest as he prepares to load matchlock. He seizes powder-filled wooden container hanging from his leather bandoleer, popping it open with his thumb. He then drops charge down the muzzle and seats the ball over this. At top left, he then primes the pan. The match is then carefully placed into the serpentine. He then aims in on his target and he's ready to fire, resting the heavy gun in a forked stick. These seven drawings appeared in The Management of Arms, Arquebuses, Muskets and Pikes in 1606. This was an official guide to musketry exercise until the matchlock was replaced by wheellocks.

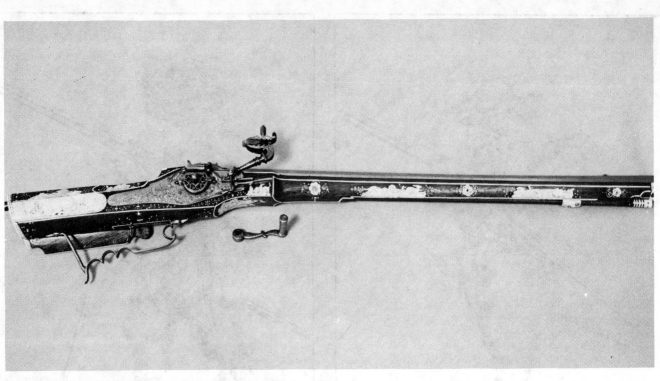

This modern reproduction of the wheellock design rifle is an example of the artistry used to make each gun one of a kind. Note the key in upper photo used to wind lock, which threw sparks toward shooter.

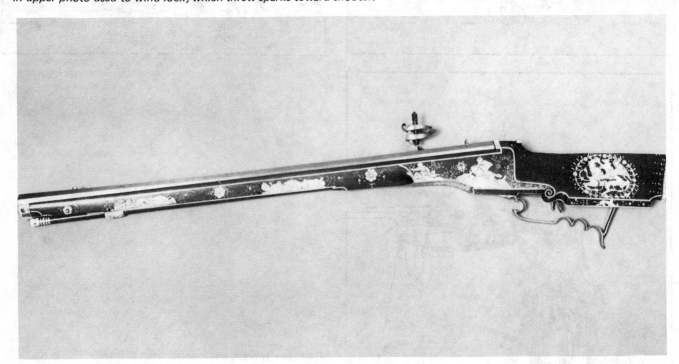

its hardness, it wore the peaks off the roughened surface of the wheel. Pyrites was softer and would ultimately see use in a system known as the pyrites lock. Grand-daddy of the flintlock, the pyrites lock seems to be a logical stepchild of the matchlock. Variations involved only the substitution of a "cock" for the earlier serpentine and a roughened plate, called the battery or frizzen, for the pyrites to strike. The brief appearance of the pyrites lock is mainly significant because once again, an attempt had been made to get rid of the match and its inconveniences. The difference this time was that it had been done without approaching the com-

plication of an alarm clock.

At about the same time, still in the middle of the Sixteenth Century, the snaphance or "snapharmce," made itself known. This one reached back and picked up one of the good ideas that had been put to work in the design of the wheellock, namely a covered flashpan as featured in yet another of its variations, the miquelet. Pyrites lock, snaphance and miquelet seem to have been different names for guns that, except for variations of mechanical detail, were essentially the same.

Admirers of matchlock, wheellock and the pyrites-snaphance-miquelet trio just described continued to tug in different directions (probably to the snickering of loyal bow and arrow enthusiasts) until the first part of the Seventeenth Century. Gunmakers of the era at last agreed to advance from the confusion of over two centuries with a uniform effort in the interests of standardization. The resulting harmony of thought and idea crystallized in the form of a better gun, the flintlock. It preserved the simplicity and low manufacturing cost of the matchlock, with a lock time that rivaled that of the wheellock. Coupled with its use of flint, more generally available and less given to crumbling than pyrites, the flintlock had retained such features of convenience and safety as the covered flashpan, unhesitatingly hailed as an outstanding advantage of the wheellock.

This early 1500 woodcut by Erhardt Schoen depicts the firemaster of a mercenary force. His task was to supply fire for matchcords and braziers, as well as cooking fires. At left an arquebusier loads his matchlock.

This 16th Century Arquebusier is armed with a spring driven matchlock. The cost of these weapons was so great that many countries had to continue arming their forces with the older matchlock until the discovery of flintlocks.

No agreement with respect to measurement of shot was to come until the middle of the Sixteenth Century. Throughout Europe medieval "wildcatters" sought to promote their own system of bullet measurement, knowing certainly that they would thereby achieve a sort of paper immortality. As measurement of lengths, widths, depths, et al., varied in different areas between inches and millimeters, the only hope rested in some system that correlated values of weight.

In England, royal proclamation officialized the pound in favor of commerce. Each pound contained a prescribed number of ounces, each of which was divisible into scruples, grains and so on. Scales with surprisingly high capabilities of accuracy aided in establishing the number of lead balls of a given size needed to constitute a total weight of one pound. The number thus required, sixteen, for example, was assigned to every ball of that particular size. Henceforth, every gun taking such a ball could be referred to as a "sixteen bore." There were numerous bore sizes and an equally wide assortment of balls, some more popular than others. In modified form the bore system reamins with us today and is used in references to shotgun gauge.

The transition in usage from "bore" to "caliber" brings to light an interesting bit of word history. At first the word "caliver" (corrupted pronunciation can be blamed on medieval Englishmen) was used to name a particularly awkward eleven-bore with an overall length of about six feet. In weight, the caliver would challenge the heftiness of many of today's benchrest rifles. Regardless, the word has no roots in common with the origins of any gun: In mean-

Sic fluuialis Anas capitur cane fulminis ictu,   Dum percussus obit, pennasque in flumine spargit

77.

*From a 1566 book entitled The Hunt of Beasts, Birds and Fish, this
woodcut engraving by Jan ver der Straet shows common people hunting
ducks. This book was one of the earliest to depict firearms use
for the taking of wild game, probably the first to show bird hunting.*

ing, "caliber" is directly attributable to a contraction of the Latin "qua libra," a phrase that asks, "How much?"

Just how much shooters have loved the flintlock over the centuries can, to some extent, be appreciated with the knowledge that thousands of them are still in use today! Author Charles Edward Chapel, writing near the close of the 1930s, made clear reference to flintlock rifles still being used in this country, not necessarily as novelty arms but as practical tools of hunting and home defense. True though it may be that the bulk of flintlock arms in use today are in the hands of black powder hobbyists, no concession is made as to the practical usefulness of these guns. They have, by reason of sound design and practicality, managed to outlive numerous systems which were said to be superior.

The piercing of armor by the rifle ball established a significance for the shoulder weapon in military matters. In an attempt to re-establish a comfortable degree of invulnerability for knighthood, tailors of armor, for want of superior metallurgy, made thicker plates. The process continued to ridiculous extremes. Knightly knees wobbled and the mighty steeds of combat snorted under the growing burden of iron.

Even as the warring nobility collectively sweated and swooned beneath their useless shell, others found pleasure in the leisurely indulgence of hunting. On the Continent, large parties of bird hunters flaunted nature's abundance by amassing kills that numbered in the hundreds as the result of a single day's slaughter. In the name of sport, deer by the thousands were shot by hunters who knew neither the limit of law nor conscience. We must remember, however, that the term "deer" was used by many to describe just about any animal of the forest. Carnage in the name of target practice and gentlemanly pastime persistently foreshadowed the coming of more and more restrictive hunting laws.

Records do not generally show the popularity of large and extravagant hunting parties in Britain. The hunter existed somewhat more within the bounds of sportsmanship. While he may at times have been wasteful of game and given to indiscriminate plinking, he hunted as much out of necessity as for recreation. Had not the political and economical significance of the common peasant been altered by the gun? In addition to soldiering, his training and familiarity with firearms had taught him to hunt in order to augment his family food supply.

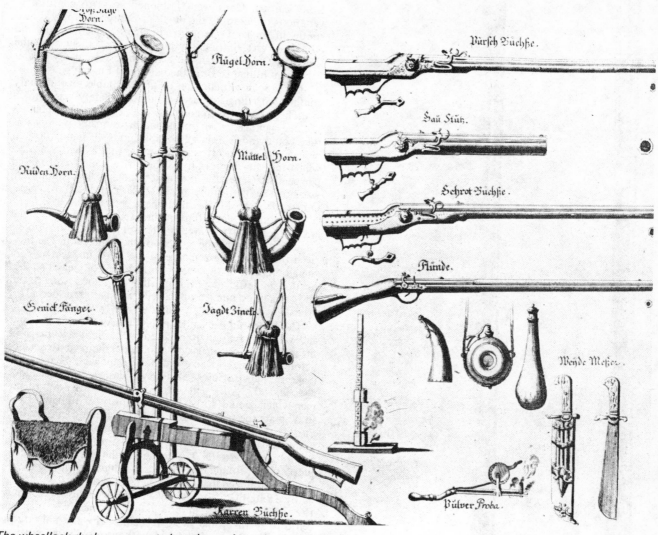

The wheellock duck gun mounted on the carriage, the three wheellocks and flintlock, five horns, two knives, game pouch, three powder flasks, and two powder testers are all 17th and early 18th Century hunting implements. Duck gun would fire several pounds of shot at waterfowl.

The classic Puritan of Seventeenth Century England who sought freedom and a new life in the world to the West considered his destiny somewhat less uncertain because of his confidence in the gun. Whether matchlock, wheellock or flintlock, it was his companion in defense as well as his assurance of food when game was available. The Algonquin hosts of the New World may in some measure have been responsible for an enhancement of appreciation of game animals as a natural resource. Although the colonist was far from conservation-minded, at least it seemed that the slaughter parties common to Continental Europe would not establish themselves in America...not until annihilation of the buffalo absorbed the attention and energy of his descendants in the decades ahead.

No view of early American pilgrims seems complete without at least token attention to the blunderbuss. If a carbine existed in relationship to the long Brown Bess flintlocks, it would have had to be the short, Dutch "thunder gun." Popularized in history and subject to an immortality of exaggeration and falsehood, it probably drew the greater part of attention because of its odd, funnel-shaped barrel. Its value seems to have been based on its handiness, credit the short overall length, and its capabilities for short-range shooting. The stubby barrel, incorporating no choke, suggests that the blunderbuss would have been well adapted to the rapid dispersement of birdshot.

It looked like a cartoon gun and in "blunderbuss" found a name that added to its clumsy appearance. The term is a translation of the Dutch, "donderbuchse."

For all its usefulness, the blunderbuss did not enjoy the popularity of its longer kin. The English shoulder gun of wide use by the middle of the Eighteenth Century was the Brown Bess. Bess, for Queen Elizabeth, who is said to have endorsed the making of the prototype and brown, in description of a color that was imparted to the metal through a process of oxidation.

Despite the known superiority of accuracy possible for bullets shot from twist-rifled barrels, the majority of guns used by early Colonials were smoothbores. "Musket" was the accepted name usually applied to these. German guns of the American Colonies were mostly of the rifled type, probably because both the grooving and spiraling had been a result of German thinking. Yet, while the rifled barrel held greater possibilities for accuracy, the smoothbore was the more versatile by reason of its ability to handle either rifle ball or birdshot.

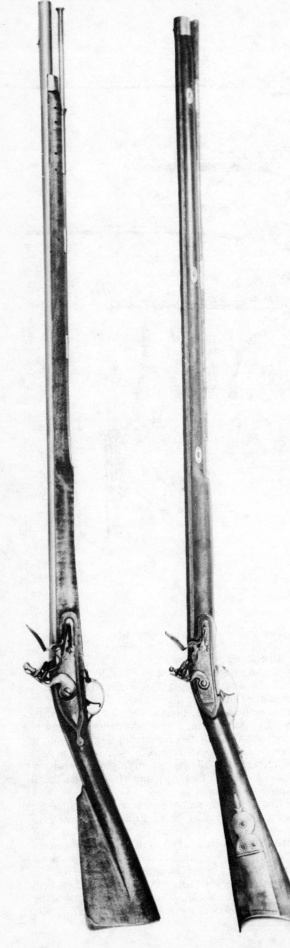

American makers of long guns in the years before the Revolution were dependent on the importation of locks from Europe. Guns were fashioned so as to conform to variations imposed by the origin of European supply. Locksmiths in England, Germany, France, the Netherlands and Austria sent flintlock systems for use on guns of the Colonies. Overall design, however, took a decidedly greater balance of influence from the pattern of English guns.

In 1775, in anticipation of the inevitable revolutionary conflict with England, a Committee of Safety was formed in each of the thirteen colonies. Each committee appointed selected gunmakers to manufacture as many weapons as they could and, within all possible limits, to standardize on design and caliber. It was, however, that a lack of accord which left any uniformity of bore size a matter of ragged perspective. Generally, the most popular caliber, about .75, was ruled by that of the most popular gun, the Brown Bess. Others of .70 to .80 are said to have been used.

The simplicity of flint raking across roughened metal was to continue to have its irresistible appeal to shooters far and wide until the middle of the Nineteenth Century. Even thereafter, the romance of the flint guns was to earn the admiration of shooters who had guns of greater sophistication and efficiency. It is possible for a good thing to survive something our reasoning tells us is better...especially if it challenges our primitive wiles.

The Reverend Alexander Forsyth, Scottish experimenter and wildfowl hunter, is credited with taking advantage of the explosive properties of fulminates, known to science before his time, for the ignition of powder charges. To make the most of his idea, Forsyth designed a special lock and, in 1807, got a patent for it. His idea involved a hammer which would strike a tiny quantity of fulminate and thus create the spark of ignition. The Reverend's inspiration and its consequent development represent strides of immense significance in the story of firearms and, indeed, ammunition itself. The usage of the pressure building properties of fulminates served as a foundation in the development of breech loading and metallic cartridges.

By 1836, the advantages of Forsyth's percussion cap and the Forsyth lock, in production for nearly a quarter-century by that time, were recognized by the military in Britain. The Brown Bess could, without prohibitive expense or difficulty, be converted from flintlock to the new system. It is said to have seen its first use in the hands of British troops in China in the year 1841. By the middle of the Nineteenth Century, American shooters also were in full appreciation of the percussion cap.

Subsequent evolution from muzzleloading to breechloading and, eventually, to self-contained ammunition seems to have taken nothing from the intrigue of the flintlock. For all their practicality and superior technology, the later innovations did not possess the primitive mystique generated by the sound of stone on metal.

Today, the flint and pyrites guns exist in distant harmony with the modern generation of firearms whose roots trace themselves to the authorship of Alexander Forsyth's invention. Each extreme in technology represents a branch of firearms history that is distinguished by reason of its deep-felt influence on virtually every aspect of our lives. For evil and for good, the discovery of the fire drug has meant much to us all in terms of our social lives, our economics and, in fact, our sciences. Those Taoist alchemists would be impressed. — *Dan Cotterman*

Two early flintlocks used in this country were the Brown Bess (left) and various styles of long rifles such as the one shown on the right. The Brown Bess was the official arm used by British troops in Colonial times, long rifles were used by colonist to hunt game and during Revolution.

CHAPTER 3

A History Of Handguns

The Chronological Evolution Of The Handgun From Its 14th Century Beginning To The Introduction Of The Cartridge And Smokeless Powder.

JONATHAN SWIFT, THE IRISH-BORN satirist, philosophized at the turn of the Eighteenth Century that necessity is the mother of invention. Necessity did have much to do with the early development of firearms, especially handguns.

Although it isn't totally agreed upon by historians, the introduction of the smallarm appeared in the form of a crude hand cannon sometime during the third quarter of the Fourteenth Century. However, in the monastery of St. Leonardo in Lecetto, Germany, paintings clearly depict soldiers carrying and firing small handgun tubes around three feet in length. These early scenes had been painted by Paolo del Maestro Neri during the period from 1340 to 1343.

primer for the main charge in the chamber. More often than not though, the touchhole went straight through to the charged breech.

Hand cannoneers never were far from the frypanne, a pan or brazier of hot coals, usually heated until they glowed. These were for heating the touche — a short piece of wire, a burning stick or even a hot coal.

Taking a somewhat hasty aim in the general direction the projectile was intended to fly, the cannoneer would ignite the charge of powder by inserting the touche through the touchhole or by igniting the priming powder just above the touchhole. If the hand cannon didn't explode in his face, killing him and anyone foolish enough to be standing close at hand, the round was on its way, more or less in the

Hand cannon, such as this, first appeared sometime during the 14th Century. This particular hand cannon is much more refined than the majority, displaying the well advanced styling of the modern day pistol.

Even though these paintings supposedly are the same as the original artist had done them, some historians feel that the hand cannon may have been added by a later artist who tried to modernize the image projected by the scenes. If these paintings are original and untouched, they may well be the first to depict the use of handgunnes, as they later became known in Britain.

Military ledgers and log books of the last quarter of the Fourteenth Century and the first quarter of the Fifteenth Century make mention of the use of and procurement of touches, drivells, tampions and frypannes.

To load his gun or piece, the cannoneer first charged it by pouring a desired amount of powder down the muzzle. This usually was done with the use of an elongated hollow tube, the end of which was cut to form a scoop. The tampion — a wooden disk used to separate the powder from the ball and to form greater chamber pressures for harder hitting shots — then was seated over the powder.

The cannoneer seated the tampion firmly over the powder with the drivell — referred to today as a ramrod. Next, the ball was seated above the tampion. The balls used for these early black powder guns were made usually from lead or brass, but those made from bronze or even iron are not uncommon. If supplies were limited or required too great a length of time in acquiring, soldiers occasionally used balls that had been hewn from stone, just as the balls for cannon were made, except somewhat smaller in size. The bores of hand cannon rarely exceeded three-quarters of an inch in diameter, although many of the early wood-cut scenes and paintings show hand cannon with bores better than twice that size.

Occasionally the touchholes required that the cannoneer place a minute amount of powder into it to serve as a

direction of the target.

Being a cannoneer had its problems, not only in being a poor way of arming oneself but in that the deadly bow and arrow remained superior when it came to accuracy and speedy reloading. It wasn't until sometime around the end of the first quarter of the Fifteenth Century that cannoneers began thinking of ways to improve their abilities by devising ways of aiming their armament.

This had been done previously to some extent by merely sighting down the top of the barrel and lining up on the target, be it man or animal. This again proved a problem in itself.

To aim in on the target in such a manner required the cannoneer to use both hands in order to hold the gun steady. Who then would apply the touche to the touchhole to ignite the round? Had man been created with a third hand, all would have been well enough. As it was, however, the cannoneer was very ineffective unless a means of aiming or firing the cannon could be established.

As a remedy to this problem, some forces enlarged the size of the hand cannon and assigned two men to aim and fire each. While one man aimed and supported the gun — by now better than five or six feet in length and having a bore in the neighborhood of .80 or .90 caliber — the other would apply the touche upon command of the first or when he signaled that the gun was aimed in on the target. This worked to a certain degree, but it then jeopardized two men instead of one once the gun had been emptied into the ranks of the enemy.

As an even more practical remedy — in a way giving the cannoneer a third hand — someone at an unknown date in an unknown country built the first matchlock. Historians have pondered these two unanswered mysteries and, although not backed by any historical documents or significant happenings, Genoa, Italy, may have been the place and about 1440 the date.

In this original form of matchlock hand cannon, the lock was nothing more than an S-shaped lever to which a slow burning piece of cord or match was attached. When aiming the gun all the cannoneer had to do was grasp this lever with several of his fingers and lever the match into the touchhole as soon as he was lined up on his target. To keep the match from accidentally setting off the powder charge, the lower half was made longer and heavier purposely. The extra weight balanced the arm in a vertical position, keeping the match away from the touchhole, which was now the flashhole.

Up to this point, the hand cannon had been the early development for both the shoulder weapon and the handgun. With the introduction of the matchlock, the two forms began to develop in their own forms even farther.

The majority of the matchlocks were built as shoulder weapons, but a few were fashioned after the earlier hand cannon, but given a short one-handed handle to serve as a grip. These were fitted with shortened barrels — less than two feet in length. Crude in design, the match still had to be levered into the touchhole that was located atop of the breech, requiring use of both hands.

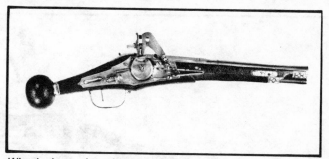

Wheelocks, such as this late 16th Century Austrian, revolutionized the pistol, allowing for the first time a gun to be loaded, primed and stored or carried, but ready to shoot.

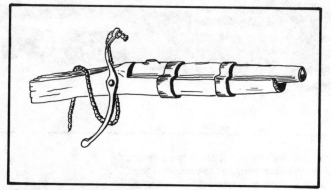

This sketching depicts the design similar to the first matchlock small arms. The serpentine holds the matchcord in the nose of a pivoted arm, is levered into touchhole.

It wasn't long before the matchlock won wide acceptance and replaced the touchhole hand cannons. It was evident, however, that the location of the touchhole was rather precarious. As a deterrent to the hazards that rain and wind had on the exposed touchhole, it was moved to the side of the breech, appearing in the form of a pan.

Along with the improvement of the flashhole — some having a plate that would slide or slip over the priming powder to prevent it from spilling or being blown out by the wind or even dampened by an unexpected shower — came improved matches. Early matches consisted of nothing more than twisted cords, which probably were hard to get burning, let alone keep burning for any length of time. It was found that, by soaking the cord in various solutions of saltpeter and allowing them to dry, the matches would burn better and for a longer period of time; these eventually became known as slow matches.

The true mechanical matchlock was developed sometime during the third quarter of the Fifteenth Century. Together the matchlock and the improved match remained the principle means of armament of the world's forces until the Seventeenth Century.

Although the development of the matchlock was instrumental in the evolution of the handgun, a pistol fitted with this type of lock saw little use in Europe. Several pistol-like arms were made at this time, but these, for the most part, were produced in Japan and India. With the exception of a few matchlock pistols made in Poland during the Eighteenth Century, European armsmakers considered a firearm of this sort to be of such uselessness as to not even warrant limited manufacture.

With the coming of the wheellock, handguns took a giant stride forward. As with the origin of the matchlock, hand cannon and black powder itself, the inventor of the wheellock is yet another mystery to arms buffs. Many believe that the first wheellock was the result of the work done by several men. One such man was Leonardo da Vinci, who designed an early form of the wheellock as early as 1508.

Along with the wheellock came the first practical pistols. This lock allowed a short, easily maneuvered gun to be carried and fired with a one-handed hold. The absence of the burning match also made it possible to hide or conceal the arm, or at least to have a gun that would readily fire without having to worry about adjusting the match.

The pyrite or flint of a wheellock pistol is held in the jaws of the dog head — the vise like section of the cock — and the wheel is spanned, or wound in place. The pyrite then is placed against the area of the wheel that is located nearest the flashpan. If the powder and ball have been loaded in the proper sequence, the rotation of the wheel should provide enough spark from the iron pyrite to ignite the primed pan as the trigger is released and the pistol should fire.

As mentioned, the date and place of the first wheellock is not clear, but it is certain that they were being used widely during the first quarter of the Sixteenth Century. The development of these locks met some opposition from a large number of people. Many were not familiar in how they worked and classified them as being dangerous. Emperor Maximilian I made it illegal to manufacture the dangerous wheellock in 1517. His actions were followed closely by similar authorities, all contending that such guns made the job of thieves and robbers easier by affording them a gun that could be hidden and concealed.

Europe was war-ridden during the first half of the Sixteenth Century, giving the wheellock ample opportunity to prove its value as a military arm. Attacking or defending forces would line up in ranks, many of them armed with nothing more than pistols, and fire in volleys. While the front rank would be firing, the others would be busy reloading their pistols; the ranks continuously going forward and falling back to reload.

Wheelocks were expensive to produce and perhaps this is why many of the major armed forces continued to use matchlock rifles until the Seventeenth Century. With the exception of some military pistols that were made more functional than fancy, pistols were the property of wealthy gun enthusiasts. These were usually decorated with numerous inlays of ivory, bone, horn or mother of pearl. The metal on these guns usually was ornately engraved and

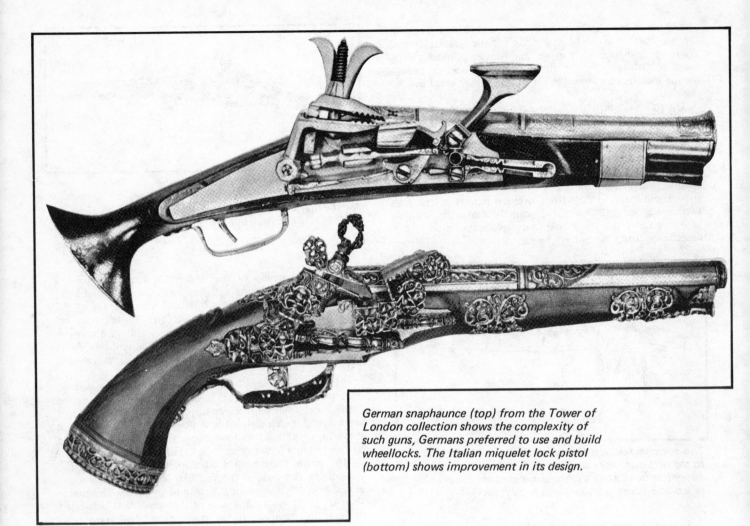

German snaphaunce (top) from the Tower of London collection shows the complexity of such guns, Germans preferred to use and build wheellocks. The Italian miquelet lock pistol (bottom) shows improvement in its design.

sported gold and silver inlays. The lock, barrel, trigger guards and mounts were also blued, richly browned or even enameled.

Gunsmiths all across Europe tried feverishly to produce work superior to their counter-parts in yet another country. The result of this competition is evident in many of the exquisite guns of the period that are now in many private collections and on display in museums. The word pistol itself is of reputed origin, possibly the result of such international pride in craftsmanship.

Italy, in which many paintings show the early use of handguns, has some claim to being origin of the wheellock pistol, the name supposedly derived from the city of Pistoia. Czechoslovakia also lays some claim to origin of the word, the word coming from a short Bohemian handgun known as a pist'ala or pipe.

Use of flint and steel to ignite a primed flash pan was established through the use of wheellocks, but the expense of producing them made it impossible for common working people to afford such guns. Breaking away from the complex design of the wheellock, the Dutch snaphaunce did much to do away with the smoldering match of the matchlock and the expense of the wheellock.

This lock was an early forerunner to the flintlock, as also was the miquelet. All three types of locks used the flint against steel to produce spark principle. To fire, the cock or hammer was drawn back and held under the tension of a spring by some type of sear. As the trigger was pulled, the sear released the hammer and the tension of the spring

drove it forward, causing sparks as the piece of flint held in the jaws of the cock struck against the steel arm located above the flash pan.

These sparks are actually minute particles of molten steel being scraped away from the hardened frizzen or pan cover. By dropping into the primed flash pan, they ignited the priming powder and the gun would discharge.

The first snaphaunce locks appeared during the late Sixteenth Century and were made in and around the European countries of Germany, England, and France, although there is evidence of such locks from as far south as Italy. The sear protruded through the side of the lock plate on the earliest of these locks. This would engage a notch on the cock itself, either on the rear of the cock or a slot that had been milled or cut into the inner face.

To prevent the powder from spilling from the pans on these early handguns as they were being carried in whatever way the owner saw fit — belt, makeshift holster, lanyard, et al. — the flash pans were fitted with a cover that mechanically slid out of the way as the pistol was cocked. Few, if any, of these pistols featured a half-cock position.

Miquelet locks were an improved version of the flint and steel or snapping lock. Two different styles of this lock were common to the mid-1500s: the Spanish miquelet and the Italian miquelet. Although there is considerable debate over just where this type of lock first appeared, it is believed that the Spanish were the first to utilize it on pistols. If Spain had been the first country to use the miquelet lock at all, it may be the first time credit can be given the

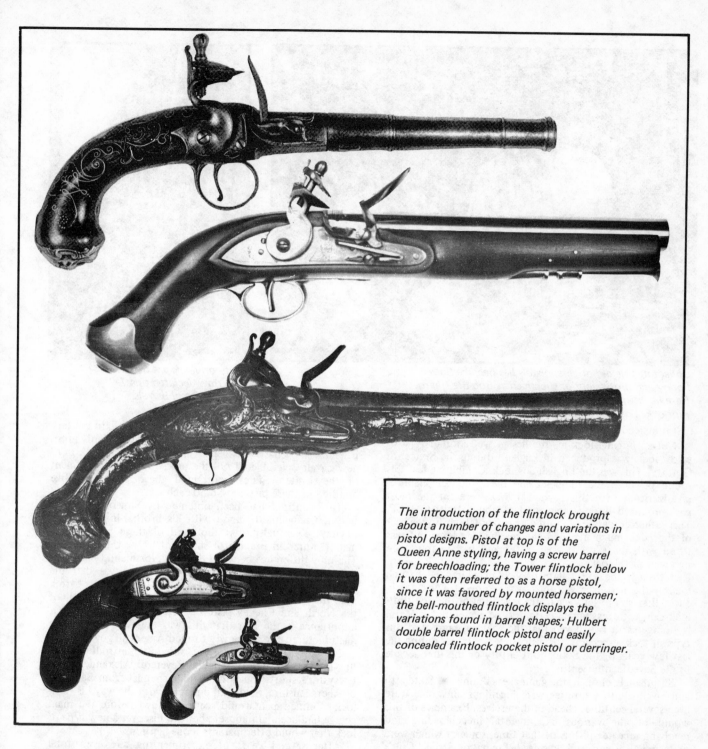

The introduction of the flintlock brought about a number of changes and variations in pistol designs. Pistol at top is of the Queen Anne styling, having a screw barrel for breechloading; the Tower flintlock below it was often referred to as a horse pistol, since it was favored by mounted horsemen; the bell-mouthed flintlock displays the variations found in barrel shapes; Hulbert double barrel flintlock pistol and easily concealed flintlock pocket pistol or derringer.

inventor. Supposedly the lock was invented by Isidro Soler, a Madrid gunmaker.

There were several differences between snaphaunce pistols and miquelet pistols that made the latter superior. First of all, the miquelet was the first to utilize the pan cover as the actual frizzen. On pistols with snaphaunce locks the cover and striking arm — frizzen — were two separate parts. Combined into one L-shaped part, the combination frizzen and pan cover made the lock simpler by doing away with internal parts that were needed to move the pan cover as the lock was cocked.

Another desired feature on this newer lock was the addition of a half-cock or safe position of the hammer. This was made possible by the addition of a second sear. This sear — on both Spanish and Italian versions — worked horizontally through the lock plate. On the Spanish miquelet, both sears passed through the lock plate. The half-cock sear appeared as a stud and the full-cock sear as a flat blade. On the Italian version, half-cock was achieved by one arm of the sear engaging the toe of the cock; full-cock was achieved by the second sear to the rear of the cock engaging the heel.

The use of the Spanish miquelet lock for pistols never really caught on throughout the rest of Europe, but handguns made in that country continued to be so produced until the end of the flint and steel period. Even more backward were the oriental countries, still relying on the match principle until introduction of the percussion lock in the 1860s after Perry's opening of the Eastern Empire; they never really went through the flint transition period, but

Collecting fine old original pistols has become both hobby and profession for such men as Bob Elz (right). Here he examines one of a cased pair of fine Manton flintlock. Looking on is collector Gary Saunders.

Many originals are fitted with now declared unsafe damascus steel barrels.

past it instead.

Not an original lock in true design, yet another type of pistol lock was produced in England during the Sixteenth Century. This was the English dog lock. Combining features found on both the miquelet and the earlier snaphaunce, pistols fitted with this particular lock were for the most part produced during the period of about 1640 to 1650. This rather crude lock featured a horizontal sear to the rear of the cock much like had the snaphaunce lock, but was fitted with the L-shaped pan cover and frizzen found on miquelet pistol locks.

Although the exact date or year in which the French lock — the first true flintlock as we know it — was introduced first isn't exactly clear, the invention of the first flintlock can, with reasonable certainty, be accredited to Marin le Bourgeois. It is believed that the first appearance of this type of lock, especially for pistol use, was either during the last few years of the Sixteenth Century or the first decade of the Seventeenth Century.

Surprisingly enough, the gunmakers during the Sixteenth and Seventeenth Centuries were ingenious and some were even several centuries ahead of themselves. Examples of this would be the various experimental breechloading and revolving repeater pistols of that time, some of which were quite practical and well advanced. Pre-dating Samuel Colt's famed introduction of the revolver are quite a few practical revolving handguns. Repeaters and breechloaders were too complicated for the period, however, and perhaps this is why they weren't refined until later dates.

The flintlock remained the most commonly used pistol until the first percussion locks had been perfected during the early 1800s. With the exception of a few small, privately run gun shops, the American armsmaking industry didn't start taking shape until the turn of the Nineteenth Century. American revolutionary forces had been armed mostly with guns that had been stockpiled as they could be obtained and were nearly all manufactured in European plants.

One of the biggest problems encountered in the manufacture of early pistols was the lack of standardization. By 1763, however, the French had remedied this problem to

some degree and began producing the first standard military flintlock pistol. Some fourteen years later the plants in St. Etienne and Charleville began producing the Model 1777 new cavalry pistol. In 1799 the newly formed government of the United States contracted these plants for five hundred of these pistol at $6.50 each.

This contract had been obtained by Simeon North of Berlin, Connecticut, along with his brother-in-law, Elisha Cheney. Eventually two thousand of these pistols were manufactured in France for shipment to the United States. The only difference between the U.S. North and Cheney, as they were known, and the French pistol was that the former had an extra inch added to the length of its barrel. Also the French pistol was fitted with a belt hook; none of the North and Cheney pistols sported this attachment. Of importance is the fact that this was the first pistol to be manufactured for the newly formed American government.

Necessity again played a vital role in the introduction of the first percussion type lock. Reverend Alexander John Forsyth, a sportsman and amateur chemist from Belhelvie of Aberdeenshire, Scotland, unhappy with the way his flintlock's primed pan would scare wildfowl before the main charge had been ignited, set about to discover a new type of lock that would offer instantaneous ignition.

After several years of experimenting and even total rejection by the military, Forsyth took out a patent on his new lock and, with the assistance of one James Purdey — later to become renowned in the firearms field — set up business at No. 10 Piccadilly, London, in 1808. Their first successful lock was the of scent bottle type. This type of lock was used on some of the Joseph Manton pistols made after the introduction of the Forsyth lock.

A number of different handguns with locks similar to the principle of the Forsyth lock cropped up during the years between 1810 and 1820, most of which had little appeal to handgun fanciers or were of such uselessness they were dropped from further testing.

Several handguns were fitted with locks that were primed with a formed priming charge that appeared in the form of a round ball. This was placed in a shallow receptacle that formed a sort of flash pan. A solid nose striker would ignite the globule of powder and discharge the main body of powder inside the breech. The biggest downfall of handguns featuring such a lock was that the priming charge was easily knocked from its position and was susceptible to moisture.

A few other handguns were manufactured about this time that used a tubular percussion cap-like ignition system. The tube lock was primed with a copper tube five-eighths of an inch in length and approximately a sixteenth of an inch in diameter. This tube was open on both ends and filled with percussion powder. To prime the lock, the tube was inserted into the flashhole until about an eighth of an inch protruded; this rested on an anvil-like piece of metal that acted as a sort of flash pan. The impact of the blunt nosed hammer or striker ignited the powder inside the tube, which in turn ignited the loaded charge. In addition to occasionally throwing sparks back into the face of the shooter, this lock proved undesireable in that it had a tendency to crimp the tube to a point that it would lodge in the flashhole.

A percussion cap is nothing more than a small copper cup about an eighth inch in depth and diameter. Open on one end, a minute amount of fulminate of mercury is placed on the inner surface of the closed end. This is placed over a short hollow nipple, the inner passage leading to the powder charge in the breech. As the blunt nosed hammer falls on the cup when the trigger is pulled, it explodes the fulminate of mercury and sends most of the flash or sparks down the hollow cavity of the nipple to ignite the main charge of powder.

With the percussion cap, shooting was immune to weather, misfires and hangfires, providing the caps had been manufactured with good quality. The change in pistol locks — and rifle locks — from flint to percussion was the swiftest ever to take place. By 1830, the percussion caps had all but replaced flintlocks. The shooters of the latter were greeted on the field with the same amusement as today's black powder shooter.

During this period James Purdey left Forsyth to open a business of his own, today a world famous name in firearms. Some of Purdey's first guns were beautifully designed

Developed during the first quarter of the 19th Century, the percussion caplock was the first really dependable ignition system.

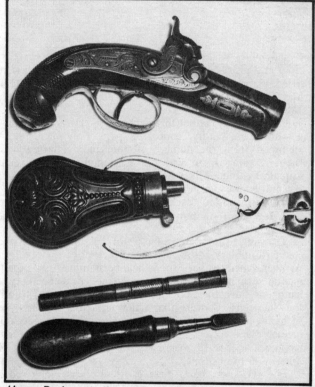

Henry Deringer built pocket pistol similar to the one used in the assassination of President Lincoln, such pistols since then have continued to be classified as derringers.

All of these, however, were early forms of the percussion cap lock; all working on the principle of igniting the priming powder by striking it between two hardened surfaces — the blunt nose of the hammer and whatever the globule of powder or tube rested on.

The first true percussion cap appeared sometime between 1814 and 1820, possibly invented by an American or an Englishman. There is some controversy over the originator of this principle. But by the mid-1820s pistols featuring a true caplock appeared in both countries. The percussion cap operated on a simple principle and, with its reasonably reliable firing capability, won the acceptance of shooters world-wide.

percussion combination duelling and target pistols. These first guns were all handmade and, since they were intended for the defense of one's honor or for just plain plinking, they were made without provisions for attaching the ramrod. This usually was kept in the pistol case along with all the other loading accessories.

The simple design of the percussion lock made it possible to produce pistols that would fit easily in pockets, boots or wherever the owner desired to conceal his miniature firepower. These small percussion pistols were known as pocket pistols, later to become known as the derringer.

Henry Deringer was an American gunsmith who started business in Easton, Pennsylvania. He later moved to

Although still predated by numerous early revolving handgun designs, the Collier flintlock revolver was probably one of the first actual practical designs. Type of ignition robbed it of becoming popular.

Philadelphia, where he began to produce guns. His first rifles and pistols began appearing around 1806 and all were fitted with the principal lock of that time, the flintlock. Many of these guns were produced under contract for the U.S. Army.

The notoriety, rather than fame, of the Deringer pistol — a short and easily concealed percussion handgun — stemmed from the number of homicides comitted with them. Among these was the assassination of President Lincoln by John Wilkes Booth. The public identification of the murder weapon resulted in the international use of the word, derringer, to describe the type of pistol, the second 'r' added to differentiate the Deringer-made pistol from the general type.

The single-shot percussion pistol continued to be the standard military handgun until perfection of the revolver. As mentioned earlier, there had been numerous experimental versions — many quite practical — of revolving type handguns since the Sixteenth Century, but it wasn't until the Nineteenth Century that actual refinement of this type of handgun took place. One reason for this late development of the revolver can be accredited to the fact that there had been a lack of machinery for the manufacturing of firearms until this time.

For the most part, these early revolvers employed a crude or unorthodox mechanism to rotate the cylinder or relied upon the shooter to manually turn the cylinder and line up the chamber and barrel by hand. Perhaps the earliest practical automatic cylinder rotation appeared on a revolving handgun built by John Dafte of London in about 1680. The method used to rotate the cylinder is nearly the same as that used later by Colt and may possibly be the source of the idea for his first single action cap and ball revolver. Actually, the same principle is used on Colt single action Army revolvers still being produced. The Dafte revolver, however, used a snaphaunce type lock.

One of the first revolvers to appear in the United States was the Collier. This five-shot flintlock — the accredited invention of Captain Artemus Wheller of Concord, Massachusetts — appeared around 1820. The handgun had one strike against it; it featured a flintlock instead of the percussion cap that was increasing in popularity. Later percussion models were introduced, but they never became

popular and were discontinued.

Although Samuel Colt can hardly be given claim for the invention of the handgun, he probably did more in the development of such guns than any other individual. The first revolvers produced by Colt were several different versions of the folding trigger Paterson model, so named since they were manufactured in Paterson, New Jersey. Colt ran a business that was constantly on the verge of going bankrupt, until he landed a government contract for one thousand revolvers in 1847.

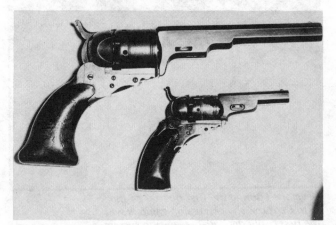

Colt Paterson was the first of the famous Colt made percussion revolvers to be produced. Top revolver was known as the Texas Model, bottom pocket pistol known as a Baby Paterson.

Mass-produced for Colt by Eli Whitney, Jr., in his Whitneyville, Connecticut, plant, these pistols were issued to the U.S. Mounted Rifles for use in the Mexican War. To aid in the speedy production of the Colt Whitney Walker Model, production also was moved to several different shops in Hartford.

With business now booming, Colt began to refine the revolver even further. By the time of the outbreak of the Civil War, Colt had refined his wares to the point of near absolute perfection. Revolvers had become the accepted handgun and Colt soon found himself contending with

First of the Colt Dragoon pistols was the Whitneyville-Walker of 1847. This percussion revolver gave U.S. troops the added firepower needed to help win the Mexican War.

numerous counterfeiters, making nearly exact reproductions of his originals. A number of European revolvers were spawned at that time also. Among these were many Colt look-alikes that were manufactured under the authority of Colt.

The Civil War brought about the manufacturing of even more copies of Colt's revolvers, especially the Navy and Army model revolvers. Most of these domestic imitations were made in Texas for use by Confederate troops and, since most employed a considerable amount of handwork, they usually varied some from one to the other.

In America, the firm of E. Remington and Sons of Ilion, New York, was Colt's chief competitor. In 1857, Remington started production of the firm's first percussion cap and ball revolver. This gun had been designed and patented by Fordyce Beals, also the designer of the famous walking beam model. Patented in 1854 and manufactured by Eli Whitney, Jr., the Whitney Beals featured a solid frame that encircled the cylinder completely, something that Colt revolvers lacked.

The Remington Beals First Model of 1857 differed from the Whitney Beals in that it featured a conventional means of rotating the cylinder. On the Whitney Beals the cylinder had been rotated by first forward movement of the trigger, the rotation ending as the trigger was returned to the original position. The gun then was fired by pulling the trigger in the regular manner, by squeezing it to the rear.

Several early models of the Remington revolver saw use before the production of the Beals Army revolver from 1860 to 1862. Users generally favored the solid frame and the more robust feel of this revolver over that of the Colt. So it was only a matter of satisfying its public that Remington introduced a near identical version of this gun in the smaller .36 caliber instead of .44. Improved models of the Beals Army and Navy revolvers appeared in 1861 and were referred to simply as the 1861 Army and 1861 Navy, being .44 and .36 caliber respectively. These guns remained basically the same until the introduction of the Remington Army Model cartridge revolver in 1875.

Undoubtedly the revolver was produced in larger

numbers in the United States than anywhere else in the world. The Civil War demanded a step-up in their production so great that U.S. and Confederate manufacturers couldn't meet the demand of their armies. To solve this problem, both sides turned to foreign manufacturers, both occasionally buying arms from the same source.

In addition to the revolvers made throughout Europe for the American forces, many fine sporting cap and ball

The New Model 1858 Army was designed for Remington by Fordyce Beals, who seemed to favor the solid frame. The design proved so successful that the 1861 Navy Remington (below) remained practically unchanged.

6 Combustible Envelope
CARTRIDGES,
Made of American Powder Co's Powder,
FOR REMINGTON'S, COLT'S & OTHER
Revolving Holster Pistol,
44-100 inch Calibre.
WARRANTED SUPERIOR QUALITY.

Combustible cartridges
were commercially made
and sold during the 1860s.
They made loading cap and
ball revolvers less tedious.

This Remington Beals First
Model pocket revolver is an
example of the various types
of designs introduced during
the percussion revolver era.

Many Colt replicas appeared
during the Civil War, top
revolver is a Metropolitan
made Navy replica, middle
pistol is authentic Colt.
Bottom revolver is an early
Belgian pin fire revolver.

revolvers were also produced. Much to the surprise of many Americans who believed that today's modern design of handgunnery originated in the United States as a result of Yankee ingenuity, such developments as the first solid frame revolver and double action revolver were invented and saw their first commercial use in Britain.

Perhaps the earliest form of a double action revolver to see commercial production was Robert Adams' self-cocking revolver. Actually, this British five-shot featured a trigger action instead of a true double action, not allowing the hammer to be cocked manually. Through its internal design, lifting and camming action — the hammer was drawn back mechanically — and released as the trigger was pulled. There was no means of cocking the revolver manually and there was no half-cock position, but instead a hammer catch that would allow the hammer to be drawn back and locked in place for ease in loading and rotating of the cylinder.

The first true double action revolver was the Beaumont-Adams revolver of 1855. The appearance of this pistol and that of Adams' pistol of 1851 patent is nearly the same. The loss of accuracy with a gun that required a tug of the trigger to fire it apparently became noticeable to both shooters and its inventor. To remedy this, a small spring-loaded pawl and an extra notch on the breast of the hammer were added. This allowed the 1855 Beaumont-Adams to be manually cocked and fired, at the same time offering the shooter double action firing for point blank shooting when accuracy wasn't critical.

Paper cartridges for cap and ball revolvers appeared in many makeshift forms, usually contrived by the individual shooter for the sake of convenience. These usually were nothing more than the bullet — a round ball in most cases — and the powder rolled together in a piece of paper. The problem with this was the necessity of removing powder and ball from the wrapping before loading them into the chamber. What was really needed was a loaded unit — ball, powder and paper — that could be seated hastily in the chamber and fired.

The Remington Army Model of 1875, although having a reliable extraction system, didn't become as popular as Colt single actions due to excessive fouling and its often difficulty of operation.

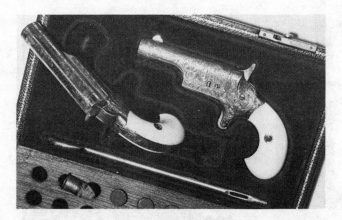

The Colt No. 1 derringer was chambered for the .41 short rimfire cartridge. These small guns were a favorite of gamblers and others of similar professions from the days of riverboat fame.

A number of experimental cartridges resulted from this need. In addition to a cartridge that would have to be completely combustible, the round would have to be durable enough to withstand reasonable handling and, to some degree, impervious to moisture. Among the first early attempts that proved successful was a cartridge wrapped in a paper hull made of gunpowder and collodion; although burning completely and reasonably waterproof, it proved too fragile.

The most successful of these attempts was the skin cartridge of Captain John Montague. As described in his patent of September 1856, "a skin or membrane (prepared from the gut of animals, pigs or birds or reptiles) is used instead of paper for cartridges, which are made without a seam. A covering of net-work or thread may be used to strengthen the cartridge."

Following the paper cartridge era, or overlapping and running concurrently with it, were experiments in developing the breechloading arm and ammunition, some of which featured either internal or external ignition. The first satisfactory self-primed metallic breechloading cartridge was the pin-fire cartridge. This type of cartridge is known to have been around as early as 1841, but development of its potential didn't really occur until the late 1850s.

In its original form, the pinfire case was similar to the paper shotgun hull, having a brass base and paper walls. Later pinfire cartridges appeared in an all-brass form. Both types had a small hole through the case wall near the head of the brass. A percussion cap was pressed into this small hole, followed by a small pin.

The cap was retained in position by the pin and the walls of the chamber. The pin protruded through an opening of the loaded chamber and the round was fired by the force of the hammer striking the pin, which, in turn, exploded the priming cap. Many European cartridge companies manufactured pinfire pistol cartridges up until the mid-1930s.

The first self-priming cartridges resembled a percussion cap that had been increased in size. The idea of the cartridge — a brainstrom of Louis Nicolas Auguste Flobert — was derived probably from the percussion cap, since it used the same principle. These cartridges were intended for indoor target practice, so didn't feature any range or great amount of velocity. The copper case wasn't much larger than the standard percussion cap and the bullet was propelled by the fulminate, also used as the primer. These cartridges didn't support the rim that is so prevalent on today's .22 rimfire, but the rear area of the case was swelled to prevent the case from being driven all the way into the chamber as the hammer struck the rear of the chambered round.

Further development of the rimfire cartridge was done by the American plant of Smith and Wesson. Developed by Douglas Wesson during the years of 1856 to 1858, the No. 1 Pistol Cartridge or .22 short was an advanced form of the Flobert cartridge. There was a difference in bullet design, however, and the brass case also contained three and four grains of black powder in addition to the fulminate priming. This cartridge and the pistols chambered for it won such wide acceptance that by 1871 more than 100,000 of these cartridges were being produced each day.

Many of the existing cap and ball revolvers were modified to accept rimfire cartridges as those in suitable calibers were produced. A number of new make handguns also were produced to handle the rimfire cartridges, including numerous derringers. One such pistol was Colt's No. I Derringer chambered for the .41 short.

The development of the metalic rimfire cartridge and the later introduction of the primer-ignited center-fire cartridges put an end to the muzzleloader and cap and ball revolver era.

By the turn of the Twentieth Century the handgun had evolved as we know it today; smokeless powders and automatic handguns the chief advancements in the last quarter of the Nineteenth Century. — *Toby Bridges*

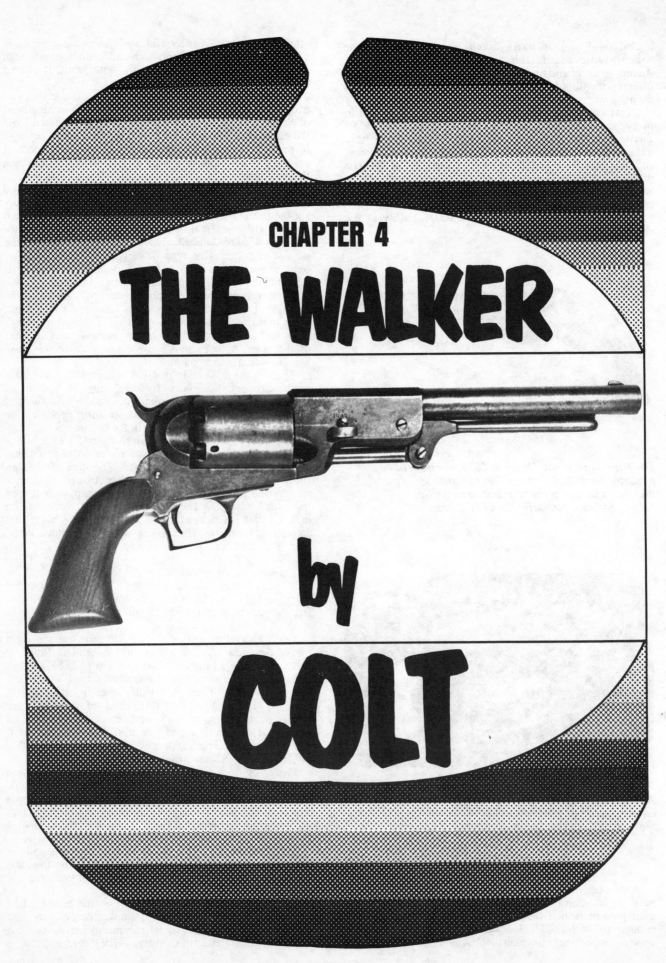

CHAPTER 4
THE WALKER
by
COLT

Lost For Many Years, Captain Samuel Walker's Colt Is Found Among A Southern California Collection!

THE ORIGINAL "WALKER" COLT – the Colt's Army Revolver, .44 Caliber, Model 1847 – which was the personal property of its designer, Captain S. H. Walker, is in the collection of Shelly Horton of Santa Ana, California.

At the time of manufacture in late 1846, two of the revolutionary handguns with numbers 1009 and 1010 were specifically marked as personal arms to be sent to the soldier and gun designer, who at that time was involved in the Mexican War.

The gun in Horton's collection bears the stamped serial number "1010," and has been certified as one of the handguns made especially for presentation to the captain by Samuel Colt; the other still is in the family of Captain Walker in Baltimore.

This particular Walker was "lost" for many years. It had disappeared and no trace of it was found until it came into the possession of the present owner in about 1940. According to Horton, his late father an avid collector purchased the black powder revolver from a stranger, ascertaining only that it was a "Walker" Colt, but not checking the number until several days later. By that time, the seller had disappeared, leaving no means of tracing the hands through which it had passed since its manufacture.

In all, there were only 1100 of the Walker Colts manufactured. A special lot of 1000 was turned out for the United States Mounted Rifles, a new cavalry unit to which Captain Walker had been assigned. The other log of 100 was turned out as presentation pieces for such persons as Walker and other notables.

Of the original lot of 1000 of the .44 caliber handguns, today there are approximately 85 known to exist, most of them in the hands of collectors and museums. Of the additional 100, the location and existence of 15 has been verified to date.

The order manufactured exclusively for the Mounted Rifles was divided into lots of 200 handguns each, with each revolver in each lot having the letter designation of the military company stamped on it with the numbers from "1" through "200" following. Companies of the U.S. Mounted Rifles were designated as running from "A" through "E." The additionally produced 100 handguns, of course, bore no letter and were numbered consecutively from 1001 through 1100.

Walker, a professional soldier and lawman, first had served in the army as a corporal in the Florida Indian Wars of 1837. Later, as a Texas Ranger, he had become familiar with the deadliness of Colt's Paterson revolver. He had made several visits to Colt, suggesting improvements in a handgun which he had in mind specifically for the mounted soldier. Finally, prior to his assignment to duty in the expeditionary forces in Mexico, he worked out the model for the "Walker" Colt and was instrumental in having it ordered by the War Department.

The model designed by the soldier was patterned to a large degree after the .36 caliber revolver produced earlier by Colt, but had numerous refinements. In addition to being more compact, it was much better suited to the needs of a fast-charging cavalryman.

At Walker's suggestion, a loading lever was fashioned as a part of the handgun, working on a hinge; a precaution against the lever being lost during battle or at a time when

The big Walker Colt disassembles for easy cleaning. Enclosed trigger and loading lever were big improvements over earlier Paterson.

Both Shelly Horton (right) and his brother, Roy are avid collectors. Even after more than a hundred years of hard use, machine marks are still evident on the Colt Walker below.

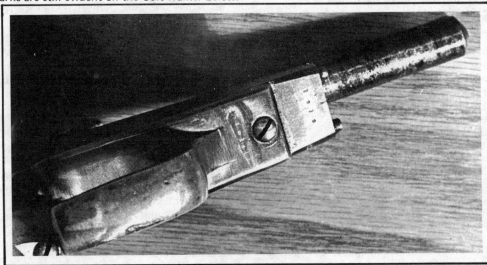

the horseman or soldier might need it most.

Colt, of course, had secured his first patent on a revolver in 1836 at the age of only 21 and is said to have drawn plans for his first practical model while serving as a plain seaman on a voyage to India. He later formed the Colt Patent Arms Manufacturing Co. at Paterson, New Jersey, with his father and 25 stockholders, turning out his earliest models.

At the time Walker had convinced himself of the need for the new .44 caliber model for his U.S. Mounted Rifles, Colt had suffered some financial reverses and it was necessary to have the handguns made at the musket factory of Eli Whitney, Jr., son of the inventor of the cotton gin.

Since a model of the earlier .47 caliber handgun was not available from which to draw plans for the new pistol, Colt copied it entirely from memory, incorporating the new innovations supplied by Captain Walker. At the time, Whitney was intensely worried about getting his money for turning the new model in its limited order in spite of the government contract which Colt had received. The "Walker" Colt, as it is popularly known rather than by its official designation, was purchased by the Army for $28 each.

(The original price is of interest when compared to the amount which a Walker Colt is considered to be worth in this day and age.)

Under the terms of the government contract, the first 1000 .44 caliber Colts were completed on July 6, 1846, and arrangements made to ship them to the supply unit of the Mounted Rifles. The weapons did not catch up with the cavalry unit until it already was involved in the Battle of Vera Cruz; the heat of battle was not considered the ideal time for uncrating the revolvers.

As a result, although there is considerable dissension both pro and con, it is doubtful whether Captain Walker ever actually received the two Colts — Nos. 1009 and 1010 — which had been sent for his personal use. He was slain in the battle, when a Mexican civilian killed him with a wooden spear.

Under the terms of the Army contract, the Walker Colt was to be .44 caliber (using 32 conical and 48 round balls to the pound); the barrel, nine inches in length, was marked with the words: ADDRESS SAMUEL COLT NEW YORK CITY.

The handgun boasted a cylinder measuring two and seven-sixteenths inches in length with six chambers, as well as oval locking slots and one locking pin at the rear. On the 1000 revolvers turned out for the Mounted Rifles, there was the design of Indians and soldiers engaged in a battle scene engraved in the metal. The barrels and cylinders all were fashioned of Sheffield cast steel.

The all-important loading lever was designed without an end catch. Instead, it was held in place by a slender "T"-shaped spring, which entered a slot in the lever near the plunger joint.

On the Walker Colt, the trigger and bolt screws did not pass completely through the frame; in later models — improvements upon this pistol such as the Dragoon — the screws penetrated completely through the frame.

Walker's improved model boasted a "V"-shaped mainspring, while the frame was curved in at the rear, where the grips were designed to enter. The grip-strap was of iron, the trigger guard of heavy brass, while the rear housing was angled at the junction of grip and frame.

The grips themselves, sometimes referred to as "Slim Jims," were in one piece and fashioned of black walnut holding a particularly deadly grace.

The wedge, holding the revolver firmly together, entered from the right side of the barrel. When well oiled, it could be driven out with the haft of a light knife or even with pressure from the fingers, making the handgun easy to dismantle.

The cylinder, barrel and gripstrap of each pistol had a blued steel finish, while the loading lever and hammer were case hardened. Weight of the handgun was standardized at four pounds, nine ounces.

Clumsy though it may appear by today's standards, the Walker Colt constituted a major improvement in firearms, as did Colt's first revolver. The improvements designed by Walker — including the loading lever — were included in the Dragoon model, which also was .44 caliber and was manufactured for the Army from 1848 to 1860.

Horton's Walker Colt No. 1010 is in excellent shape considering the fact that it is well over a century old; it still fires and Horton's father, the late Roy S. Horton, a retired optometrists, conducted target practice with the handgun on numerous occasions.

The lost years of its history before it came into the possession of the present owner probably will never be recounted, but it is not unlikely that the revolver saw service along the frontier, helping to win the West in the days after Captain Walker was slain. — *Jack Lewis*

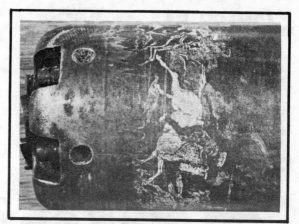

With chalk rubbed into the lines of the cylinder engraving, the scene sketched by Captain Samuel Walker is clearly seen on Walker's revolver.

The barrel and loading lever assembly are fastened to the frame — holding cylinder in place — by a metal wedge. Below, the serial number 1010 is stamped several times.

CHAPTER 5

THE ORIGINAL REPLICAS

Sam Colt Called Them By
A Less Refined Term: Counterfeits —
And Devised Ways To Tell The Real Thing!

REPLICAS ARE NOTHING new. Even as early as the 1840s Samuel Colt himself was hard pressed to discourage the illegitimate production of his cap and ball revolvers. The idea of a repeating handgun was beginning to win wide acceptance and more than one get rich quick armsmaker tried his hand at copying any of the several designs produced by Colt during the period of 1836 to 1872.

An unusual and distinctive feature of the original Colt revolvers produced during this period were the scenes that encompassed their cylinders. The large and heavy .44 caliber Walker and Dragoon revolvers made during 1847 and 1848 were engraved with a panoramic view of mounted troops battling a horde of Indians. Pocket revolvers had a stagecoach holdup scene with one of the passengers blazing away at the fleeing bandits — presumably using one of Colt's pistols — stamped on its five-shot cylinder. Engraved upon the cylinder of Colt's famous Navy revolver was the scene of warships of the era engaged in battle.

Often looked upon as an ornate addition to the handgun's design, these engravings are really more. Although the fact is only vaguely understood among many collectors, Colt included these engravings as a means of telling his original pistols from fakes, or as we have come to call them today, reproductions.

The numismatist — a collector or individual that studies coins, tokens, medals and other similar objects — often numbers among his cherished possessions an illustrated sheet showing a vignetted illustration of numerals and other banknote details known as a counterfeit detector. Most of these originally were issued to bank tellers to enable them to readily identify or to check the authenticity of monies or banknotes from other such firms.

For this reason, Colt marked the cylinders on his handguns with scenes that could be readily identified. He then issued his own form of counterfeit detector. The only one that was ever issued, however, appears to have been printed in 1849. In addition to the scenes printed on the counterfeit detector there was a peculiar design of the Dragoon type revolver also printed in assembled and disassembled form. It is believed that this was an experimental model that was produced in that same year.

Samuel Colt had the uncanny knack of always choosing the right man for the right job. Perhaps this is why he chose W. L. Ormsby to engrave the three scenes previously mentioned.

Ormsby, a banknote engraver by profession, occasionally put his artistic talents to work on other projects, among which were the patterns for the Colt cylinders. Although the scenes on the Walker and Navy were his renditions of sketches forwarded to him for copying, the engraving on the cylinder of the pocket pistol was entirely of his own design.

Of these three Colt Dragoon type revolvers and the Walker below, only two are actual Colts. The Dragoon at top on opposite page is authentic Colt, as is the Walker, other two are replicas.

Sam Colt's own form of counterfeit detector.
W. L. Ormsby, a professional banknote engraver,
engraved all three scenes. The Indian fight
and Naval battle scene were done from drawings,
hold up scene depicts Ormsby thrwarting hold up.

The story has it that Ormsby was travelling aboard the ill-fated stage on his way West when the holdup occurred. It is believed that he was armed with one of Colt's older model Patersons with a folding trigger. Since the first of the new pocket pistol models were first produced in 1848 — the same year in which Ormsby allegedly thwarted the holdup with his Colt revolver — it is not impossible that he might have been armed with one of these.

The first of this Colt design to be produced were engraved with a portion of the fight scene which appears upon the cylinders of the Dragoon and Walker models. It was also during this time that Colt revolvers came under their heaviest attack by counterfeiters.

The scene which appears on the Walker and Dragoon pistols was done from a sketch by Captain Samuel Walker of the U.S. Mounted Rifles, also a former member of the Texas Rangers. Armed with Colt Paterson revolvers, Walker and about fifteen members of the Texas Rangers attacked a large force of Comanche braves that had them outnumbered by better than five to one. Putting them to flight, they managed to kill or wound nearly half of the raiding renegades.

Due to the fire power of their six-shooters, the Rangers managed to escape the battle with only minor wounds. Although Captain John Coffee Hays was in charge of the command at the time of the battle, it was Walker — impressed with the extra fire power of the sixgun — who later encouraged the supplying of pistols of this type to mounted troops.

Prized by collectors today, the Walker Colt had Indian fight scene engraved on its cylinder, big gun weighed nearly five pounds loaded.

Colt had an abundance of competitors during the 1848-1850 period. He travelled all over Europe selling production rights to numerous minor gunmakers to make and market his patterns. Under Colt's Austrian PATENT 1849, for example, Joseph Ganahl of Innsbruck was licensed to make Dragoon revolvers. The same type of agreement was made with some of the Liege, Belgium gunmakers also.

Most of these production rights were made under the stipulation that the manufacturers would not export these weapons back to the United States or to England, where Colt also had his London plant. To help with the production of guns in Liege, he even shipped sets of unfinished parts. Once the parts had been finished, the Belgium gunmakers would stamp the parts with the markings COLT BREVETE, which meant that they had paid Colt ten Belgian francs royalty.

As agreed, most of these guns were marketed only in the European countries, but the American market seemed more appealing to some. So, eventually many of the guns started filtering back into the United States.

The cylinders on the European made revolvers — with the exception of some Belgium-produced guns — lacked the engraving of the Colt produced revolvers. To avoid being undersold by a product of his own design, Colt began printing his counterfeit detector. This way a dealer or purchaser could at least assure himself of buying an original instead of a foreign made copy.

Drawn up by Ormsby — who had originally sculptured the engravings — the counterfeit sheet was marked with the firm's name and address, ordering instructions, the warning BEWARE OF COUNTERFEITS & PATENT INFRINGEMENTS, and Sam Colt's signature. With the exception of a very few Belgium made imports, the fashion for engraving American pistols did not spread abroad.

Even among the arms manufacturers here in the United States the practice of cylinder engraving did not spread, except for maybe an occasional presentation gun. The only exception to this rule would probably be the Whitney arms, but even so, there were few mass produced revolvers that bore engraving to match the intricate Indian fight, Naval battle and holdup scenes used by Colt.

As Benjamin Franklin once said, there is much difference in imitating a good man and counterfeiting him!

It is also interesting to note that, although engraved on the cylinder, there was no known comparison or counterfeit sheet printed for the Paterson. Perhaps at that time Colt hadn't thought of the possibility to use the engraving as a means of detecting originals from fakes that were made outside of his Paterson, New Jersey, plant without his permission.

Why Walker was chosen to lead the U.S. Mounted Rifles during the Mexican War is still a mystery; there were many other better qualified military men at the time, including Hays and Ben McCulloch. It is said that his brother, Jonathan, had many political ties in Washington and was instrumental in getting him the command

Walker, however, made several design recommendations to Colt and was influential in the remodeling of the handgun. Produced by Eli Whitney, Jr., in his Whitneyville, Connecticut, factory, the new model was designated the Whitneyville-Walker Dragoon pistol. The gun later became the official sidearm of the U.S. Mounted Rifles and the cylinder of the large revolver — weighing approximately four pounds — was engraved with the Indian fight scene sketched by Walker during his earlier Texas Ranger service.

In the sketch, Walker depicted himself in command of the charge, although it was Hays who actually was commanding the troops. Since Hays was riding a white mule during the battle, it is believed that it is he that Walker sketched riding just to his rear, partially hidden by his dark mount.

The Navy pistol scene bore stampings that depicted the Texas Navy and Mexican Navy battling it out in the shallows of the Gulf. This scene also commemorates one of the early exploits of the Colt Paterson and, incidentally, is the same batch of revolvers later used by the Texas Rangers during the Indian fight.

The cylinder of this Colt Pocket Model also includes the gun's serial number. Engraved metal is evidence that this was presentation gun; note the words COLTS PATENT on gun.

On May 16, 1843, the Texas armada — quite the worse for wear and drastically undermanned — met with Mexico's well armed and heavily manned warships near the port of Campeche.

The Mexican ships were well built shallow draught steam vessels and were well suited for use in shallow flats of the Gulf. The Texas ships, on the other hand, were nothing more than some old sloops and schooners that had been hastily prepared for use as armed warships.

Under the command of Commodore Edward W. Moore, the Texans sent shot after shot crashing into the heavily manned Mexican ships. Hardly a shot was fired that did not hit its mark, taking some of the attackers with it. Mexican shells did a considerable amount of damage to the Texas ships, but since they were undermanned, many of the rounds failed to hit anybody.

During a later visit to New York in 1850, Moore — excited in telling of the battle — sketched out the battle scene for Colt to use on the cylinder engraving on his then new model Navy revolver. This gun was to replace the earlier pistol as the official issue gun for Naval forces.

To manufacture the engraved cylinders, the scenes were first cut into a plate of iron. Through a hardening process the iron plate was then turned into a somewhat soft grade of steel, from which yet another impression was made onto another soft piece of iron. This second piece of iron was in the form of a roller. After the sculptor had made any last minute changes or touchups that he cared to, the roller was hardened into steel.

The cylinder blank — already bored and milled out for the placement of nipples and cylinder locks — was then placed in a device resembling a lathe. The engraving roller was then brought against the cylinder blank under a considerable amount of pressure. In doing so, the raised etchings of the scene were incised into the much softer metal of the cylinder.

On the early engraved scenes were included the markings COLT'S PATENT. The cylinder engraving on the Whitneyville-Walker and the Whitneyville-Hartford Dragoons were additionally marked MODEL U.S.M.R., later on the First Model Hartford Dragoons appeared the stamping U.S. DRAGOONS. The pocket pistol and Navy revolver cylinders were also marked with the gun's serial number. — *Toby Bridges*

Although worn through years of hard use, the Naval battle scene on this Colt Navy is clearly legible; revolver was .36 cal.

CHAPTER 6

FIREPOWER ALONG THE MASON-DIXON

It Took An Assortment Of Rifles And Muskets To Fight The Civil War. The North Found Quantity An Asset Over Quality When It Came To Markmanship!

WAR ALMOST ALWAYS NECESSITATES an extreme step-up in the production of suitable arms for the armies involved. The great Civil War between the North and the South was no exception.

Although the Northern states were much better prepared to meet the increasing demands of the wartime forces, they too were hard-pressed to maintain an adequate supply of such guns flowing from their arms plants. The South, however, was far worse off. They were hardly prepared to meet the demands of war when the first shots rang out over Fort Sumter.

For the most part, the majority of the arms used by the South's ill-equipped forces at the outbreak of war were guns that had been captured from such raids as that at Harpers Ferry. Despite the beliefs that such raids did much to arm the South's soldiers, the take from those raids was relatively small, when compared to the great number of rifles, handguns and artillery pieces that it would take in later attempts to defend their homelands from the invading Northern forces.

The lack of standardization of armament on both sides resulted in a motley assortment of firepower. Hardly a single unit was uniformly armed. The South's raids had

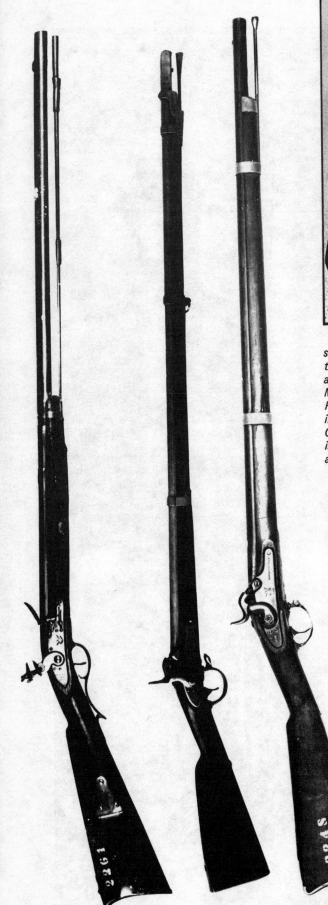

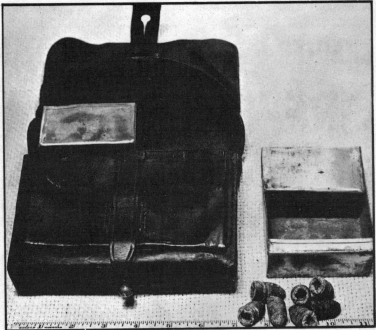

Early in the war, Confederate soldiers carried such guns as the 1814 Harpers Ferry flintlock at far left and the 1842 Model Mississippi rifle (middle). Rifled musket at right was made in a Fayetteville, North Carolina, armory. Pictured above is a Confederate cartridge box and .577 caliber Minie bullets.

mostly resulted in obsolete military guns, many of which were flintlocks that had to be converted to a percussion ignition system before they were of any value. The lack of these large captures in early battles, however, would probably have resulted in an early collapse of the Southern armies.

The rifles and muskets used by the Confederate forces fell into eight different categories. During the early days of the war, Southern armory-made rifle and 1855-61 musket models became standard issue. Another favorite was the .54 caliber M1842 Mississippi rifle. In 1858, the .54 caliber bores on some of these guns were bored out to take the .58 caliber Minie. These were also fitted with adjustable sights and issued to U.S. Army troops as an infantry rifle.

The third type of rifled musket used by the Southern forces was the imported British Enfield and the South made copies of this particular gun. This was a fifty-four-inch rifled musket of .577 caliber. Adequately named the short Enfield, a shortened version of this gun was commonly used by mounted infantry units. Not an actual carbine in the true sense, the short Enfield was nearly as accurate as the full length musket while being somewhat manueverable like a carbine, only more effective.

Muskets were almost always accompanied by some sort of blade. Note the difference between the Enfield bayonet above and Dahlgren design below.

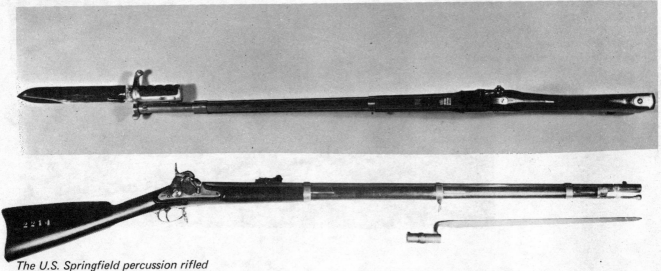

The U.S. Springfield percussion rifled musket model of 1855 was the standard armament of the Federal troops. This one is fitted for Maynard tape-priming system.

Although scattered Southern records don't reveal the exact number of these guns used by Confederate forces, it is believed that some 700,000 Enfields were obtained through purchases, captures and the constant supply of blockade runners.

The fourth type of Confederate shoulder armament was the Austrian or Texas Tyler rifle. This gun appears to be a cross between the Austrian Lorenz rifle and the French Minie. This same type of cross is prevalent in the Tallassee carbine produced at the Tallassee Armory in Alabama. In lock and fittings this rifled musket resembles the Enfield, but the stock lines followed more along the lines of the U.S. musket; in 1864, this firearm was adopted as the standard pattern for the Confederate cavalry.

The fifth type of long gun to appear in the South was the breechloading cavalry carbine. A number of novel breechloaders were produced in the South's armories, but the most interesting was a slightly modified version of the

Sharps that was produced in Richmond, Virginia. Among numerous other breechloaders, the Tarpley and Perry stand out as fairly good breechloading designs.

The sixth group of rifles to arm Confederate soldiers were those made abroad for the Southern forces. The Calisher & Terry was one such rifle that saw some use during the Civil War. In Great Britain, where the gun was manufactured, United Kingdom services passed over this gun in favor of the arms produced by Westley Richards.

Other imported guns were far less popular, such as the different Belgian guns. A good number of those muskets were so unreliable that they were properly labeled worthless by the troops who were so armed. Many a Southern soldier quickly rid himself of the arm the first chance he got, usually to replace it with one of the North's finer rifles — which was commonly picked up from the battlefield.

Such battlefield salvage can be considered as the seventh category of Confederate armament. Many of the Enfields

Springfield musket (top) was produced in a contracted armory, markings include 1861 date and stamping "Trenton." Colt revolving rifle (middle) was early repeater. Regular issue, custom cased Sharps (below) were reliable armament.

and Springfields of the Northern forces were almost always the first to be picked from the battlefields. Many of these may have needed repair work done but the South's armories were capable of doing this; it was far easier to repair a gun than to produce one from scratch.

The final category of the South's rifles and muskets were the flint and percussion guns that had been stored in the U.S. arsenals. Many of these guns were of patterns dating from as far back as the late 1700s and were originally to be used to arm the state militias; in 1808 an act by Congress established a system of arming able-bodied men in the event of state emergencies. A considerable number of these guns were originally fitted with flintlocks, but had been converted to accept the percussion system.

Springfield muskets were the standard firearms used by the Northern Union forces. Eli Whitney, along with numerous other armorers, produced some 670,000 of these rifled muskets for the Union armies. In addition to these,

the Springfield Armory produced another 793,434 of the guns that bears its name from the period of 1861 to the end of 1865.

A big .58 caliber infantry gun, the Springfield rifled musket was quite accurate. A few old sources claim that ten-shot groups having a twenty-seven-inch diameter could be made at five hundred yards and that the 550-grain Minie fired from one of these rifled muskets would easily penetrate four inches of pine at a thousand yards.

Coupled with the devastational powers of the Minie bullet, the muzzleloading Springfields, Enfields and numerous other imported and domestically produced rifled muskets were unquestionably the most employed firearms of the war. Actually, when speaking or referring to the guns of the Civil War, the topic is more on guns that were produced before the war began.

By 1860, Colt had developed his revolver about as far as

Members of Berdan's so-called "Dead Shot Brigade" advanced through open wheat fields using shocks as only cover to spearhead Union victory at Malvern Hill during the Seven Days battle.

they could before the introduction of rimfire cartridges. Remington had done the same with their solid-framed Beals' designed cap and ball revolvers and the general design of the rifled musket had remained the same since about the end of the first quarter of the century; the only changes being improved ignition systems. Of course, there were other revolvers and rifled muskets produced and used in addition to the ones we have already discussed here, but few are of general interest.

What about the guns that actually were developed during the Civil War? Actually, only a few new designs came about at that time, as most of the changes were just improvements over existing patterns. To win a war, however, one of the opposing armies must have a definite edge or advantage over the other. Additional firepower on the battlefield

could be credited as an added advantage and it is a good bet that such was the idea during the development of the first really successful repeating rifle and carbine designs.

The Civil War was the first modern war: Mathew Brady recorded the actual bloodshed through the lens of his camera; important messages could be sent in a matter of minutes instead of days through the telegraph, and the greatest development in armed warfare since the Minie came into being – the repeating rifle. Although Colt's revolving percussion carbine and several other percussion repeaters had been around since the early 1850s, it wasn't until March 6, 1860 that U.S. Patent 27,393 was granted to Christopher M. Spencer for the first really successful repeating cartridge rifle.

A seven-shot repeater, the Spencer was slow to win acceptance by the Army Ordnance Department. Spencer had managed to impress Commander John A. Dahlgren, inventor of the famous Dahlgren naval cannon, and Chief of Navy Ordnance Andrew A. Harwood during a demonstration at the Washington Navy Yard in June, 1861.

During the two-day test fire, he had demonstrated the effectiveness of the gun by successively firing 250 rounds each day without stopping to clean the rifle. During this initial introduction of his rifle to the war department officials Spencer even surprised himself by surpassing his own estimated rate of fire of fifteen shots per minute by increasing the number of shots to twenty one rounds per minute. Harwood was so impressed that he immediately put in an order for seven hundred Spencers to be used by the Navy.

The Army Ordnance Department apparently wasn't as enthused about the repeating Spencer as were the Navy officials. Most of this hesitation to accept the new rifle has been credited to the then Chief of Army Ordnance,

Sharpshooter's badge (left) worn by Berdan's marksmen displays a long range sniper rifle and the reliable Sharps. Lieutenant George A. Custer (below left) and General Plesanton shortly before Custer's promotion to general.

Spencer's seven-shot repeater was slow to be accepted by Ordnance Department officials but soon became a favorite of the troops.

Union cavalry commander, Major General Phillip H. Sheridan in photo taken by Matthew Brady. Cavalry troops found the Spencer to be an ideal choice of firepower.

Brigadier General James W. Ripley. Often described as "old Army," he apparently still favored the muzzleloaders over Spencer's new repeating concept.

The majority of the Spencer rifles and carbines used by Federal troops were of .50 caliber and were chambered for the .56-56 Spencer rimfire cartridge, having a big 350-grain bullet propelled by 42 to 45 grains of black powder. The magazine on these rifles and carbines was located inside the butt stock and was virtually protected from possible damage should the arm be dropped.

Although Spencer had made a government contract to deliver 10,000 of the guns on December 26, 1861, delivery of the arms didn't start until better than a year later. It is believed that this delay was caused by the design change of

the extractor. The first of these repeaters were fitted with an extractor that closely resembled the edge of a saw blade. As the action was worked the teeth on the extractor would latch onto the rim of the cartridge and pull it from the chamber. This was later changed to a superior side position extractor.

Spencer's seven-shot repeaters saw their first real action during the extremely bloody battle of Antietam. Until then, the Southern sharpshooters, many of whom had been firing their armament since their rural boyhood days, had brought heavy losses to the Northern forces. Perhaps this is one of the reasons for adopting the superior cartridge breechloaders and repeating Spencers and Henrys.

In an indecisive battle, both North and South suffered

heavy losses at Antietam, but the repeating Spencers had given the inexperienced Federal troops the added firepower they needed to turn Lee's first attempt to invade the North. The battle had proved one thing however: The repeater was to see further use during the war.

Some sources claim that as many as 200,000 Spencer rifles and carbines are thought to have been used during the war. Procurement records, however, clearly show that only 94,196 Spencer carbines and 12,471 rifles were purchased officially by the Ordnance Department during the period of January 1, 1861, to the end of the fiscal year, June 30, 1866; this is not counting the seven hundred rifles purchased by the Navy.

In addition to these purchases, better than 58,000,000 of the Spencer cartridges were purchased, many of which were used in the Ballard and Joslyn carbines of the same .56-56 Spencer caliber.

The Spencer became so popular among troops that when units were denied issue of such arms they occasionally took it upon themselves to personally purchase the guns. One such case was the order of 4000 Spencers by Colonel John T. Wilder to equip the men of his brigade. Actually, he had no authority to make the order and the Ordnance Department promptly refused to purchase the guns for him. Wilder asked his men if they would mind purchasing the guns with their own money and the brigade voted in favor of his suggestion.

Armed with the seven-shooters, Wilder's brigade soon won the title of The Lightning Brigade as they turned the Confederate troops from Hoover's Gap in the Cumberland Mountains. With the Confederate troops unable to reinforce those already at Chickamauga, Union soldiers won the battle in a smashing victory several weeks later.

The most widely used repeating rifle of the Civil War, the Spencer wasn't the only one to be employed. In the opinion of many modern Civil War buffs the fifteen-shot Henrys were the best rifles available during the war. Although about 10,000 of these repeating lever actions were eventually purchased by individual soldiers, not one was officially purchased for issue to Federal troops.

An extremely accurate close range arm, the Henry was fitted with a twenty-four-inch barrel that was first bored to .42-inch and then rifled to .43-inch. The .44 Henry Flat, the rimfire cartridge for which these guns were chambered, lacked something in the power department. Propelled by 26 to 28 grains of black powder, the 200-grain bullet was pushed from the muzzle at a velocity of around 1100 feet per second, developing a muzzle energy of just under 600 foot/pounds. Even with this power shortage it nonetheless became a popular sporting cartridge. These early Henrys were the first milestones for the later Winchesters, which were greatly improved through the use of such center-fire cartridges as the .44-40.

Combined with the fact that the Spencer was slow to be fully adopted for use by Union cavalry units, the limited use of the Henry may have added to the length of the war. Many historians and arms buffs believe that if the Spencer had been adopted earlier and produced in large enough numbers, along with full utilization of the Henry's firepower, the war could have been shortened by as much as a year, maybe two.

Burnside, Joslyn, Merril, Gallagher, Maynard, Remington, Smith, Starr, Ball, Gibbs, Hall, Ballard, Linder, Palmer, Warner and Cosmopolitan are a few more names that were known among arms producers of the Civil War.

For the most part these were carbines and, although many gave good service, they never quite matched the firepower of the big bore muzzleloaders or repeaters such as the Spencer. – *Toby Bridges*

Union cavalry soldier in full uniform, including sabre and Spencer repeating rifle. While mounted, rifle was carried in this manner, attached by lanyard.

Big Civil War cannon (right) were a problem to move over rough terrain. Cannon above was made in Selma, Alabama, armory. Below, rear of the Brooke cannon was built to withstand much pressure.

Above, shells for the seven-inch Brooke, such as well taken care of model shown below. The seven-incher at bottom right is on display at Ft. Morgan, Alabama.

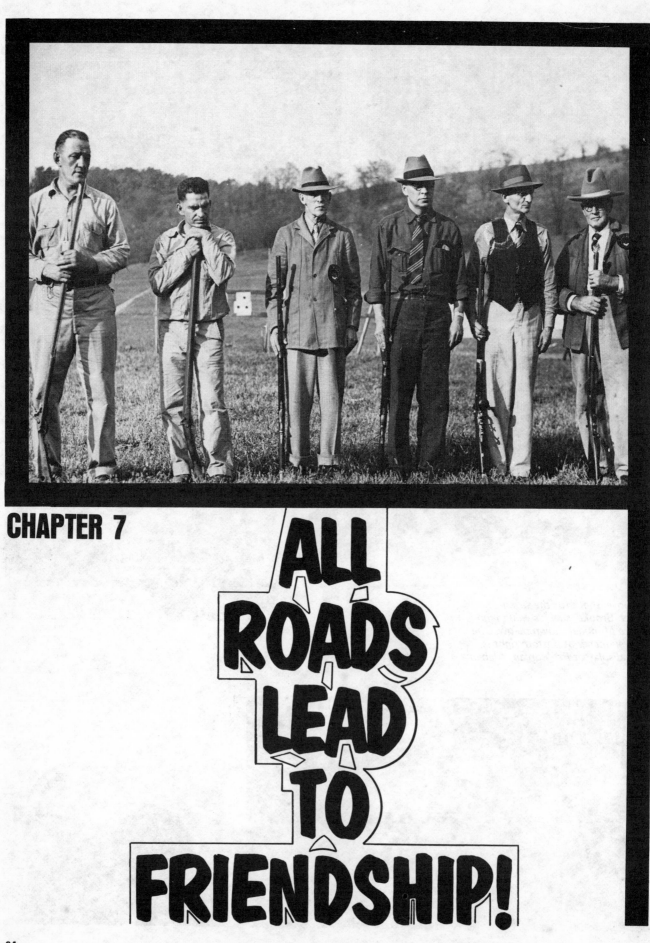

CHAPTER 7

ALL ROADS LEAD TO FRIENDSHIP!

IN THE GENTLY ROLLING, wooded hills and farm lands of southern Indiana lies the village of Friendship, population 120. Here, fifty miles west of Cincinnati, is a piece of Hoosierland from the pages of James Whitcomb Riley, where you can see and take part in competition in historical America. Here, too, you can see and take part in competition in not just plain target shooting, but marksmanship with muzzleloading guns firing only black powder. There are matches for pistols, rifles and shotguns.

Each Fall, a six-day shoot is held to determine the muzzleloading champion of the United States. This Fall shoot always ends on Labor Day. In addition to "this big one," a two-day Spring shoot is held as well as a two-day turkey shoot in November.

The National Muzzle Loading Rifle Association conducts these matches on its own ninety-two-acre range located on the eastern border of the town of Friendship, north of Laughrey Creek.

On August 24, 1781, a band of Indians attacked the command of Colonel Lochry, which was on its way to join Clark's forces at Vincennes. The colonel and thirty-six of his men were killed and the survivors made British prisoners. This action took place on the north bank of the stream that somehow became Laughrey Creek.

The NMLRA Labor Day Shoot is, to the black powder fan, what the World Series is to a baseball fan, what Camp Perry is to the breechloading clique — pure magic. You rarely hear the shoot called by its correct name; rather it is referred to as, "the shoot at Friendship," or just plain "Friendship." So, if you should hear a couple of characters mumbling something about "friendship," with a queer look in their eyes, they aren't talking about undying loyalty to each other, they're discussing ways and means of getting to the Big Shoot back in Indiana.

Just how old the sport of marksmanship is, no one knows. Civilization started to emerge from the mists of time when man and vegetation appeared in the forms we recognize today; we are told this was at the end of the Pleistocene Epoch, about one million years ago. It is not improbable that some Stone Age kids became the world's first marksmen by throwing stones at some whitening skull. The adults were too busy fishing and hunting to play games.

We read of a Roman Emperor during the Second Century A.D. who must have been the greatest marksman of them all. Once he killed a hundred raging lions in the great arena with exactly one hundred arrows.

By 1375 the crossbow began to supplant the long bow and shortly after 1400 A.D., the sound of firearms was heard at the shooting festivals.

At Augsburg, Germany, home of many of the best artist-armorers of the Dark Ages, handguns and muskets were used in the 1429 matches. The 1508 match was attended by 544 bowmen and 919 gunners. This great turnout so protracted the meet that thereafter efforts were made to limit the number of invitations to four hundred.

Today, all the best traditions of the ancient shooting festivals are still carried on at Friendship. The NMLRA, with its 7,500 members, 150 affiliated clubs and the wonderful ninety-two-acre shooting facility didn't just spring into being; it did have a double start, though, because two separate groups started about the same time and, when they joined forces in 1935, the NMLRA was formed.

Early in 1931, E. M. "Red" Farris and Oscar Seth of Portsmouth, Ohio, decided to hold a shooting match with oldtime muzzleloading guns. The event was held February 22, 1931, with great success, as sixty-seven shooters attended.

Every Sport Has Its Big Yearly Event And, For Nearly A Quarter-Century Now, This Indiana Annual Meet Is It For Muzzleloaders!

BRIDGE OVER HAYES BRANCH - STATE HIGHWAY 62 - NEAR DILLSBORO, IND.

The next year, another shoot was held at Portsmouth. In 1933, an organization was formed with Seth as president and Farris as "ramrod." The hat was passed and there was ten dollars in the treasury. Radio WLW of Cincinnati featured a popular story teller known as Boss Johnson. Boss had an especial friend among his host of followers, W. F. "Pop" Neighbert, storekeeper and police chief of Friendship, Indiana. These two cronies decided to hold a black powder shoot.

Boss "talked it up" on WLW and the response was all they hoped for. He asked his boss, Powell Crosley Jr., owner of WLW, to put up a prize. It was a silver loving cup about the size of an umbrella stand and was hotly contested for; today nearly forty years later it is still being battled over and is the most important single trophy of all, next to the National Championship Cup.

Some of the other awards for that first Friendship shoot were: A pair of rubber boots donated by S. H. Sickerman, a hunting coat donated by Neighbert, a suede jacket offered by the Friendship State Bank, a half barrel of flour by the Friendship Milling Company and several more of which I have no record.

Today, the first three places in every event are awarded medals: gold, silver and bronze. In many cases, the winner receives a handsome trophy in addition to his gold medal. There are fourteen different championship aggregates consisting of two or more of the seventy events and in a

The atmosphere at Friendship is a relaxed one during the yearly shoot. Umbrellas are used to ward off the scorching sun.

Wearing authentic costume and beard, this shooter appears as if he just stepped out of the pages of a history book. Not all shooters are quite this authentic in dress.

Slug gun shooters and spectators both enjoy an informal practice session before the heat of the actual competition is on.

Firing their heavy barreled black powder rifles, competitors shoot for top honors in the Alvin York Match. Shooter above is Bill Furst.

Floyd Resor of Union City, Indiana, is a regular at Friendship. He is known for his extremely accurate black powder guns.

number of cases, a single event may be part of several different aggregates.

In 1935, the two groups joined to form the NMLRA with Boss Johnson as president. The 1937 shoot was held at Rising Sun, Indiana, next year the matches were moved to the Sugar Bowl, amid the larch and maple trees, one time camping ground of the Shawnees near Dillsboro, Indiana. The Dillsboro Health Resort became the association's headquarters for the next two years. This establishment is the nearest complete hotel accommodation to Friendship; Del Ross, Margaret Turner and the rest of the staff always do everything to make the visiting shooter happy.

Since 1938, all matches have been held on the association's own range, a piece of land bought from the late Walter Cline, author, a founder and long time M-L enthusiast. The present range is named the Walter Cline Range. The association's monthly magazine, Muzzle-Blasts, was started in September, 1939, and goes out monthly to each member.

No organization grows without the leadership of industrious men of ability. Only a few can be mentioned in a short story like this. In addition to those mentioned above: Walter Grote, Bull Ramsey, Clarence McNeer, James Lemon and about a dozen others should be listed as founders. B. LeRoy Compton, M. G. Van Way and James Lemon are some of the businessmen who helped the lusty infant reach its present status. Today the headquarters address is: P.O. Box 67, Friendship, Indiana 47021.

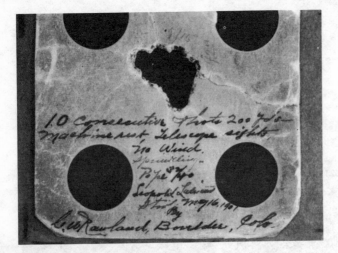

Somewhat of a record at the annual muzzleloading meet is this ten shot, two hundred yard group made by C.W. Rawland.

The purpose of the association remains the same as the day it was founded: To promote shooting, collecting and building muzzleloading guns and equipment, along with the joy of research into the history of these items.

Each year, when the order to commence firing is given, some are made bold, some irresolute, some strengthened and some paralyzed by buck fever. Some consider the loss of an event the way most people would regard the loss of an eye. Others are as keenly downcast, but hide behind a stoic front. To be a winner, you have to be a competitor;

With the competition still not underway, the parking lot at the Walter Cline Range fills rather quickly with arriving shooters.

this spirit of competition seems to be what brings us back each year, for maybe "the next time," our efforts to excel will pay off. The rifle events — both round ball and slug, offhand and bench — make up the bulk of the program on the 175-position rifle range.

Over the years, complete and detailed rules and procedures have been developed and are published in the NMLRA Rule Book. All round ball rifle events are five-shot matches, the slug-gun and pistol events are ten-shot affairs and the number of birds for the shotgun matches varies. Each string of five shots must be fired in forty-five minutes, then the range is closed for fifteen minutes while the crews change targets. Firing starts at 8 a.m. and continues straight through until 5 p.m. All scores are posted hourly on the seventy different event sheets. Each shooter selects the events he wants to enter and he may fire these events in any order he chooses. Because of this, the winner of every event is in doubt until the final relay on Labor Day morning.

Most competitors enter the four events, the aggregate of which makes up the National Championship. These events are: the Mike Fink Match, twenty-five yards offhand, any iron sights; the Powell Crosley Match, fifty yards, benchrest, open iron sights; the Alvin York Match, fifty yards, benchrest, any iron sight and the Walter Cline Match, one hundred yards, benchrest, any iron sight.

Your gun will qualify, if you can lug it up to the firing line, it shoots black powder, is loaded from the muzzle and can be fitted with the specific sight equipment and fires the proper bullet for the match — either a round ball or a slug. Several events do have a weight limitation on the gun, but its vintage is of no importance. Loading benches are provided to the rear of the firing line, but a sturdy folding shooting bench and chair are a must.

Because each man and woman is firing the events of his choice in the sequence of his choosing, the outcome never "hangs on the next shot." This does not make for keen spectator interest; after the novelty of the flash, boom and smoke has been observed, a muzzleloading match is about as exciting to the casual observer as watching grass grow.

To a competitor, it is a different story. If he has turned in a good score the first day, he finds himself checking the score sheet for that event several times a day to learn whether anybody has beaten him yet. If his score holds up, the suspense grows.

The pistol range and of course the trap field hold more

spectator value. To add more color for everybody's enjoyment, shooters and their families are urged to wear authentic costumes of earlier days, especially for the Sunday morning parade to church. The Lutheran Church of the nearby hamlet of Farmers Retreat conducts services Sunday morning. All shooting is stopped for an hour while the Jim Bridgers, Wyatt Earps and Colonial girls parade to church and for a moment barbers, salesmen, lawyers, doctors, engineers, laymen and ministers lose their identity and become characters of the past. Those not attending church use the time to renew cherished friendships or repair a piece of equipment. The ladies of the church also operate the dining room in the club house, as well as the lunch stand outside throughout the shoot. Three meals a day are served and the menus range from hot-dogs to a full chicken dinner, including all the trimmings — even blueberry pie. A feature of the noon meal is the special fast service table for shooters only.

each state. The registration area is on the main floor near the west door. Scoring is done on the second floor, secure from helping hands. South of the clubhouse the camping area is laid out in "streets" with 110-volt juice available for the individual lots. Modern rest rooms and bath houses are permanent installations. The shooter's camping equipment ranges from a sleeping bag under the sky to the most luxurious self-contained house trailers. A strict five-mile per hour speed limit is enforced throughout.

Commercial Row lies to the west and here permanent wooden booths flank a wide street area to accommodate our modern gold and silversmiths. If the demand for space overflows the booths, space for tents is made available. All kinds of equipment and supplies are for sale. Remington still makes percussion caps, Hodgdon has black powder and the ancient art of flint knapping flourishes in Brandon, England. In recent years, several new sources of flints have been developed in our South.

This photo, taken in 1953, shows the interest already prevalent at that time. These shooters were busy practicing for match four days before.

A few years ago a new event was added: the Seneca Running Offhand. Here the contestant — preferably in buckskins — must fire five shots from five widely separated stations on surprise targets. Each man must be fully equipped to load between stations and, since a time element is involved, each must move at a fast trot and after the last shot race back to the starting point. The shadows of Colonel Lochry and his men must certainly watch in approval; for the Seneca course is laid in the bed of Laughery Creek.

Any person shooting a five-shot possible in competition automatically joins the exclusive 50 Club and receives a gold lapel button, is a guest at the 50 Club dinner and may enter the 50 Club Match.

The two-story clubhouse is equipped with kitchens, dining room and a main hall capable of seating five hundred people. The great memorial fireplace contains a stone from

The number of shooters registering each year varies from 500 to 600. They come, some with families, from virtually every state and territory. On the holiday weekend the crowd exceeds 2,000.

So, we come to the real purpose of the whole enterprise: The shooting events, the best individual shooter, etc. In my opinion, the greatest individual accomplishment was the 100 — 9x record score fired by John Baldinger in the two hundred-yard Billinghurst match, not only because of this record, but because John was seventy-eight years old at the time. What a wonderful example of the joy a target shooting competitor can experience long after more strenuous sports have to be given up.

For a fine outdoor hobby for the entire family, try muzzleloading target shooting and, if you do I hope you never have a misfire. – Bob Furst

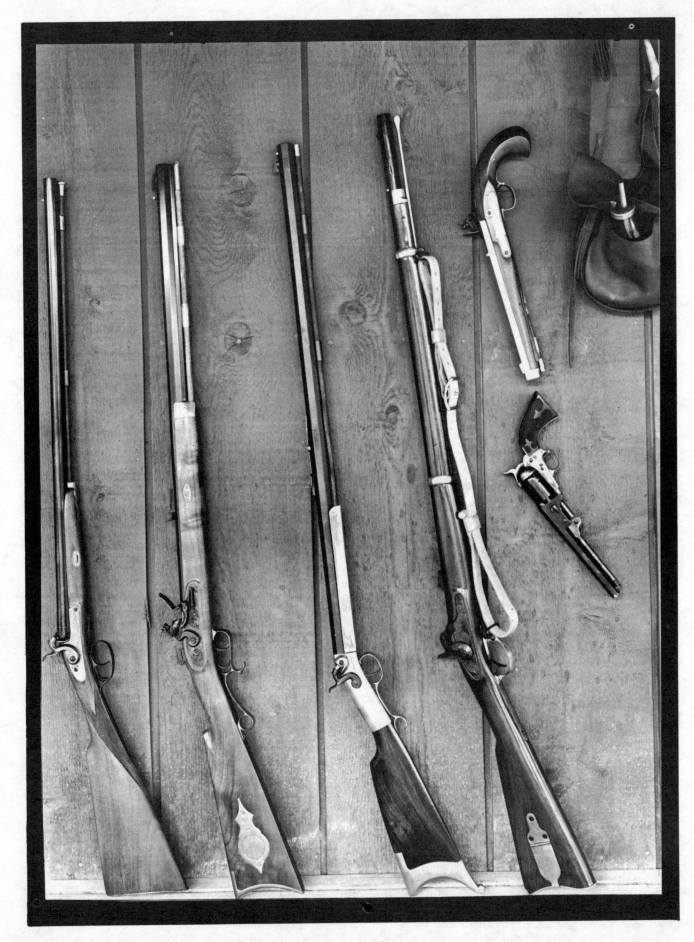

REBIRTH OF AN ERA

Nostalgia, Low Cost And Anti-Gun Laws Have Much To Do With The Rebirth Of The Black Powder Sport!

THE SCARCITY OF fine old original black powder arms in safe shootable condition can be accredited for the introduction of the numerous replicas and reproduction guns that are being offered today. Few, if any, serious collectors would even entertain the thought of putting such fine old originals through the rigors of everyday shooting. Once these guns are lost to irreparable damage, they are lost for good.

The idea of producing a modern reproduction or replica of these early arms took hold in the second half of the 1950s and, through the efforts of such men as Val Forgett of the Navy Arms Company and Turner Kirkland of Dixie Gun Works and others, there now are a good number of replica models to choose from. For the most part, the majority of these guns are almost exact reproductions of the originals they copy. There are changes on some, however, that actually make these guns far superior to their predecessors. Most of these changes are internal, making the guns more dependable without changing the overall appearance.

It's hard, if not impossible, to credit any one individual with the introduction of replicas. It's a known fact that Sam Colt, himself, was hard pressed to discourage the illegal manufacture of Colt copies and there are a number of guns still around that were assembled from surplus original parts, many known to have been produced well before the rebirth of black powder shooting in the last several decades.

In 1955, Turner Kirkland began marketing his Dixie

Ruger recently entered the black powder field
with this percussion version of their famous
Blackhawk single-action, dubbed the Old Army.

squirrel rifle. Made in Liege, Belgium, this rifle was the first modern-made black powder muzzleloading arm to be introduced in the United States. As could only be expected, this .45 caliber rifle was accepted quickly by the contemporary black powder crowd.

The shortage of vintage Kentucky and Pennsylvania long rifles, coupled with the fact that the vast majority of these guns were handmade, and the growing rarity of such guns caused the prices to skyrocket out of the average shooter's reach. The Dixie rifle, however, had two extremely pleasing features. In addition to being reasonably priced, the gun actually was superior to most of the originals in that it utilized much stronger modern steels in its construction.

Dixie Gun Works' rifle opened a new field and it wasn't long before other replicas and reproduction guns began to hit the market. In 1958, Val Forgett formed the Navy Arms Company; his first gun was a near exact replica of the 1851 Colt Navy. This was the first of the cap and ball revolver replicas to come into this country.

The story behind producing this first pistol is somewhat interesting in itself. It seems that Forgett experienced some trouble from the Italian customs people in trying to get an original Colt Navy to Brescia gunmaker Vittorio Gregorelli. Customs officials wouldn't allow the pistol to be shipped to the gunmaker, who hadn't received a license to produce firearms. This problem was easily solved, however, by calling on a friend, who was in the service and stationed in Italy at the time, to deliver the gun to the armsmaker.

Of the first sixteen of these guns produced — ten copies of the original Colt Navy and six of the Confederate Griswold & Gunnison brass framed .36 caliber Army revolver — Forgett quickly noticed nearly a dozen changes in their design. These were all prototypes and he soon had them straightened out.

The Italian hand craftsman had changed the bead front

sight to a dovetailed blade and among the other changes that robbed the guns of an original appearance were the enlarged screw heads of the guard screws and the extra width of the brass guard plate. The inner curve and beveled angle on the back of the guard plate was deliberately changed slightly to distinguish the copy from the original. This also results in yet another slight change in the shape of the grips.

Replicas and reproduction guns have come a long way since the introduction of the aforementioned two. Today's black powder enthusiast finds a large number of such guns available at most any sporting goods store and through a multitude of arms distributor catalogs.

Why all this fuss over shooting dirty, smelly and ballistically inferior black powder guns?

Of all the logical reasons, from nostalgia to the growing legal complications involved in possessing and discharging firearms of modern design, especially handguns, perhaps the single best reason is that black powder guns are fun. How many times have you been firing at a range with your conventional armament to suddenly notice a giant puff of smoke belch forth some ways down the firing line? It sure catches your interest and, before the day is over, it's a good bet that you'll mosey on over and see what said shooter is firing. Black powder guns are interesting!

Beginning muzzleloader and cap and ball revolver shooters would be wise to stay away from the cheapies on the market. Even though these guns are fully proof-tested before being imported into this country and are declared safe for shooting, their sloppy manufacture make them undependable and the trouble they present detracts greatly from the pleasure of shooting them.

As with modern cartridge-type guns, black powder guns are classified into one of three main categories: rifles, shotguns and handguns. Each of these categories can be broken down even further — single-shot, multiple-shot, double barrel, single barrel, etc. — but for this brief introduction of replicas and reproduction guns we will leave them in the three main categories. Subsequent sections will go into detail on the background and development of many of these guns. This is a look at some of the better black powder pieces available on today's market.

CENTENNIAL ARMS has been in the black powder arms business since the early 1960s, following closely the developments made by Val Forgett. Among the numerous pieces now offered by them, two stand out as about as close a reproduction as can be obtained — their New Model Colt Army replica and 1863 Zouave Remington reproduction.

Both of these guns are imported from Italy and both are strong, well built shooters. The Army replica is .44 caliber and has an eight-inch rifled barrel. A big .58 caliber, the reproduction of the Zouave is a perfect choice for North/South Skirmishes or big game hunting.

COLT: Getting back into the black powder scene this early developer of the cap and ball revolver has again begun reproduction of the 1851 Navy. This is a top quality cap and ball revolver that is not a replica, but a reproduction of the same gun. Colt had to work out a few bugs when production was first started on these revolvers, but they are now stronger shooters than the originals.

Lyman — long known for its sighting and reloading equipment — is another new entry. This is the .36 caliber New Model Navy revolver. The firm also produces a .44 caliber New Model Army and numerous other black powder shooting aids and accessories.

DIXIE GUN WORKS: A pioneer in the replica business, Turner Kirkland has built this firm into one of the largest black powder gun distributors in the country. Among the numerous replicas now offered are the Dixie Deluxe Pennsylvania rifle and the Dixie First Model Brown Bess. The Dixie Pennsylvania rifle isn't an exact replica of any given make, but is a copy of the general type, roman nose shaping of the butt stock, beautifully inlaid brass patchbox, cherry-stained hardwood stock. The Dixie Brown Bess is a big .75 caliber long land smoothbore musket and is about as close a reproduction of the original available today.

ESOPUS: A division of Port Ewen Products, Incorporated, the Esopus Gun Works has introduced a new pair of black powder rifles. Both guns are considerably different from any other rifles on the market. The Pacer is a .45 caliber rifle featuring a unique side lock mechanism. This lock automatically places the rifle's safety in the on position as it is cocked. The other rifle from Esopus is a two-shot swivel-breech double rifle; a good hunting rifle offering two spontaneous shots. Both of these guns are one hundred percent American-made.

LYMAN, a firm well known for its sighting equipment and reloading presses, now offers two cap and ball revolvers. The Lyman New Model Army is a six-shot, .44 caliber revolver and the Lyman New Model Navy is its smaller .36 caliber version. Both guns are made in Europe under Lyman's supervision and the result is two fine black powder revolvers that are dependable. Both the Army and Navy follow the solid frame Remington pattern, a design favored by shooters interested in installing adjustable target sights.

NAVY ARMS, known for its spearheading the development of replica cap and ball revolvers, offers a complete line of single-shot percussion and flintlock pistols. The Navy Arms Kentucky pistol is a copy of the type of pistol used during the late 1700s and early 1800s. Having a .440 bore diameter, this is a reliable shooter backed by an experienced distributor of black powder guns; it is available in flintlock or percussion.

For the serious competitor, Navy Arms also offers special target percussion revolvers. These .44 and .36 caliber revolvers are of the solid frame design and have full-length top ribs with ramp front sights and fully adjustable rear target sights.

NUMRICH ARMS: For some time now this developer of the Hopkins & Allen underhammer rifles has offered a complete line of wares for the hunter and serious competitor. The H&A Deluxe Buggy rifle is a light, short rifle that makes an excellent hunting piece in brushy country. This rifle is in .36 or .45 caliber. Available in the same calibers, the Heritage Model features a thirty-two-inch rifled octagon barrel and is a dependable offhand target rifle.

MARIETTA REPLICA ARMS is known for its complete line of replica revolvers. This Ohio-based firm also distributes a well built replica of the Cecil Brooks rifle called the Plainsman. Available in .38 and .45 calibers, this is one of the finest muzzleloading rifles on the market.

Replica Arms also offers an extremely well built and dependable double-barrel muzzleloading shotgun. This 12-gauge front-loading scattergun features a checkered French walnut stock and is one of the few that offers choked barrels; the twenty-eight-inch barrels are choked full and modified.

RICHLAND ARMS, new to the field of muzzleloading arms, is a longtime distributor of fine imported breech-loading shotguns but now offers a 12-gauge muzzleloading shotgun. This gun sports twenty-eight-inch barrels that are cylinder bore. It is a rugged lightweight shotgun and should make an excellent upland bird hunting gun. The walnut stock is set off by the engraved lock plates — purposely left in the white — and the beautifully plum-colored browned barrels.

THOMPSON/CENTER, of Rochester, New Hampshire, is producing an American-made modern version of the Hawken rifle. This rifle was the prized possession of the westward adventurer and today is one of the most sought after collector pieces. Thompson/Center's modern reproduction differs slightly from the original, utilizing modern coil springs in place of the original flat type springs in the lock work. The rifle, however, maintains the husky and robust feeling of the original.

RUGER now is producing a black powder .44 caliber version of its famed single action Blackhawk. Featuring a completely modern internal mechanism, this is one of the most dependable cap and ball sixguns. The revolver, dubbed the Ruger Old Army, features a fixed blade front sight and fully adjustable rear target sights. In appearance, the Old Army is similar to the firm's line of cartridge revolvers, the frame being modified to accept the loading lever, substituting a capping groove in place of the loading gate.

There are numerous other top quality replicas and reproduction guns available. As mentioned, there still are cheap black powder guns on the market even though the trend is toward quality. Never settle for anything less than top quality. It pays in the long run, even if it costs more initially! – *Toby Bridges.*

THE CONFEDERACY'S LAST ARSENAL!

Turner Kirkland's Tennessee Arms Stronghold Is Enough To Stagger The Civil War Buff's Imagination!

NEED A NEW hammer for your well-used 1819 Halls rifle? What about an original main spring for that mint condition Charleville musket hanging over the fireplace – which could have been in the boat with Washington as he crossed the Delaware? Or perhaps your needs are more in the line of an original lock for a rare Green carbine.

An old gun fancier could spend a lot of time searching for any of these parts. Charleville muskets are hard to come by and it's doubtful that a collector owning one would be willing to part with his main spring anyhow. Equally rare are Green carbines – with less than a thousand produced in 1856 and 1857 – so chances are that, if you could locate a hammer for the 1819 Halls rifle, it would be quite the worse for wear. As a matter of fact, replacement parts for just about any antique firearm is near impossible to locate, unless you happen to know where to look!

One such place is Dixie Gun Works of Union City,

Rebirth Of An Era: Part B

Tennessee. Here, Turner Kirkland — founder and president of the firm — has stockpiled an unknown quantity of old original parts for these guns and many others. Today, Dixie Gun Works is perhaps the largest retail black powder catalog order store and antique gun parts supplier in the country. How it grew to reach this status is a story in itself.

"The first gun that my father bought me — being quite young at the time, I paid for the gun, but father bought it — was an old Colt 1849 Model .31 caliber pocket pistol that

Remington pistols, not to mention near mint condition Civil War rifles and muskets could be had for as little as fifty cents each, with mint condition guns bringing as high as two or three dollars. Collecting these guns had not yet reached the level of interest we know today and there were plenty of guns to be had; nearly every home had at least one or two just collecting dust.

"Of course, he said he was buying them for me," recalls

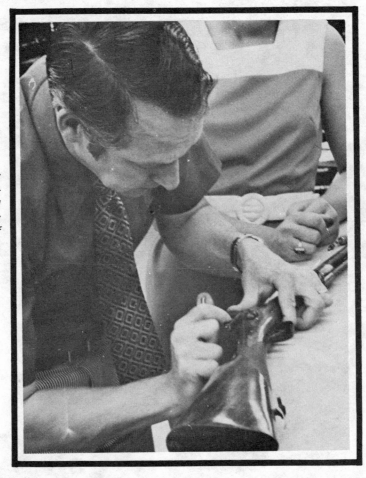

Dixie Gun Works' vice president Ernest Tidwell replaces faulty nipple on one of firm's muzzleloaders.

was pretty well used up. But the gun only cost seventy-five cents, so I couldn't complain much about that. I liked the gun so well that I would carry it to bed with me each night," states Kirkland. "I loved that gun better than just about anything else."

He had no idea at the time, but that worn out old Colt probably was part of the foundation on which Dixie Gun Works was formed. It was 1932 and the country was suffering from the effects of the depression. Small businesses folded under the stress of just day to day living; in short, it was hardly a time to be spending money on guns.

Kirkland's father, however, ran a small men's clothing store that just managed to survive the times. Although his sales were small, he always managed to scrape together enough money to buy an occasional rifle or pistol.

Money was scarce and hard to come by and, when anyone did manage to earn a few dollars, it almost always went for food to feed the family; rarely was it spent on guns. Consequently, fine original Kentucky rifles, Colt and

Turner Kirkland, "but really I think he was just buying them to hang on the walls in his store so they would help bring in a little more traffic and consequently make people spend a little more money.

"I didn't really know the difference between gunpowders then and didn't even know that black powder was available, but I would take firecrackers and stuff them in the end of the old Colt's barrel and light them, holding the gun out while it shot. A couple of years later, about 1934, I took out the silver powder by cutting open and unrolling the firecrackers. I loaded this into one of the chambers of an old Remington revolver.

"Well, the gun blew up! The solid strap on the frame that ran across the top of the cylinder just disappeared into thin air when the powder ignited. The chamber of the cylinder blew outward and, of course, ruined the gun. I can't remember what I ever did with that particular gun, but I guess I traded it off to someone way back. Anyway, I had learned my lesson about using smokeless powder in a black powder gun!"

Kirkland would travel with his father to visit relatives in Memphis every chance he got or at least that's the excuse he used to go along on the trips. Almost as soon as they would roll into Memphis, Turner would just disappear, but could always be found at York Arms, looking at their great display of guns and ammunition. "I was in my seventh Heaven visiting York Arms," recalls Kirkland today with a faint smile.

At that time York Arms was selling black powder for around sixty-five cents a pound, percussion caps ran around fifteen cents for a tin of a hundred. Today, Dixie gets nearly three dollars for that same pound of powder and a tin of percussion caps runs a dollar.

Five years after buying his first gun — the old Colt 1849 pocket pistol — Kirkland had managed to build his collection to more than a hundred guns of various makes. For the next few years, college took up most of Kirkland's time and gun collecting underwent a temporary set back.

When World War II broke out, he joined the Army and for the first time began meeting other gun collectors. Looking back, he remembers that "during the war I began to run into other collectors and started going into gun stores, among which was Bannerman's in New York City. I would spend hours walking around in Bannerman's just looking around.

"I couldn't afford to buy anything, but my mouth watered when I saw all the bargains they had. Back then you could buy a Sharps rifle for around $3.50 and good Spencer rifles were only $3. Mint condition .58 caliber Civil War muskets with bright and shiny bores could be had for less than five dollars apiece.

"Bannerman's even had new cast model cannon barrels for sale. Because I saw these at Bannerman's and liked them so well, is the reason I sell them today."

After the war — even more interested in gun collecting

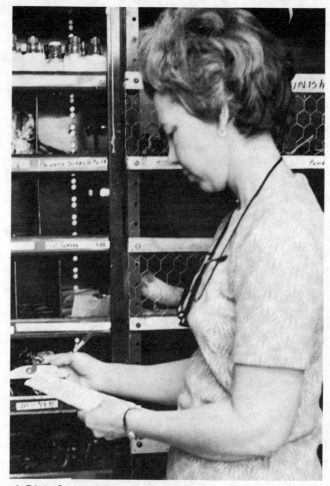

A Dixie Gun Works employee fills an order from the numerous bins filled with old gun parts. Many of these parts are near impossible to find.

In addition to an outstanding collection of old guns, Dixie's Turner Kirkland is also an old car fancier; has many of them displayed in his antique car museum located next to gun works.

If you can't find it on display, look it up in the catalog. If you can't find it in the catalog, no problem, just ask at the counter!

than he had been before — Kirkland began trading off the hundred-gun collection he had acquired before WWII. This was not to get rid of his guns, but instead to upgrade each piece in this collection.

There were few serious collectors in western Tennessee, so he did most of his trading and selling with collectors in other states through the mail. This was when he first discovered that there was a good demand for selling and buying through the mail.

Business continued to grow and in the May, 1948 issue of Muzzle Blast Magazine, Kirkland ran his first commercial ad. It was short and to the point: He had ten muzzleloaders — giving a very brief discription of each — he wanted to sell and he was looking for prospective buyers. In a very short time, all ten of the muzzleloaders were sold and Dixie Gun Works became a consistent advertiser in several of the shooting magazines.

In 1950, Turner Kirkland took a job selling jewelry and found himself doing a lot of travelling throughout his home state of Tennessee and neighboring Arkansas. Most of his work was done during the day and he had a lot of free time on his hands at the end of each day. To pass this time, he began to look up local gun collectors in each of the towns he travelled. Carrying quite a stock of merchandise with him, he did a lot of swapping and buying out of the trunk of his car.

His magazine advertisements began to receive a lot of attention from gun dealers all over the country and Europe. As a result, he made important contacts in England, Belgium, Spain and Italy.

During his jewelry selling travels he discovered there was a definite need for replacement locks, triggers, tenons, barrels and various other parts. He began importing these from manufacturers all over Europe and his business prospered even more.

He then purchased a small metal working lathe from

More than a dozen different kits are available from the Union City, Tennessee, firm. There are an even dozen displayed here but there are several not shown.

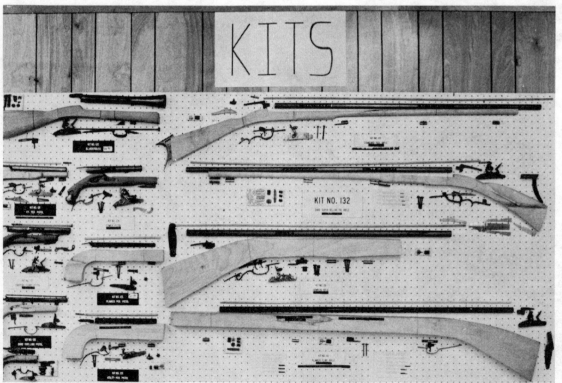

Two of the numerous visitors to Dixie Gun Works are almost lost among the forest of gun barrels as they browse through the old guns on sale there.

Part of the Dixie collection that isn't for sale. Many of these guns were a part of Turner Kirkland's early gun collection.

Sears-Roebuck and began milling bullet moulds out of commercially made cast iron hair straighteners. The demand for these moulds was so great that he could make as much as a hundred dollars a week making and marketing them in his spare time.

By 1954, mail order for his imported parts and bullet moulds, not to mention the occasional batch of guns he advertised for sale or trade, reached the point of forcing him to quit his selling job. He moved the business into a revamped coal house and this was Dixie Gun Works' first home.

Six months later Dixie Gun Works offered its first catalog, a twelve-pager selling for twenty-five cents. Business really boomed and in less than a year, the operation outgrew its coal house facilities and had to be moved into a larger building.

In 1955, Dixie Gun Works introduced the first reproduction rifle ever to be marketed in this country. Built in Belgium to Kirkland's strict specifications, the Dixie Squirrel Rifle was an exact copy of the type of rifle that is referred to so fondly as the Kentucky rifle. The gun featured the rounded symetrical lines of the original Kentucky types and the quality of the Belgium-made rifle soon won wide acclaim among the growing black powder crowd.

Dixie Gun Works continued to grow until it once again outgrew its existing facilities, doubling in size in five years.

In 1961, the firm moved into yet a larger building, where it was based until 1968, when it had again increased

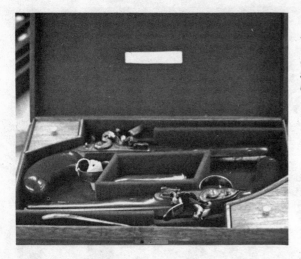

Among the many replicas
for sale are actually
quite a few antique arms,
such as this cased pair
of duelling type pistols.

It's always hard on
muzzleloaders to dry
snap them. Visitors
that must snap a gun
are given the chance,
but with a flare pistol.

to the point of having to be moved into a still larger structure. Today, Dixie Gun Works occupies a spacious 31,000 square-foot building on the outskirts of Union City.

Turner Kirkland today is as fascinated with firearms as he was when he bought that first 1849 Colt. He now spends a good part of his time travelling throughout the country and Europe trying to locate forgotten stockpiles of antique gun parts, old leather goods and other relics, including medieval armament, antique reloading equipment — and even scalplocks.

Dixie Gun Works has done much to promote the sport of shooting black powder guns, as evidenced by their participation in the National Spring Shoot of the National Muzzle Loading Rifle Association at Friendship, Indiana, each year. The firm has been represented at every match since 1951, with Kirkland attending most of the matches himself.

The initial success of Dixie's Squirrel Rifle reproduction led to an ever-growing market of reproduction black powder guns. Today the firm imports close to forty different makes of replicas, as well as being a distributor for many of the other replicas being made or imported by

Coon skin cap???
Prospective buyer
gets the feel of
a reproduction gun.

Customer explains to a Dixie Gun Works employee the parts needed to restore two fine antique arms.

The Belgian-made Dixie Gun Works' black powder rifles are authentically built in every detail; strong and accurate shooters.

numerous other firms.

If you are the type of gun fancier who likes to thumb through gun magazines, you've probably come across a short seven-word ad that reads, "Visit Dixie Gun Works for Antique Arms." Turner Kirkland encourages anyone that might be travelling through that section of the South to stop in and visit.

A visit to Dixie Gun Works is like walking through an antique firearms museum and, better yet, many of the old guns are actually for sale. There are countless old military muskets and rifles filling the spacious gun racks, several showcases jammed full of hundreds of mint and near-mint condition Colt and Remington cap and ball revolvers. Adorning one complete wall of the building is Kirkland's personal collection of fine old original Kentucky rifles and rare and unique military arms. Some of these have been in his collection since before World War II and a few now have collector values of over $2,000.

The current Dixie Gun Works catalog is a far cry from the twelve-page 1954 catalog that sold for a quarter. To get all of their wares into a single publication, the present day catalog consists of some 362 pages, selling for two dollars.

Having become known as an authority on antique firearms, especially on Philadelphia derringers and Kentucky rifles, Kirkland receives as many as a hundred inquiries each day concerning old guns that someone is interested in buying, selling or repairing. Their questions range from "what is the gun's value?" and "can it be repaired?" to "would you like to buy it or know of anyone that might?"

Kirkland is always interested in buying old guns, but to answer questions such as the first two, he has included in his latest catalog more than fifty pages of helpful information on how to clean, care, repair, test and determine the date of manufacture for many of the more common black powder guns. Also listed are several pages on Civil War proofmarks that help give the reader some personal information on guns made during this era. – *Toby Bridges*

A NAME TO REMEMBER!

Part C: Rebirth Of An Era

Today's Burgeoning Business In Black Powder Replicas Is A Phenomenon Of Fairly Recent Growth And This Is The Saga Of A Man And His Company Who Helped Pioneer It!

Nearing nine inches in length, this fourteen pounder James projectile is just one of the many types Forgett encountered on Bannerman's.

"THE WHOLE ISLAND had been cleaned off in keeping with my contract and that was probably one of the oddest documents in history," Val Forgett, a quiet, soft-spoken gent, recalls. "It was necessary to take off everything of an explosive nature before the insurance company would even allow anyone else on Bannerman's Island."

The boat was about to pull away from the pier that jutted out from this castle on the Hudson River, but Forgett noted that, at the end of this dock, there stood like flanking sentinals two naval war shells from the Spanish-American war. They were some fourteen inches in diameter and at least nine feet in length.

"With a Stillson wrench in my hand, I shinnied up one of the shells like I would a palm tree. I unscrewed the plug and discovered that the shell was still loaded!

"It had been sitting out there in summer suns, hot and ready to go, since 1898 or thereabouts. And as I looked into that supply of powder, I suddenly had the feeling I might be the first man on the moon. And that was before anyone learned to spell astronaut."

Undaunted, the man from Teaneck — then his home — climbed the adjoining shell, removed the plug from it and, just before he and his boat sailed away into the sunset of the Hudson River, he tipped the two shells off the pier — and into fourteen feet or so of soft mud!

This experience has much to do with Forgett's initial success in the field of antique arms sales. As the story goes, the insurance agents covering what was known officially as the Bannerman Island Arsenal, a 5½-acre piece of land loaded with obsolete but nonetheless dangerous explosives, had sought to have the Army, the Air Force and even the Marines send demolitions experts to defuse what could have created the greatest stir in Greater New York since the last passing of Halley's Comet. By everyone's admission, the island — loaded with decomposed Civil War and Spanish-American War explosives — was a bomb that was simply waiting for the right opportunity to do its thing.

At the time Forgett was contacted and contracted to clean up the island arsenal, his own business, Service Armament, was in being and doing well, dealing largely in antique and war surplus armament, most of it out of the muzzleloading era.

Forgett long had been a student of the armament of the Civil War and the decades following and, in addition, had a thing about cannon. He had, at one point, as many as sixty Civil War artillery pieces on his farm. His idea of a quiet Sunday's entertainment was to load one up and hold target practice at several hundred yards. He since has cut the collection to some eight prime pieces.

While Service Armament already was a thriving business even Forgett admits that the old arms he purchased from the Bannerman arsenal did much to make the business even better known. After all, Bannerman's had been a leader in the surplus business after the Spanish-American War and, at one point, had advertised in several New York City newspapers that they had just received three whole trainloads of

A front view of Bannerman's Island Arsenal. Despite everlasting appearance of the building, poor concrete caused the castle to crumble.

In this view of the Bannerman castle, the cannon are pointing out above the portcullis; cannon balls used as decoration.

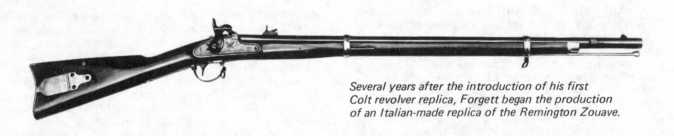

Several years after the introduction of his first Colt revolver replica, Forgett began the production of an Italian-made replica of the Remington Zouave.

war surplus goods, much of it captured from Spain.

The near legends regarding the so-called Bannerman castle are countless, but most have a basis in truth. For example, the Bannerman firm admitted the manner in which the huge structure came into being in the first place. It seems that a soldier of fortune approached the firm with the idea of purchasing arms to begin a Latin-American revolution. The Bannerman's, of course, refused such an arrangement and the adventurer went elsewhere to find the needed goods.

He eventually was arrested, along with his supply of contraband armament. All of the smallarms had been dismantled and hidden in bags of cement.

When the Federal Government ordered the arms — and the cement — sold at auction, it was the Bannerman's who purchased them. The armament was put up for sale and the cement was hauled to the island to be used in building the

vast structure that sprawls across the 5½ acres.

The erstwhile gunrunner may have had the final laugh, however. The cement was of low quality as might be expected. The structure was hardly finished before it began to show crumbling fissures and wide cracks in the concrete.

The breakwater flanking the castle had been created by driving the barrels from artillery pieces into the mud until they formed a continuous series of pilings. The cannon from the flagship of Admiral Farragut, the naval hero, was emplaced on the top level of the castle to guard the entrance.

In these surroundings, one would expect to find a hoard of collector trophies that should be worth thousands upon thousands of dollars — and a few of these were found, Forgett admits. But for the most part, the valuable collector items long since had been sold through the Bannerman operation. What remained was largely rubble. In one court-

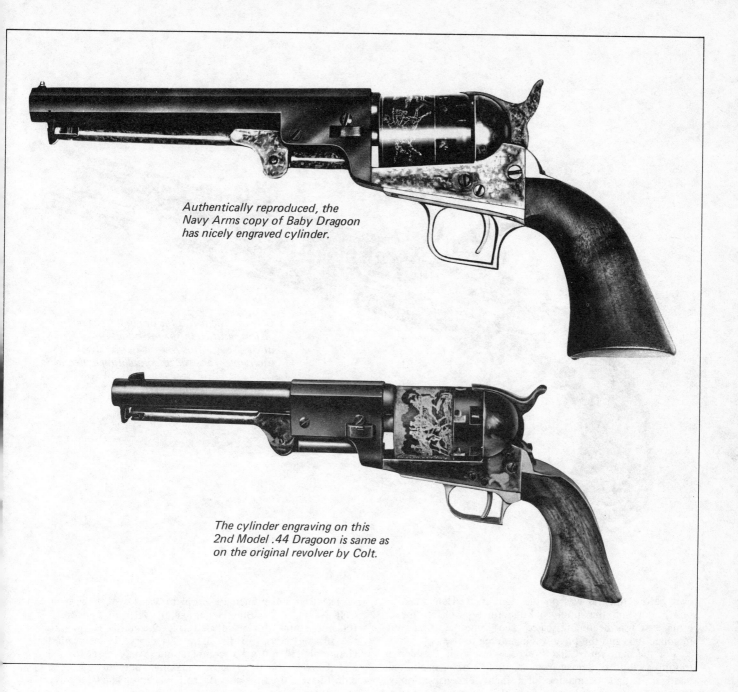

Authentically reproduced, the Navy Arms copy of Baby Dragoon has nicely engraved cylinder.

The cylinder engraving on this 2nd Model .44 Dragoon is same as on the original revolver by Colt.

yard, there were thousands of pith helmets strewn about, literally all that remained of the once proud British regiments that had fought in North Africa and India in the last century.

Countless Gatling guns had been smashed by vandals, the brass fixtures hauled to the mainland and sold as scrap. A number of the watchman hired over a period of years also seem to have made up for the low pay by going into the scrap iron business on their own. And almost everywhere were unexploded shells, some of them nearly a century old, when Forgett and his own small crew of explosive experts landed on the island to make it safe.

According to Forgett, the State of New York wanted, at that time, to purchase the island for recreational purposes, but the sale was being held up by the fact that those insurance companies would have nothing to do with it until the island was literally defused.

With only forty days in which to accomplish this monumental chore, Forgett had to draw upon his own experience, designing special tools for dismantling some of the shells.

As they were disarmed, some shells were turned into scrap and hauled away to a smelting plant in Pennsylvania, while some of those in better shape were made into safe collector items. In fact, Forgett put together a collection of every shell known to have been used by either side during the Civil War, disarmed the lot, then donated them to the Smithsonian Institute.

This explosive adventure took place early in 1958 and more than a decade later, when the Bannerman Arsenal finally did catch fire — again the victim of vandals, it is reported — it was not the holocaust that it once could have been.

But that experience convinced Val Forgett more than

Collector demands for original Kentucky pistols resulted in the introduction of the Navy Arms Kentucky pistol, an economical answer to completing collection.

ever before that he was on the right track. Here again he had noted that the supply of collector type black powder armament was becoming scarce. The prime pieces all were in collections and the price was beginning to rise.

For the man who – like Forgett – reveled in the idea of loosing a cloud of smoke from the muzzle of a cap and ball handgun, it had the makings of a mighty expensive hobby. In fact, at the prices that original black powder guns were bringing, it was not wise to shoot them. It just wasn't the economic thing to do.

In 1956, several businessmen met in Alexandria, Virginia, to discuss the feasibility of having replica revolvers made abroad. After some debate and considerable study of the venture, it was determined there might possibly be a market for this type of gun. No one was certain, it was a hit or miss proposition, but the deal was on. A replica Colt Navy would be made in Italy for importation into the United States.

Actually this informal business meeting was the beginning of the Navy Arms Company. One of those men bold enough to take the gamble of producing a replica cap and ball revolver was Forgett, now president of the aforementioned firm as well as Service Armament.

There was more to getting an authentic looking replica built in Italy than just a handshake with a couple of business associates, as Forgett soon found out.

The first and immediate problem was to get an original Colt Navy to the Brescia gunmaker, Vittorio Gregorelli. Italian customs officials refused to let the gun be shipped to the subcontractor for the Beretta factory. It seems that Gregorelli did not make complete guns; only parts for the M-1 Garand for Beretta; not making complete guns, he didn't have a firearms manufacturing license. The Colt Navy was returned.

The problem was remedied by delivering the Colt in person to Gregorelli and the latter soon had the prototype run of sixteen guns under way; ten were copies of the 1851 Colt Navy and six had brass frames and round barrels, like that found on the Confederate .36 caliber Griswold & Gunnison Army revolver.

When these guns finally reached Forgett's office, it didn't take him long to notice nearly a dozen design changes. The majority of these changes were of minor significance and were easily cured.

Most detectable was the change of the original front sight bead to the more conventional dovetailed blade. Another change was the size of the guard screw heads. These were much larger than should be. Also, the guard plate had been widened to surround the larger screw heads.

These changes were transformed back to the original pattern and the first production run got underway. The inner curve of the replica was purposely changed slightly as the Italian craftsmen had done so on the prototypes. This was to ensure an accurate means of determining an original from the replica.

The black powder revolver, marked NAVY ARMS CO. along the barrel top, began to hit the U.S. market in 1958. Built from quality materials and assembled by hand, the replica was accepted immediately by modern black powder shooters and collectors needing such a copy to fill a gap in their collection.

With the success of the Colt Navy replica, Forgett considered producing a replica black powder rifle. His choice was the Remington Zouave — often referred to as the most colorful of all Civil War guns. The rifle was also a success and the Navy Arms Company was now a well established business.

Val Forgett (left) and assistant deactivate Bannerman shells. Flasks at right are among Navy Arms' accessories.

Since the introduction of the Colt replica in 1958, Forgett has built Navy Arms into what is possibly the largest black powder gun supplier in the country. Since then he has introduced a number of near exact replicas of many famous guns, the originals of many which are all but impossible to find for sale or otherwise.

A favorite of North/South Skirmish shooters, the Navy Arms' reproduction of the 1863 Zouave is so exacting that the firm claims that parts from it will interchange with those on the original. The big .58 caliber rifled musket is fitted with a thirty-three-inch rifled barrel and is fitted with a folding rear sight that adjusts in elevation for ranges from one to three hundred yards.

Another authentically reproduced gun is the firm's Harpers Ferry musket. In .58 caliber, this rifled musket sports a thirty-five-inch rifled barrel, but instead of being blued, it features a browned finish, as did the originals. This gun is of the half-stock design and has a flintlock; the walnut stock on the Navy Arms' gun is fitted with a large hinged patchbox as were original Harpers Ferry muskets.

For percussion revolver fans — especially Colts — Val Forgett is importing numerous different revolver replicas. A copy of the Colt 2nd Model Dragoon in .44 caliber is about as exact a copy of that revolver as can be found. The frame and loading lever of this revolver are beautifully color case-hardened and are set off by the deep bluing of the barrel and cylinder and the polished brass frame and back strap. The cylinder of this gun is engraved with the same Indian fight scene found on the original.

Competitive cap and ball marksmen usually favor the solid frame Remington design over that of the Colt. Reasoning is simple; the Colt's open frame doesn't allow the installation of adjustable sights, whereas the Reming-

As found on Bannerman's Island, cannon from Admiral Farragut's ship was covered with vines.

ton's solid top strap is ideal for such sights.

Navy Arms has redesigned the Remington Army Model revolver by fitting these replicas with a set of micro adjustable target rear sights. Often considered the magnum of Civil War revolvers due to its ability to withstand greater pressures, the Navy Arms' target version of this gun is no exception. The quality of the material used in the construction of the solid frame allows the use of heavy maximum charges. Late outdoor writer and pioneer of handgun hunting Al Georg killed a near record black bear with a prototype of this particular gun. – *Jack Lewis*

AUCTION TO ARMORY

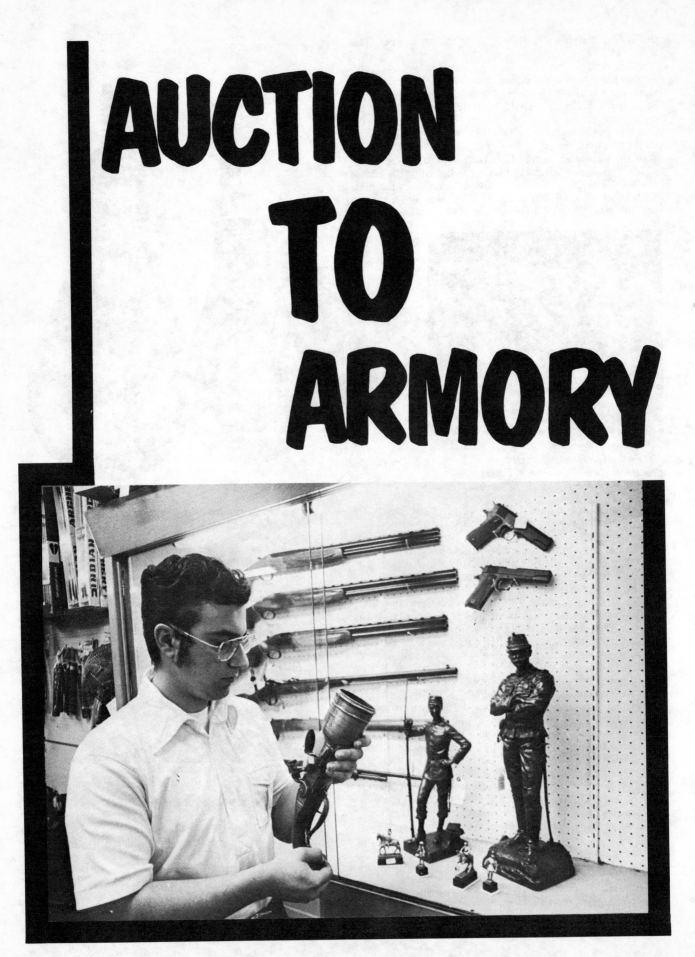

Centennial Arms' Beginnings Were Almost Accidental, Resulting From Sale Of A Collection!

Part D: Rebirth Of An Era

"IT WAS ALL A MISTAKE."

Sig Shore, behind his desk at Centennial Arms Corporation, was referring to his entry into the antique and later the replica firearms business, that has made him one of the nation's leading dealers in the field.

Auctioneering has been the Shore's family business for three generations. Sig Shore's father and grandfather before him were auctioneers in the Chicago area and founded Shore Galleries in Lincolnwood, Illinois, which is also the home of Centennial Arms.

Entering the firearms business was a result of Shore Galleries auctioning a large estate that included a fine antique firearms collection.

"The response was so amazing and people so fervent in their enthusiasm that I decided the gun business was for me," Shore recalls. "After that auction in 1958, I went out looking for antique firearms. We found that collectors are much more enthusiastic over their purchases than the average person buying daily needs. The fever in collectors is high enough that many sacrifice a necessity so that they can buy that particular gun, coin or what have you, to add to a collection."

Shore became fascinated with the business of buying and selling antique guns both at auction and through the gallery. As time passed and money became more plentiful with today's affluent society, Shore found that most of the larger collectors were not selling their priceless antiques, but there still was a growing demand for the guns of our country's historic past.

During 1960, the company started selling replicas to fill the demand from collectors and a growing public to own a firearm related to America's history.

Centennial's first replica was the 1860 Army Colt, a .44

cap and ball revolver. The pistol featured an engraved cylinder eight-inch barrel, walnut grips, blue finish, round cylinder mounted on a steel frame. This gun was a copy of the famous Civil War issue revolver used by both the North and South. Surprisingly, this same 1860 Colt replica still is one of the biggest sellers at Centennial Arms.

Shore points out that the Civil War and the nostalgia of the Old Wild West are really our only heritage in the antique firearms field. The Revolution was fought with European-made arms and it wasn't until the Civil War that American-made guns became prominent, being used by both the Union and Confederate forces. The guns of that era stretched across the wild western frontiers of the United States and became more famous than the men who carried them.

The collecting of American pioneer items such as firearms has become a booming business even in Europe. Our movies have played a large part in bringing that era of history to the masses and countless millions seem to want to be a part of this saga of the early days of the Wild West.

Sam Colt patented and manufactured the first revolvers in 1836 and, by the time of the Mexican War in 1849, the gun was a standard of the U.S. Army. These first cap and ball revolvers were American-made and not a heritage from the old country, allegedly the reason for their continued popularity today.

Shore sells his replica arms to a wide section of the population. The collectors and shooters come from every walk of life: blue collar workers, plumbers, carpenters, electricians and, at the other end of the spectrum, company presidents and board chairmen of some of the largest corporations in the country. Even women are becoming interested in collecting and shooting the black powder arms, Shore has found.

Another reason for the growth and popularity of black powder arms is that there are no federal restrictions for the purchase of these replicas and they can be shipped to the customer and ordered by mail without a Federal firearms permit. However, it is recommended that one check with local officials to insure there is no local law preventing the

Sig Shore, founder and president of Centennial Arms, with early bladed fighting instrument; a part of his collection.

The showcases at the Lincolnwood, Illinois, firm are packed full of various modern made black powder replicas and reproduction guns.

Personnel at Centennial Arms find the arms trade a fast moving business, working hard to meet and fill orders from all over U.S.

use or shipment into your area. Centennial Arms also makes it mandatory that all customers submit a statement that they are over 21 years of age and no local laws prohibit black powder guns.

The replicas are manufactured in Europe for Centennial Arms. The first were produced in Belgium, but because of devaluation of the dollar, Shore has shifted most of the firm's business to Italy where prices are still reasonable enough to meet the competitive market.

Under Shore's guidance, Centennial has sold thousands of real antique guns and, in recent years, developed a long line of the replicas. The company also carries a line of powder flasks and bullet moulds.

Replicas sold by Centennial range from thirty bucks to more than $100. They are fairly accurate, considering the design and type of firearm. Many have used these modern replicas for hunting with great success in states where there is a special black powder season. The effective range for a black powder pistol is twenty-five yards. The rifles are good up to about one hundred and twenty-five yards.

The future of replicas is unlimited, according to Shore.

"It is one of the fastest developing businesses in the nation. Not only are they sought by the avid collector and shooter, but many people just like to decorate their homes with a piece of Americana from the nostalgic past."

The Centennial folks come out with a new model each year, sometimes replacing one of the less popular guns. Many of these have been replicas of Civil War era guns but some have also been "firearms that could have been," dreamed up by Shore and his staff.

Even to the casual observer visiting the Shore Galleries in Lincolnwood, Shore's statement that "it was all a mistake" seems pretty far from the truth. What once housed a successful auction business now is a complete sporting goods store. The stock includes guns, fishing equipment, camping gear, tennis and golf equipment and, of course, the line of Centennial replicas.

The firm still is in the auction business and Shore may hop a plane tomorrow to globe trot and bid on a collection of fine antique arms or visit the factory in Italy to start things going on the next replica model. – *Chuck Tyler*

CHAPTER 9

This Muzzleloading Classic
Heals Old Wounds While
Increasing Black Powder Interest!

N

S

SKIRMISH

A CHILLING MAY rain cascaded from dark storm clouds as five men, attired in the drab gray uniform of the Confederate Army, marched onto the small Maryland clearing, stepping in rhythm to the tune of Dixie. From the opposite side of the clearing, carrying their Civil War style .58 caliber muskets and wearing the blue uniform of the Union Army, five Yanks moved on line across the same clearing.

At a range of twenty-five yards, both teams stopped, brought their muskets to their shoulders, aimed ever so cautiously and fired.

Had the time and place been nearly a hundred years before, this same incident at the Berwyn Rod and Gun Club probably would have become a part of history as the Battle of Berwyn, the Siege of Berwyn or perhaps even Berwyn Run. The truth is, neither of the two rifle teams actually was aiming and firing at the other. Instead, the shooters were firing at some thirty balloons, fifteen each, that had been attached to the twenty-five-yard target frames.

As the smoke of that first volley cleared, it was clear that the Norfolk Gray Backs had proved themselves the deadlier of the two teams, taking five of their targets with their first five shots, while all fifteen balloons stared back at the Berwyn Bluebellies.

Good times and rain seldom go hand in hand, but these members of the Washington Blue Rifles don't seem overly upset about the damp conditions, while they practice the manual of arms, which is part of competition.

Both teams then reloaded as fast as possible and sent another volley on its way, then another, and another, until the cry of "cease fire" echoed across the clearing. The Confederate team had won the first event easily.

Firing at standard match type targets from the fifty-yard line, the Confederate team also managed to walk away with the honors in the second and final event of the day. There were no bitter feelings, however. This had only been a friendly shooting match between two musket teams that had decided to make things a little more colorful by wearing uniforms of an an era when the North and South had met on less friendly terms.

Since that first meeting of North and South in May of 1950, the number of participating shooters has grown from the original two five-man teams to more than 2,000. Also spawned that day was the North/South Skirmish Association, which now is the overseeing organization of the twice-a-year event.

Representing over 150 regiments that had comprised the majority of the original units that had participated in the Civil War, these dedicated black powder shooters flock to rustic Fort Shenandoah, Virginia, twice each year to participate in a few days of marksmanship competition. A walk through the parking lot will show license plates from nearly

every state in the Union — even those that had not taken part in the first original North/South skirmishes of the mid 1800s.

Even so, shooters without units or regiments get to shoot; everyone shoots, as a team or individually. For shooters without a team with which to participate in the team matches, volunteering is allowed when one of the teams suddenly comes up a man short. It's not unusual to see someone from the West Coast firing with a unit from Georgia, Mississippi or Tennessee. Then there are always the individual competitions, where the lone shooter can display his expertise with one of the charcoal burners.

Safety becomes a prime factor when this many shooters get together. All events are scheduled, thus limiting the number of shooters on the line at any given time. To make things even more safe, all loading is done by the numbers, or at least on the command to load.

A large number of the musket shooters prefer to use homemade paper cartridges instead of going through the bothersome measurement of powder charges from flasks or horns. There are several preferred ways to make these cartridges, but one of the most simple methods is to use a small paper or cardboard tube as the body or casing.

The paper hull can be formed by rolling up heavy stock brown wrapping paper or cutting cardboard tubing of the right diameter to the desired length. The tube should be small enough in diameter to allow it to be almost inserted down the muzzle — but not quite, for obvious reasons.

One end of the tube is sealed off. Cartridges made out of brown wrapping paper may be merely tied off with string and those utilizing cardboard bodies can be sealed by plugging one end with a cardboard insert.

A measured amount of powder then is dropped into the tube, with the Minie ball large enough in diameter to plug the open end of the cartridge. Usually this ball has a tight fit and is inserted to the first or second lubricating ring. The finished cartridges are most likely to be carried in leather cartridge boxes that hang from the shoulder by a wide leather strap or are fastened to the belt.

To load, all the shooter has to do is reach down, grab

Even this wild assortment of clothing would have conformed to regulations during the Civil War. Quite often uniforms of the times matched even worse.

Replicas of the Remington Zouave share the rack with well preserved Civil War Springfield as this unit sits waiting for its turn to fire.

Cannoneers move away from cannon as fuse is lit. North/South Skirmishes include competition even for these beastly bored black powder shooters.

Officials of the North/South Skirmish Association watch closely as individual shooters compete. Targets are clay pigeons attached to the target frame.

These two shooters alternate, as one fires the other glasses through scope. Individual shooters without a team can occasionally fill in on short team.

Timer and safety officer monitors the firing line.
Some volunteering is permitted if a man does not
have a team to shoot with or one is short a man.

one of the cartridges, pull the Minie ball from the mouth of the cartridge with his teeth, dump the powder charge down the muzzle, drop in the lead ball, run it home with the rod, slip on a percussion cap and he's ready to fire. It is hardly poetry in motion, but experienced shooters can go through the entire loading procedures in less than twenty seconds.

Jeff Davis, with Generals Grant and Lee would probably turn in their graves, if they could witness what takes place when the gray and blue uniforms start to mingle at Fort Shenandoah for the semi-annual shootouts. It's a good time for all. Troubles are left at home with the roof that needs fixing, screens that need repairing and the doors that need painting. When the carpenter from Indiana, the farmer from Missouri or textile worker from Alabama slips on his regimental colors, it's time for some serious shooting.

At first glance the Virginia camp grounds resemble a Boy Scout jamboree, especially with all the uniforms being proudly displayed. Except for a few well intentioned jeers about the time someone's original unit got lost behind enemy lines or the day that one regiment whipped the daylights out of another, it is difficult to realize that all this fun is the result of what originally had been a war within this country.

Instead of harboring information and giving only name, rank and service number, a visiting shooter seems to take pride in sharing his shooting experiences, boasting of his personal little tricks that might give him an edge over his competition. A few even go so far as to give away secret recipes for patch lubricant that have been handed down by forgotten ancestors.

More often than not, these passed-on homemade lubricants end in disaster with a gooey cartridge box or a fouled bore. Many of these concoctions spew forth odors that are strong enough to clear the sinuses of a dead man or at least bad enough to get you — and your pot of goodies — run out of the basement by your wife.

Although it wasn't around at the battles of Shiloh, Bull Run or even Gettysburg, one of the most widely used lubricants at the North/South Skirmish matches is Crisco vegetable shortening. Also growing in popularity are such ready-made lubricants as Hodgdon's Spit Patch for cap and ball revolvers and Spit Ball for muzzleloading rifles and muskets.

There are undoubtedly mixed feelings at the sight of an authentic Harper's Ferry or an original Smith carbine being put through the rigors of continuous competition. Die-hard collectors tend to weep over such sacred items actually being put to the purpose for which they were designed.

There are now numerous well made replicas on the market that are actually better built than the originals. Utilizing stronger steel as well as better construction, most of these reproductions are capable of withstanding powder charges that would probably result in damage to an original. Before any replica is allowed in actual match competition, however, it first must be approved by the North/South Skirmish Association.

The .58 caliber Remington Zouave reproduction being offered by Navy Arms is an example of a quality replica. The original, with its 33½-inch rifled barrel, was the most accurate rifle of its time. Since accuracy is the name of the game when Rebs and Yanks assemble at Fort Shenandoah, its not unusual to see even entire teams armed with the Navy Arms copy.

Competition is divided so that individual matches are held on Saturday and the team matches on Sunday. Typical individual competition consists of fifty and hundred-yard match targets for musket and carbine shooters and twenty-five and fifty-yard targets for the handgun shooters.

Team competition, with eight men comprising a team, varies from one match to another. It is admissable for a regiment to host as many as four eight-man teams. Most units, however, have only an "A" and "B" team.

To give spectators something to view, some of the targets are made of objects that not only break but disintegrate when contact is made with one of the .58 caliber slugs — or whatever hits it. These targets may consist of the standard clay pigeons or perhaps clay flower pots. Reasoning behind this is simple; a spectator can see, without a doubt in his mind, when a competitor has scored a hit.

One of the most popular strings of fire consists of a board suspended in a frame as the target. A vertical line is drawn down the center of the board, serving as the point of aim. The object is to hit the line in such a manner that the impact of the slug splits the board down the middle.

Other targets consist of the standard silhouette, water-filled beer cans or even styrofoam cups, with variations running from match to match. All events are timed and the team utilizing the shortest amount of time to hit or break all of its targets is the winner.

After a busy day of shooting, a good portion of the evening is spent in cleaning the black powder guns. There are numerous cleaning solvents that do a fine job of turning a powder-fouled bore into the bright and shining cylindrical drilling it had been before the day's shoot. BlakSol and Bucheimer's black powder solvent are two of the commercial solvents that have won wide acceptance, but for many shooters there in no replacement for the old favorite standby — hot, soapy water.

Regional shoots of the North/South Skirmish Association are held from spring through summer, into fall, whenever there are enough shooters to participate. Black powder shooters are a minority when compared to the number of shooters comprising such shooting sports as trap, skeet and benchrest competition. The dates for the Nationals varies from year to year, but is always divided into two matches, the Spring and the Fall Nationals.

Nostalgia probably accounts for the reason why a large number of the North/South Skirmish Association members drive thousands of miles, just to slip on a blue or gray uniform that could probably withstand a little repair work, just to see all of his efforts go up in a puff of FFFg smoke, as the Minie makes its way to the target.

Then again, maybe they're just true Americans wanting to relive our American heritage. — *Toby Bridges*

The length of hair and beards of these shooters add to the authenticity of the uniforms worn by these shooters of the 17th Virginia Infantry, Joe Leisch, Jr. (left) has played Lincoln on TV often.

The 17th Virginia Infantry fire at their
assigned targets during one segment of the
competition, when all targets have been hit
closest shooter must push button for time.

Teams continue to fire until all targets are
hit or broken, team hitting all of the targets
in the least amount of time is the winner.

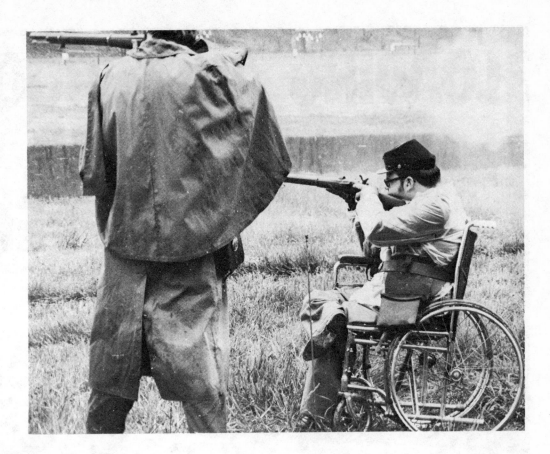

Physical handicaps are all but ignored, as this shooter aims in on his target.

Although it is not uncommon to see mint condition originals, such as these Smith carbines, being fired, most North/South shooters now use the better replicas.

Shooter creates a cloud of smoke as he unleashes a shot with a Remington cap and ball revolver, competition covers handgun marksmanship also.

LOADING AND SHOOTING BLACK POWDER GUNS

A Complete Step-By-Step Guide To Loading And Shooting Cap And Ball Revolvers, Single-Shot Pistols, Muskets, Rifles And Muzzleloading Shotguns!

CHAPTER 10

As authentic looking as any hundred year old handmade original, the powder horn above is commercially produced. Also being commercially produced today are a number of black powder shooting aids, such as lubricants shown at left.

DROP A CHARGE of black powder down the barrel or into the chamber mouth, seat a round lead ball or conical minie over this powder, prime the flash pan or place a percussion cap on the nipple and you're ready to indulge in some black powder shooting!

Sounds like a simple operation, doesn't it? Really it is quite simple, provided the proper components have been used in the loading process. Even so, how these components are loaded can make a big difference on just how well the rifle or handgun will group its shots on paper or bring down game.

A question most commonly asked by the beginning black powder shooter is, "how much powder is actually too much?" A good rule to follow when working on starting loads is to begin by matching the caliber of the ball with the same number of grains of powder.

For example, a good starting load for a .36 caliber rifle would be in the neighborhood of 35 grains of FFFg. Although this rule will apply to most of the replicas on the market today — as well as their originals — there will be an occasional case where it will not hold true.

A good example of this would be the Colt 1862 Police pistol. Try as you like, about all the powder you can get into the small revolver's chambers is in the neighborhood of 20 grains. Although the police pistol resembles the New Model 1861 Navy in appearance, it is more like the 1849 pocket pistol in actual size. Even with as little as 20 grains of powder, it sometimes is difficult to seat the lead ball far enough below the one-half fluted and rebated cylinder's

chamber mouth to allow it to rotate freely enough to fire.

Black powder is available in several different grades, based upon the fineness of the granulation. Powder with a single Fg designation is quite coarse and is used mostly in many of the old black powder center-fire cartridges and muskets with bores as big as the .70 caliber Brown Bess. This overly bored shoulder arm fires a patched .680-inch ball powered by 70 to 80 grains of Fg powder. Powder of this granulation will pass through a screen opening of .0689, but not through a .0582 screen opening.

Used extensively for the loading of muzzleloading shotguns, FFg powder is somewhat finer than Fg. This powder also is a good choice for loading big bore rifles and Tower-type pistols having a bore diameter of .540 to .690; having a faster burning rate, it is still popular among old arms buffs that handload .44 Colt, .44 Webley and .45 Colt center-fire black powder cartridges.

Perhaps the most commonly used, FFFg powder is used in loading practically all of the cap and ball revolvers, small-bore single-shot pistols and rifles ranging from .36 up to and including some of the .54 calibers. This powder has a much faster burning rate than the two grades previously mentioned and is a better choice when loading short-barreled guns.

Black powder guns are practically immune to being overloaded, although heavy charges many times are the most inaccurate. When loaded with too much powder — which has an extremely slow burning rate when compared to smokeless powders — a black powder rifle or handgun will merely expel the excess charge out the muzzle as it is fired.

If you ever have watched a cannon being fired you've probably noticed all the fire and sparks that shoot from the muzzle. This is the excess powder still burning as it leaves the barrel. This is also the reason why most black powder rifles have long barrels; to utilize all of the propelling force caused by the burning powder by allowing it to be ignited fully while still in the barrel.

The following chart from Dixie Gun Works clearly shows how the velocity is increased as the barrel length is increased:

VELOCITY TABLE*
CAL. .40 DIXIE CAPLOCK RIFLE
Barrel Charge Wts. in Grains Of DuPont FFFg Blk. Powder

Length	38	47	56	65	75	84	94	104	114	120
40"	1551	1770	1884	1987	2059	2178	2260	2356	2437	2463
38"	1567	1747	1879	1992	2099	2216	2306	2347	2359	2398
36"	1543	1735	1836	1994	2079	2189	2194	2301	2274	
34"	1493	1610	1828	1966	2063	2186	2272	2246		
32"	1527	1654	1819	1913	2017	2098	2199	2233		
30"	1460	1642	1796	1932	1984	2052	2088	2064		
28"	1492	1623	1742	1903	1973	2095	2089			
26"	1445	1596	1734	1838	1902	1944	1952			
24"	1449	1593	1710	1784	1894	2019	2092			
22"	1468	1553	1668	1733	1844	1879	1937			
20"	1420	1509	1631	1703	1818	1863	1976			

* Velocity averages, expressed in feet per second, are for 5-shot strings. Firing with increasingly heavy charges was discontinued when recoil and muzzle blast became objectionable.

Solid framed Remington design revolvers are broken down by dropping loading lever, pulling cylinder pin forward and rotating cylinder out of the frame.

Extremely fine in granule size, FFFFg powder seldom is used, except for priming the flash pans of flintlocks. On occasion it is used for loading small pocket pistols and smallbored derringers of a .31 caliber or less. This is the fastest burning grade of black powder and, although many shooters claim that FFFFg burns much too fast and creates pressures that are too excessive for most black powder guns, there are those who argue the point that it is safe and that it gives a hunting rifle a little more punch. This is something of a personal debate, but certainly FFFFg should not be used in guns that are in poor condition. Usually these guns shouldn't be shot with any grade of powder!

In loading each type of muzzleloading firearm, each varies a little from the others, but basically they are loaded all the same — from the front to the rear!

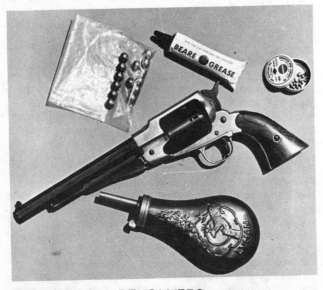

CAP AND BALL REVOLVERS

Samuel Colt, Eli Remington and a few other early arms-makers probably would turn in their proverbial graves should they witness the large numbers of reproductions —

many of which actually are built better than the originals — that are being made to exact specifications of some of their early designs.

The cap and ball revolver is being produced in larger numbers today than at any other time in history. Nostalgia probably has accounted for the largest number of the modern day sales, but a few shooters have made tack drivers out of some of the better made replicas.

Navy Arms, Replica Arms, Dixie Gun Works, Centennial Arms, to name a few, all import modern-made replicas. Although basically the same as the originals in design, these are produced from materials superior to those used a century or better ago. These guns are fully proof tested before leaving the factories in Belgium, Spain and Italy for export to the United States, today the largest black powder shooting country in the world.

A black powder revolver is simple in design and operation, but there are a few steps which make loading, shooting and caring for them a little simpler and a lot more enjoyable.

Presuming you have just purchased your black powder cap and ball revolver, there is an important task one must take care of immediately before trudging off to the range with the expectation of punching a few holes into a paper target or two. As packed in the factory, most replica revolvers are doused thoroughly with a number of different types of lubricants. If not cleaned from the chambers of the cylinder, the first attempts to load them can end in one gooey mess.

Colt replica revolvers can be broken down easily for cleaning by removing a small wedge located just forward of the cylinder. The wedge is tapped back through its slot from the right side of the revolver.

Placing the hammer on half-cock, rotate the cylinder until the end of the loading lever will make contact with the metal between two of the chambers when levered down. This works as a lever and removes the barrel and loading lever unit from the frame and cylinder pin.

This initial cleaning doesn't have to be an out and out complete scrubbing of each and every part, especially if you plan to go right out and do some shooting with the gun as soon as you finish cleaning it; that's what you'll have to do

Colt replica is broken down by first removing wedge located in front of the cylinder. Such replicas as the Lyman below are actually safer than originals.

The Remington-type revolver has a solid frame that completely encircles the cylinder. To remove the cylinder from this type of gun is simpler than with the Colt type.

The loading lever is brought down as if a round is being loaded into the chamber. With the lever in this position, grasp the T-shaped wedge that rests tightly against the flat bottom area of the octagon barrel and pull it toward the muzzle. By placing the hammer on half-cock and returning the loading lever to its upward position, the cylinder should rotate out of the frame.

The cylinder then is cleaned the same as the cylinder from the Colt-type replica. The barrel on the Remington-type revolver, however, does not separate from the frame and must be cleaned from the muzzle. Cleaning techniques and the care of cap and ball revolvers are covered in greater detail in another section.

Before loading the revolver, place a percussion cap on each nipple and snap it. By doing so, the explosion of the percussion cap will remove any dirt or grease that may be blocking the ignition from reaching the chamber. Unless the cylinder was scrubbed thoroughly, it might be a good idea to place a second cap on each of the nipples and snap it again, burning any oil that is remaining inside the chamber.

Percussion caps are available in a wide range of sizes and it sometimes is a problem to find the size that fits best. Trying to match one manufacturer's size designation to another's is like trying to break a secret code of some sort.

For instance, the Eley No. F4-21 is nearly identical to the No. 11 Winchester cap, both having a .175-inch inside diameter. Unless the manufacturer designates in the literature that comes with a new cap and ball revolver the size and make of cap to use, about the only way to get the proper size is by the old trial and error method, actually fitting the caps to the nipple.

Most of the modern made nipples measure .163-inch across the top and taper to about .168-inch in diameter at the point where they thread into the cylinder. If it is impossible to find the exact cap size, it is wise to buy the size on the larger side. The larger cap can be pinched slightly with the fingers, giving it a tight fit on the nipple.

After the caps have been placed on the nipples and snapped, place the revolver's hammer on half-cock to allow the cylinder to rotate freely. Using a powder flask or some other means of dropping a measured charge of powder into the chambers, charge each chamber with powder. The amount of powder to use will vary with the caliber and model of gun. It is, however, impossible to overload a cap and ball revolver with black powder. There isn't enough room to allow for an over-charge of powder and still have room to seat the ball.

The soft lead ball used to load cap and ball revolvers is always oversize and is swaged with a tight fit. To load a .44 caliber Colt Dragoon, for example, a .453-inch ball is used. A good powder charge for this hefty handgun — the gun weighing in the neighborhood of four pounds — is 40 grains of FFFg behind the 145-grain lead ball.

As the oversize .453 ball is seated in the .440 chamber, a thin ring of lead is peeled off the sides of the ball to form at the chamber mouths. This is a good indication that the ball is being swaged tightly. It's important that the ball fit snugly in the chamber; if it doesn't, the ball would have a tendency to work its way forward as the gun is being fired.

This, in itself, would prove no great problem during the first shot or two, but there is a chance that the ball could work its way far enough forward that it would protrude from the chamber mouth and catch onto the frame as the cylinder rotated. The ball catching onto the frame wouldn't allow the cylinder to turn.

again when you're through firing it.

A quick examination of the insides of the chambers will probably reveal that they are well coated with lube. To clean this out rather quickly, simply dip a cotton swab into a cleaning solvent such as Hoppe's No. 9 or Birchwood-Casey bore solvent.

Swab out the insides of the chambers with the solvent, making sure that you clean all six — or in the case of five-shot cylinders, all five. Surprisingly enough, its easy to lose count!

Next, place the cylinder — chamber mouths down — onto a folded piece of cloth or paper towel to drain. You might have to swab the chambers first with a dry cotton swab, if you splashed on the solvent rather heavily. The paper or cloth will absorb the excess as it drains out.

While the chambers are draining, it might be a good idea to make a few passes through the barrel to remove any lube that might be packed into the rifling. Using a wire brush of the right caliber, make several passes through the barrel. Hold it up to the light and visually check to see if it is clean; if not, push the brush through a few more times, this time using a little solvent on it. Run a clean patch or two through it and it should be clean enough for firing.

By this time, the chambers should have drained any excess solvent. If there still is solvent visible, either let it drain a while longer or swab it out. Reassemble the gun in reverse of the way it was broken down.

CHART OF BALL SIZES TO USE IN REPRODUCTION GUNS		
Revolver	Chamber Size	Ball Size
1860 Army, .44 cal. Centennial	.446	.450
1860 Army, .44 cal., Replica	.446	.450
Reb, .36 caliber	.375	.376
Model 60 Army, .44 caliber	.447	.451
Wells Fargo, .31 caliber	.315	.320
Patterson, .36 caliber	.378	.380
Yank, .36 caliber	.375	.376
Sheriff's Model, .36 caliber	.375	.376
1861 Navy Colt, .36 caliber	.375	.380
Baby Dragoon, .31 caliber	.316	.321
Leech & Rigdon .36 caliber	.375	.376
Walker, .44 caliber	.440	.441
Dragoon, .44 caliber	.440	.441
Remington Revolving Carbine, .44 caliber	.450	.454
Remington Army, .44 caliber	.450	.454
Remington Navy, .36 caliber	.375	.376

Once the ball has been seated in each of the chambers, a grease-type lube should be placed over each chamber mouth. This prevents the possibility of a chain fire — having more than just the intended chamber firing. This is not a recommended way of grouping the shots on the target and is dangerous to the shooter, most of the time resulting in a ruined gun.

Numerous types of lubricants can be used to prevent a multiple discharge; Crisco shortening is one of the most widely used. Hodgdon now offers a commercially made lube which is called Spit Ball. It comes in a hip

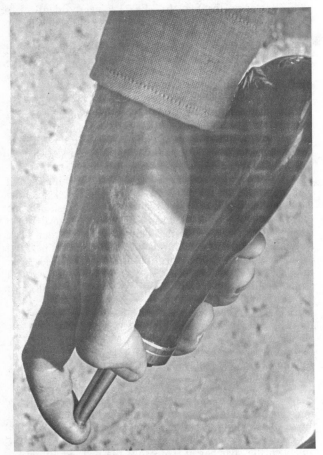

The charger on this flask measures out one exact charge for a .36 caliber cap and ball revolver such as this Colt Navy. Thumb opens and closes charger opening.

pocket-size plastic bottle that has a flip open or shut nozzle that allows you to get the lube down into the chamber mouth and completely cover the seated ball. In addition to

preventing a chain fire, this lube is also supposed to improve accuracy. Lubes of this type help prevent powder fouling from buidling up in the bore. There are several such commerical products now available.

As a rule, the hotter the powder load used, the less consistent accuracy you'll get from a black powder revolver. It is best to experiment with the gun until the right load is segregated. Usually this load is just enough powder to get the lead ball from the muzzle to the target with the least amount of drop in its trajectory. Hot powder charges have a tendency to spew the balls erratically and seldom puts them anywhere near the same point of aim for each shot.

The following chart is of recommended loads for certain models and calibers. These loads may seem on the mild side to you, but these are the loads we feel will give consistent accuracy.

Revolver	Ball Diameter	Apprx. Wt. in Grains	Charge in Powder	Grains
.31 Colt Pocket Pistol	.321 (0 Buck- shot)	45	FFFg	15
.31 Remington New Model Pocket Revolver	.321 (0 Buck- shot)	45	FFFg	15
.31 Remington Rider Double Action Revolver	.321 (0 Buck- shot)	45	FFFg	15-18
Other .31 caliber American revolvers	.321-.310	40-45	FFFg	8-18
.36 Colt Navy	.376-.380	80	FFFg	22
.36 Remington New Model Belt Pistol	.376-.380	80	FFFg	20-22
.36 Savage Model 1861	.376-.380	80	FFFg	20-26
.36 Modern Manufacture Reproductions	.380	80	FFFg	18-22
.36 Colt Police Pistol	.380	80	FFFg	12-15
.44 Colt Dragoon	.451-.453	140	FFFg	40
.44 Remington New Model Army	.451-.453	140	FFFg	26-30
.44 Rogers and Spencer	.451-.453	140	FFFg	30-35
.44 Modern Manufacture Reproductions	.451	140	FFFg	28-30

With hammer at half-cock the cylinder on the Navy Colt replica can be easily rotated to charge each chamber with FFFg powder from charger on the flask.

Although cap and ball revolvers normally are loaded without any kind of wad or patch, there are those who choose to place a treated felt wad between the ball and powder charge. These wads are made by treating a piece of thin felt — like that used in the making of your favorite Stetson — in a melted liquid consisting of beeswax and beef tallow. The felt material then is laid out to dry.

Wads are cut to the exact chamber size with a wad cutting device, which is simply a punch with a recessed head and sharpened edges. This is placed on the material and

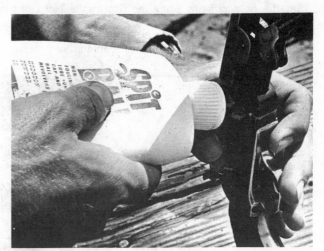

The final step to loading a percussion revolver is to place a lube of some sort over loaded round. This seals the round and prevents a possible chain fire.

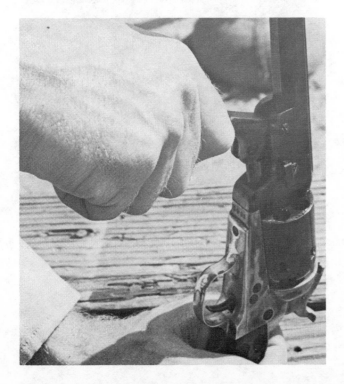

Slightly oversized soft lead ball is placed sprue down or up over the charged chamber. Cylinder is then rotated until ball is directly below loading lever. Below, the ball is firmly seated over the powder by fulcrum action of loading lever.

heartily rapped with a hammer; cutting a circular wad from the felt the exact size of the chamber diameter.

When loading with felt wads, the powder charge is dropped in the same manner as before. Instead of seating the ball directly over the powder charge, however, the felt wad then is inserted, the ball seated over this wad. Lubricant at the chamber mouth no longer is needed, as the wad completely seals off the powder charge from any possible exposure to the flash as another chamber is being fired.

Wads are a little less messy and easier to load than smearing grease at the chamber mouth, but they do little to help prevent powder foulings in the bore and make sustained firing of the revolver more difficult.

If you've ever watched a shooter at the local rifle and pistol range make several trips back and forth to his car before he is ready to do any shooting, you probably realize that shooting a cap and ball revolver requires more than just the gun and a few bullets. There are numerous accessories that aid in shooting these black powder sixguns.

There is probably nothing more frustrating than trying to fit a percussion cap onto a nipple with the fingers. Half the attempts resulting in a cap lost in the grass or among the piles of .22 brass that are a part of almost every range.

If a capping device is used, however, it then becomes a simple operation; simply slip the cap on the nipple and pull the capper away, moving to the next nipple until all the chambers have been capped. Most of the large black powder gun suppliers carry a capper of this sort. Dixie Gun Works even handles the circular spring-loaded capper for the Paterson Colt.

If Crisco is your favorite lube at the chamber mouth, for both economic and acquisition reasons, a good way to dispense it into the chambers is by filling a cake decorator with the shortening, then squirting it over the loaded chamber. This not only speeds the process, but helps keep the Crisco in the chamber and not all over the hands and, eventually, the gun.

MUZZLELOADING SINGLE-SHOT PISTOLS

Single-shot muzzleloading pistols have come to be known as pirate pistols, duelling pistols and even a few are referred to as horse pistols. Although they vary greatly from one to the other — from the extremely short barreled derringers of riverboat fame to the duellers used in the early 1800s — they are all loaded in just about the same manner, with the only variance being the size of the ball and the amount of powder used.

Certainly you wouldn't load a short, three-inch barreled derringer of .44 caliber with the same amount of powder as

This well photographed explosion of a primed flash pan should be enough to convince anyone why it causes flinching.

you would a Kentucky pistol of the same caliber having a nine-inch or longer barrel. With chamber and barrel being the same — one-piece barrel and breech — more powder can be loaded into this type of handgun than with the revolving cylinder type. With the cap and ball revolver, the ball must be seated below the chamber mouth to allow the cylinder to rotate. If the ball is left protruding partially from the chamber, more likely than not, it will catch on the frame as the cylinder rotates.

Being a single-shooter, the muzzleloading pistol has no moving or rotating chamber that must be aligned with the barrel before it can be fired. Consequently, the ball does not have to be seated to any significant degree.

A shooter should be ever cautious when loading this type of gun. It is easy to overload these guns accidentally, usually a double charge dropped from the powder flask. Occasionally a shooter can't remember whether he's already charged the gun with powder. This is especially true when busily engaged in conversation. So, it is wise to pay attention to what you're doing.

If the gun is well made and manufactured from strong modern materials, it should be able to withstand the double charge. The problem would be the effect on the shooter. As an example, the .58 caliber Springfield pistol of approximate 1855 manufacture usually is loaded with 40 grains of FFg or FFFg powder behind a 265-grain .570-inch ball. A double charge of 80 grains is 20 grains more than the recommended load for the .58 caliber Zouave rifle. In probability, the excess powder would only be expelled from the muzzle, the gun's short barrel not allowing the slow-burning powder complete ignition.

Unlike the cap and ball revolver, the single-shot pistol always is loaded with a ball actually smaller than its bore diameter. This is patched with a thin piece of cotton or linen to fit the ball tightly against the rifling, if the pistol happens to be rifled.

Many original flintlock and caplock pistols, as well as some of today's reproductions, are fitted with smoothbore barrels. These guns were intended originally for use at rather close range and longer range and pinpoint accuracy wasn't one of their better virtues. The exception to this rule

might be some of the early military wheellock designs, with barrels as long as eighteen inches, and a few of the duellers.

Today, numerous smoothbore muzzleloading pistols are being imported from all over Europe. These can be loaded just as their rifled relatives or without the patching material, if the gun is going to be fired as soon as it is loaded. The patching keeps the ball from rolling back out the muzzle, if the pistol is going to be carried with its muzzle toward the ground. In addition to loading with the lead ball projectile, this type of gun can be loaded with birdshot much the same as muzzleloading shotguns are loaded.

The following chart gives recommended loads for several of the various types of derringers, duellers and horse pistols.

Pistol	Ball Diameter	Powder	Charge Weight in Grains
.28 caliber derringers made under various brand names	.260	FFFg	10
.31 caliber derringers made under various firm names	.300	FFFg	10
.36 caliber Dixie target pistol	.355	FFFg	22
.36 caliber Hopkins & Allen Boot Pistol	.340	FFFg	18-22
.41 caliber Dixie brass frame derringer	.395	FFFg	10
.40 caliber Dixie Flint Pistol	.395	FFFg	25
.44 caliber Replica Arms Kentucky percussion pistol	.410	FFFg	25
.45 caliber Hopkins & Allen Boot Pistol	.435	FFFg	25-28
.45 caliber Dixie Flint and Percussion Pistol	.445	FFFg	25
.54 caliber U.S. Pistol Models 1819-1842	.535	FFFg	30-35
.56 caliber Navy Arms 1806 Harper's Ferry Pistol	.555	FFFg	35
.58 caliber Navy Arms Harper's Ferry Dragoon	.575	FFg or FFFg	35-40
.58 caliber U.S. Springfield Pistol Model 1855	.570	FFg	40
.67 caliber Tower Flint Pistol	.650	FFg	40

Flintlock pistol fanciers usually have two powder horns. The larger horn carries the powder for the main charge, the smaller horn holds the powder for charging the pistol's flash pan.

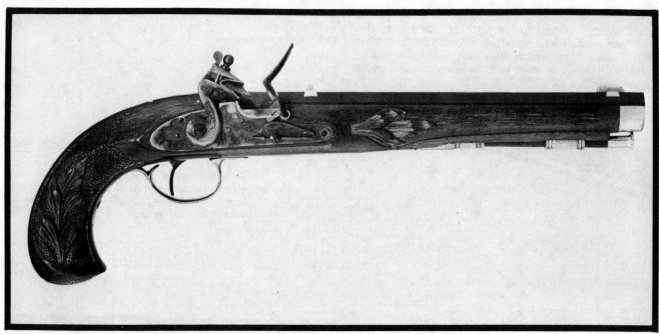

Some of today's black powder guns are copies of the general
type, such as the Replica Arms Kentucky pistol above. Others
are exact replicas, like the Navy Arms 1855 Harpers Ferry below.

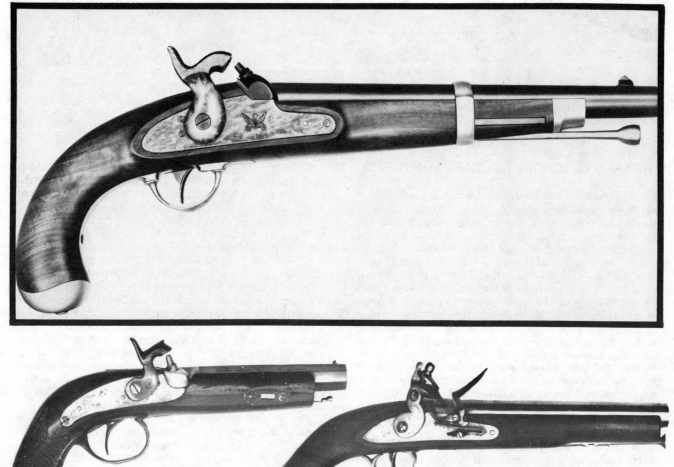

Two more of today's replicas to show
the wide variety available are the
Hawes derringer and the Tower flintlock
pictured at left. All imported guns
are fully proof tested and quite safe.

If continuous shooting is planned for the better part of an afternoon, it is best to use patching material that has been dampened with sperm oil, Hodgdon's Spit-Patch lubricant or something similar. The lube will keep powder fouling soft and allow more shots between cleaning, which is necessary when accuracy is the goal.

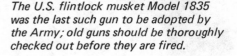

The U.S. flintlock musket Model 1835 was the last such gun to be adopted by the Army; old guns should be thoroughly checked out before they are fired.

There are now several .58 caliber replicas of this original 1841 Mississippi rifled musket on the market; original was .54 cal.

THE MUZZLELOADING MUSKET AND RIFLE

WEBSTER'S DICTIONARY DEFINES nostalgia as a wistful or excessively sentimental, sometimes abnormal, yearning for return to or of some past period or irrecoverable condition. Certainly the yearning to shoulder a long barreled black powder rifle and to wander almost aimlessly through the timbers, fields and over hill after hill can hardly be defined as being abnormal. It may be the result of some nostalgic feelings, but whatever the reasons, this is an enjoyable pursuit that can be made even more pleasant through proper loading of the rifle or musket being carried.

Although basically the same in design and functioning, there is a world of difference between the heavy-barreled Kentucky, Hawken and Pennsylvania rifles and their distant relative, the thin-barreled rifled or smoothbore musket. How the two types of guns are loaded also are similar in many respects, but there is a difference here too. Although not a complete loading guide for shoulder weapons, this section should help you find the right load for the type of rifle or musket you shoot.

As already mentioned, the main difference between the muzzleloading rifle and musket is the thickness of the barrel walls. Rifles almost always have rather thick and heavy rifled barrels, while the musket — which may either be rifled or left smoothbore — is fitted with a barrel that more resembles the barrel of a shotgun than the rifle. For this reason, the musket should not be loaded with a patched ball. Instead, it is loaded with a conical minie bullet.

There are still quite a few shootable original .58 caliber Civil War muskets to be had. The prices of these will make the average black powder shooter's wallet suddenly lose weight and result in the silent treatment from his wife.

During the 1930s and 1940s, these guns could be ordered from Bannerman's in New York for the lordly sum of three to five dollars apiece. Today, this same gun, in good condition, will bring upwards of $200 and, even if in poor condition, in the neighborhood of a century note. By the time the latter has been restored to shootable condition, it is probably worth more than the musket in good condition that originally cost twice as much.

The .58 caliber muskets of the mid-1800s receive more attention from black powder enthusiasts than probably any other make or design. To cope with the shortage of fine old originals — that really shouldn't be shot anyway — a number of firms are importing from European manufacturers a variety of reproductions that are quite safe and fun to shoot.

One of the most copied and currently reproduced versions of this type of early military shoulder arms is the .58 caliber Remington Zouave. Navy Arms' copy of the 1863 Zouave is about as fine a reproduction of this type that you're bound to find and, selling for just under a hundred dollars, it is within the price range afforded nearly any shooter's budget.

There are numerous other reproductions for less money, but their quality seldom matches that of the Navy Arms Zouave. Before being imported into this country, however,

The Navy Arms firm imports from Italy a well built replica of the Zouave rifled musket. This was the general type of gun used during the Civil War and best results are obtained when firing Minie bullets such as those below; hollow base expands into rifling.

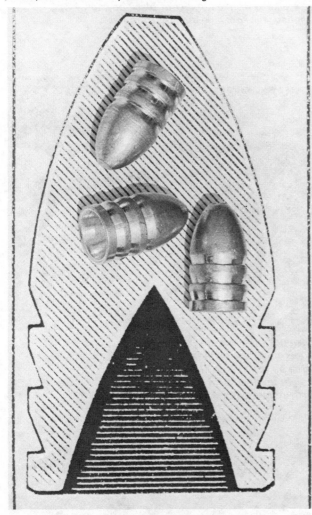

complete scrubdown of the musket, but should be thorough enough to remove excess oil and lube from the barrel and breech. Usually a swab dipped in the soapy solution and run the length of the barrel several times should do the trick. It is also a good idea to place the hammer at half-cock and make sure that some of the cleaning solution is forced out through the nipple or vent hole on the downward stroke of the rod and cleaning jag.

The wet, soapy patches should be followed by several clean, dry patches to absorb any water left in the bore. A few patches slightly saturated with a bore solvent, such as Hoppe's No. 9 or Bucheimer's black powder solvent, should be run through the barrel, allowing some to trickle through the vent. The solvent will help prevent rust, the worst enemy a muzzleloader can have. To remove any excess solvent, shove another dry patch down the bore. Now you're ready to do some shooting!

Even after thorough cleaning it is a good practice to snap a few caps on a percussion rifle before loading it.

all of these guns are proof-tested with a charge of powder that exceeds any that should be used during day-to-day shooting.

As with nearly all guns that come straight from the factory, these guns usually are well lubricated and will have to be cleaned before they are loaded and fired. If there happens to be quite a bit of lube down the breech, the result can be a gooey mess, if the powder charge is dropped in before cleaning.

Hot soapy water is as good as anything else with which to scrub the bore. This initial cleaning doesn't have to be a

If this first outing is to be done at a local rifle range, remember to keep the muzzle pointed downrange. Place a percussion cap on the nipple, if the gun happens to be a caplock, and snap it. This should remove any grease that might be obstructing the nipple vent; if the explosion of the percussion cap reaches the breech, a small amount of smoke will be emitted from the muzzle.

It is a good idea to carry a nipple prick — a piece of wire small enough in diameter to be inserted through the flash hole of the nipple — to punch through any obstructions in the nipple. Unless percussion caps are hard to come by in your area, it also is a wise practice to snap two, maybe three,

A perfect powder charge can be weighed out each time with the Lee powder dippers, great for range shooting, not while hunting.

Adjustable powder measures such as this are available from a number of black powder suppliers; never charge directly from flask.

more caps before loading.

When dropping the powder charge down the muzzle, always hold the muzzle out and away from your body, keeping your hand away from it at the same time. Never charge a muzzleloader directly from the powder flask! This is only asking for trouble in the event that there is an accidental discharge — having a flask full of powder explode in your hand can prove quite discouraging.

If the musket being loaded is of the flintlock type, it is best simply to make sure that the flash hole is clear by punching it with the nipple prick, which, in this case, becomes a vent prick. It is, however, a common practice to prime the pan and dry fire the gun to check whether the flint and frizzen are sparking enough to ignite the FFFFg powder used to prime the flash pan.

In either case, loading a caplock musket of the Zouave type or a flintlock musket of the Brown Bess type, always keep the muzzle at a safe distance.

The .58 caliber musket can be loaded with either FFg or FFFg powder. While many black powder shooters swear by FFg powder, others faithfully stand by FFFg. So, it is best to experiment to see which powder best suits your wants and needs. It is actually safe to use either powder since black powder will not create pressures enough to create a problem in this caliber.

The .575 diameter minie used in the .58 caliber Zouaves weighs in at just around 500 grains, enough lead to drop just about anything that wanders the North American continent provided the shot is well placed. A good starting load for this caliber would be 65 grains of FFg or 60 grains of FFFg. This load is good for a muzzle velocity just around the 1000 feet per second mark and enough foot-pound energy to knock game as big as moose off its feet for good one-shot kills.

There are a number of ways to measure the correct amount of powder to drop for each charge. Occasionally you will probably run across a musket shooter that uses the "looks like enough to me" system, guessing at the charge weights. This is hardly recommended since rounds so loaded are usually very inconsistent.

If shooting is confined to just target shooting at rifle ranges, the No. 230 dipper from the Lee powder measure kit is the answer for consistent charge weights. A level dipper full of powder will measure out a consistent 60 grains of FFFg every time.

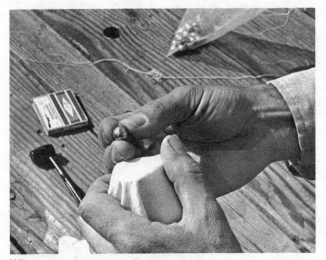

When not using pre-cut patches, drape proper thickness material over muzzle. Sprue on ball should either be seated straight up or straight down. It can be partially pushed into muzzle with thumb.

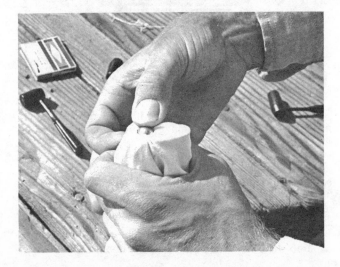

If small plastic containers are available, these make excellent powder containers. Using a powder scale of reputable manufacture, an exact powder charge can be poured into each of the containers before heading for the range or out to fill the freezer with a winter's meat supply.

With the muzzle held out at an arm's distance, drop the pre-measured powder charge down the muzzle, making sure that the finger tips are clear of the barrel opening.

The conical minie is then started into the barrel with the finger tips. Always take care to make sure that it is started into the muzzle as straight as possible. Next, pull the ramrod from its position beneath the barrel and firmly seat the bullet over the powder charge. Never slam the bullet down the bore; instead, take care and try not to batter the soft lead.

If hunting in the field, replace the ramrod in its original position below the barrel; if at the range, it can be laid on the bench. Place the hammer at half-cock and place a percussion cap on the nipple, pressing it down firmly with the thumb to make sure that it is firmly seated. Bring the hammer to full cock and aim in. The gun is ready to fire, providing the components have been loaded properly.

Of course, the .58 caliber Zouave wasn't the only military musket, but it was one of the best known during the Civil War. In addition to the muskets used during that period, there are a number of carbines and rifles ranging from .54 to .75 caliber that are loaded in this same manner; many of these so-called rifles are really muskets that were designated rifles because of their rifled bores.

Above: After the ball has been pressed into the muzzle, the excess patching material is cut off with a knife. (Below) The patched ball then is started into barrel. The instrument being used is termed a short starter.

The means and equipment for patching the round ball are almost as old as black powder, but less complicated.

MUSKET/RIFLE	BALL DIAMETER	POWDER	CHARGE GRAINS
.54 caliber U.S. Mississippi Rifle	.535 or minie	FFFg	75
.54 caliber U.S. Rifle, Models 1804-1814-1817	.535 or minie	FFFg	75
.577 English Enfield Rifle	.570 to .575	FFg	60
.58 caliber Civil War Muskets (Confederate)	.570 to .575 or minie	FFg	60
.58 caliber U.S. Civil War Rifle, Models 1855-1861-1863	.570 to 575 or minie	FFg	60
.58 caliber Navy Arms Model 1863 Remington Zouave	.575 or Lyman No. 575213, 575494, or 575602 minie	FFg or FFFg	60-65
.69 Whitneyville Plymouth Navy Rifle	.680	FFg	70
.69 caliber U.S. Muskets Models 1808-1842	.680	FFg	80
.69 caliber U.S. Muskets Models 1821-1840-1842, re-rifled from smoothbores	.680	FFg	70
.70 caliber Navy Arms Brown Bess	.680	Fg or FFg	70-75
.75 caliber Dixie Gun Works Brown Bess	.740	Fg or FFg	70-80

After the ball has been seated four to five inches into the barrel, ramrod is used to seat it over powder charge.

There are actually no set rules to loading and firing muskets. True, patched balls can be fired in them, but seldom do they perform as well as the minie bullets. The musket just doesn't allow enough powder to be loaded to get the utmost accuracy from their large bores with round ball projectiles. The one exception to this would be the Brown Bess musket.

Dixie Gun Works now offers a reproduction of this once favorite arm of the early East Coast settlers — provided they could get one from an unsuspecting British soldier. This particular gun is fitted with a forty-two-inch smooth-bore barrel and is loaded with a patched 610-grain .740-inch ball in front of 70 to 80 grains of FFg.

The following chart is by no means a complete list of loads for the different guns listed, but instead gives some

Black powder rifles don't have to be all old fashioned. The above shooter has scope sighted his hunting rifle. Such changes add greatly to the effectiveness of a big bored muzzleloader.

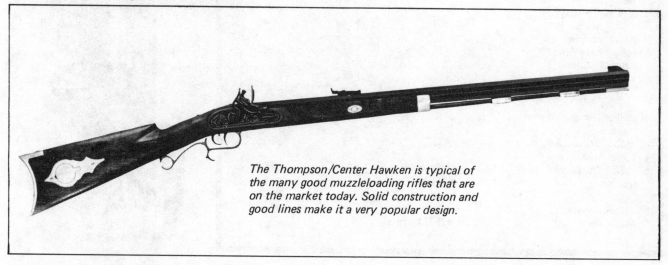

The Thompson/Center Hawken is typical of the many good muzzleloading rifles that are on the market today. Solid construction and good lines make it a very popular design.

good starting loads for the given guns and calibers. There were numerous foreign-made muskets that were made especially for the Civil War and imported to the United States, some being sold to both Union and Confederate forces. As a rule, these are basically built to the specifications of the Springfield rifled muskets and should be loaded as such. Calibers may vary, so it would be wise to learn the exact caliber before attempting to shoot any of them.

The loading and shooting of heavy barreled muzzleloading rifles is basically the same as with the thinner barreled musket. For better accuracy, however, the long barreled Kentucky and Pennsylvania rifles, as well as the short barrel Plains and Hawken type rifles, always are loaded with a patched undersize ball.

The Minie bullet at left is superior to the round ball when it comes to speedy reloading. Patched ball, however, usually proves to be the most accurate of the two.

RIFLE	BALL DIAMETER	POWDER	CHARGE-GRAINS
.36 caliber Hopkins & Allen Offhand Rifle	.340	FFFg	35-45
.38 caliber Replica Arms Plainsman Rifle	.360	FFFg	40-45
.44 caliber Navy Arms Kentucky Rifle	.434	FFFg	45-60
.45 caliber Dixie Gun Works Standard Percussion or Flint Rifle	.445	FFFg	65
.45 caliber Thompson-Center Hawken	.440	FFFg	50-65
.45 caliber Hopkins & Allen Target Rifle	.435	FFFg	55-70
.50 caliber Thompson-Center Hawken	.490 or No. 445599 Lyman minie	FFg	50-70
.58 caliber Hopkins & Allen Deer Stalker	.570 or No. 575213 Lyman minie	FFg	60-70

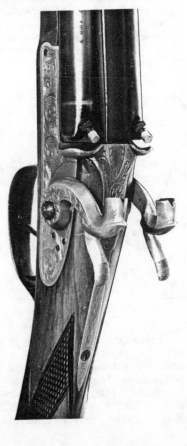

Reproduction muzzleloading double barrel shotgun is copy of type of gun used a hundred years ago.

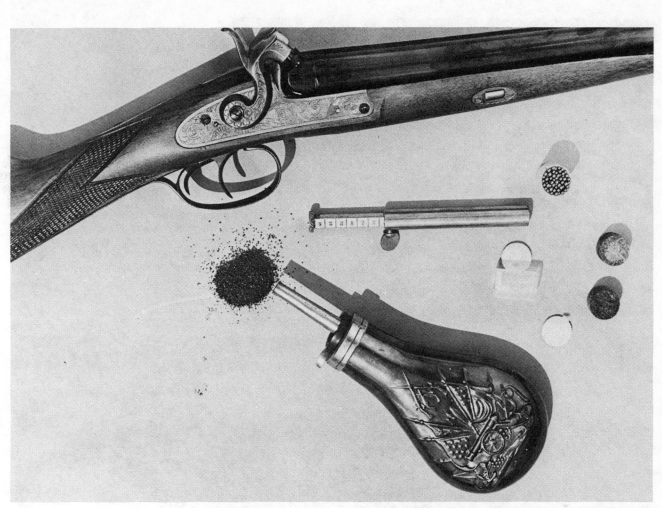

The muzzleloading double from Richland Arms, some shot, powder, wads and percussion caps are the ingredients for a day of shotgunning.

MUZZLELOADING SHOTGUNS

To ram the Powder well, but not the Ball (shot);
    One Third the well-turned Shot superior must
Arise, and overcome the nitrous Dust,
    Which, dry'd and season'd in the Oven's Heat,
Has stood in close-mouthed Jarr the dampless Night.
    Now search for Tow, and some old saddle pierce:
No Wadding lies so close or drives so fierce.
    And here be mindful constantly to Arm
With Choice of Flints, a Turn-Screw and a Worm;
    The accidental Chances of the Field
Will for such Implements Occasion yield.

Written in 1727, this segment of a poem entitled *Pteryplegia: Or, The Art of Shooting Flying* by A. B. Markland goes into some detail concerning the components needed to load an early fowling piece, the early name for the muzzleloading shotgun. The poet even goes so far as to warn of some of the hazards and the need of a turn screw and worm to remove the loaded components from the breech should they fail to fire.

With "One Third the well-turned Shot superior must Arise," Markland was trying to get across the point that as much as one and one-half as much shot is used as powder. When referring to the search for tow or saddle pierce, he

Same flask used to charge the percussion revolver will double as shotgun powder container, Lee dipper measures the charge.

115

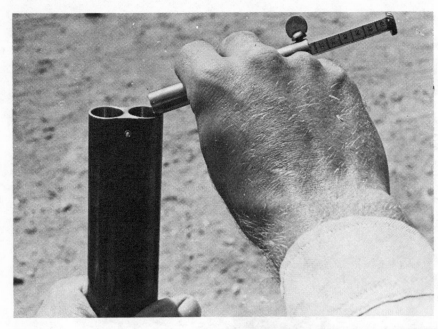

Measured powder charge is loaded into muzzle (left). Above, the wads used to comprise load and what they should look like loaded.

Felt wad of right thickness is first inserted over powder (right). Plastic shot protector such as that available from Federal is then inserted.

was referring to the most commonly used materials for wadding between the powder and shot.

Black powder apparently was not the propellant that we know today. For one thing, powder mills were usually just small businesses employing little, if any, quality control over their product. Atmospheric moisture must have been something of a problem then also, since Markland writes of placing the powder in a "close-mouthed Jarr the dampless Night" to dry in the warmth of the oven's heat. Hopefully, the powder was kept well away from the flame!

Just as these early fowling pieces were loaded in 1727, the currently made muzzleloading shotguns also are loaded, except that you don't have to place your powder in a jar to dry overnight or rip apart old saddles to get the tow padding to use as wadding. The components, though, are basically the same; powder, wadding, shot and a wad over this to keep the shot from rolling out the muzzle.

Missing, however, from many of the modern black powder shotguns are the forty-inch or longer barrels that were used on the early fowling pieces. This, perhaps, is where the idea of an extra long barrel giving a shotgun added range originated. This is true with shotguns that are loaded with black powder, since the long barrel gives the powder more distance to be completely burned or ignited.

With breechloading shotguns using smokeless powder shells, this isn't the case. The powder, in most cases, is completely ignited by the time it has traveled less than half of the gun's twenty-six or twenty-eight-inch barrel. With these guns, the longer barrel only tends to improve the gun's pattern at maximum ranges, not make it shoot farther.

As a starter, if the gun happens to be a new black powder reproduction, clean the bore to remove the excess lubricant that usually is all but poured down the bore at the factory. Muzzleloading shotguns can be cleaned in the same manner as the rifled or smoothbore musket.

An over-the-shot cardboard wad is seated over the shot to keep it from running out the barrel; this should be firmly seated.

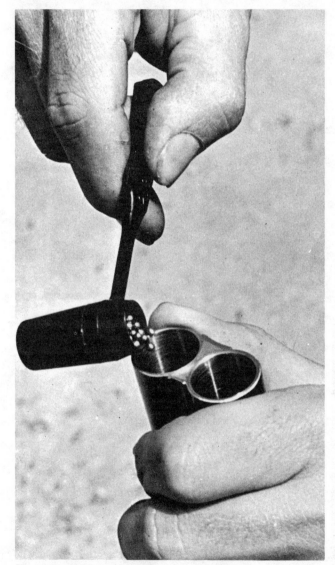

Proper load of shot is poured into the muzzle of the shotgun. Muzzle should be held away from body for each loading step.

If the gun happens to be a caplock, snap a few caps to clear the nipple and burn any moisture away that might be in the breech. In the event that the gun you are shooting is

fitted with a flintlock, prime the pan with just enough FFFFg to insure that the flint is sparking enough to ignite the powder; clean the flash hole leading from the pan to the breech.

A muzzleloading shotgun is loaded in almost the exact manner as a shotgun shell; it might not be a bad idea to cut open a shell and examine how it is loaded.

A measured charge of powder is first dropped into the breech through the muzzle. The amount of powder used will vary according to the intended target. If claybirding is the afternoon's activities, a good medium velocity load is best. Again this will vary, according to the gauge of the shotgun.

The powder is followed by a thick felt or cardboard wad. This should measure around 3/32 to one-eighth inch in thickness. If the gun's bore is close to being the exact diameter of one of the standard 12, 16, 20 or 28-gauge breechloading shotguns, there is a wide variety of components in the line of wads that can be used in the black powder gun also. This includes plastic shot cups that will greatly improve the gun's pattern.

Lightweight 12 gauge double belches forth
lead and smoke as black powder enthusiast
Toby Bridges swings on a clay pigeon.

Powder having FFFg granule size tends to throw the shot in erratic, inconsistent patterns that vary too much to be dependable. Most muzzleloading shotgun manufacturers and shooters who have done countless experiments with the guns agree that the best granulation to use in shotguns of 12, 16, 20 and 28-gauge is FFg. Shotguns of 10 gauge or larger should be loaded with Fg powder.

With the wad seated over the powder, drop in the shot. Lead shot comes in a variety of sizes and — again depending on the target — there is a proper size shot. For the medium velocity trap or target load, No. 7½ and No. 8 shot work the best. The small size of the shot allows more pellets to be loaded in a given 1-1/8 or 1-1/4-ounce shot charge, making the pattern more dense.

To keep the shot from rolling out the end of the barrel, another thin felt or cardboard wad should be seated in front of the shot. Tissue paper that has been blotted with a commercial lube such as Dixie Gun Work's Bear Grease or Hodgdon's Spit-Patch makes an excellent over-the-shot wad. The lube helps hold the wad in place and allows more shots between barrel cleanings.

The following chart gives light, medium and heavy loads in drams. To figure how many grains each load is made up of, simply multiply it by 27.34 grains; a one dram equivalent. It is recommended that you start by loading the light load first, then if it doesn't seem to be up to your desires, go to the medium, then to the heavy, if even more is needed.

GAUGE	DRAMS POWDER	SHOT CHARGE (OZ.)	
4	10	3	Medium
8	5-1/2	2-1/4	Medium
10	5	1-3/4	Heavy
10	4-1/2	1-1/2	Medium
10	4	1-1/2	Light
12	4-1/8	1-3/8	Heavy
12	3-3/4	1-1/4	Medium
12	3-1/4	1-1/8	Light
16	3-1/8	1-1/8	Heavy
16	3	1	Medium
16	2-1/2	1	Light
20	2-3/4	1	Heavy
20	2-1/2	7/8	Medium
20	2-1/2	3/4	Light
28	2-1/4	7/8	Heavy
28	2	5/8	Medium
28	1-3/4	5/8	Light
32	1-3/4	5/8	Heavy
32	1-1/2	9/16	Medium
32	1-1/2	1/2	Light
.410	1-1/2	5/8	Heavy
.410	1-1/2	1/2	Medium
.410	1-1/4	1/2	Light

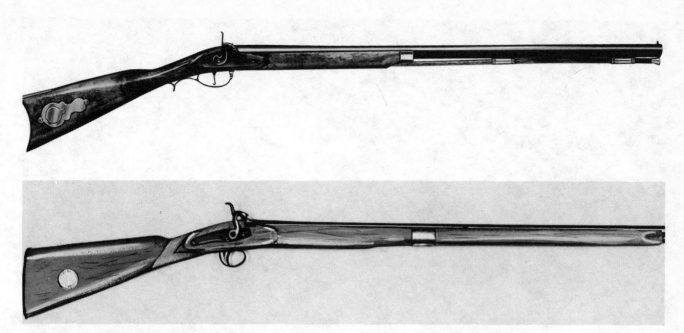

All loads are based on the use of FFg powder. If FFFg powder is used on the smaller 28 gauge, 32 gauge and .410, reduce the load slightly.

At one time it was common practice to use the smoothbore muzzleloading shotgun to hunt big game, especially the large bore 4, 8 and 10 gauges, which were used on dangerous game in Africa. The smaller gauges were used extensively for taking whitetailed deer and black bear in this country and Canada. Of course, these weren't loaded with regular lead shot, but with a large round lead ball that is referred to as a "pumpkin ball."

These are loaded just as the regular shot load, except that the ball is used instead of the shot. The following chart from the Dixie Gun Works gives recommended loads for firing round lead balls from muzzleloading shotguns.

The shotgun at top is a lightweight 12 gauge from Numrich Arms, below is a full-stock 28 gauge from Century Arms, as is fowler shown below left. Double is imported by Dixie Gun Works.

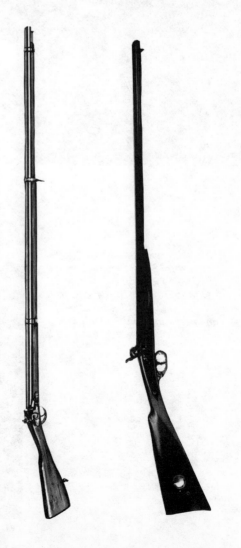

GAUGE	POWDER GRAINS	DRAMS	BALL GRAINS
4	273	10	1531
5	213	7-15/32	1217
6	179	6-17/32	1025
7	154	5-5/8	889
8	135	4-15/16	793
9	122	4-15/32	725
10	109	4	656
11	96	3-1/2	574
12-13	89	3-1/4	547
16-18	75	2-3/4	437
19-21	68	2-1/2	383
22-30	55	2	328

Although the loads on this charge hold true for loading today's modern muzzleloader, it was originally compiled in February, 1896 by the Gunmakers Company and the Guardians of the Birmingham Proof House under the authority of the Gun Barrel Proof Act of 1868. All charges were based on FFg powder for those gauges of 12 or smaller and on Fg powder for the larger bores.

It does prove that muzzleloading scattergun loads have changed little in the past century! – *Turner Kirkland*

The replica of the .44 Walker Colt belches lead and smoke in Skelton's hand. Holstered sixgun is a Ruger fired for comparison purposes.

(Right) with two-hand hold, Bridges fires the 1862 Police replica at a fleeing jack rabbit. Not to his surprise it was another miss, but so were all of his other shots. The two-handed hold is for placing an accurate shot, not recoil.

CHAPTER 11
ROUNDUP FOR REPLICA

Here's One Midwest Company That Is Making A Career

Of Reproducing Oldies — But Goodies!

IN THIS AGE OF flat shooting, hard hitting, high velocity, not to mention deadly accurate firearms, why would anyone even consider going afield or gracing the firing line armed with a dirty, noisy, smelly and ballistically inferior black powder gun?

Perhaps to this hardy group of practicioners, the glory of the challenge means more than being able to make a three hundred yard shot on a woodchuck with a long range varmint rifle equipped with a scope that is nearly as long as the rifle's barrel. Or perhaps, being able to punch out the centers of a target with each shot from a finely tuned match pistol.

Toby Bridges had always wanted to try hunting with one of the black powder cap and ball handguns and when an invitation to do some rabbit hunting with Ron May and Mike Arnold of Norco, California, coincided with doing a field test with the new 1862 Police Pistol from Replica Arms, he had the makings for an interesting hunt.

After a fast breakfast of hot coffee and sweet rolls, our trio of bunny busters strolled up the side of Rattlesnake Mountain in quest of cottontails.

"We hadn't gone forty yards when a bunny burst up the hill. Being the only one clear for a shot, I swung the bead front sight of the black powder handgun on the rabbit much as I would have had I been packing my trusty old Beretta over and under. There was a loud *kwmp* as I pulled the trigger and the whole mountainside was obliterated from sight by a cumulous-sized cloud of smoke," Bridges reports.

"Running around the self-inflicted smoke screen, I saw the rabbit as he topped the ridge and was soon hot in pursuit.

"Reaching the crest of the ridge, I saw the rabbit sitting next to a large boulder around forty yards away. Using another large rock for a rest, I aimed in on the bunny again and let another round fly."

"He went up that valley over there," yelled Mike

Arnold, from the ridge as I strained my eyes looking for a kicking rabbit lying next to the boulder.

"I took off up the valley, determined to get that rabbit if it took me the entire day. Half a flask of powder later, a pocket full of balls poorer and dead tired from chasing that darned rabbit over hill after hill and through valley after valley, I decided to conserve what energy I had remaining to make the trek back down the mountain. I had reached a conclusion, though: either I wasn't destined to kill a rabbit with a cap and ball revolver or that Replica Arms' 1862 Police Pistol had been designed for use other than hunting, but I had enjoyed it."

To meet the demands of the shooting public, firearm companies and importers have introduced a large number of well built shootable replicas. Incorporating quality control with stronger construction, these modern duplicates are, in most cases, far superior to the originals.

It had been more than a century since the Colt Firearms Company had mass produced their last cap and ball revolver when, to meet the whims of the gun-buying public, the firm began to reproduce the famed Navy Colt last year. The Colt revolvers used during and before the Civil War probably have been copied more than any other handgun designs during this spreading of black powder mania.

Replica Arms of Marietta, Ohio, now is importing from Italy a copy of the conclusion to Colt's percussion revolver era, the 1862 Police Pistol. The design, resembling a scaled-down version of the famous Navy Colt, encompassed many improvements and modifications of the earlier revolvers. Designed primarily for use in police work, the model was popular with Army officers during the Civil War due to its efficiency, light weight and nice balance.

Colt offered the pistol in three barrel lengths; 4½, 5½ and 6½ inches. Utilizing the small frame of the Colt Pocket Pistol, the 1862 Police model weighed only twenty-six ounces with a 6½-inch barrel. Unlike the Pocket model, it was equipped with a round barrel instead of the octagon barrel.

The semi-fluted five-chambered cylinder on the original occasionally was stamped with the markings, "Pat. Sept. 10th 1850." The barrel was stamped with either "ADDRESS COL. SML COLT – NEW YORK U.S. AMERICA," "ADDRESS SAML COLT HARTFORD CT." or "ADDRESS COL. COLT – LONDON," depending on where the pistol had been made.

The Italian-made replica is almost an exact copy of the original made over a hundred years ago. With a 6½-inch barrel the copy still weighs in at twenty-six ounces and also is available with 4½ and 5½-inch barrels. As on the pistol of Colt manufacture, the replica is equipped with a brass trigger guard and grip straps.

The case-hardened frame, hammer and loading lever combined with brass trigger guard and backstrap, deep bluing of the barrel and cylinder and the fine figuring of the one-piece walnut stocks make the replica eye pleasing. Unlike the originals, however, the only markings on the revolver are the proof stampings, serial number, the importer's name, "Made in Italy," the caliber and "Black Powder Only."

By removing a single screw and wedge located directly in front of the cylinder, the revolver can be broken down into its three basic parts; the barrel, cylinder and receiver. It's necessary to break the gun down after every firing session to clean the residue left from firing the black powder loads. The barrel and cylinder may be washed in a hot soapy water solution, then dried off and coated with a rust-preventing lubricant. To protect the finish of the walnut grips, it is not recommended that the receiver be submerged in the soap and water. An old toothbrush dipped in the solution is perfect for scrubbing the powder fouling from the receiver.

As the warning stamped on the barrel indicates, "Black Powder Only!" Smokeless powders create pressures that are too excessive for guns designed for shooting black powder. Hodgdon's black powder manual recommends loads of 15 to 20 grains of FFFg as the appropriate charge for .36 caliber cap and ball revolvers, Replica Arms recommends a load of only 18 grains. Using black powder, however, it would be virtually impossible actually to overload the cap and ball revolver, since the ball must be seated below the chamber mouth, thus limiting the amount of powder one can get in the chamber.

Conical bullets and revolver balls are always oversize and firmly seated with a tight fit. When swaged, they usually leave a thin ring of lead around the mouth of the chamber. Balls ranging in diameters of .368 to .400 inch will fit revolvers of .36 caliber adequately, although those of .375 to .380 inch are suited best for this caliber. The mould-lead cast balls used during the test firing of the replica averaged 80-84 grains each and ran approximately 86 to the pound. Conical bullets, which weren't available for testing in the revolver, usually average around 140 grains each and run an average fifty to a pound. The tight fit of the ball is necessary to keep them from being jarred out as the revolver is fired.

With the chambers charged and Hodgdon's Spit Ball at the chamber mouths, a percussion cap is fitted to the nipple, this is final loading step.

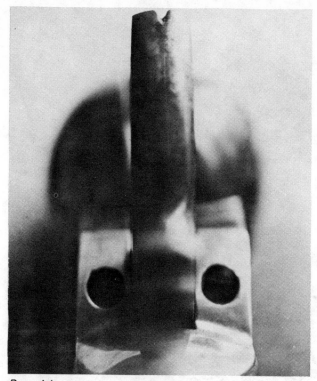

Rear sight aperture on the 1862 Police replica is hardly more than a notch in the top of the hammer. Front sight is a shotgun-type bead.

only.

Smaller than the cylinder of the .36 caliber Navy Colt, the chambers of the 1862 Police will not hold as large a charge as the larger pistol. Using the Lyman black powder flask, which was designed for use with their entry in this rebirth of black powder shooting, a maximum charge of almost 21.0 grains of Hodgdon's FFFg can be dropped, leaving barely enough room to seat the ball. Although this is a maximum load for this revolver, only because this was all the powder that could be gotten into the small chambers, the recoil of the fired round was about equal to that of a .32 S&W.

In shooting any pistol for accuracy, the heavy loads are consistently the least accurate. Firing the aforementioned maximum charge, groups were spread out and averaged close to ten inches at twenty-five yards.

The sights of the replica are a far cry from match sights, consisting of a small shotgun type bead front and a V-notch rear sight, which is located in the nose of the hammer. Even so, groups were reduced considerably when the powder charge was lowered to 18.5 grains of FFFg. This charge was attained by using the .069-cubic inch powder dipper from the Lee Loader measuring kit and behind the .375-inch

A curious young passerby stops long enough to watch Bridges load the 1862 Police. With the proper instruction, black powder guns are easy to load, care for and, most of all, fun to shoot.

Before firing, as with any other new black powder gun, the Replica Arms copy of the Colt 1862 Police was broken down into the three basic parts and cleaned as mentioned previously. All oil was removed from the chambers and, to clean oil and dirt from the flash holes of the nipples, a cap was placed on each of the five nipples and snapped. The explosion of the percussion cap removes accumulated dirt or fouling from the nipple and may prevent a chamber from failing to fire during actual firing.

To load the revolver, the muzzle is pointed skyward and the hammer is placed on the half-cock notch. By doing so, the cylinder then will rotate freely and allow a premeasured charge of powder to be dropped in the cylinder chamber. The ball or conical bullet is placed at the mouth of the chamber and is seated firmly against the powder with the loading lever. Caution should be taken not to crush the powder.

To minimize the chances of spilling powder from charged chambers, it is best to charge and seat the ball on only one chamber at a time. As a safety precaution, grease or a commercial lube such as Hodgdon's Spit Ball then is placed in the chamber mouth over the ball. This serves two purposes: As a seal which prevents the flash of the firing chamber from igniting the powder in a chamber that isn't aligned with the barrel and as a prevention of barrel leading and powder fouling. Many of the commercial lubes claim to improve accuracy also.

The final step in loading the cap and ball revolver is to seat a percussion cap firmly on each of the nipples. Sometimes it is difficult to find caps that fit perfectly. If the nipples of a revolver require a half size, one size being too large and the next smaller size being too small, it is best to buy the larger size. By pinching the open end of the cap slightly, it will fit snugly over the nipple. This is the only answer to the problem since caps are made in full sizes

Light recoil of a maximum charge in the .36 caliber handgun is comparable to that of a .32 S&W. Note how little the gun jumps when fired.

diameter ball, groups of seven inches at twenty-five yards were fairly common during the test firing.

Reducing the charge to 12 grains, the groups shrunk to a little less than five inches. This charge was so mild an infant probably could have handled the revolver with ease. Without any adjustment for elevation, the revolver seemed to hold its group about ten inches above the point of aim at twenty-five yards.

Although cap and ball revolvers usually are loaded without any sort of patching or lubricant other than that placed on top of the loaded chambers, Replica Arms suggests using a treated felt wad between powder and ball. They recommend using felt — like that used in felt hats — treated in a solution of one-half pound paraffin, one-half pound beeswax and one-fourth pound beef tallow.

The mixture is melted in a shallow pan over a low flame and the pieces of felt are dipped into it. The treated felt then is palced on a flat surface and allowed to dry and harden. Using the proper size wadcutter, the wads are punched out to the exact diameter as that of the chamber. Using this type of wad makes it unnecessary to use the grease at the mouth of the chamber. The felt wad seals the charge from possible accidental ignition as another chamber is fired. Not wanting to carve up my favorite Stetson, the tests were made with Hodgdon's Spit Ball at the chamber mouth.

The rifling in the barrel of the replicas are made shallow for a reason. The Marietta, Ohio, firm claims that the shallow grooves allow shooters to fire the revolver quite a few times between barrel cleaning sessions. They reason that the shallow rifling will not be clogged as easily with lead or powder foulings as would a barrel incorporating much deeper rifling.

The grips of the replica 1862 Police are on the small side, as were those on the originals. A shooter with large or even average-size hands will find his pinky looking for a place to hang on. Light in weight and recoil, the revolver is an excellent gun for the young shooter who has been bitten by that incurable black powder bug. If the "missus" is always complaining about the long hours you spend at the range, the easy handling and dependable performance of the 1862 replica make it an ideal lady's gun.

Shoot a black powder gun and you're bound to draw an audience, as Bridges discovered. A group of young BB gun shooters take a break from their lizard hunt to watch the man with the "funny gun." Firing reduced load, 12-year-old Gary Arnold experienced no recoil.

MEANWHILE, SOMEWHERE IN Texas, a delivery-man made his relieved getaway down the dusty street, while Skeeter Skelton, our Man on the Rio Grande, sat staring unbelievingly at the array of cap-and-ball sixguns, powder flask, moulds and sundry accessories that tumbled from their packages. "It'll take me six months to count this stuff, let alone test it," he moaned.

And it did. But Charles A. Skelton, handgunner, border rat and originator of the six Margarita lunch, slugged his way through what turned out to be one of the most pleasurable field tests of his experience.

The cornucopia of black powder hardware coming from Replica Arms, Incorporated, of Marietta, Ohio, was enough to turn the head of any bargain-hardened Colt collector. First out of wraps came a monster Walker replica. Weighing in at four pounds, nine ounces, this Mexican War magnum is an extremely faithful replica of the original, a collector's specimen which commands prices starting at $2,500 and soaring skyward.

The half-round, nine-inch barrel is blued and stamped U.S. 1847 – MADE IN ITALY. The cylinder, also blued, has oval bolt stops and displays a close reproduction of the original rolled-on engraving of a soldier and Indian scene

Firing the .36 caliber Navy replica and shoulder stock combination, Skelton uses the pistol's butt for rest. Escaping gases from any revolver make it unwise to place hand in front of cylinder.

and the legend, Model U.S.M.R. – Colt's Patent. Backstrap is blued iron and the square-backed trigger guard is rich looking, polished brass. Frame, hammer and loading lever are case-hardened in color. The one-piece grips on Replica's Walker, like the wood on all their test guns, are of good quality, well figured European walnut and fit the straps better than those of most of the Colt and Remington "copy" percussions seen today.

The 1860 Army .44 – dubbed the Trooper – and the round-barreled 1861 .36 Navy Officer both are styled after the desirable original four-screw models, and are cut for shoulder stocks. Both have "creeping" loading levers that gear the rammer home to seat balls with considerable ease and both feature classic naval engagement engraving on the cylinders. The .36 Navy has an iron backstrap and trigger guard, the .44 Army sports iron backstraps, brass guard. Lock work on both these models is crisp and true, with the cylinders lining up precisely and locking down tight for each shot. Some attention apparently has been given to the innards of these guns, Skelton finding mainsprings light, for easy cocking, and trigger pulls clean and running around an acceptable four or five pounds, with the exception of the Walker, which was heavier.

Next up were two petite ante bellum belly guns, 1848 Baby Dragoon and Wells Fargo models. From the barrels back, these little .31s appear to be identical, with square back, brass guard and straps and the same Indian fight scene engraving on the cylinder of each. The Baby Dragoon has a six-inch octagon barrel with case-hardened loading lever; the Wells Fargo is five-inch octagon, with no loading lever.

Four bullet moulds were included with the test guns. Three are excellent, brass duplicates of the old Colt moulds, with tough, case-hardened steel sprue cutters, cherried for both round and conical bullets in .31, .36 and .44 caliber. The fourth is a copy of the original .44 Walker iron mould, its sprue cutter having a long, thin handle.

Using pure British pig lead, Skelton whomped up a mess of pellets for all three calibers, sticking with the round ball half of the moulds, since this is a favorite missile of black powder buffs. Wanting to try the Walker with its heaviest bullet charge combination, though, he ran off a few conicals with the Walker mould.

Probably the most notable feature of the Replica Arms inventory is the great number of accessories it offers.

Ken Phelps, ramrod of the Replica outfit and a charcoal burner of some thirty-five years' practical experience, seems to know what he wants – and what he wants makes for a comprehensive list. Hence a brass Walker powder flask, ornamented with stands of flags on both sides and equipped with a plunger type spout adjustable to drop a charge of 30 to 60 grains of black, with a bullet compartment on one side. Other flasks include a purple copper 1860-1861 adjustable model and the small, .31 eagle flask with 10-grain spout.

Shoulder stocks are offered for both the 1860 Army and 1861 Navy models, our specimen being for the .36 Navy. This stock is fashioned of a particularly handsome piece of dense, dark walnut, with brass butt plate, yoke and blue steel saddle ring and retaining clamp. It fits perfectly on an original four-screw Navy Colt found in a Texas collection.

All Replica models can be cased with accessories in walnut or leather and plenty of such minutiae as nipple wrenches, extra nipples and combination tools are rolling off the Italian assembly lines. Purists may even ask for and get 1872 Colt conversion loading gates from the good Mr.

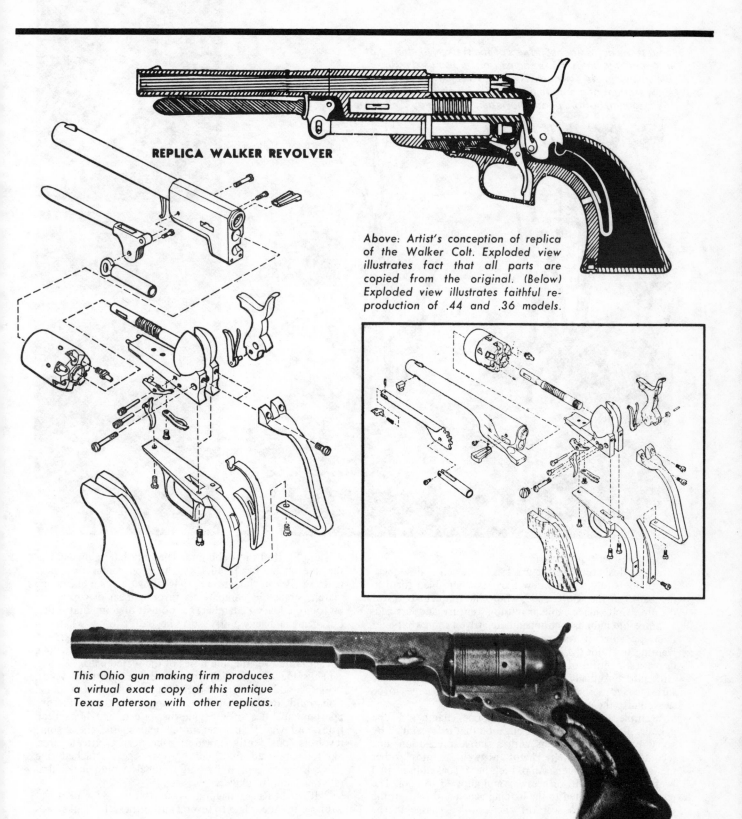

REPLICA WALKER REVOLVER

Above: Artist's conception of replica of the Walker Colt. Exploded view illustrates fact that all parts are copied from the original. (Below) Exploded view illustrates faithful reproduction of .44 and .36 models.

This Ohio gun making firm produces a virtual exact copy of this antique Texas Paterson with other replicas.

To test the devastational powers of the Walker, Skelton shot into mesquite limbs. For a comparison he also used a Ruger Blackhawk in .44 magnum. The photo at top right and center show sections of mesquite limbs that were hit by the Ruger .44 magnum, bottom photo shows damage done by Walker replica.

Phelps, president of Replica.

A practical sort, Skelton was less interested in how these frontloaders looked than how they shot, and hied forth to the banks of the Rio Grande, where the frequent barks of the first Colts made familiar music a century and less ago.

Since the moulds mentioned here arrived somewhat later than the guns, it was necessary to scrounge for fodder. Wanting to shoot the pretty little thirty-ones, Skelton came up with a handful of No. 1 buckshot, which is supposedly .30 caliber. Actually, the intrepid Texan had to carefully sort the shot, as there were some balls too large to be swaged into the chamber with the rammer.

Multiple discharge — more than one chamber of the cylinder firing at once — is a bugaboo that is forestalled by savvy percussion pistoleers with a simple precaution, one recommended by Ken Phelps as well as most other meticulous cap'n ballers. An old felt hat is soaked in melted beef tallow, paraffin or beeswax and allowed to cool. The resultant mess is toted to the loading bench and wads of the correct diameter to seal off the powder charge in the revolver's cylinder are cut. These wads, seated by hand between powder and ball, effectively block the entry of the flame of a round shot while in battery position. Too, they lubricate and partially clean the bore of the revolver during every shot, allowing continued firing without barrel fouling for a much longer string of firing.

Here Skelton drew the line. The only hat he owned was the one on his head and it was in good condition, a near new 5X Beaver bought in 1946. Having read that some match percussion competitors favor a smear of cup grease on top of a loaded chamber, he thought of going that route, but being a backwoodsy sort, he didn't know what cup grease was. So, in lieu of cup or bear or transmission grease, he used Crisco. It worked fine when daubed on with a pocket knife over the dull noses of the seated balls.

Thus loaded, the tiny thirty-ones, in Skelton's words, "Done good." The grip-to-barrel angle of the pocket model Colts and Replica's replicas emphasizes the instinctive pointing qualities of the gun. In spite of the brass bead front and wiggly hammer notch rear sights, these small revolvers consistently stayed on a beer can at fifteen yards. Skelton observed that, with proper sights attached, the Baby Dragoon and Wells Fargo models would make first rate quail and frog killers.

With a .44 Ruger magnum as control, the .44 Walker was wrung out. According to several authorities, the Walker was the most potent revolver manufactured until the advent of the modern magnums. Its chamber will hold 50 grains of FFFg black powder under a 220-grain conical bullet. Compare this with the later .45 Colt cartridge flashing a 250-grain slug over 40 grains of black, which attained a muzzle velocity of 910 fps and muzzle energy of 460 foot pounds.

Granting that the Walker revolver utilized its powder with the same efficiency (and powder should be burned more completely in its nine-inch barrel), the 220-grain Walker conical would walk along at 1085 fps, with a contingent energy at the muzzle of 575 foot pounds.

Green, 2½-inch mesquite limbs were attacked at a range of five feet, Lyman's .44 semi-wadcutter No. 429421 over 21 grains of Hercules 2400 in the Ruger regularly cleaved them in two, leaving frayed ends of the broken halves. Round balls over a chamber full of Triple F in the Walker ripped hell out of 'em, too, but less spectacularly.

The rather tough trigger pull of the Walker didn't do much for groups, but consistent mankilling hits were made on a twenty-yard silhouette target.

Skelton's best shooting was done with the .36 Navy with shoulder stock attached. This little carbine arrangement is especially rigid when backed snugly into the shoulder by a steady pull exerted on the revolver's grip.

When kept clean and well lubricated with Crisco, the .44 Army produced the best offhand groups, its best five shots staying in three inches at twenty yards. Series were shot in all the Replica sixguns without benefit of treated wads or grease, to see how long they would retain their accuracy. With each gun, accuracy suffered after five shots (one chamber being left unloaded for safety in carrying), and barrel leading and fouling became so severe after ten or fifteen rounds as to impair the rotation of the cylinder. This is no defect in the Replica product; the same results are obtained when other percussion revolvers are so mistreated.

Full charges of black powder give the best accuracy in these smokepoles, reduced loads invariably widening groups. Lacking a measure set for the exact charge, full loads are put together by filling the chamber almost full of powder, leaving a space about two-thirds the diameter of the round ball, so that when the ball is seated firmly the powder will be slightly compressed. Unlike most smokeless powders, black works best with this little bit of compression, which makes for more uniform ignition and burning. These charcoal burners are good shooters as well as eye-catchers. Johnny Reb, who had no aversion to using copies of the Colts of his day, would have liked them.

Not tested were Replica's Paterson .36, which comes with all accessories and in various barrel lengths, and a Second Model Dragoon.

To allow for thorough cleaning of all parts, black powder revolvers are easily broken down. This 1862 Police is disassembled by removing screw and wedge in front of the cylinder.

CHAPTER 12
THE MEAN BOAR CAPER

After chasing the dogs for better than two miles, the author stops to take a five minute rest, listens as dogs pursue the fast boar.

Pig Busting In The Heart Of Dixie
Proves To Be Quite A Challenge
For This Muzzleloading Enthusiast!

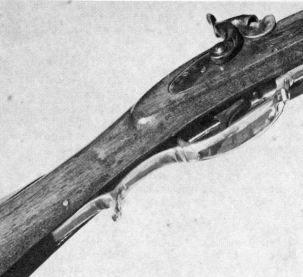

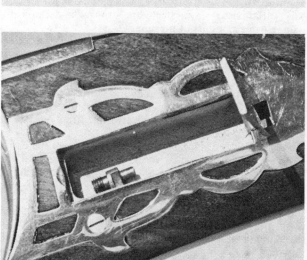

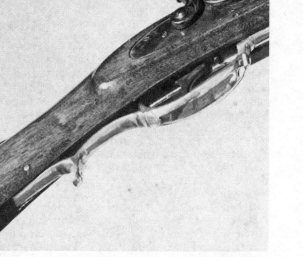

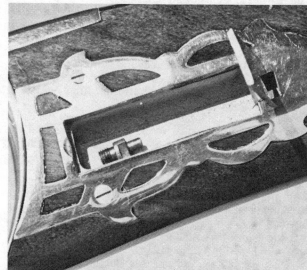

The dark red cherry stained stock is set off by polished brass furniture. The trigger guard (top photo) is contoured for fingers and bears the serial number. Schnabel and Kentucky type front bead are made of brass.

Featuring Roman Nose shaping of the butt stock's comb, the Dixie Pennsylvania rifle sports a brass butt plate that is contoured to fit into shoulder (top). The inlaid brass patch box carries extra nipple, jag.

"DAMN FOOL DOGS," muttered Ben Burton, as we hurried down the narrow Tennessee logging road, trying to catch up with them. "They must be headed for the next county!"

"Stop griping and keep running. It's good for your health!" I chided, as we trotted down the muddy dirt road. "Just keep reminding yourself of all the fun you're having and you won't even notice those sharp pains shooting through your chest."

Several hours earlier, after plowing our way through rain-soaked fields and over dirt roads rutted by continuous use, we had released the dogs from the pen that Burton had built in the bed of his four-wheel drive pickup. Within minutes, the dogs were in hot pursuit of an animal that Tennessee has become noted for — the Russian wild boar.

"They're having trouble with him," gasped Burton, as we temporarily halted our mad rush to catch our wind. "Guess I'll have to go back to the truck and let Ol' Spot go in and show 'em how it's done. Why don't you all find yourself a good stand just in case they turn that fool boar

back this way?"

Burton was referring to Fred Bryce, a Michigan bow-hunter who had driven to Tennessee with hopes of skewering a boar with his broadhead-tipped arrows, and myself. As Burton trotted down the road to where the truck sat bogged down to its axles in mud, Bryce and I moved up along the ridge that ran parallel to the wilderness expressway.

Bryce decided to make his stand along a fairly open section of the ridge, while I moved on up to the crest. Sitting with my back to a large hickory tree, I examined the rifle sitting across my lap.

While visiting the Dixie Gun Works in Union City, Tennessee, several days earlier, I was so impressed with their Deluxe Pennsylvania rifle that I acquired one for the purpose of using it on this hunt. The .45 caliber percussion black powder rifle is an exact reproduction of the original Pennsylvania rifles made more than a hundred years ago.

The stock appears to be made of maple, stained to take on the appearance of cherry, having a reddish tint. The right side of the butt section of the long, one-piece stock is equipped with a beautiful brass patch box. The color of the stock really makes the patch box stand out, as it also does the brass butt plate, trigger guard, schnabel and rod guides.

The stock of the Pennsylvania rifle varies from that of the Kentucky rifle. Although it retains the rounded features and lines of the Kentucky rifle, its butt section has considerably more drop at the heel. The comb of the stock is much more rounded than that of the Kentucky, taking on a shape that has come to be known as Roman nose styling.

The Dixie Pennsylvania rifle is fitted with a rifled thirty-eight-inch barrel with a bore diameter of .450-inch, or .45 caliber. The firm offers the rifle in either flint or percussion lock. Since it was early spring and torrential downpours were not infrequent, I had chosen the percussion lock for the hunt, being more impervious to moisture than the flint-lock model.

During my visit with Turner Kirkland, founder of Dixie Gun Works, he explained to me, "Our rifles are made as authentic as possible. The locks, trigger assemblies and the lines of the stocks remain the same as on rifles of more than a century ago. The quality of the metal used is perhaps the only variation. Today's steels are stronger and can withstand greater amounts of pressures.

"One of the best methods of testing a modern reproduction is to load it with a double charge of powder, then seat two balls. Of course, this should be done with the rifle braced against something and a string tied around the trigger so that you can get far enough away not to be injured should the rifle not be strong enough to handle the charge. We have yet to have anyone get hurt while firing one of our rifles!"

We didn't drop a double charge of FFFg down the barrel of the Dixie Pennsylvania rifle or seat two balls over the charge, but we did give it a good test firing before the hunt. Using 60 grains of FFFg behind a patched .440-inch diameter ball of approximately 128 grains, both Kirkland and I put our shots five inches high of the point of aim when firing the rifle from a range of twenty-five yards. With the rainbow trajectory of black powder guns, we figured this load would hit right on at around seventy-five yards.

Driving some three hundred miles east of Union City to Crossville, I met up with my host for the hunt, Ben Burton. Managing the 6,000-acre Renegade Hunting Range nestled among the mountains just east of Crossville, Burton makes hunting his living.

Inquisitive as to how the wildlife management area received the name, Renegade Range, I was told several different stories by some of the local townspeople, but the best and most logical reason is explained in the brochure that Burton sends out to hunters inquiring about the hunting there.

It seems that outcasts from the various Cherokee Indian tribes banded together and made the rugged mountain terrain a sanctuary from which they would raid the scattered homesteads. Later, during the Civil War, deserters — both Union and Confederate — made the area a base for their raids.

Today, Renegade Range still harbors some mean and nasty inhabitants, the ill-tempered wild boar. In addition to trophy boar, the high ridges and deep valleys are now home for such exotic imports as Babiroussa and Mouflon rams, fallow and Sika deer, Spanish goats, as well as the native whitetail deer, black bear and turkey gobbler.

The sun was just clearing the peak of a distant mountain as our group of hunters piled into Burton's four-wheel drive pickup. Armed with the .45 caliber black powder rifle, I was the only gun hunter in the group. The other three hunters were all hunting with bows.

Once the dogs had hit a track, we split up. Two of the bowhunters — Bob Polito from New Mexico and Butch Kochen from Illinois — went with their guide, Bob Harvelle, in an attempt to get in front of the chase. Fred Bryce and I went with Burton, trying to keep up with the dogs, should they bring the boar to bay.

Several hours and three or four miles later, Burton decided that the chase was getting out of hand and went back to the truck to release his "special boar dog," as he referred to it.

"Ol' Spot ain't got a lick of sense," Burton remarked earlier. "He gets himself so torn up it's just pitiful. I don't know what I'll do if he ever manages to get himself killed, best dog I got."

Sitting next to the tree, the dogs were barely audible as I took stock of my loading components. In one pocket were the percussion caps, patches and the wooden short starter, in another, premeasured charges of black powder in small plastic containers. Yet in another pocket were a dozen or so 250-grain Minies.

I had found that reloading succeeding shots — should they be necessary — would be difficult if using the patched round ball. The round ball, however, had proved the most accurate, so I loaded my first shot with a patched ball relying on the Minies for quick reloading. The Minies can be loaded without any sort of patching and are seated easily atop the powder charge.

Cocking back the hammer of the percussion rifle, I visually checked to make sure that the percussion cap was seated firmly on the nipple. Aiming in on a stump, I discovered that the long barrel made it difficult to aim the rifle while sitting, so I stood up and used the hickory tree for a rest. Aiming in on the stump again, my hold was much steadier.

"Get ready!" yelled Bryce as the dogs finally managed to turn the boar. "I think they're coming our way."

The chase had changed course and now was heading toward where Bryce and I were waiting. I brought the rifle's hammer to half cock to make sure that the percussion cap was firmly seated on the nipple. The yapping of the hounds grew louder and louder and I strained to see what was running ahead of them.

Something moved in and out of the underbrush as it made its way up the ridge. The early morning shadows made it difficult to distinguish whether it was a trophy boar or just another wild hog. Less than forty yards away from where I stood squinting down that rather long sight radius, the large boar stepped clear of the thick mountain laurel, looking back in the direction from which it had just come to see how close the pack of hounds was getting.

I quickly settled the front sight blade on the boar's front shoulder and squeezed off the round. As the hammer fell, a cloud of gray smoke blocked the boar from sight. The loud whump of the lead ball striking flesh and the loud squealing and grunting that followed assured me that I had hit my target, but that it was far from being done in.

Just before the hunt Bob Harvelle had commented, "If you get a shot at a big boar and don't kill him with that first shot, don't move. Freeze in your tracks and he won't know where you're at and won't be able to charge you."

Apparently he forgot to tell this boar just what he was supposed to do, as I tried to make myself as immovable as the hickory tree I was using as rest for the muzzleloader's long barrel. As soon as the boar was back on his feet, it didn't take him long to figure out which was the hickory tree and which was the hunter.

I managed to elude the wounded boar by getting a large fallen tree between the two of us. Several minutes later the dogs caught up, Ol' Spot leading the charge. He latched onto a rear quarter and the two went crashing through the underbrush squealing, growling and grunting, making it hard to distinguish which was doing which. Two or three other hounds moved in to give the dog a hand.

Bridges inspects the ivory of his Tennessee razorback. The boar sustained three hits from the big caliber .45 muzzleloader before finally going down for keeps. The thick brush made accurate shooting quite difficult.

Turner Kirkland, founder of Dixie Gun Works, test fires the rifle used on the hunt. The rifle shot high when fired on his twenty-five yard range, but hit right on at fifty yards.

Fumbling through the pockets, I somehow managed to come up with the ingredients to load for a second shot. I was so excited it's a wonder that I didn't drop in the Minie before the powder charge, but somehow I had everything in the right order.

With the rifle reloaded, I moved into the underbrush from which all sorts of ungodly sounds were bellowing forth. It should be mentioned that this was done with some deliberation. About the time I was entering the scene the boar decided it was time to depart it, with my entrance his only exit. As the boar charged out, he must have recognized me from our earlier encounter, for he didn't waste any time in getting me back on the other side of the fallen log.

The dogs were just about to resume their attack when I took aim on the boar's spine for the killing shot, or so I thought. The shot went off and the 250-grain Minie completely knocked the boar off his feet, but not for long.

He turned on an old bluetick hound with the intention of doing a little dissecting with the wicked tusks protruding from his lower jaw. The dog soon found himself the pursued and took an evasive course. Right around the log that I had chosen to hide behind!

I didn't lose any time getting out of the way. Luckily, the boar kept after the dog instead of me. By now the entire pack had caught up to all the action. While they kept the hog busy, I reloaded another round.

Apparently the 60-grain charges of FFFg didn't give the Minies the penetration necessary to finish the boar, so I increased the charge to 65 grains. Moving in for the kill, I took aim on the boar's shoulder and waited for the dogs to move out of the way. Just about the time I started to

squeeze the trigger, the boar made one last rush at me. Firing at almost point blank range, I hit him in the top of the skull and he went down for keeps.

Later — while skinning out the boar — I discovered that my first shot probably would have done the job. It had entered the chest cavity just behind the front shoulder and had punctured the hog's left lung, collapsing it. The second shot had missed that spine by less than an inch, angling forward and lodging itself in the rib cage. The final shot killed the boar almost instantly, entering the brain.

Later that evening — with four trophy boars hanging from the meat pole — we engaged in a little shooting match, Tennessee style. Harvelle placed an old tin can atop a fence post and I loaded the rifle, handing it to Burton. He handled the rifle as if he had been packing one around for years, except for one thing — he missed the can!

Harvelle was having the time of his life teasing Burton as I loaded the rifle again. This gaiety was cut short as I handed the rifle to him. Burton stood there smiling as Harvelle managed to shoot a limb off a nearby tree.

"Lets see you knock it off!" retorted Harvelle as he handed the rifle back to me. "How do we know that you didn't get lucky and accidentally hit that boar of your'n?"

With a fresh charge in the breech, I stepped up to the makeshift firing line. Remembering something I had seen in an old Gary Cooper flick about a famous Tennessee sharpshooter, I wet the tip of my thumb with my tongue and drew it across the front sight blade.

"What was that for?" asked Harvelle inquisitively.

Looking over my shoulder at him, I smiled and remarked, "Wetting the front sight blade is an important part of successfully shooting one of these long shoulder pieces. It knocks down the glare and sort of makes aiming easier."

I could see some doubt in his eyes as I told him this. There must have been something to it, however, since that rusty old tin can flew off the top of the fence post as the muzzleloader belched forth.

The last time I saw Harvelle he was still shaking his head back and forth and mumbling to himself, "Damndest thing I ever saw."

RETURN OF THE HAWKEN

Thompson/Center's Modern Reproduction Of The Hawken Half-Stock Rifle Is One Of The Finest Muzzleloaders Available Today!

CHAPTER 13

THE PROFESSIONAL HUNTER and mountain man of the early 1800s usually carried among his prized possessions a short and heavy barreled half-stock muzzle-loading rifle. For the most part, these were nearly always well built and were so made that they would withstand a considerable amount of hard use, be it on the trapline, following the buffalo herds, putting camp meat on the meat pole or fighting Indians, the latter being a peril often en-countered while in pursuit of the first three.

One such rifle favored and highly prized by these hardy individuals was produced by Jacob Hawken and later by his brother, Samuel, at their St. Louis, Missouri, plant. Jacob was the first to go into the gunmaking business and perhaps the earliest remaining record of his exploits in the manu-facture of firearms is his listing in the 1821 St. Louis directory. It seems that all records of the Hawken factory

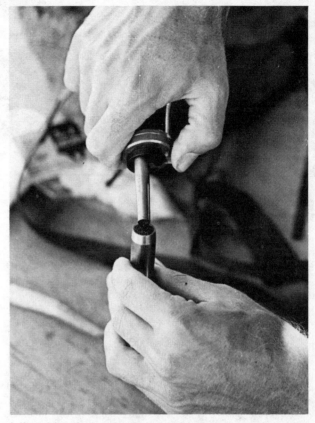

Not an exact copy of the original, the Thompson/Center Hawken does feature the styling and feel of the famous Hawken gun.

were destroyed upon Jacob's death during the cholera epidemic of May, 1849; the loss of all such record is perhaps the reason that a cloud of mystery and uncertainty hangs over the authenticity of many early Hawken type rifles of reputed manufacture. Genuine Hawken-built rifles are among today's most sought collector pieces and their value is so great that few, if any, are taken to the field for actual hunting or continuous firing.

Originally built as an extremely rugged hunter's rifle to withstand the hardest of use, the Hawken rifles featured heavy octagon barrels and were commonly of large caliber for use on game as large as buffalo or elk. The stocks almost always were cut and shaped to be strictly functional without any fancy frills; for the most part these were of half-stock design, although there were a few full stock Hawkens produced. Since these guns were handmade there were slight differences from one rifle to another; placement of sights, shape of the iron butt plate, stock lines, et al.

Ten years after his brother's death, Samuel Hawken moved the gunmaking operation to Denver, Colorado. With the assistance of his son in carrying on the family tradition, he continued to produce the Hawken rifles in Denver until 1861, returning to St. Louis and reopening the shop there once more. A year later, he sold the shop to former employee John P. Gremer, who continued to turn out rifles under the Hawken name for some years.

Through the popularity of such rifles, the name Hawken is occasionally used to describe the general type of buffalo, plains or mountain man rifle built on the lines of the Hawken-built originals.

With collectors placing high value on original Hawkens, such rifles are nearly always only seen at gun shows. For the hunter wishing to own this type of durable hunting black powder rifle, however, a reproduction of the Hawken now is being produced at the Rochester, New Hampshire, plant of Thompson/Center Arms Company.

Available in .45 and .50 caliber, the Thompson/Center Hawken does feature some design changes, a number of which make the reproduction gun even more reliable that were the originals. The rifle does, however, retain the husky feel and eye-pleasing lines of the original; the firm admits that their Hawken isn't an exact replica, but is a well built and dependable gun of the general type.

Unlike the iron furniture found on the original Hawken-built rifles, the Thompson/Center rifles sport polished brass

Adjustable powder measure makes weighing exact charges simple. Below, the patched ball after the excess patching is trimmed.

135

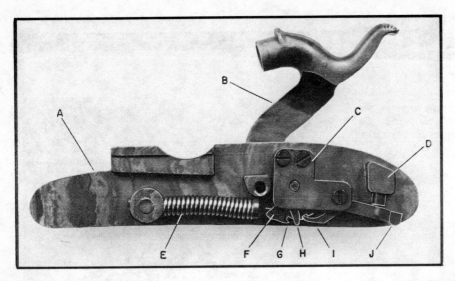

Hawken lock: (A) lock plate; (B) hammer; (C) bridle; (D) sear spring; (E) coil main-spring; (F) tumbler; (G) half-cock notch; (H) detent; (I) sear nose engaging full-cock notch; (J) sear. Below middle, ball is started down barrel with wooden short starter. Bottom, flash pan of flintlock is primed.

ramrod thimbles, butt plates, patch boxes, and nose caps on the short half-stock walnut stock; few originals were fitted with patch boxes. The trigger guard on guns produced before 1972 were made from beautifully color case-hardened iron. Since then, however, the firm has been installing polished brass trigger guards on the new Hawken rifle.

The double-set triggers on the new rifle are designed so that the rifle can serve a dual purpose, as both a fine hunting rifle and a reliably accurate target rifle. The clever design makes it possible to fire the Hawken by completely bypassing the rear set trigger, should a snap shot present itself while hunting. On the other hand, the front trigger can be set so that it will release at the slightest amount of pressure by first pulling the rear trigger. This hair trigger makes the Thompson/Center gun a fairly accurate off-hand or light benchrest target rifle.

A feature that should be equally pleasing to the black powder shooter who can't stand the messy chore of cleaning his favorite smokepole after an afternoon of shooting it is the easy removal of the Hawken's barrel from the rest of the rifle. This is accomplished through the patented or hooked breech system; the rear of the breech plug forms a hook that fits into a recess of the tang and the front of the barrel is held in place by a wedge that travels through two plates in the stock and a loop located on the bottom flat of the octagon barrel.

To remove the barrel, the ramrod is first removed from the thimbles and placed aside. The hammer is then placed at half-cock, or in the safety position. The barrel wedge is carefully tapped from the slot through which it holds the barrel in place. With this done, all that remains to do is grasp the barrel near the muzzle and lift upward until the hooked breech frees itself from the recess in the tang. This makes cleaning easier and prevents accidental staining of the stock with strong solvents.

With the barrel removed, the breech end of the Hawken's barrel can be placed into a pail of hot soapy water. The ramrod – with the cleaning jag attached – and a cleaning patch are inserted into the muzzle. Each time the ramrod is drawn toward the muzzle the air-tight fit of the patch will cause a vacuum and the soapy solution will be sucked into the barrel through the vent hole. This pumping action will keep a constant fresh supply of hot water coming into and leaving the bore of the barrel and results in as clean a barrel as possible. As soon as all powder foulings are removed the barrel is removed from the water and swabbed with dry patches until it has cooled; this is followed by running a patch lightly coated with lubricant

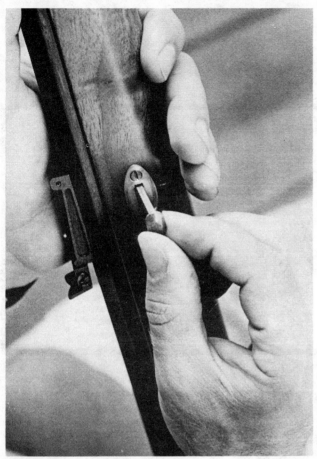

T/C Hawken barrel is held to stock by a wedge that travels through brass plates.

Above, hooked breech for easy take-down and the advantage of this system shown below.

the entire length of the barrel.

Of all the design changes on the new Hawken, perhaps the most interesting are those that have been made in the lock itself. On both the flintlock and percussion lock models, the flat springs usually found in these mechanisms have been replaced with coil springs. A flat spring may be more original, but the coil springs are less likely to break, especially the heavy duty type used in the new Hawken. To utilize the coil spring, however, several other internal designs had to be changed; such changes may make the lock different from the original on the inside, but the outside appearance remains basically the same as that of locks found on rifles manufactured better than a hundred years ago.

Both the .45 and .50 caliber Hawkens are fitted with a twenty-eight-inch button rifled barrel. This high quality octagon barrel features a one turn in forty-eight inches twist rifling. To the beginning black powder enthusiasts this may seem rather slow, and it is. Black powder rifles have to be rifled with long land patterns to make them accurate since they have relatively slow muzzle velocities.

When care is taken to load the Hawken properly, it is about as accurate a black powder rifle as can be found. Fitted with a high-bladed front sight and an open rear sight that is fully adjustable for windage and elevation, the gun is an ideal hunting rifle. Although not standard equipment on the rifle, Thompson/Center also manufactures an accurate vernier tang rear sight. This aperture type "peep sight" is easily attached to the barrel tang which is already drilled to accept the sight.

Packed with each rifle that leaves the factory is an in-

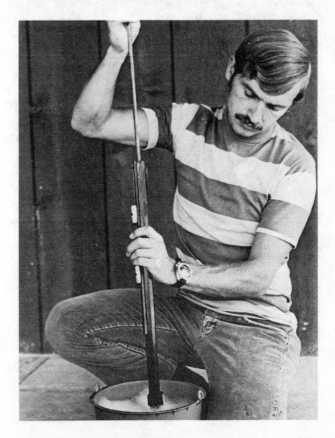

formative booklet containing information that the beginning black powder shooter would be wise to know before venturing afield with the new Hawken. Within its sixteen pages, the booklet explains how to care for the rifle, gives some background on its original manufacture and most important, it gives good starting loads for the beginner.

Thompson/Center recommends the following loads:

POWDER CHARGE	CALIBER/BALL DIAMETER	MUZZLE VELOCITY	MUZZLE ENERGY
50 grains FFFg	.45 caliber/.440 ball	1605 fps	732 ft. lbs.
50 grains FFg	.50 caliber/.490 ball	1357 fps	761 ft. lbs.
60 grains FFFg	.45 caliber/.440 ball	1720 fps	841 ft. lbs.
60 grains FFg	.50 caliber/.490 ball	1434 fps	850 ft. lbs.
70 grains FFFg	.45 caliber/.440 ball	1825 fps	947 ft. lbs.
70 grains FFg	.50 caliber/.490 ball	1643 fps	1115 ft. lbs.
80 grains FFFg	.45 caliber/.440 ball	1929 fps	1054 ft. lbs.
80 grains FFg	.50 caliber/.490 ball	1838 fps	1396 ft. lbs.
90 grains FFFg	.45 caliber/.440 ball	2003 fps	1140 ft. lbs.
90 grains FFg	.50 caliber/.490 ball	1950 fps	1570 ft. lbs.
100 grains FFFg	.45 caliber/.440 ball	2081 fps	1231 ft. lbs.
100 grains FFg	.50 caliber/.490 ball	2052 fps	1739 ft. lbs.
110 grains FFFg	.45 caliber/.440 ball	2158 fps	1324 ft. lbs.
110 grains FFg	.50 caliber/.490 ball	2135 fps	1883 ft. lbs.

Toby Bridges takes aim on his target with scope sighted .45 caliber Hawken with percussion lock. He classifies this combination as one of the best hunting rifles available today.

Although the loads having the greatest amount of powder displayed more punch — on both ends — we found that most of the milder loads were the most accurate. Tests were made with both a .45 caliber percussion lock and a .50 caliber flintlock Hawken, in both guns patched round balls were used for the most part; some tests were made with Minie bullets moulded in a Lyman No. 445599 mould.

Working with the .45 caliber percussion Hawken first, 50 grains of FFFg printed five of the patched 128-grain .440 round balls into something resembling a group eight inches below the point of aim when fired from a hundred yards; 60 grains brought the shots up to the point of aim but did little to improve the group tightness.

An increase of another ten grains proved too much as far as accuracy was concerned; dropping to 65 grains of FFFg the Hawken consistently printed its shots into the four-inch bullseye. One charge of 100 grains was all we needed to decide that it was more than necessary, sending burning

powder several feet from the end of the muzzle; the short twenty-eight-inch barrel didn't allow enough room for this much powder to be ignited completely and we doubt if those flames chasing the ball to the target are that beneficial once it leaves the barrel.

This rifle had been fitted with one of Thompson/Center's Puma pistol scopes before test firing. This scope is easily fitted to the rifle and requires no additional drilling on the octagon barrel. To install, the rear sight of the Hawken is removed by unscrewing the two small screws in its base. The base of the scope is then attached to the barrel by the same screws and holes, both matching perfectly. The scope tube is then attached to the base mount by two hex screws that align with two notches in the flat rail that travels the bottom length of the 1½X scope.

Using the standard open sights that come on the Hawken, there was little difference in the results obtained

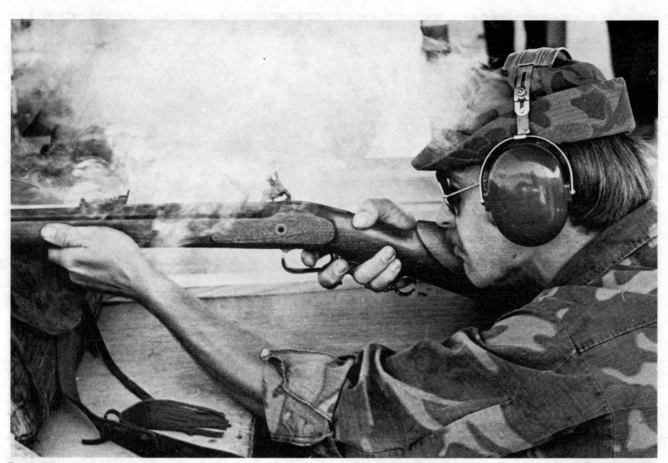

Smoke from flash pan all but hides target as shooter squeezes off a round in the .50 caliber T/C Hawken flintlock. It's no wonder that exposed flash causes flinching.

Bridges explains merits of loading and shooting black powder rifles to curious Boy Scout. Muzzleloading interest is growing into a major shooting sport.

with .50 caliber flintlock. We did notice, however, that the pre-ignition of the primed flash pan was enough to occasionally cause the shooter to flinch slightly and ruin his groupings. Working with a variety of powder charge weights, we finally established 70 grains of FFg as the best all-around load; 65 grains of FFFg worked nearly as well but the groups weren't as tight. One thing was evident: These .50 caliber balls carried a lot of punch, making the rifle an ideal choice for primitive weapon big game hunts.

Thompson/Center recommends that the patching be lightly coated with lubricant such as Vaseline, Crisco or one of the commercially produced black powder rifle lubes. Hodgdon's Spit Patch was used extensively during the test firing and worked very well. We did find it necessary to wipe the bore partially clean of powder fouling after every six to ten shots, varying according to the amount of powder used; the more powder used, the more the bore would build up.

The nipple of the .45 caliber percussion rifle uses standard No. 11 caps; although the sizes of caps have a tendency to vary from one source to another — like trying to fit a pair of number seven shoes on a number eight pair of feet — both No. 11 caps produced by Remington and those offered by Navy Arms fit the nipple with just the right amount of snugness. The flash pan on the flintlock is best primed with FFFFg black powder, but FFFg will work almost equally as well.

Selling at $175 for the percussion and $190 for the flintlock, the price seems quite reasonable when you consider that Thompson/Center backs these guns with a lifetime warranty. For $20 more the guns come complete with an accessory kit that includes everything to get the purchaser to the range and the bullet to the target — except for the black powder, cap and balls, that is! – *Toby Bridges*

139

THE GREAT KENTUCKY COME BACK

CHAPTER 14

Navy Arm's Reproduction Of The Kentucky Pistol Is A Boon To Both The Serious Collector And Shooter!

OFTEN SOUGHT by today's dedicated antique arms collectors, the Kentucky pistol was the first truly domestic handgun of the United States.

Prior to the Revolutionary War, American gunmakers were practically nil. Almost all arms still were being produced in Europe, where gunmakers had been in the business for several hundred years. It was during the years leading into the Revolution, that U.S. armsmakers began to produce their long rifles, most of which are erroneously labeled as Kentucky rifles. It was through this mislabeling, though, that the Kentucky pistol may also have received its unwarranted title. Actually, the majority of both pistols and long rifles were handcrafted by gunsmiths in other gunmaking states, such as Pennsylvania, New York and a few other East Coast colonies.

In form, the Kentucky pistol was commonly far less fancy than those produced in Europe; ferrules on the forestock were often left off, ramrod thimbles were simpler in design, and the barrels — sometimes made of brass — were commonly much heavier than, say, a British dueller. The pistol did, however, fulfill the need for an accompanying sidearm for the American long rifle.

Now considered an important piece of Americana, collectors have placed so much emphasis on Kentucky pistols that it is about impossible to find them at any price — reasonable or otherwise. As mentioned, these pistols were produced before the introduction of mass production, being completely assembled from parts made entirely by the same method.

To make available a pistol of this type for those collectors and shooters that can't afford an original — or can afford but are wise enough not to subject them to the rigors

of everyday firing — several of today's black powder gun distributors are offering modern-made replicas of the general pattern.

One such replica that stands out in both quality and authenticity is the Kentucky pistol available from the Navy Arms Company. This particular pistol is the result of years of studying the Kentucky pistol designs and the evaluation of numerous prototypes by Navy Arms' president Val Forgett.

Like the first American-made pistol of nearly two hundred years ago, this Italian replica is assembled by skilled hand craftsmen. The parts, however, are produced in larger quantities through modern mass production. Actually these parts are probably much more uniform than the handcrafted ones built during the late 1700s, each built to a standard pattern. Original handmade gun parts almost always varied from one piece to another, even when built by the same gunsmith.

Truthfully, a pistol of this type has little practical use in the field. The fixed sights are hardly target quality, the cumbersome shape of the gun makes it impractical to carry for any length of time and its single-shot concept practically rules it out as a choice for a hunting arm. They are, however, an economical answer to filling the gap left in many collections that are in need of such a gun.

The Navy Arms Kentucky pistol is available in either percussion or flintlock. Both guns are fitted with an oil-finished walnut stock as well as a 10¼-inch rifled brass barrel. The lock plates, hammers and flash pan on the flintlock models are beautifully color case-hardened. The lock screws that run through the stock are held in place by an inlaid press side-plate on the left side, screwing into the lock plate itself on the right.

The solid walnut stock is set off by polished brass thimbles, trigger guard and forend schnabel. The ramrod appears to be made of hickory, stained with walnut tones so it matches the stock. The metal tip on this is also made of polished brass.

Of all the Italian proof marks on the .44 caliber brass barrel, two are easily identified. One appears as two bayonet-equipped rifles in the crossed position, backgrounded by a hammer. This is encircled by an outline resembling a medieval shield and topped by a single star over something resembling a toothed gear. This is the house proof mark of the Gardone Val Trompia Proof House. The other proof mark is yet another gear background star over the upper case letters PN. In 1950, this mark was adopted to distinguish black powder arms that rated a definitive proof of 8,800 psi.

The lock bolt plate on the replica is similar to the lock design used on the pistols produced by Joseph Long in his Snyder County, Pennsylvania, gunsmithery around 1800. The stock, on the other hand, is quite different from Long's pistols. Instead of the rounded butt commonly found on early Kentucky pistols, the Navy Arms model features a definite edge in place of the rounded contour.

The barrel is well inletted into the stock, as is the lock and brass trigger guard. The two brass ramrod thimbles are attached firmly to the stock by several pins through the wood and matching holes in the ferrules.

Although the sights are fixed and, as mentioned, are a far cry from target sights, the gun shoots with fair accuracy. The best results were obtained when firing a patched .430 ball in front of twenty-six grains of FFFg powder. When a ball closer to the actual .440 diameter bore was used, the patching wouldn't allow the lead ball to pass into the muzzle at the projectile's widest point.

Several shots were made with just the ball and without the patching. As can be expected, the results were less than desirable. No two shots flew in the same direction; one shot would hit high and to the left, the next low and to the right, etc. The smaller the ball — of less diameter than that of the bore — the more erratic the placement of the shots.

Possibly the gases escaping around the open space left by the smaller projectile can be credited with the extreme deviation of the points of impact. This theory is partially backed by the betterment of the results as soon as cotton patching of .011-inch thickness was used.

With the aforementioned 26-grain loads and the patched .430 balls, the placement of the shots were a little more consistent. By consistent, it is meant that they at least hit the cardboard holding the target — and occasionally even hitting the latter — from a range of twenty-five yards. If the groups were to be measured, it is a safe estimation to say that ten shots were placed into an area of around two feet in diameter, hardly a match winner!

Surprisingly enough, quite a few shooters become so accustomed to firing a pistol of this type that they become quite proficient with it. Usually, this is after many test firing sessions to find just the right load for that particular gun and, more often than not, after some tinkering around with the sights; with usually around an eight to ten-inch barrel, it only stands to reason that such guns should be somewhat accurate.

Originally these guns were built as a sidearm to accompany the early domestic long rifles, so what could be more challenging than to carry a replica of this particular design as a back-up gun when hunting with a black powder rifle? This should have a certain amount of appeal if the target of the hunt is to be such ill-tempered game as the wild boar.

Lock plate of the Navy Arms Kentucky pistol is color case-hardened and adds greatly to the overall appearance of reproduction gun.

Of all the proof marks on the 10¼-inch rifled brass barrel, shooter would be wise to follow warning to use only black powder in pistol.

The dovetailed brass front sight blade is similar to those installed on original pistols of more than a hundred years ago. Schnabel and ramrod fittings are also made of brass.

As a safety precaution, shooter at left first measures out correct powder charge with the aid of powder measure.

With Kentucky pistol braced against knee, patched ball is seated.

Although the barrel of the Navy Arms Kentucky pistol is longer than that found on the majority of the black powder pistols, it still isn't long enough to allow large charges of powder to be fully utilized. Simply, this means that large amounts of powder will only result in much of this powder to be still burning as the ball leaves the barrel. This does little to improve accuracy or increase the projectile's penetrating capability.

It was found that any charge of more than 33 grains of FFFg was only a waste of powder when fired from the 10¼ inch brass barrel. This load, however, proved to be one of the most inaccurate, but displayed the most penetrating power — a good point to keep in mind if the gun is to be used as a back-up gun on a primitive hunt. With this load the soft lead ball easily penetrated the thickness of a two by six pine board, good enough to put the finishing touch to a wounded wild boar, bear, cougar or other game that could be listed as being dangerous, especially if wounded.

The Kentucky pistol leaves a lot to be desired when it comes to target shooting or hunting, but they are an interesting part of American history and still are a lot of fun to shoot. — Toby Bridges

Pistol of the Kentucky type are awkward to load, best method is to place butt against the ground and keep muzzle away from face (right). The flash pan is primed (below) and the pistol is ready to fire.

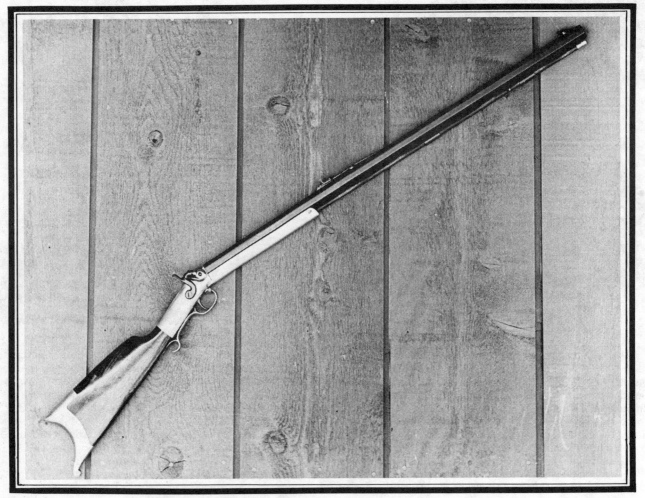

CHAPTER 15
MOWREY'S ETHAN ALLEN RIFLE

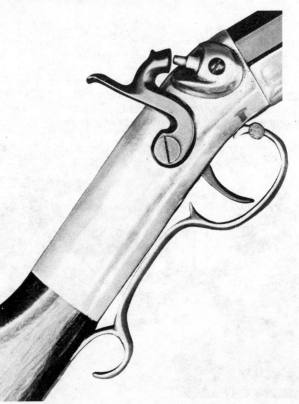

As discussed here, the action is notable for its sleek lines and simplicity. Round object at the front of the trigger guard is a nail which supports it on wall.

Once A Favorite Of Early Frontiersmen, The Allen & Thurber Rifle Is Once Again Being Built For Today's Discriminating Black Powder Enthusiast!

Reduced charge of FFFg proved entirely ample to take this coyote with the caliber .50 A&T rifle. Below: a simple blade foresight is attached near the muzzle by means of a dovetailed base mount.

OF ALL THE MUZZLELOADING RIFLES produced by the Nineteenth Century gunmakers, the excellent long rifles produced by Ethan Allen at his Grafton, Massachusetts, gunmaking facilities are probably the least understood — and undoubtedly the least written about.

Little known, except by those dedicated to studying the history of the firearm in the United States and the serious antique arm collector, is the fact that Allen actually was the first maker of pepperbox pistols in this country. In 1834, he was granted the first U.S. patent for handguns of this design. His was a revolving pepperbox, no doubt a refinement of similar guns being built in Europe at the time.

For a number of years after he began production of his pepperboxes, he was the only mass producer of such handguns; his competition was mainly from numerous small gunsmithing firms, most of which either soon folded or sold out to larger operations.

In his book, "Roughing It," Mark Twain's writings concerning the Allen pepperbox pistol made the gun famous, if not notorious. The small multi-shot handgun delivered tremendous firepower considering its size and was easy to conceal, a perfect choice of armament for some shady characters. The majority of today's so-called up-to-date and comprehensive publications on firearms, however, fail to make any mention of the rifles made by Allen. Even when the authors and editors of such books cast some light on this mystery to the black powder shooter, they usually do so briefly.

As mentioned, Ethan Allen began producing his pepperbox pistols in his plant at Grafton, Massachusetts, after receiving his patent of 1834. Several years later, in 1837, he formed a partnership with his brother-in-law, Charles T. Thurber, and the firm's name was changed to Allen & Thurber. Under this name — at the Grafton, Massachusetts,

The highly polished brass butt plate is fitted
meticulously to the walnut of the stock, which
has had ten hand-rubbed coats of oil finish applied.

location — they continued to make pepperbox pistols, some
single-shot pistols and an accurate, well built rifle.

Apparently, family ties weren't all that strong between
Allen and Thurber, for in 1856 Allen dissolved the partnership with his by-marriage relative, only to form yet another
partnership with another brother-in-law, Thomas P.
Wheelock.

Under the firm name of Allen & Wheelock — located in
Worchester, Massachusetts, having moved from Norwich,
Connecticut, yet another previous move made while still in
partnership with Thurber — they continued to produce
their line of wares on through the Civil War.

In 1865, the name was changed once more, this time to
E. Allen & Company and was so named until Ethan Allen's
death in 1871. Allen's two sons-in-law, Sullivan Forehand
and Henry Wadsworth, took control of the company and
ran it under the name of Forehand & Wadsworth; in 1890
this was changed to the Forehand Arms Company.

Although at one time or another the Allen firm, run by
him or by later members of his family, produced numerous
styles and designs of both percussion and cartridge revolvers, rifles, pistols and even shotguns, it is the rifles produced
under the name of Allen & Thurber that are probably of
the most importance to today's black powder enthusiast.

Allen & Thurber rifles aren't as well known as their
pepperboxes, but those shooters and collectors that are

familiar with them consider them of top quality. Of simple
design and solid construction, many a westward traveller
and frontiersman chose to shoulder one in place of such
well known rifles as the famous guns produced by Jacob
Hawken in his St. Louis shop.

The W. L. Mowrey Gun Works of Olney, Texas, now is
producing an exact replica of the Allen & Thurber rifle for
those shooters wanting what the makers consider the
ultimate in a black powder hunting muzzleloader. As on the
original Allen & Thurber, simplicity of design is one of the
rifle's strongest selling points.

Unique in design, the lock features only two actual
moving parts, the trigger and tumbler. The lack of numerous moving parts on this simple lock almost guarantees the
shooter years of trouble-free shooting. The internal lock
work is housed inside a hollow, high density brass casing.
This brass action housing also serves as the wrist of the
stock, breech plug and nipple seat; even the cleanout screw
threads into this.

In addition to the trigger and tumbler, the lock is made
up of two springs and a single pin. The shaft of the tumbler
passes through the right side of the brass casing and
attaches to the hammer on the outside. Anyway you look
at it, it's about as simple as you can get!

The thirty-one-inch barrel features eight-groove rifling;
the lands and grooves of about equal width. Although only

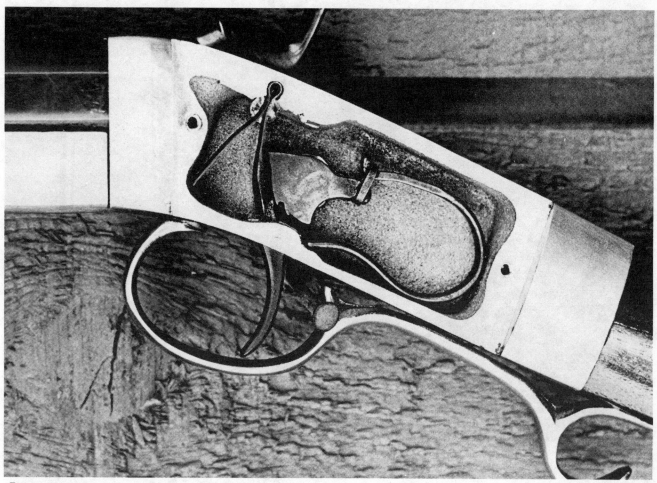

Extreme simplicity of the lockwork can be seen here. Trigger and tumbler are the only moving parts.

.010-inch in depth, shallow rifling of this type has actually proven superior to rifling with much deeper grooves. As black powder burns, it tends to leave a considerable amount of residue within the barrel. Deep grooves only result in a bigger build up of this residue and actually make loading subsequent shots only more difficult.

By utilizing eight-groove rifling in the Mowrey replica of the Allen & Thurber, the shallow .010-inch lands and grooves hold the patched ball just as securely as six or four-groove rifling having a deeper cut. Not only does this make it possible to load more shots between barrel cleanings, but it also resists stripping under heavy charges.

Conventionally, the barrels on muzzleloading rifles have a twist somewhere in the neighborhood of one turn in forty-eight inches. The Mowrey, however, has a somewhat slower rate of twist in its barrel, at one turn in sixty inches. Combined with the thirty-one-inch length of the barrel, this slow twist allows the usage of heavy charges without noticable loss in accuracy. Again, the slow twist resists stripping of the bore when heavy charges are being used; this is especially an added advantage when target shooting or hunting on a windy day.

Each gun produced at the Olney, Texas, plant can be considered sort of a semi-custom job, with many of the processes in its manufacture being either done partially or completely by hand. One example of this is the beautiful

walnut stock. Each stock is custom fitted to the rifle, a process that can only be accomplished through hand labor.

In addition, each stock receives ten coats of hand-rubbed oil finish to give the walnut the high luster it deserves. As on the Allen & Thurber replica, only the butt-stock is of walnut, the forend is made from the same Inco brass used in the action housing. The result is a good looking and well balanced rifle well suited for either bench or off-hand shooting.

Available in .45, .50 and .54 calibers, this long barreled black powder rifle is capable of developing muzzle velocities around 2200 to 2400 fps, which should interest hunters who choose to go afield each fall after their buck with a muzzleloading rifle. When loaded with 115 grains of FFFg powder, the patched .490 ball of the .50 caliber leaves the barrel at around 2250 fps and has enough energy at fifty to a hundred yards to drop even the biggest buck in his tracks.

When firing the .50 caliber Mowrey Allen & Thurber rifle, however, I achieved the best results with powder charges ranging from 70 to 85 grains. Even a charge of this mildness pushes the patched 175-grain ball out of the muzzle at around 2000 fps and still has enough punch to bring down game as big as deer and black bear, and although not exactly an ideal small game rifle, it is still a good choice for some of the larger varmints in the coyote

Serial number of the rifle is stamped on brass butt plate along its lower edge.

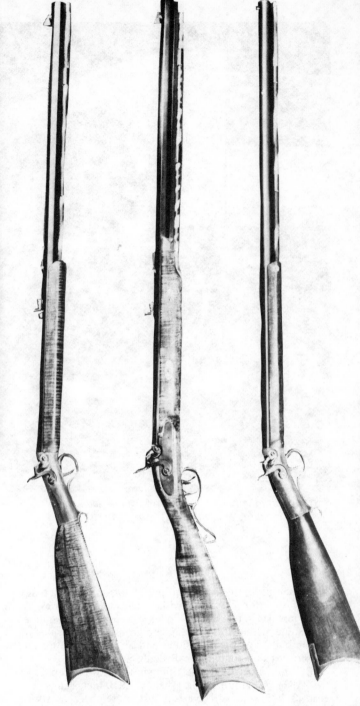

From left: the Mowrey Hawk has wood forend and Hawken -type butt plate, as does same firm's Hawken model; at right is Mowrey 12-ga shotgun.

and bobcat class.

During the testing of the .50 caliber rifle, I packed it along with an array of other guns on one of my coyote calling sessions. After pulling a sixty-yard, one-shot kill on a coyote called in with the aid of a Circe jackrabbit distress call, I had nothing but praise for the gun.

Several weeks before the hunt I began taking the rifle with me to the range during my visits there several times each week. Working with the gun on numerous occasions, I consistently achieved the best accuracy with a load of 75 grains of FFFg and the patched .490 ball.

Mowrey claims that anywhere from a 100 to a 125 grains of FFg powder is the ideal load for this gun. When I tried this granulation of black powder, however, I found that it delivered its best groups when reduced to anywhere from 80 to 90 grains. But the results were no better than what I had previously gotten with the finer FFFg powder, which I have plenty of on hand for my smaller caliber black powder rifles.

The combination of 75 grains of FFFg and the .490 ball weighing in the neighborhood of 170 to 180 grains was more than ample to drop the coyote I called in. Truthfully, I don't think he would have noticed the difference had I been shooting twenty or thirty more grains of powder. He

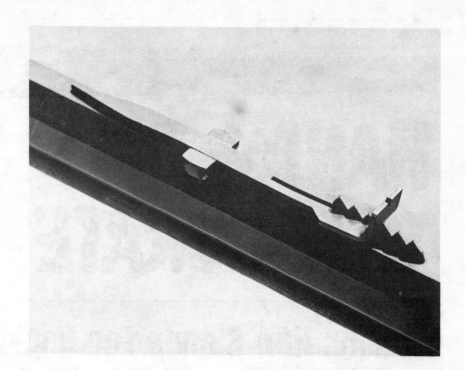

Above: Rear sight is adjustable for elevation by means of notched blade.
Lower: Thimbles for rod are well made.

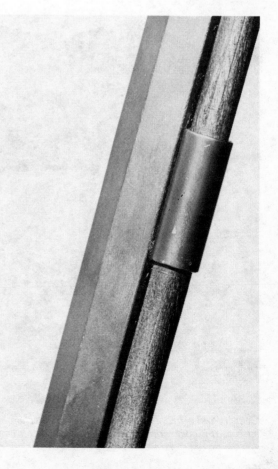

was dead by the time I covered the sixty yards separating us.

The Mowrey replica of the Allen & Thurber rifle is an extremely well balanced gun, well suited for carrying in the field and for off-hand shooting. It was a pleasure to shoot and bearable to carry!

Presently selling for $149.50, the Allen & Thurber is probably one of the best muzzleloading buys on today's market. For twenty bucks more, a presentation model of the gun featuring a hand-rubbed northern maple stock and furniture made of bronwite — having an appearance similar to nickel silver — is available.

Other fine muzzleloading guns from Mowrey include a wooden forend model dubbed the Allen & Thurber Special. With the exception of the wooden fore-stock, this is basically the same rifle as the Allen & Thurber replica. Also of similar design but having a Hawken-type butt plate is the Mowrey Hawk; Mowrey's 12-gauge shotgun also features the enclosed lock and Hawken style butt plate.

Of completely different styling than all of the other Mowrey guns, the firm's Hawken half-stock replica is an exacting reproduction of the gun once favored by the hardy mountainman. This is built only upon special order and to the individual shooter's or collector's specifications. The gun features a select hand-rubbed maple stock, polished Inco brass furniture, percussion lock and double set triggers. Interesting to note is that each and every part used to construct the Hawken half-stock is completely hand shaped and fitted.

Mowrey has a lot to offer the discriminating black powder shooter, most of it at a reasonable price and built to last the owner a lifetime. — *Toby Bridges*

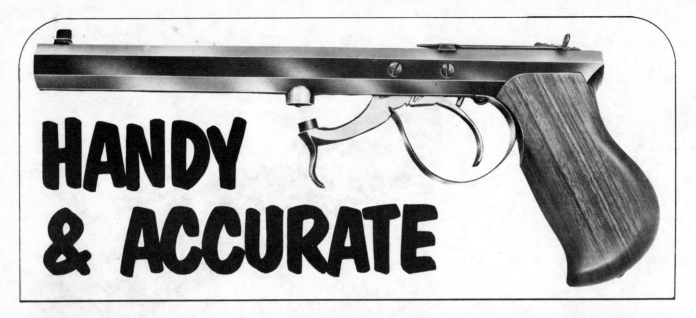

HANDY & ACCURATE

Actually, H&A Stands For Hopkins & Allen, Original Builders Of This Design Which, Again, Is Winning Popularity! CHAPTER 16

Century-old originals and custom-built underhammer rifles such as this cost more than the average shooter can afford.

Numrich's Hopkins & Allen rifles are reasonably priced
and author was pleased with accuracy at one hundred yards.

THE UNDERHAMMER RIFLE first appeared in New England during the 1830s. Unlike the side action locks of the earlier Kentucky and Pennsylvania long rifles, the understriker action on these percussion hunting and target rifles was completely of American design, perhaps making these rifles more distinctly American than any other domestically produced arm up until that time.

Simplicity of the lock made the underhammer a favorite among hunters, while instantaneous ignition proved a boon to the serious target competitor. The sad fact is, though, few underhammer rifles ever were produced. Firearms development was going through a rapid change in design and the birth of breechloaders was just around the corner.

Although target competitors hung onto the underhammer design for several decades after the introduction of breechloading rifles, hunters all but abandoned their use. Besides being usually superior in design and more accurate, the breechloader was far easier to care for and less tedious to load. The underhammer muzzleloader wasn't singled out as an inferior pattern to be discriminated against, for metallic cartridges were slowly putting an end to most muzzleloading guns.

Today it's not unusual to encounter an occasional muzzleloading benchrest shooter meticulously loading and firing a rifle of underhammer design. Many of these are century-old originals that probably couldn't be bought from said shooter for any price, and if one could be purchased, probably for more than the average shooter is willing to fork over. Not all such guns are hundred-year-old originals, but the price for such guns is still astounding, since they are almost always custom built to the individual shooter.

For the budget-wise shooter wanting a top-quality underhammer rifle at a reasonable price, Numrich Arms of West Hurley, New York, markets a complete line of Hopkins & Allen underhammer rifles. Completely American-made, the Hopkins & Allen line includes a model to whet the appetites of most all muzzleloading aficionados, whether serious target shooter, hunter or plain plinker.

At the top of the Hopkins & Allen underhammer line is the Heritage model. As on all the rifles comprising this line, the action is extremely simple. The only two moving parts on the lock are the trigger and the hammer; the trigger guard doubles as the mainspring. The underhammer is fitted to the solid metal receiver by a fairly large bolt, as is the trigger. The result of this simple design is a solid lock that is designed to give the rifle's owner years of trouble-free shooting.

A unique feature of the Heritage — as well as on the rest of the Hopkins & Allen rifles — is the rifle's easy takedown. A single tapered pin holds the barrel and fore-stock to the receiver. For easy storage during transportation, all of the Hopkins & Allen underhammer rifles can be broken down into the two pieces.

Available in .36 and .45 caliber, the thirty-two-inch barrel of the Heritage is precision rifled from a 15/16-inch octagon blank. The name of the model appears on the octagon flat immediately to the right of the barrel's flat/matted top. Although the rifle comes equipped with a receiver peep sight, there also is a square notch rear sight. The front sight is a hooded post and, when used with the

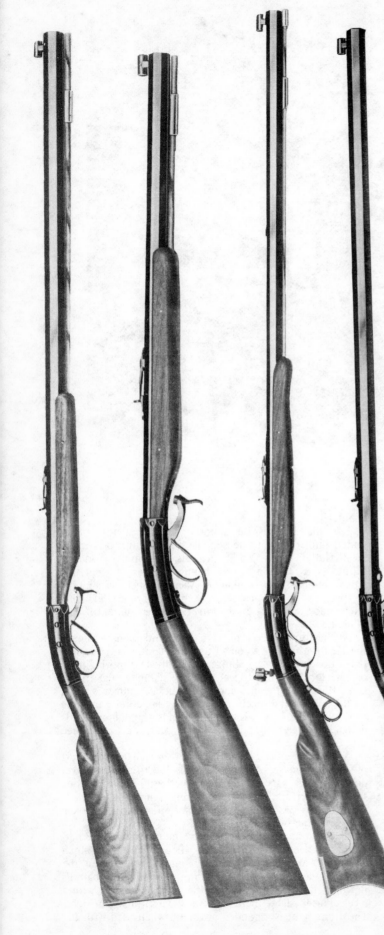

aperture rear peep sight, the rifle makes an excellent offhand target or hunting rifle.

Simple is the word best used to describe the brass furniture on the stock. In keeping with the rifle's simple utility design, Numrich Arms has avoided getting fancy with the rifle's functional patchbox, butt plate, trigger guard and single ramrod thimble. The oval-shaped patchbox on the butt stock can hardly be described as precision inletted, but on the other hand, it is a far cry from being crude and sloppy.

Working with one of the Heritage models in .45 caliber, my best groups were attained with a load of 72 grains of FFFg powder behind a patched .435 ball. First attempts to load with patching having a thickness of .016 proved unsuccessful. Combined with the diameter of the ball, the heavy material made it difficult to start and seat the patched ball. The recovery of one of the patches showed that the fit was too tight; the material was slitted where it had ridden on the rifling. Switching to .010 thick cotton patching, the fit of the ball in the barrel was perfect.

Groups of five to six inches at a hundred yards weren't uncommon. although most were around eight inches in diameter. When the powder charge was increased to 85 grains of FFFg, groups began to open up to twelve or more inches. Any attempts to go farther were dropped.

Slower burning FFg resulted in a considerably larger cloud of smoke at the muzzle and did little to improve accuracy. Using powder of this granulation in the Heritage did prove one thing, however, involving the difference in the pressures obtained between it and finer FFFg. Without measuring, I still believe that most of the groups obtained with FFg printed themselves on the paper a good three to four inches lower than those using FFFg.

Out of sixty or seventy shots fired with the Hopkins & Allen Heritage, I never experienced one misfire or hangfire. The direct path of the ignition flame into the charged chamber undoubtedly can be the reason; a hotter flame to ignite the main powder charge.

With the ability to group well within six inches from one hundred yards, the Heritage and the less fancy Offhand Deluxe model are both muzzleloaders well suited for packing in the field in hope of bagging that big racked buck or hard earned black bear. Basically, the Offhand Deluxe is the

Some of the rifles comprising the Hopkins & Allen line are, from left, the Deerstalker, the Deluxe Buggy, the Heritage and the all new .45 Target rifle.

Above left, the Heritage's ignition system. Hunter, below left, found the Heritage adequate for Eastern whitetail. The hooded front sight (below) found on each of the Hopkins & Allen rifles.

same rifle as the Heritage, only it lacks the brass trigger guard extension, patchbox, butt plate and the aperture rear peep sight. The two rifles sell for $99.50 and $87.95, respectively.

Perfect for carrying in brush country where extremely close snap shots usually are the order of the day is the Hopkins & Allen Deluxe Buggy rifle. This twenty-inch barreled muzzleloading carbine is actually just a shortened version of the Offhand model that was designed specifically for the Seneca Match competitor. Since its introduction, however, the short and light rifle has become very popular among black powder hunters that do their buck busting in close-range brush country. Like the Heritage and Offhand models, the Buggy rifle is available in .36 and .45 caliber and sells for $84.95.

Few if any hunters would attempt to use a .36 caliber muzzleloader for deer, most favoring the larger .45 caliber. Deer hunters demanding an even larger bore should find the Deer Stalker the ideal rifle. A bigger .58 caliber version of the Offhand, this rifle should give the hunter more knockdown power than should ever be needed. When fired from the thirty-two-inch rifled octagon barrel, .575 diameter

Minies should be extremely accurate.

With the growing interest in black powder competition, Numrich has introduced a special target/benchrest version of the Hopkins & Allen underhammer, the .45 Target. This rifle is produced without a forearm or ramrod ferrules, the lack of these combined with the heavier 1-1/8-inch rifled octagon barrel make the .45 Target an ideal benchrest rifle. Before the introduction of this mass-produced benchrest muzzleloader a shooter wanting an understriker competition gun could expect to pay well within the $300 margin for such a rifle. The price of the Numrich rifle is only $84.95 at this writing.

In addition to the Hopkins & Allen line of underhammer rifles, Numrich Arms also offers two more top quality rifles. The Minuteman is a beautiful reproduction of the long rifle of early America that has become known as the Kentucky rifle. The other rifle is the firm's two-shot swivel breech rifle, perfect for the hunter wanting two spontaneous shots. Yet another gun available is the Hopkins & Allen Boot pistol, a six-inch barreled pistol of the underhammer styling. – *Toby Bridges*

CHAPTER 17
CENTENNIAL'S ZOUAVE

This Remake Of An Epic Arm Has Scored High On The Black Powder Hit Parade!

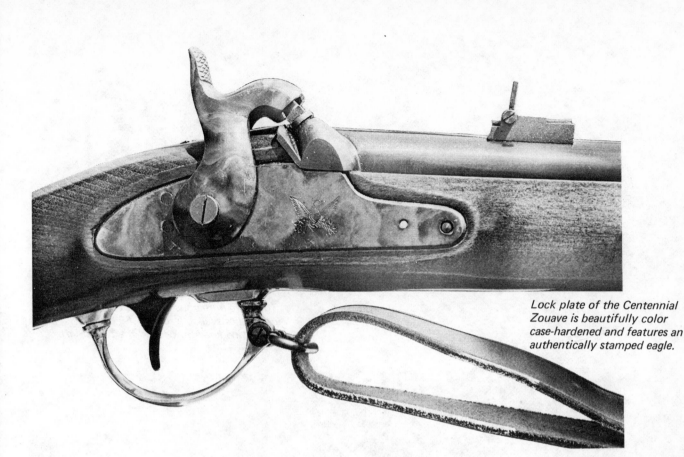

Lock plate of the Centennial Zouave is beautifully color case-hardened and features an authentically stamped eagle.

"THESE RIFLES ARE TO BE .58 inch caliber, and to have a three leaf rear sight, and cupped ramrod, with sword bayonet stud similar to those of the Harpers Ferry rifle, Model of 1855, in other respects of the pattern of rifles without bayonets heretofore made by you for this department."

Accepted by Eli Remington on August 6, 1861, this order for 10,000 of the described rifles from Chief of Ordnance General James Ripley marked the introduction of the famed Remington Zouave. Although only 10,001 Zouaves ever were produced, with an even less number of these seeing actual field use during the Civil War, the .58 caliber rifled musket still is considered to be one of the best and most colorful guns produced during that era.

Little is documented on the actual issue of the prized Remingtons and a large number of these guns in new condition are known to have been shipped to a number of Liege, Belgium, gunsmithing shops post war; many of these guns unfortunately were rebored to smoothbores to be used with shot and then were sent to Africa or South America. Combined with the scarcity of the Zouave due to its limited production, this rendering them into junk guns is enough to make any North/South Skirmish shooter cringe.

Though most U.S. Zouave regiments were armed with many different makes of foreign guns and even some transformed Springfields, the title also was used to describe the colorful Remington rifle, even though few Zouave regiments were lucky enough to be so armed. Exceptionally accurate, the dependable Remington was much like the graceful and elegant French Chasseurs de Vincennes rifle in appearance, having eye-pleasing styling and plenty of bright brass trimming.

The term, Zouave, is also of French origin and is used to denote a French Algerian military unit that became widely known for its colorful dress. Even more distinctive, however, was the Algerian unit's quick spirited drills. Later this title was used to acknowledge a light and highly mobile regiment.

Today, as was the case more than a hundred years ago, the individual fortunate enough to own one of the Remington Zouave rifled muskets is not apt to part with it. When such a gun is in mint or near-mint condition, it also is unlikely that said owner will pack it out to the local shooting range and put it through the hardships of firing the much desired collector's piece.

Centennial Arms of Lincolnwood, Illinois, is one of several muzzleloading arms distributors now offering reproductions of the famous Zouave rifled musket. The Centennial Zouave is so authentic that the original inspector marks are included on the stock.

Dubbed the Model 1863 Zouave Remington, the Italian-made replica is an exceptionally good looking and well built arm. The deeply blued thirty-three-inch barrel features three-land and three-groove rifling of the conventional right-hand twist. A close examination of the reproduction proved this three-land rifling to be about the only really distinguishing difference between it and the original Remington, which had five-groove rifling.

Just as Ripley had ordered on the Remington in 1861, Centennial Arms had the Antonio Zoli & Co. — the name of the Italian gunmaker as it appears on the Zouave's .58 caliber barrel — include the Harpers Ferry type bayonet mount. It is authenticity such as this that makes this modern day Zouave one of the most favored by North/South Skirmish shooters.

The nearly full-length walnut stock — ending approximately five inches from the muzzle — has a glossy oil finish and is accentuated by the polished brass butt plate, patch

There are numerous different types of lead projectiles available for the .58 caliber muzzleloader. Author used the two at left.

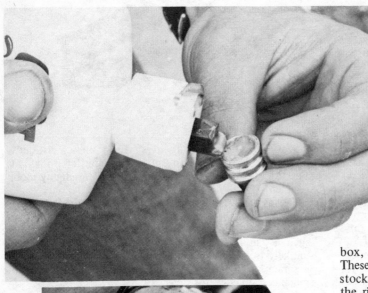

To prevent a build-up of powder fouling, author filled hollow base of Minie bullets with lube. Minie bullet, (bottom) is carefully started into muzzle; note cupped ramrod tip.

box, trigger guard, removable barrel bands and schnabel. These barrel bands are slipped into recessed grooves on the stock and are held in place by a spring that protrudes from the right side of the stock. To remove the barrel the tang screw must first be loosened, then all that remains to do is depress the band springs and slip the bands off; the barrel then should just lift out of the stock for easy cleaning.

The all-metal ramrod slips into a slot running the full length of the fore-stock. Keeping with the design of the original Zouave, the tip of the ramrod is cupped to prevent possible damage to Minie type bullets when being seated.

Other reproduced features that make the Centennial rifled musket authentically detailed is the color case-hardened lock plate, sling swivels and original type sights. The front sling swivel attaches to the front barrel band with the rear swivel located on the front curve of the brass trigger guard.

The three-leaf rear sight, graduated in increments of one, two and three hundred yards, intrigued me, as I studied it before making a visit to the local rifle range. A simple arrangement, the rear sight consists of three leaves that fold down and out of the way to allow the use of either a higher or shorter V-notch. The three hundred-yard notch is nearly a half-inch higher than the notch used for ranges of a hundred yards or less. This higher rear sight makes it necessary to elevate the muzzle in order to draw a bead on the

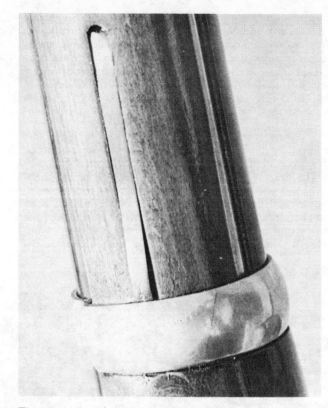

The brass barrel bands on the Zouave musket are slipped on/off, held in place by spring. Photos (below right) show the bayonet stud and rear sight.

group with the Minies, I was in store for a second surprise when I found that my next four rounds all hit within six inches of that first shot.

Patched with the heavier pillow ticking, the .562 balls gave equally pleasing results. Working with both patched ball loads I finally settled for a load of 55 grains of FFg as the most accurate for the .575 ball and 65 grains of FFg for the .562 round ball. During the hundred yard firing with the previously described loads, the barrel on the Centennial Zouave was wiped clean after every five shots. To see just how many shots could be fired with the patched balls without cleaning, I fired the next twenty shots without running the cleaning rod down the barrel.

Starting with the .575 ball — the patching receiving an application of Hodgdon's Spit Patch lubricant — the bore build up was so great after seven shots that the ball would no longer seat, with shots five, six and seven doing so after considerable wrestling with the ramrod. At the end of the twenty-shot test, however, the smaller .562 ball still could be seated without too much difficulty.

After cleaning the barrel with Bucheimer's black powder solvent and one big pile of patches, I fired the Zouave at two and three hundred-yard targets. Using the Lyman Minie — the preferred round of the Civil War — I found it quite difficult to keep any hits at all on the longer three hundred-yard target. Out of ten shots fired at this target, only two printed on the paper.

Things were a little different on the two hundred-yard target, with nine of the ten shots fired hitting the two foot square piece of paper. After that demonstation, and my shoulder feeling the afternoon's firing session, I have a little more respect for this piece of Civil War armament. – *Toby Bridges*

target which in turn results in a rainbow trajectory from the muzzle to said target.

Curious to just how accurate the Zouave replica would be at the longer ranges, I concentrated the majority of my shooting with it at ranges of a hundred yards or more. Both .575 Minie bullets and patched .575 and .562 round balls were used with various loads of FFg and FFFg powder.

Firing a load of 65 grains of FFFg behind the Lyman No. 575602 Minie, I was really surprised when I put three consecutive shots right over the top of a hundred yard target. By dropping back to 50 grains of the same powder, the next three printed on the paper but in no way could they be considered a group; better than twelve inches separating any two hits.

Switching to FFg, a charge of 60 grains kept the shots on the paper and brought the "group" back to around ten inches. An attempt to load the round .575 ball soon had me digging through my box of loading accessories in search of thinner patching material. The .011-inch thick cotton pillow ticking I usually find ideal was much too thick since the ball was nearly the same diameter of the .58 caliber bore. When a small amount of .006-inch thick linen cloth was finally found it too gave an extremely tight fit, but it worked after a considerable amount of effort on my part.

With the .575 ball weighing in the neighborhood of 275 grains, I reduced the load to 50 grains of FFg as a starter. The thinner barrel walls of a musket won't withstand the pressures of heavier rifle charges, so it is a good practice to use some caution when firing patched round balls; these almost always, or should, weigh more than the Minie, resulting in increased barrel pressures.

With no adjustment for windage, there was little I could do as the first shot printed itself on the target just outside the last ring at approximately ten o'clock. After the last

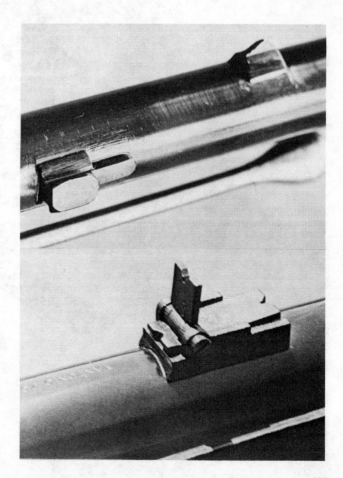

WHEN YOU CHECK OUT Ruger's newest black powder cap and ball revolver, don't expect to find a replica model of any specific, historically famous gun. Neither will you find that the Ruger team has borrowed extensively from internal designs prevalent during the first dawnings of percussion pieces. Instead, you will note that the mechanism of Ruger's "Old Army" has much in common with their "Super Blackhawk" model.

All things considered, this new percussion revolver is an original Ruger design. It retains traditional handling and firing characteristics, while incorporating numerous improvements which mark the first significant advance in percussion revolver construction in more than a century. Needless to say, this new Ruger is intended solely for use with black powder. Never, under any circumstances should it be loaded with any other type of powder, no matter how light the load.

Like all other Ruger products, the Old Army has been manufactured entirely in this company's Southport, Connecticut, and Newport, New Hampshire, plants. It is, as they say, one hundred percent Yankee-Doodle, with quality ordnance steels and music wire coil springs used throughout. Stainless steel nipples are standard and grip panels are turned from American walnut.

During the period since the first prototype, certain minor changes have worked their way into the design of the revolver. Nipple holes have been enlarged slightly and hammer fall beefed up for an even greater guarantee of cap ignition. Beyond this, few changes were found to be necessary, none altering the overall appearance of the gun.

The caliber, as already stated, is .44 percussion; it has been designed to use a .457-inch diameter round ball or conical bullet of pure lead. The use of jacketed or alloy bullets is not recommended as accuracy is generally not as satisfactory as with the pure lead bullets. The bore of this percussion piece is .443, with a groove of .451 inch. The

THE OLD ARMY GAME
CHAPTER 18

Something Old – And A Great Deal That's New – Are Involved In The Design Of This New Black Powder Entry

With powder expended or in safe place, Bill Ruger (left) watches Steve Vogel fire the cork from a champagne bottle in preparation for tail-gate party in the field.

barrel measures 7½ inches and features six grooves with a right twist of one in sixteen inches. The sights are the same as those on Ruger Blackhawks and Supers – a target rear, adjustable for elevation and windage, plus a ramp front with a one-eighth-inch wide blade, matted to eliminate glare. Weight is forty-six ounces, just three ounces lighter than that of their .44 magnum/.44 Special.

When it came time for field testing sessions with two of these percussion revolvers, I was allowed to choose at random from the current Ruger production run. Both of these cap-and-ballers boasted serial numbers under 100. As for their finish, both showed the results of careful polishing and were richly blued/anodized. If it weren't for the variation in frame contour, the loading lever and plunger unit, the different appearance of the threaded nipples at the rear portion of the cylinder, the Old Army could almost pass for a Super Blackhawk.

When Bill Ruger learned that his newest offerings were

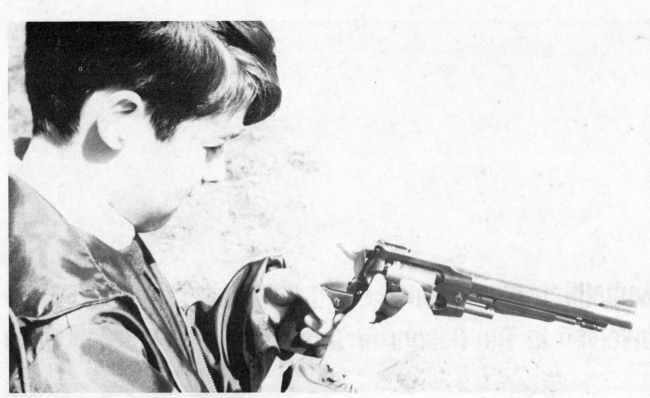

Kurt Vogel preferred to seat No. 11 Remington cap individually, not adapting to the in-line capper.

Author, wearing Don Hume custom holster rig, displays targets shot on snowy day in New England. Six-shot groups measured 1-3/8 inches, fired from benchrest at 25 yards.

scheduled for test sessions, he voiced a desire to be on the scene and offered us the use of a large tract of land that he maintains in a rural sector of Connecticut. Before the day was over Steve Vogel, a Ruger executive, and his young son, Kurt, volunteered their services. Almost immediately so did one Sandy Gleacher, obviously one of the world's youngest, ablest groomers of horses. Sandy is one of the prettier fixtures at the Vogel diggings.

Once it was learned that Bill Ruger actually wished to see how young tads and lasses could handle his cap and ball newcomer, my own secretary, Heather Williams, was recruited by way of a Ruger invitation, to join the festivities.

On the appointed Saturday the parade left the Ruger/Vogel chateau. My station wagon led the way, as Bill Ruger's Ferrari loafed along in our slip-stream. Upon leaving the black top for Bill's cowpath-type entrance road, it was learned that Ferrari's do not necessarily negotiate rutted, high-crowned dirt roads as can an especially built Ford wagon. Not unless you are willing to carry it in your arms.

It had been planned we would all celebrate at the end of our session, assuming all went well with the day's shooting. For this purpose we were prepared for a tail-gate feast of imported cheeses, salami, wursts and soda, plus an ample supply of champagne and fine cognac slated for senior members of the entourage. Powder and grog do mix, so long as the powder and guns are layed away before popping the corks!

Bill Ruger shares the opinion of this editor in feeling that shooting is not solely an adult sport. With proper supervision, it is both enjoyable and challenging to the younger set. Young Kurt, as an example, has become an exceptionally competent shooter in two short years, thanks

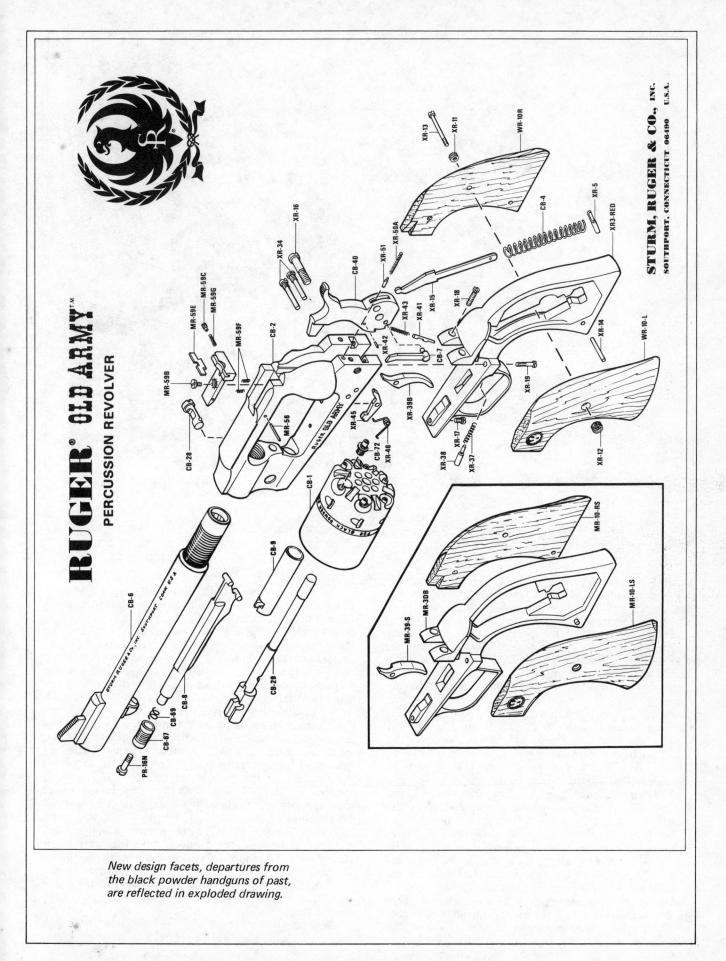

RUGER® OLD ARMY™

PERCUSSION REVOLVER

STURM, RUGER & CO., INC.
SOUTHPORT, CONNECTICUT 06490   U.S.A.

*New design facets, departures from
the black powder handguns of past,
are reflected in exploded drawing.*

Finding right hold on lever in order to seat bullet properly was problem for the younger set, as evinced by Kurt Vogel. Steve Vogel, Sandy Gleacher observe.

in large degree to the patient efforts of his sports-minded dad. Naturally, it was Kurt that we chose to ready the two new percussion revolvers; without being told, he cleared the nipples by placing a Remington No. 11 cap on each nipple ...after ascertaining that the chambers still were unloaded.

The reason behind this, as most all know, is to guarantee that the nipple passages are rendered both clear and dry. This basic procedure completed, he then was ready to get down to the business of actually loading the revolver for firing.

As Bill Ruger and I pointed out to Kurt, Sandy and Heather, though it is completely safe to use as much black powder as the chamber will hold, leaving room for the bullet, such maximum loading is rarely the most accurate loading. End results of Ruger staff tests, along with my own, show that a good starting accuracy load, using a pure lead .457-inch diameter ball, is 20 grains of FFFg, plus sufficient filler (we used corn meal) to seat the ball approximately one-sixteenth inch below the chamber mouth.

For those who do not wish to bother with the extra step of using filler, then let me recommend 45 grains of FFFg. This gives excellent accuracy, though target sessions would seem to point out that the most consistant accuracy was attained while utilizing the filler over 20 grains.

Do not try 20 grains, unless you use filler. There will be no contact with the ball, for one thing, and there is good chance that you will have occurrences where the detonating cap will fail to ignite the angled amount of powder lying in the chambers.

For those not yet initiated into the black powder fraternity, here is the procedure for loading as it applies to the cap and ball percussion revolver:

After clearing the nipples, you are ready to charge the chambers; now, place the hammer in the half-cock (loading) position so the cylinder is free to rotate in a clockwise direction. If you bring the hammer back too far, or if the hammer is put into the loading position by easing it forward from full cock, the cylinder will not be free to rotate.

Next, with one hand, hold the revolver by the grip with the barrel pointing upwards, but away from your own or anyone else's face or body. Using a powder dipper or other single charge measure, pour the correct amount of powder into one chamber. I personally use a custom, calibrated powder measure that prevents any mistakes. If you are to use the 20-grain load, don't forget to fill the balance of the chamber with the filler, leaving room enough to seat the bullet properly.

Now place the bullet in the mouth of the charged chamber and rotate the cylinder, until that chamber is aligned with the rammer. To execute the next step correctly, grasp the rammer lever and, with a firm, even stroke, seat the bullet on the powder or powder and filler. For maximum accuracy, the charge should be lightly compressed by the bullet.

Be certain that you have seated the bullet deeply enough so it does not interfere with the barrel and so the cylinder is

With the exception of the cylinder, carrying stainless steel nipples, Old Army resembles Super Blackhawk.

able to rotate freely. When you look at a correctly seated ball, it will have the appearance of a wadcutter bullet and be almost one-sixteenth inch recessed. Repeat this procedure until all chambers are loaded with powder and ball.

And now you are ready for the simple chore of applying one of the commercially available bullet greases — we used Beare-Grease, produced by the Caution Tool Company, Incorporated, located in Southport, Connecticut — or one of the automotive water pump greases that also can handle the job. Whatever you choose, apply a liberal coating of the grease to each chamber mouth to cover the bullet fully and seal the chamber. The reason for this step is all-important; mainly so that the chance of a multi-chamber discharge is reduced.

And now for the capping procedure. Be sure you use only pistol caps, and that they be of good quality and the correct size (in this case No. 11). Whether you use an in-line cap feeder or one of other design, or prefer to position each by hand, the caps should be completely — and without pressure — seated on the nipples. Caps should only be tight enough that they do not fall off when the barrel is elevated. Never force a cap into place. Such extra pressure could cause it to detonate and that chain of events could put the gray into your hair.

The revolver is now ready to fire. If you do not intend to fire immediately, the hammer nose should be eased into one of the safety recesses which are provided on the rear of the Ruger's cylinder, between the nipples. This little operation must, in itself, be performed cautiously; should the hammer fall onto a nipple — you receive one demerit and a loud bang. Further, be certain the hammer is fully down in the safety recess and not just resting on the edge. The half-cock notch is provided for ease of loading only and should never be used as this revolver's safety.

With all of this data clearly explained to the troops assembled at Bill Ruger's shooting area, things progressed rather smoothly. Most of the offhand and benchrest shoot-

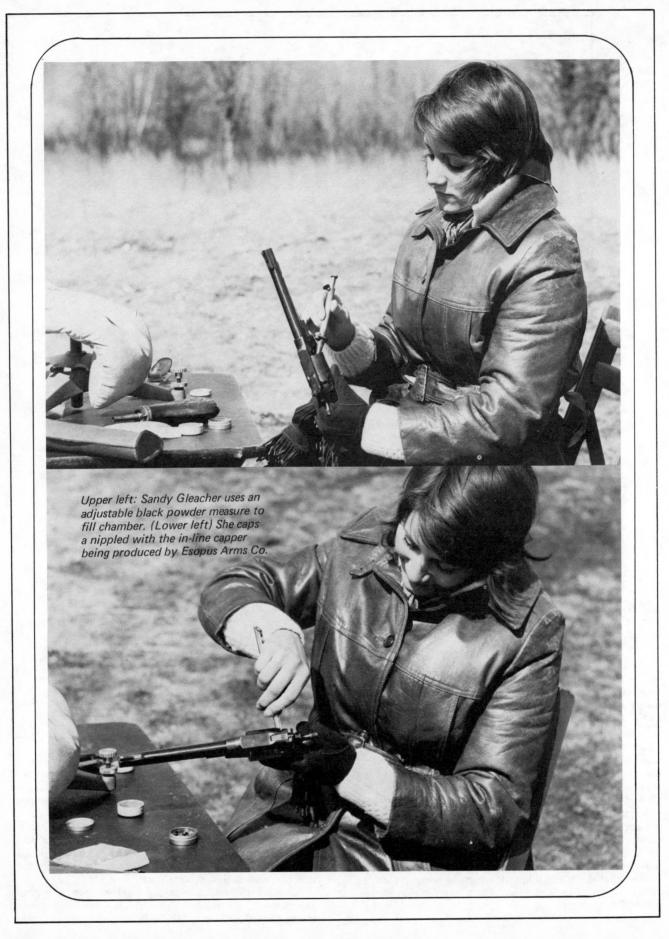

Upper left: Sandy Gleacher uses an adjustable black powder measure to fill chamber. (Lower left) She caps a nippled with the in-line capper being produced by Esopus Arms Co.

Heather Williams, representing distaff shooters, uses a two-hand hold. Note elevated barrel, resulting from recoil, after shot has been fired from black powder gun.

ing was run off from the twenty-five-yard mark. Groups, even when fired by Kurt and the two lasses, proved most satisfactory. Steve Vogel also managed to punch several dozen holes in targets, showing a not unsuspected professional hand while doing so.

There were only two slight difficulties encountered with the Old Army. First, it takes a fair amount of leverage to seat the bullet correctly in any gun of this type. This, at first, gave Kurt and Sandy a hard time; however, once the younger set got the knack of it, the problem pretty well worked itself out. Second, it does take some thought and practice for the uninitiated to disassemble the cylinder, cylinder pin and loading unit with any ease and no great loss of time.

What it takes, stated as simply as possible, is this: (Note: never attempt to remove a capped or loaded cylinder.) Place the hammer in the half-cock notch, being certain that the cylinder rotates freely. On the right side of the Ruger frame, just forward of the cylinder, you will see a large slotted pin. With a suitable tool turn this pin counterclockwise until it stops at about 160 degrees. Now, unlatch the rammer lever and pull the rammer base pin assembly forward, toward the muzzle until it comes free of the revolver. The cylinder may now be removed.

Care and cleaning are all important with a black powder revolver, just as is the case with all other black powder arms. Remember, the chemical compounds formed by black powder residue are extremely corrosive; under some conditions of humidity, rusting will begin within hours after firing. Thus, clean thoroughly and without delay following each day's use. Depending on your personal preference, it is acceptable to use either commercially available black powder solvents or a solution of soap and water.

Sight adjustment on the Old Army is there for the same reason as on any other fine shooting piece. On the Ruger, each click of the sight adjustment screws, either windage or elevation, will move the point of impact of the bullet three-quarters inch at a range of twenty-five yards. The height of the front sight has been pre-set to take best advantage of the elevation adjustment in the rear sight, considering the various ranges at which the gun is most likely to be used. Also to be considered is the simple fact that different loadings will also call for readjustment of sights.

Bill Ruger, Steve Vogel and I found it interesting to learn just how quickly our junior-achievement team of lad and lasses overrode the surprise and distraction experienced by those new to black powder shooting. After each had fired but a few rounds with the Rugers, the muffled roar and cloud of smoke no longer bothered them to any great degree. The fact that they weren't doing much flinching could be noted from the targets they each fired.

In the case of Kurt Vogel, this came as no great surprise. His pappy already has him shooting the single action .44 magnum from the off-hand position; no small feat for a tad who just about clears some guy's belt buckles.

As I see it, ol' Bill Ruger has got himself another winner to add to his lineup of top quality firearms. If cared for as cap and ballers must be, it should serve a couple of shooters' lifetimes.

Their basic percussion model, the BP-7 will list for $115, while the BP-7B, the model featuring a solid brass dragoon-style grip frame and wide trigger will bear a price tag of $130. – *Bob Zwirz*

CHAPTER 19

SON OF A GUN....

...Or How Does Today's 1851 Navy Colt Model Compare With The Original Of More Than A Century Back?

THE UNPREDICTABLE TASTES of the gun-buying public must have grayed many a hair and planted many an ulcer among the management of the venerable arms plant near the Connecticut River in Hartford over the century-plus of its activities.

Many a good model of Colt revolver has been discontinued from production, perhaps with regret, perhaps with a sigh of relief and, in later years, market conditions have necessitated setting the dies and jigs back up on the production line to churn forth additional units.

That's how it went for the legendary Peacemaker, Model of 1873: Sales had sagged to levels which made it economically impractical, so production terminated. The fickle public became ever more enamored with the charm of the cowboy's traditional hogleg, prices soared to incredible heights. Other manufacturers commenced turning out replicas to satisfy the ever-growing demands and, with handwriting clearly legible on the wall, Colt resumed production: no great tragedy, considering the influx of greenbacks generated by the western six-shooter in its second reincarnation.

So time inched forward, as it has a way of doing and that less-than-predictable group, the gun-buying public, not content to fire and admire their latter-day single action

New version carries square-backed trigger guard. On the originals, this was less common than rounded trigger guard.

As cylinder is pulled from closely fitted arbor, the spiral-cut grease grooves can be seen in latter.

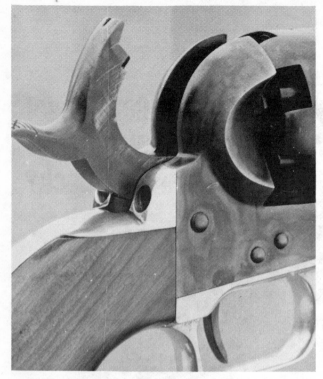

Left: Small notch in nose of the hammer serves as the rear sight when hammer is cocked. Below: With locking wedge loosened and moved to the left, rammer is positioned between two of the chambers and the loading lever is used to force the barrel forward as first step in disassembly.

six-shooters, began trending toward the old muzzleloading arms which had preceded the M1873. All of this may have disturbed the well earned rest of those earnest innovators such as Rollin White who had labored long and diligently to improve the breed by developing the principle of cartridge-loaded firearms.

Once again, the more adventurous competitors of the Colt works came forward, happily catering to this new penchant on the part of the g.b.p. and, once again, the Colt management noted substantial and growing sales which were having no effect upon Sam'l. Colt's check-stubs. It is easy — though surely not accurate — to envision some board member at Colt's as he accepted the inevitable, staring moodily out the window at the bulbuous gilt dome which has been the plant's hallmark for generations. You picture him dropping a half-finished cigar into a mirror-polished brass cuspidor, smoothing luxuriant mutton-chop whiskers and gritting, "All right! Send someone into the back room to dig out the tooling on the Navy Colt!"

That's not the way it was, but it sounds plausible in a firm that has been surviving corporate shakeups since long before the great-grandparents of most people now living were wrestling with McGuffy's spelling books.

As with many of the more successful Colt Models, the Navy Colt of 1851 went through numerous modifications in its first career of production, many of them of a minor

As discussed, the small plastic, dipper-type powder measures supplied for use with the Lee Loader kits can be used to dispense powder into front of each chamber, although the dipper is not quite as convenient as flask.

When using a powder flask, such as this one by Lyman, a finger tip is held over the nozzle, flask is inverted and the gate lever is pressed and released. This allows the measuring tube to fill with powder which then can be poured into the chamber. Details of the engraving on the cylinder are shown below and, bottom of page: In the tests, inexpensive automotive grease worked well.

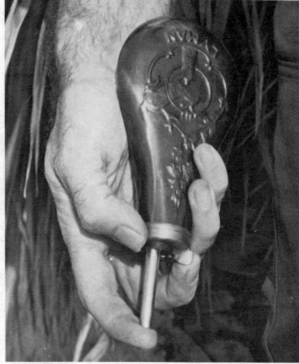

Unlike loading operations with rifles and other shoulder arms, it's common practice to pour charge direct from the powder flask into chamber mouth.

nature. Knowledgeable scholars of Coltly lore, such as James E. Serven, seem to agree that the Navy Colt was the most popular of all the muzzleloaders the firm turned out. It was the favored equalizer of the fairly late Wild Bill Hickok and a brace of them may have been tucked beneath his waistband on that fateful Dakota evening when he crumpled over his last poker hand: aces and eights, full.

The second-generation Navy Colt tips the scale at a hair over two pounds, nine ounces, carries the traditional 7½-inch octagonal barrel and its unfluted cylinder is embellished with a scene of naval combat, commemorating a successful encounter the Texas Navy had with some Mexican vessels. The words, "Colt's Patent," followed by the serial number appear on one line, and the line beneath says, "Engraved by W. L. Ormsby, New York." A third line, engraved around the forward perimeter of the cylinder, reads, "Engaged 16 May 1843." If memory serves, that was a Tuesday.

Barrel and cylinder are richly blued, with handsome case-hardening colors on the loading lever, rammer, frame and hammer. The trigger guard and backstrap — joined by a single screw at the lower front corner of the grip — are of a non-ferrous metal, presumably brass, heavily silver-plated. The stock of the Navy Colt is a single piece of wood — nut-brown on the sample gun, with attractive figuring in a deeper brown, so dark as to be nearly black, running diagonally — held by the trigger guard and backstrap encircling it in a closely fitted groove.

The trigger is blued, slender and graceful and set slightly to the left of center, as viewed from above and rearward in normal firing position. With the arm of the trigger scale positioned midway up the trigger, pull on the test arm measured approximately seventy-six ounces — 4¾ pounds — although it feels lighter when firing..

The Navy Colt field-strips for cleaning into three assemblies: barrel, cylinder and receiver. The wedge at the lower rear of the barrel is tapped lightly with a non-marring tool such as a wooden mallet to loosen it, after which it is moved on to the left. It is not necessary to loosen the screw above the wedge on the left side and this should not be done. The screw serves to prevent loss of the wedge after being moved to the limit of its leftward travel. Some dingaling, into whose clutches the sample had fallen, was unaware of this and had split one side of the screw off in a vain attempt to loosen it.

Once the wedge is moved clear, the proper way to continue disassembly is to rotate the cylinder so as to place the rammer between two chambers and actuate the loading lever to force the barrel and receiver apart. The improper way is to grab the barrel with one hand and the receiver with the other, attempting to pull them apart. As they are fitted quite snugly, they will separate with considerable force applied and it is highly probable that the cylinder will fly loose and fall to the ground: a situation with little to recommend it.

The first type of Navy Colt had a novel design feature in that the cylinder pin or arbor had an open notch on its upper surface to accept the barrel wedge. In the second type, this was changed to a rectangular slot passing horizontally through the cylinder pin. The 1971 version follows the second type as to configuration in this regard.

Accuracy requires that the cylinder be a close fit on the

Custom fitted plastic ear plugs and modern shooting glasses protect eyes and ears as loads are tested off of sandbag rest and chronographed to measure velocity.

cylinder pin and a spiral grease groove is cut around the pin for about 1-1/8 inches. Here is where the passion for authenticity shows clearly. It would be quicker and easier to cut this spiral groove on a lathe, but the sample appears to have been cut free-hand, with irregular groove spacing being clearly evident.

The front sight is a brass bead, with tapering sides and a rounded tip. A notch in the nose of the hammer serves as the rear sight. Neither are adjustable, though the side-play of the hammer, under pressure, is well under 1/64-inch, making its sight steadier than many an arm of modern design that has been tested.

The top of the barrel bears the familiar legend: ADDRESS SAML COLT NEW-YORK CITY; no period after Saml, no apostrophe, though the L is of smaller size and has a line beneath it. This is but one of at least five different markings found in this location on Nineteenth Century Navy Colts and, as with countless other details, is almost painfully authentic.

The serial number appears in at least five places: lower surface of barrel lug, cylinder, lower front of frame and on both the trigger guard and backstrap.

The trigger guard is square-backed, in the manner of the second type. The third type used a small guard, rounded front and back and made of brass. Later, the guard was made bigger, still rounded and iron was used in some units instead of brass.

Rifling of the 1971 version consists of seven grooves, fairly deep and of approximately the same width as the lands, cut with right-hand twist. This corresponds to the first models of the Navy Colt, the design being changed later to incorporate a left-hand twist. Some of the Nineteenth Century specimens are said to have had a gain twist — that is, increasing in pitch toward the muzzle — although the current production appears to be cut at a uniform rate throughout its barrel length.

Nominally, the Navy Colt, including current production, is caliber .36 — this being based upon 86 round balls to the pound, which would make it correspond to an 86-gauge shotgun, were there such an animal — although, in practice, almost any sort of leaden globule between about .368 and .400-inch in diameter can be fired with reasonable hopes of success and satisfaction.

The chambers of the cylinder measure about .375-inch in inside diameter and the ball must start its trip by being crammed down into this space, although there is a slight chamfer at the chamber mouth to accommodate lead balls of larger diameters.

Slugging the bore by carefully tapping a lead ball though it with a length of wooden dowel gave a trifle over 3/16-inch of land engagement on a ball that started out at about .400-inch diameter. When so handled, the expelled ball did not appear to have bottomed on the grooves, although it is likely that it would have done so under impetus of powder pressures.

Conical balls can be fired in the .36 Navy Colt. The oldtime logistics pegged these at fifty to the pound, which would work out to 140 grains apiece. Number 1 buckshot,

171

Round balls or – if preferred, conical bullets – are positioned into mouth of the bottom-most chamber, after charging with powder, after which they are seated by means of the rammer and loading lever before rotating the cylinder to put the next chamber into position for having same steps performed on it.

made by Lawrence, measures right around .400-inch and averages 87-90 grains. Some mould-cast balls, priced at $2.30 per hundred from a local gunstore, miked about .374-inch and weighed around 82-85 grains.

FFFg is the indicated granulation of black powder for use in the .36 Navy Colt and it should go without saying that nitrocellulose (smokeless) powder should not be used in it under any circumstances. The nipple diameter is such that the Remington number 10 caps fit perfectly.

Speaking of things not to do: Snapping the hammer on the uncapped nipple will burr and ruin the nipple quickly. Most people do not seem to know this, so you have to warn them against dry firing before letting them get their hands on a percussion firearm of any sort. The only safe policy is to warn everyone about this; if you assume the other guy is smart enough not to need warning, it's an excellent bet that you'll end up replacing at least one nipple.

Various approaches to powder measuring were used in the test firing. One of the Lee Loader measure kits was packed along and it was found that that number 108 scoop – the number indicates a volume of .108 cubic inch – worked quite well, leaving ample room for seating the round ball. Delivery with this dipper-type measure comes to 27.1 grains of FFFg black powder. Moving to the next larger size of Lee measure, the number 129, gave 31.8 grains of FFFg, which brought the charge just about level with the top of the chamber and made it somewhat difficult to ram the ball into the mouth far enough to clear the rear of the barrel during cocking. With a bit of care, the 129 dipper could be short-scooped, leaving about 1/8 to 3/16-inch of unfilled space at the top and this resulted in a workable charge of 28.5 grains, upon which the ball could

be seated easily.

The second measuring method involved Lyman's powder flask, intended for their caliber .36 black powder replica but equally well suited for use with the Navy Colt. This is a handsome production with a colorful antique patina on the copper flask and brass fittings. The technique for using it is simple, once you know how. Put a finger tip over the end of the spout, invert the flask, open the gate with the little lever, release the lever, up-end the flask and pour the contents of the measuring tube down into the mouth of the chamber. The operation is much quicker to perform than to describe. Average charge weight with the Lyman flask is 20.9 grains of DuPont FFFg, taken over ten consecutive charges.

The percussion revolver requires an application of grease over the top of the seated ball; serving at least two important functions as indicated earlier in this volume, but it deserves repetition. It reduces or eliminates lead-fouling of the bore and it prevents the uncomfortable adventure of having a second or third adjacent chamber set off accidentally by the firing of the one in line with the barrel. Further, it tends to soften and minimize the buildup of powder fouling in the bore. There are many kinds of preparations available for this purpose and priced accordingly. The lubricant used in the test was Sta-Lube type GM-21, a lithium base automotive grease containing molybdenum disulphide and priced at a rousing forty-nine cents for a one-pound can: enough for a copious quantity of shooting with percussion revolvers and there were no complaints with its performance.

Some highly self-respected authorities on the subject of firing black powder percussion arms have placed great stress

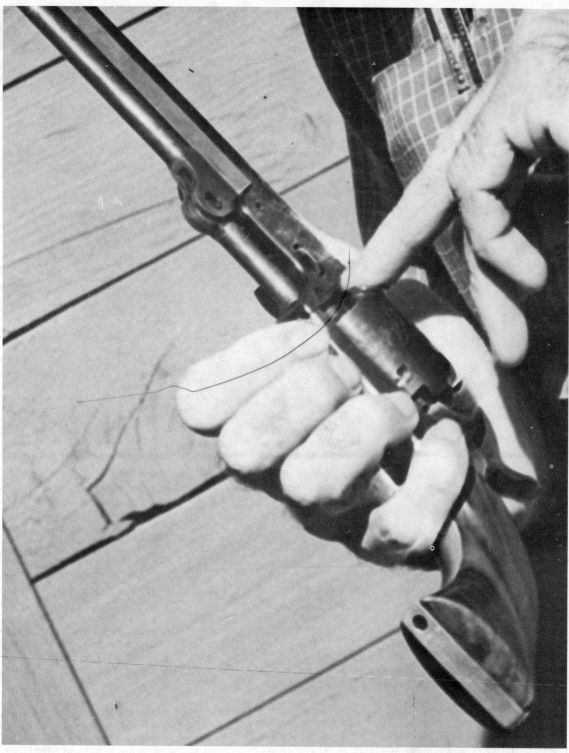

A finger tip is used to apply grease over the seated ball.

upon the need for snapping a cap in each empty chamber, so as to clear the flash hole, prior to the initial loading for each shooting session. This is, undoubtedly, a sagacious procedure if you envision the possibility of having to stop a charging grizzly with a single fast shot. However, instances of being charged by a wounded paper target are quite rare. Visual examination of the flash holes showed every appearance of being adequately clear. So the first six rounds were loaded up without wasting any caps and, to no one's great surprise, all six fired at the first drop of the hammer. Had

any of the chambers failed to fire, it was proposed to wait a decent interval, flick off the first cap and try with a second primer on the same nipple.

The photoscreen chronograph had been set up so as to permit measurement of velocity on each shot in conjunction with group testing. The obvious advantage over conventional, breaking-screen chronographs is that the latter do not permit easy sighting at a target and may produce some amount of deflection.

The charges thrown by the Lyman powder flask — with

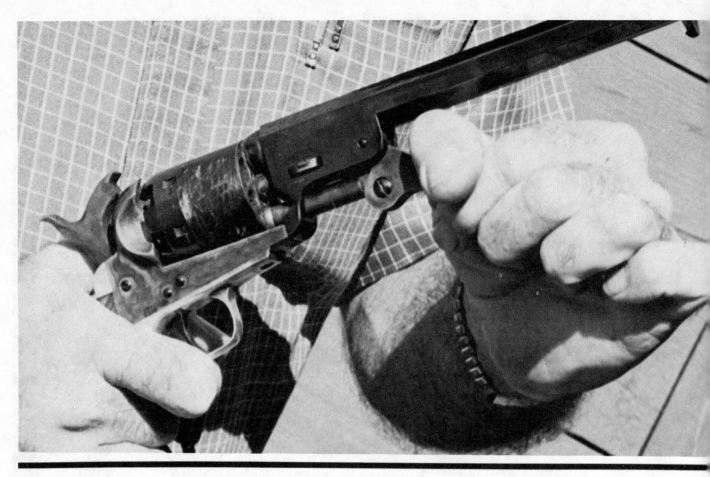

*With powder charge in place, ball is put into mouth
of chamber and loading lever is used to ram it home.*

its measuring tube intended for the caliber .36 percussion revolver sold by Lyman — weighing a hair under 21.0 grains on the average, drove the 82-85-grain moulded balls forth at a rather leisurely 680 fps average velocity. Group size, for six shots at twenty-five yards was 8.257 inches wide by 6.482 inches high. Average muzzle energy came to 85 foot-pounds.

Moving on to the number 108 Lee dipper, with its average charge weight of 27.1 grains of FFFg, the velocity climbed to an average of 813 fps with the same projectile — good for 122 foot-pounds of muzzle energy — and the six-shot group came to a more respectable 3.702 inches wide by 2.379 inches high.

Short-dipping with the number 129 Lee measure, as described previously, raised the velocity to an average figure of 941 fps on 28.5 grains of FFFg and ciphered out to a muzzle energy of 164 foot-pounds. That will shade a few of the milder smokeless pistol cartridges such as the .25 auto (73 ft-lbs), .32 auto (145 ft-lbs), .32 S&W (90 ft-lbs), .32 S&W Long (115 ft-lbs) and the .38 S&W (150 ft-lbs).

True, the Navy Colt's ballistics may seem unimpressive when rated against the .44 magnum but the same could be said of most other handgun cartridges and the Navy Colt's big brother, the awesome Walker Colt Dragoon could defend the family honor much more tellingly in the heavyweight division. It is interesting to speculate upon the possibility that Colt might tool up for 20th-Century production of that legendary hoss-pistol but there's no word to that effect out of Hartford, as yet.

The heaviest charge delivered the highest output but the group size had expanded to 4.580 wide by 4.015 inches high, leaving the dipped load from the number 108 Lee measure as the apparent best combination for this particular specimen. It should be noted that a four-by-four group is not particularly disgraceful for smokeless powder cartridges.

Certainly, it can be said that the re-emerging Navy Colt is the oldest design of handgun — perhaps you can make that "firearm" — being produced today by its original manufacturer. It is authentic Colt in every detail and it takes its glamorous final form from selected raw materials: steel, brass and wood, in the same place where the Immortal Sam'l. supervised production of the prototype, one hundred and twenty years ago.

The Navy Colt, as described here, is available in gun-only form at a retail price of $150. Available accessories — prices to be announced — include two powder flasks throwing charges of 20.0 grains, a two-cavity mould to cast one round ball and one conical bullet simultaneously, a nipple wrench, a replica of the old Eley Brothers cap container and a presentation case.

For the history-conscious and the collector, the same basic gun can be had in two commemorative versions: one honoring General Robert E. Lee and the other General Ulysses S. Grant. Total production of these will be 4750 units each, at $250 apiece, including case and accessories. In addition, there will be 250 Lee-Grant commemorative sets, containing one of each with accessories at $500 the

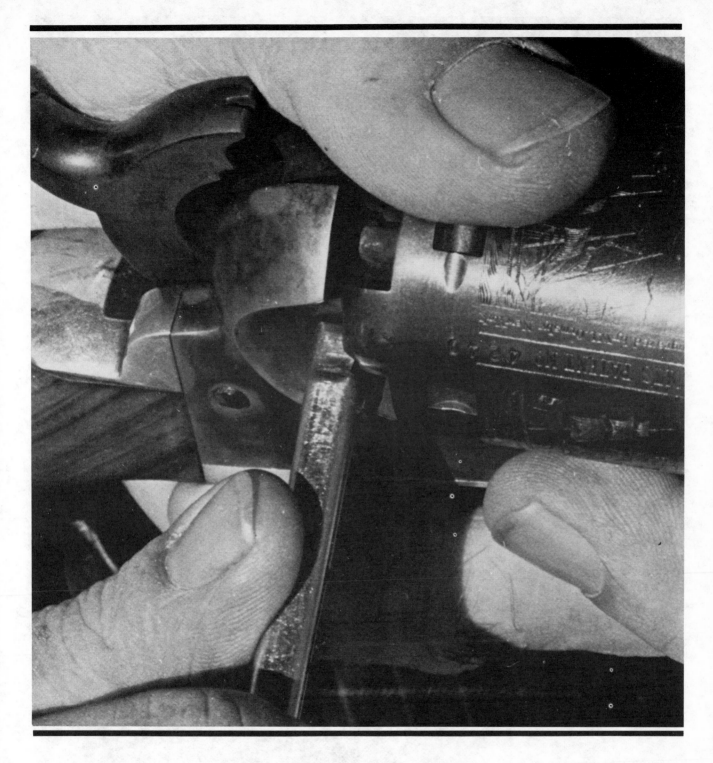

Placing percussion caps on nipples is the final step in reloading for obvious safety reasons. Here, a replica of an antique capper makes quick work of operation.

The commemorative models are identified by stamping the appropriate name on the left side of the barrel. In addition, the Lee model has the round-back trigger guard while the Grant model has the square-back guard. Among the Navy Colts left over from the Nineteenth Century production, the square-back guard is encountered less frequently.

So the ever-growing group of black powder fans can bid a hearty welcome-back to this grizzled seafaring sixgun from 'way back down the road. And you can bet that many a collector/shooter is hoping that they've got someone prowling the back room at Hartford in quest of the tooling for the Paterson Model! – *Dean A. Grennell*

THE FINE ART OF FRONT-STUFFING SCATTERGUNS

CHAPTER 20

Black Powder Shotguns Do Not Enjoy The Intense Popularity Of Rifles And Pistols, But Their Acceptance Is Growing!

THE PAST FEW CHAPTERS illustrate the development of black powder arms and their application to today's replica firearms. Samuel Colt was one of the early developers and the company bearing his name has gone full circle coming back to produce — or actually to reproduce — one of the firearms on which his reputation was built.

But there is still another facet of black powder shooting that has changed even less over the past couple of centuries. This involves the muzzleloading shotgun.

Have you ever really wondered what it was like to hunt with a muzzleloading shotgun the way your great gran'pappy used to? Today it's so easy to swing on a rising covey of quail or a brace of cock pheasant and, without too much bother, bring down a double or even a triple with the modern pump guns or that marvel of marvels, the autoloading shotgun.

Hunting with muzzleloading black powder scatterguns was all but abandoned during the first half of this century. The late 1800s saw the introduction of the break-open breechloaders that were chambered for the early black powder shotshells. Shortly after break-open single and double barrel shotguns came into being, other developments came about that pushed the front-loading shotgun even further into the past. Among these later refinements

were smokeless powders, the pump and the autoloading shotgun.

Great grandfather, however, was usually quite content with his black powder smokepole. A flask of FFg powder, a pouch filled with the size shot best suited for the game he was seeking, wadding of some sort and a tin of percussion caps or a smaller flask filled with FFFFg powder to prime the pan if the gun happened to be a flintlock were all he needed for his day afield.

It's a good bet eventually you'll find an old photo or two in the family album showing some distant relative proudly showing off a great pile of ducks, geese or similar fowl. It's also another good bet that said relative probably is tenderly cradling his prized black powder scattergun in the crook of his arm in such a manner that the photo plays as much emphasis on the firearm as it does the taken game.

It is said that man's personality is clearly reflected in the armament that he chooses. If this is true, perhaps this is the reason that such shotguns were left propped in some forgotten corner or hung over a fireplace or rafter just to collect dust and rust, as their owners turned to such repeating shotguns as Winchester's Model 1897 pump. The arms scene changed rapidly during the last quarter of the 19th Century, no one wanting to be left out. If you didn't

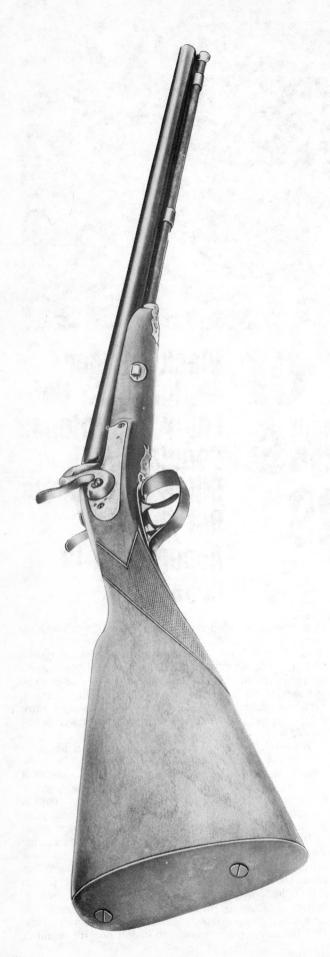

hunt with the latest of firearms, you just weren't with the times. Except for an occasional farm lad who couldn't afford anything better, shotgun shooters gave up the muzzleloading arm for the more reliable break-open singles, doubles and later the pumps and autos.

During the last decade, however, there has been growing interest not only in shooting arms of this type, but in hunting with black powder guns. Nostalgia certainly has played some role in the increasing number of muzzleloading hunters, but for many this interest stems from the real pleasure of hunting with arms of this type.

Cap and ball revolvers, single-shot pistols, rifles and muskets had received the majority of this attention with little going to muzzleloading shotguns.

As can be expected, the arms manufacturers and importers played upon the markets offering the greatest amount of sales and muzzleloading shotguns just don't fall into this category. Unlike the numerous well built Colt Army and Navy replicas, single-shot target pistols and Zouave musket reproductions, the number of modern-made shotguns is relatively small. Although there were quite a few well built originals, no exact reproductions of these are

Reproduction shotgun at left is from Navy Arms and is an example of variety of modern black powder shotguns now available. What could be more enjoyable than spending a day afield in pursuit of such game as the cottontail with muzzleloader shotgun?

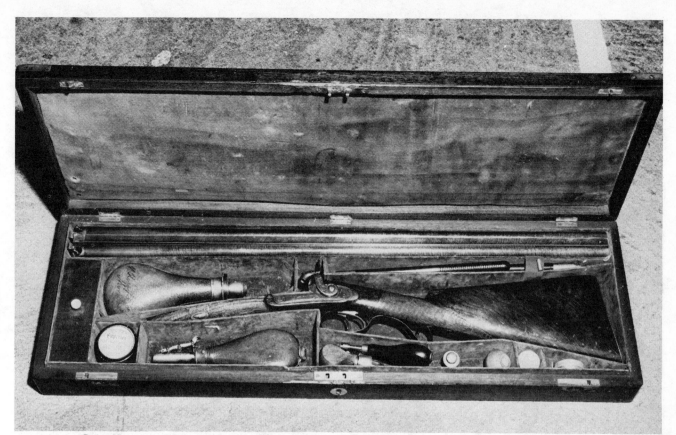

Beautiful old original shotguns as this can be bought with little harm done to shooter's budget. Barrels on old guns such as this one are commonly of damascus twist steel and can be dangerous.

CHART A

Gauge	Powder Charge	Wad Thickness	Charge Weight	
10	100 grains Fg	7/8 inch	1 1/4 oz.	Light
10	108 grains Fg	7/8 inch	1 1/2 oz.	Medium
10	120 grains Fg	7/8 inch	1 5/8 oz.	Heavy
12	70 grains Fg/FFg	3/4 inch	1 1/8 oz.	Light
12	84 grains Fg/FFg	3/4 inch	1 1/4 oz.	Medium
12	90 grains FFg	3/4 inch	1 5/8 oz.	Heavy
14	66 grains FFg	3/4 inch	1 oz.	Light
14	74 grains FFg	3/4 inch	1 1/8 oz.	Medium
14	85 grains FFg	3/4 inch	1 1/8 oz.	Heavy
16	60 grains FFg	5/8 inch	1 oz.	Light
16	66 grains FFg	5/8 inch	1 oz.	Medium
16	75 grains FFg	5/8 inch	1 1/8 oz.	Heavy
20	55 grains FFg	5/8 inch	3/4 oz.	Light
20	60 grains FFg	5/8 inch	7/8 oz.	Medium
20	69 grains FFg	5/8 inch	1 oz.	Heavy
28	55 grains FFg	1/2 inch	5/8 oz.	Light
28	60 grains FFg	1/2 inch	5/8 oz.	Medium
28	65 grains FFg	1/2 inch	7/8 oz.	Heavy
.410	34 grains FFg	1/2 inch	1/2 oz.	Light
.410	44 grains FFg	1/2 inch	1/2 oz.	Medium
.410	44 grains FFg	1/2 inch	5/8 oz.	Heavy

What size shot would work best here? Actually a load of No. 4s or 5s should work nicely.

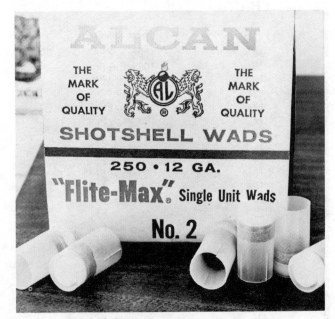

Handy to have around when figuring out loads is a dependable scale; this one is from Ohaus.

being offered currently. Instead today's front loading scatterguns are modern-made guns of the generally accepted designs.

Dixie Gun Works, Navy Arms, Mowrey Gun Works, Numrich Arms, just to name a few, all offer muzzleloading shotguns of some sort. With the exception of such guns as Mowrey's single-barrel 12-gauge shotgun, these guns are almost all made in one of three countries: Belgium, Italy or Spain. Unfortunately, some of these are cheap and lightly built guns that work fine initially, but result in a big headache in the end.

But if hunting with your lightning fast pump or auto has lost some of its appeal and challenge, give hunting with one of the muzzleloaders a try before condemning it. There's something about making a good hit on a fast rising pheasant, fleeing quail or running bunny with a flintlock or percussion caplock shotgun that adds to the pleasures of going afield.

As when hunting with the single-barrel designs, knowing that you may only get one chance, one shot, tends to make you concentrate more on making that first — and possibly last — shot count. There's nothing old fashioned about hunting with a muzzleloader, but there are certain steps that make shooting these guns simpler and increases their effectiveness greatly.

The first step toward hunting with this type of arm is to select one of the modern-made reproduction type arms or to locate a fine old original that is still in good serviceable

When available in the right gauge size, plastic wads such as these from Alcan make loading easy.

CHART B

GAME	GAUGE/LOAD	SHOT SIZE	MAX. RANGE WITH CYLINDER CHOKE
Small ducks	10 ga. medium	4, 5, 6	40-45 yards
	10 ga. light	4, 5, 6	30-35 yards
	12 ga. heavy	4, 5, 6	35 yards
	14 ga. heavy	5, 6	25-30 yards
Big ducks, geese	10 ga. heavy	BB, 2, 4	35-40 yards
	10 ga. medium	BB, 2, 4	35 yards
	12 ga. heavy	BB, 2, 4	35 yards
Pheasants	10 ga. light	5, 6	40-45 yards
	12 ga. heavy	5, 6	40 yards
	12 ga. medium	5, 6	35-40 yards
	14 ga. heavy	5, 6	35 yards
	14 ga. medium	5, 6	35 yards
	16 ga. heavy	5, 6	30 yards
	20 ga. heavy	5, 6	25-30 yards
Grouse, partridge	12 ga. medium	5, 6, 7½	35-40 yards
	12 ga. light	5, 6, 7½	25-30 yards
	14 ga. heavy	5, 6, 7½	35 yards
	14 ga. medium	5, 6, 7½	25-30 yards
	16 ga. heavy	5, 6, 7½	25-30 yards
	16 ga. medium	5, 6, 7½	20-25 yards
	20 ga. heavy	5, 6, 7½	25 yards
Quail, doves, pigeons, rails, snipe, woodcock	12 ga. medium	7½, 8	35-40 yards
	12 ga. light	7½, 8	25 yards
	14 ga. heavy	7½, 8	25 yards
	14 ga. medium	7½, 8	20-25 yards
	16 ga. heavy	7½, 8	20-25 yards
	16 ga. medium	7½, 8	20-25 yards
	20 ga. heavy	7½, 8	20 yards
Rabbits, squirrels	12 ga. heavy	4, 5, 6	40-45 yards
	12 ga. medium	4, 5, 6	35 yards
	14 ga. heavy	4, 5, 6	35-40 yards
	16 ga. heavy	4, 5, 6	35 yards
	20 ga. heavy	4, 5, 6	30 yards
	28 ga. heavy	4, 5, 6	20-25 yards
	.410 ga. heavy	5, 6	20 yards
Turkey, fox coyote, bobcat	10 ga. heavy	BB, 2, 4	40 yards
	10 ga. medium	BB, 2, 4	35 yards
	12 ga. heavy	BB, 2, 4	30-35 yards
	12 ga. medium	BB, 2, 4	30 yards
	14 ga. heavy	2, 4	25-30 yards
	16 ga. heavy	2, 4	20-25 yards
Deer, black bear	10 ga. medium	All loads made with either a bore sized round ball known as a pumpkin ball, a conical slug or buckshot.	
	12 ga. heavy		
	12 ga. medium		
	14 ga. heavy		40-60 yards depending on load.
	16 ga. heavy		
	20 ga. heavy		

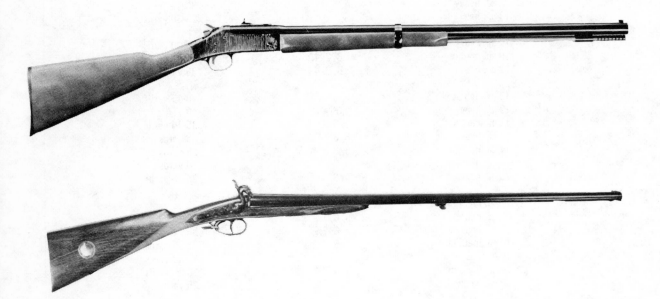

The Harrington & Richardson Huntsman (top) is one of the few domestically produced muzzleloading shotguns presently on the market. Bottom double is imported by Dixie Gun Works.

and safe shooting condition. The latter could possibly have been lying around unfired for better than three-quarters of a century, so it is wise to really check these over before attempting to shoot them.

The outside appearance of a hundred year old original can be and often is deceiving at first inspection. The outside conditions of the gun can be near factory new and the gun could still be dangerous and unsafe to shoot. This is usually the end result of some long forgotten gunowner putting the arm away uncleaned, leaving the bore's metal at the mercy of the corrosive black powder foulings still in the barrel.

Another undersirable feature on many of the originals are the damascus twist steel barrels with which they commonly were fitted. Agreed, the pattern formed from the welds that hold the strip of steel together make an intriguing-looking arm, but they just aren't safe enough to warrant day-to-day hunting use. These welds also are more susceptible to corrosion by foulings left in the bore.

The best route to take is to purchase one of the better built modern black powder shotguns. These are much safer and in the long run will probably be more trouble free. When buying an original or gun of modern manufacture, there's one important thing to look for and that is quality. Collecting antique muzzleloading shotguns hasn't reached the level of interest of collecting original long rifles or early Colt and Remington revolvers and these guns can still be had for little less than what equals one month's grocery bill. If hunting, however, is to be the gun's main use, one of the new guns would probably be the wiser choice.

Nearly all of the old guns and a majority of the new ones are made with little if any choke constrictions in the barrel. Most of the originals were made well before anyone really knew just what choking would do to improve patterns. Even after its discovery, however, the barrels on muzzle-loading shotguns were rarely choked; due to the popular belief that any constricting of the muzzle would interfere with the loading. These cylinder bores mean that the patterns are going to be quite spread out and will be a far cry from that favorite trap gun of yours.

How the gun is loaded determines just how effectively these cylinder-bore patterns will take game. Today's components are actually far superior to what granddad had available to him; his usually being what he could make at home for the most part. Wads were usually made at home by cutting out the circular cardboard-like disks with the aid of a wad cutter. Commercial wads were available then, but not in the variety that we know today.

Although the one-piece plastic wad columns are easy to load, they usually don't give very favorable results when fired from a muzzleloading shotgun. The most effective and more reliable load is to use the commercially produced cardboard and felt wads, such as those available from Smith & Wesson-Fiocchi under the brand name of Alcan. These come in a variety of bore sizes and thicknesses.

Once these have been seated over the powder charge — not so firmly as to crush or compact the powder — a plastic shot cup can be placed over the wad. Available from a number of reloading component suppliers, plastic shot cups

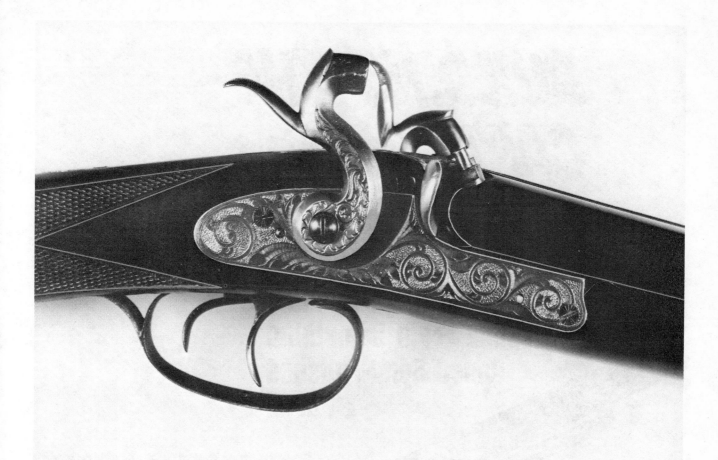

*This close-up of the locks on the Replica Arms black
powder double-barrel shotgun shows tasteful engraving.*

help hold the patterns together and prevent the deforming of the pellets from scraping against the inside of the barrel walls as the load travels through the barrel. A tight fitting over the shot cardboard wad is used to keep the shot from rolling out the muzzle when the gun is being carried in a downward position.

What loads are best for what game? As the game's habitat varies, so will the range of the shot. As a rule, however, most shots taken with muzzleloading shotguns will be done at fairly close range so the gun can be loaded accordingly.

The key factor to successful hunting lies in matching the proper size of shot to the type of game being hunted. You've no doubt heard hunters explain how the larger the shot used the farther the effective range of the load. This is true to a certain degree, larger shot does hit with greater impact at the longer ranges, but without sufficient powder to propel it, the heavier shot is no better than a shot size two or three sizes smaller.

Here again we get back to increasing the powder charge and again we encounter the problem of having the pattern blown open by the excess pressures. About the only thing we can recommend is to start by using the starting loads shown in Chart A and work from there. Some of these loads, however probably will work better in one gun than another.

* For better results use plastic shot protectors in those gauges where available. The lighter loads normally will consistently give the best patterns.

It is only logical that you wouldn't load up with No. 2 shot, if quail were to be the afternoon's target, just as it would be equally foolish to drop in a charge of No. 7½s for big ducks or geese. True, it's nearly as easy to hit game with a muzzleloading shotgun as with a gun using modern smokeless powder shotshells, but that's not entirely the idea.

The idea is to hit them with something that will bring them down and keep them there. Chart B gives the proper size of shot to use on certain game species. This chart is to be used as a guide to follow, it doesn't mean that you can't kill geese with a load of No. 6s, because its been done before and probably will be done quite a few times more in the future. Instead, this chart should give you a good idea of what size shot and load is best suited for hunting a certain type of game.

An important thing always to keep in mind is that black powder shotguns are the underdog among hunting firearms. Due to their lack of choking and slight decrease in power, ranges naturally are going to be shorter.

But that's where the challenge lies: getting close enough for the shot and, when it presents itself, to make a good one-shot kill! – *Toby Bridges*

BUILDING THE CAP'N BALL SIXGUN CHAPTER 21

...Or Adventures In Building A Replica From Something Called Semi-Finished Parts!

Finished, the Dixie Gun Works' brass frame Remington cap and ball revolver is comparable to many of today's replica guns.

AFTER READING the preceding tests of just about every type of black powder muzzleloader that is being produced today and perhaps trying some of them, one might find that he is interested in creating a black powder puffer that is strictly his own; something that he had a personal hand in creating.

With this thought, we cast about for a project that might intrigue the do-it-yourself type shooter. In checking a new catalog from Dixie Gun Works, I found that, among the new products, is a replica Remington brass frame cap and ball kit. And that's how I came to be in the gunmaking business!

A letter was sent to Turner Kirkland of Dixie Gun Works after I agreed to try my hand at gunsmithing. A week or so later I found a large and well packed box sitting on my desk when I arrived for work one morning. After a good ten minutes of sifting and digging through what must have been two, maybe three, editions of the Union City Gazette, I finally came to the conclusion that I had already found everything that was to be found from the then heaping pile of papers. Although, I must admit that I did occasionally take time to read a tidbit of news here and there, a fellow has to keep up on current events. One thing was for certain, though: Dixie Gun Works does an impressive packaging job. It would have been near impossible for any of the parts to be damaged in shipment.

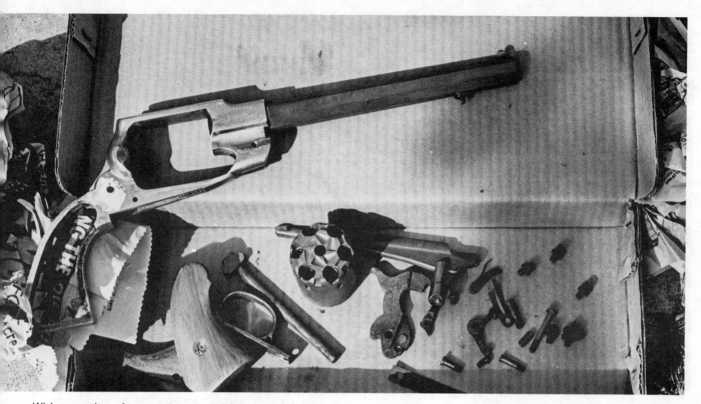

With exception of some minor finishing of the brass frame, but with barrel screwed in place, the kit arrived looking somewhat like it does above.

Taking a quick inventory of the parts included in the kit revealed that I was now in possession of a mould cast brass frame, a barrel of somewhere over seven inches long, a cylinder complete with six separate nipples, two well oversized grip blanks, a brass trigger housing, a genuine steel loading lever and a handful of internal parts, that — hopefully — would allow me to fire the handgun once it was completed.

Deciding to perform most of the major operations first, I set all of the firing mechanism parts, the barrel, cylinder and loading lever aside.

Using a Dremel Moto-Tool with a 3/8-inch diameter cone shaped emery bit, I started in on the rough cast brass frame. This is the most time-consuming phase of constructing the kit. Care must be taken not to shave too much from the soft brass frame.

The rounded cone shaped emery bit is best for knocking down the rough surface from the areas of the frame that enclose the cylinder. For the squared-off portions of the frame, such as that found on the butt of the frame, I switched to a flat surfaced 3/4-inch diameter grinding point. The frame sported a crude ridge of built up brass in this area that was left from the mould casting. The flat surfaced grinding bit makes removing this ridge quicker and easier, it also helps eliminate the possibility of accidentally giving this surface a beveled rounded edge, which would make the fitting of the grips to metal more difficult.

Before putting the final finish onto the frame, the threaded portion into which the barrel is inserted was heated slightly with a small torch and the barrel was firmly seated. If you decide to get one of these kits and do not have access to one of the small propane type torches, the barrel could possibly be seated with a chemical bonding agent such as Loc-Tite.

Next the grip blanks required minor inletting before

they would fit onto the frame. This was accomplished with the Moto-Tool with a cutting wheel inserted.

With the wood stocks fastened to the frame, a medium-toothed wood file was used to remove excess wood from the grips. This was followed by a brisk sanding with 120-grit sandpaper and a lighter sanding with 300-grit sandpaper. Before finishing the grips with Birchwood Casey Tru-Oil, the grips received a final sanding with both 400 and 600-grit papers.

The Dremel Moto-Tool and the various bits that come with it make finishing of the rough brass frame much faster and easier.

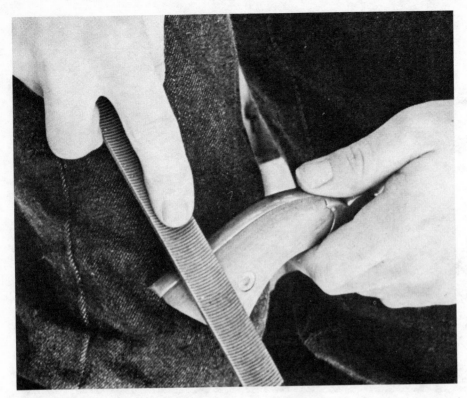

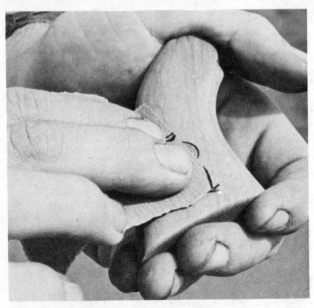

Over-sized walnut grip blanks are filed to nearly finished shape before using sandpaper for smooth finish. (Below) Naval Jelly removed the mottled finish and rust found on some of the parts in Dixie kit.

Sanding with the grain, the completely shaped walnut grip receives final sanding.

To give the wood a high gloss finish, the grips received four applications of the Tru-Oil finish. Between applications, which take approximately two hours to dry, the preceding application was rubbed down with 000 steel wool before the next coat was applied.

With the major operations out of the way, attention was turned to the parts that were to be blued. As the parts had been shipped, some were slightly pitted or not finished at all.

To remove the caked-on protective lubricant and mottled finish of some parts, they were soaked in Naval Jelly for approximately ten minutes. They were then washed in a hot soapy water solution to remove any oil that

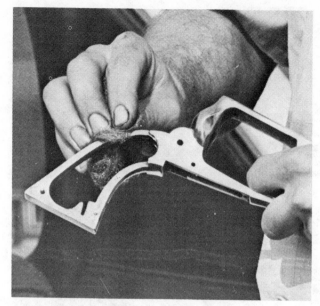

A fine grade of steel wool — 000 or 0000 — is used to remove the etched lines left by the bits of the high-speed Dremel Moto-Tool.

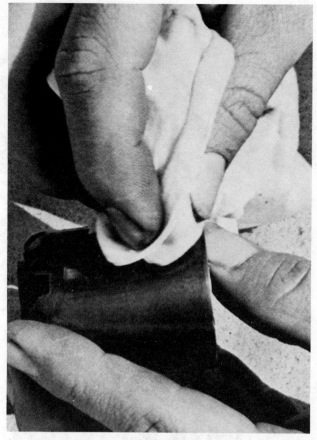

(Above) the 44/40 cold bluing is applied to degreased cylinder with clean cloth. Using nipple wrench, below, the revolver's nipples are securely tightened in place.

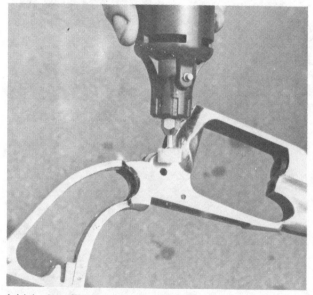

A high-gloss finish was easily obtained with the felt polishing cloth and tool's 30,000 rpm.

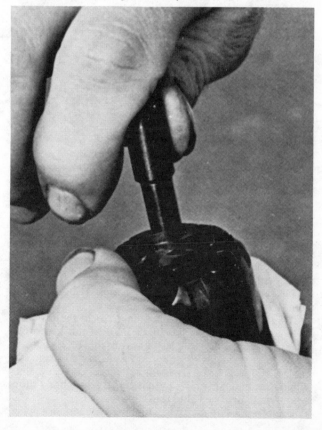

might have remained in the pores of the metal.

While the internal parts, cylinder and loading lever were soaking in the soapy solution, the area of the frame adjacent to the already fitted barrel was taped off with masking tape. The barrel was then cleaned with a dry cleaning solution known as Carbona, which has replaced the now-forbidden carbon tetrachloride.

After swabbing the barrel several times with Carbona, which was done outside where there was better ventilation, the barrel received a generous coat of 44/40 Instant Gun Blue. This bluing product begins to work as soon as it is applied to the metal surface and should be rinsed off as soon as the part or area being treated has received an application.

To give the metal a deeper finish, the first coat was worked down with 000 steel wool. The barrel was then

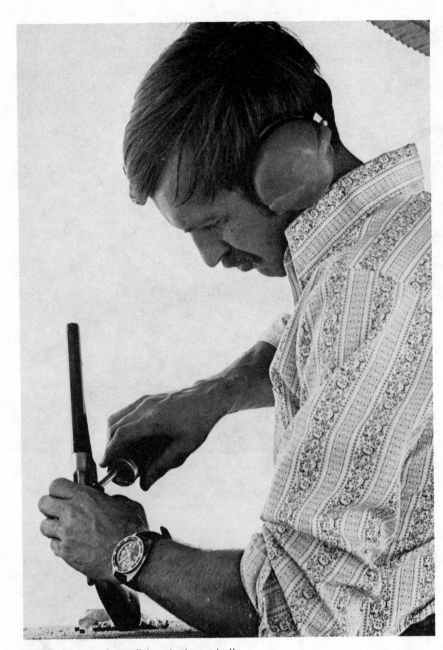

In preparation of test firing the home-built revolver, the author charges chamber with powder.

Ball, slightly over-sized, is placed over chamber, rotated under loading lever. (Below) Ball is seated over powder.

cleaned with the cleaning solution again and received an additional coat of 44/40, rinsed with clear water and dried. A coat of gun oil was applied to prevent the metal from rusting.

The remaining parts that were to be blued were also rinsed with clear water and allowed to dry. They then received the same treatment as the barrel. The result was a more than adequate bluing job.

To remove the heavily etched lines left in the frame by the emery and grinding bits of the Moto-Tool, I used 600 grit sandpaper. This also left lines in the brass that, although not evident to the touch, distracted from the revolver's appearance. To remove these, a heavy duty rubbing compound similar to that used by auto body shops to rejuvenate damaged auto finishes was used.

Several applications of the rubbing compound, applied

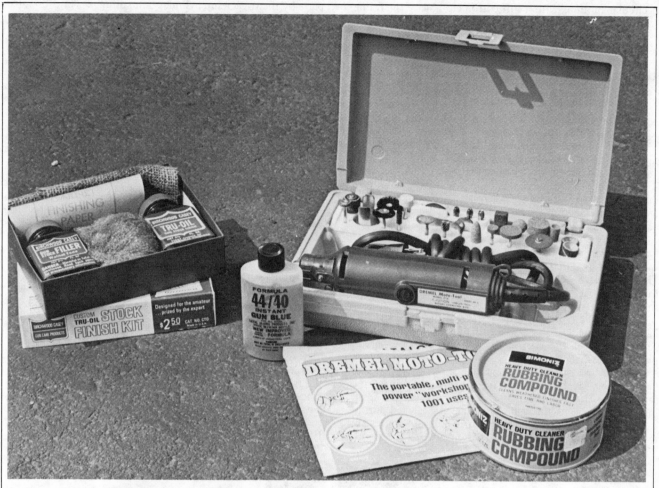

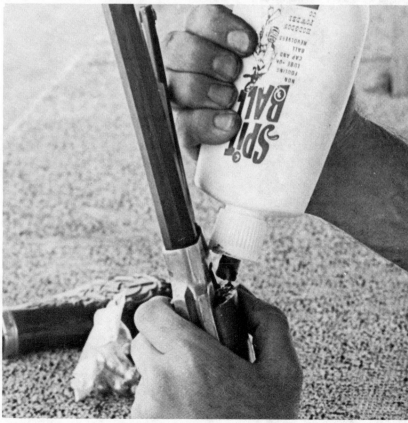

The Dremel Moto-Tool, Tru-Oil stock finishing kit, 44/40 bluing and rubbing compound used to construct the Dixie cap and ball kit. (Left) Hodgdon's Spit Ball is commercial lube used during the test fire.

in circular motions with a soft cotton cloth, gave the frame a smooth and glossy finish that was free from scratches. To give it an even higher gloss, the Moto-Tool with a felt polishing wheel inserted was used.

Now to put the revolver's working mechanism together! Really this isn't as difficult as it may sound. Even without instructions or a diagram to follow, I managed to assemble it in less than twenty minutes.

With the exception of the trigger and hammer, there are only two springs, four screws and two other internal parts. Using common sense and good judgment, anyone should be capable of figuring out what goes where.

The hammer is inserted through its slot in the frame and is worked downward until the lower end is extending from the lower part of the frame. There is a small threaded hole on the lower section of the hammer and this should fall below the lines of the frame.

Next to be installed is a small piece that has a small leaf type spring extending from it. This is the hand, the part of the mechanism that turns the cylinder during cocking. There is a narrow channel inside the frame and this is where the hand goes. The spring faces to the rear and the wedge shaped point protrudes through an opening in the area of the frame that is directly to the rear of the cylinder. The hand is fastened to the lower end of the hammer by the smallest screw in the kit and the whole assembly is held in place by one main screw.

Next to be installed is the cylinder bolt. This is located next to the trigger and both are actually installed at the same time. The cylinder bolt is inserted so that the small locking lug projects through the rectangular shaped port in the bottom of the frame. The cylinder bolt and trigger are fastened with the same screw. Tension is applied to both parts by the trigger and cylinder bolt spring. This fits directly over both and is fastened by a single short screw on the forward portion of the frame.

Next to be installed is the mainspring. This is sometimes difficult to get to slip right into place and often takes several attempts before popping into the correct position. This part rests on a tang located on the back side of the hammer, with the other end slipping into a slot that is provided in the frame. Supplying tension to the hammer, the mainspring is housed between the grips. With this part in place, the firing mechanism is completed.

The trigger guard then is fastened to the frame by inserting the notched rear section into place and then securing the forward section with a single screw.

The nipples then are threaded into the cylinder with the wrench provided. The hammer is placed at half cock and the cylinder is slipped into the frame. To secure it into position, the cylinder pin is inserted through the hole in the frame directly below the barrel. With this in place the loading lever is installed, this also holds the cylinder pin, preventing it from slipping forward.

The kit is now an assembled and shootable cap and ball handgun. Providing the builder uses a reasonable amount of care in building kit No. 140, as Dixie Gun Works has dubbed it, this revolver will handle any load that any of the numerous other preassembled revolvers are capable of firing. As with any black powder gun, however, smokeless powders should never be used. If you entertain any thoughts of getting this kit, or any other kit or assembled black powder gun, and have never fired one before, it is advisable that you get one of the black powder manuals that are now on the market, such as that available from Hodgdon Powder Company of Shawnee Mission, Kansas. — *Toby Bridges*

Both Remington and imported percussion caps from Navy Arms were of size No. 11, but the latter fit nipples much tighter.

The .44 caliber cap and ball revolver's barrel jumps
as the author fires it for first time (top). Although
quite hefty, he found revolver steady for off-hand stance.

CHAPTER 22
MINISTERING TO MUZZLELOADERS

Neglect Can Be Hard On Black Powder Firearms, But This Gunsmith Of The Cloth Turns Back The Clock As A Remedy!

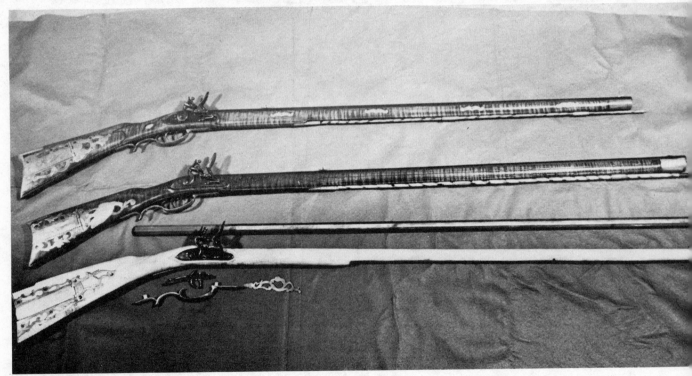

Home gunsmith Roy Miller rebuilt top rifle from parts that were salvaged from junk gun; middle rifle and the unassembled gun at the bottom built from scratch material around his shop.

The rifling bench used by Miller in his home work shop. Each gun he produces is truly a custom rifle.

THE TERM, PROFESSIONAL GUNSMITH, is used generally in describing a competent gunsmith who turns out quality work on a commercial basis. But what terminology do you use to describe a gunsmith of equal ability who works for personal pleasure? Obviously the terms, hobby gunsmith, amateur gunsmith and similar phrases fall short in their accepted meaning.

Such is the dilemma in trying to find the correct term to use in describing Roy M. Miller of Camden, Alabama, for the quality of his work is professional in every meaning of the word. Instead of making a good living as a professional gunsmith, he is a fulltime Presbyterian minister! He readily admits that his hobby usually takes a little explanation at ministerial association meetings, but he sees no conflict in the two professions. To top it all off, Roy Miller confines his gunsmithing to building and rebuilding muzzleloading rifles.

He began his gunsmithing training back in the later 1930s under William Schreckengost in Putneyville, Pennsylvania. Schreckengost was a well known local gunsmith and rifle maker who, although in his 90s at the time, was still sharp of mind and had a steady hand. A guided tour of the South Pacific during World War II as a Marine with a side excursion to Korea interrupted Reverend Miller's gunsmith training. After leaving the service, he entered the ministry. Upon graduation, he was assigned a church in Camden, in the very heart of some of the best hunting country in the South. It was not long before he

revived his gunsmithing interest, with the emphasis on muzzleloaders.

There are numerous muzzleloading rifles in various stages of ruin. Restoring these fine old rifles is a rewarding hobby both from a personal satisfaction standpoint and commercially, if you choose the latter. The stock, lock mechanism and decorative furniture restoration requires a maximum amount of elbow grease, with minimum tooling. The part that stumps most hobbyists is the barrel. If the rifling is worn badly, little can be done except to replace the barrel with a better one, either old or new, or ship the barrel to a commercial firm and have the rifling recut to a larger caliber.

Miller decided to take the big step about three years ago and, with the able assistance of Lee Davis, a local machinist and hunting buff, he designed and built his own complete reboring and rifling machines. He since has restored about a dozen shot-out barrels and made several barrels from scratch. One made-from-scratch flintlock is his favorite turkey rifle. If you have ever hunted wild turkey, even with modern equipment, you can appreciate the skill it takes to connect with a flintlock.

Old barrels turn up in a variety of places. Many are found clinging to the shattered remains of a rifle in somebody's attic, others in the corner of antique shops or under the benches of gun shops, gathering dust. One barrel picked up and restored by Roy Miller was doing duty as a fence

This close-up of the barrel reaming fixture shows the two self-aligning pillow block bearings. Large wheel powers pump, chain powers the reamer.

The ornate patch box on Miller's favorite turkey rifle features a brass-inlaid turkey above hinge.

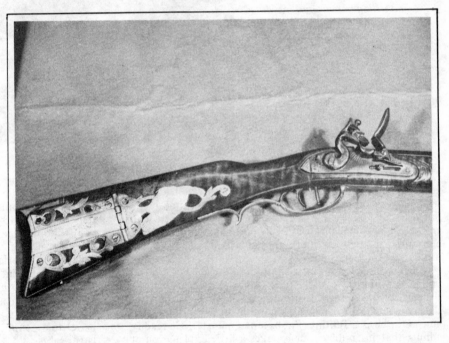

post! The major task in such cases is getting the barrel cleaned up and ready to be reworked.

The first step is to see what is down its throat. More often than not, these old barrels carry a full charge that has been down there all of those years and is ready to spew forth and give you a severe headache, if you happen to be looking down the bore when it lets go. Keep your head and other body components away from the muzzle until you are 101 percent sure that the barrel is not loaded.

To check the barrel, a long wooden dowel is needed, but a metal rod can be substituted. Push the dowel or rod down the bore as far as possible and mark the rod at the muzzle. Remove the rod and lay it alongside of the barrel. The end

of the rod should reach fully to the rear of the barrel when the mark is realigned with the muzzle. If not, chances are that the barrel is loaded and care must be taken to prevent a discharge. Quite often, dirt and a thousand other things will prevent the rod from going all the way down what is actually an unloaded bore, but take no chances. Treat it as loaded!

Lightweight penetrating oil poured down the bore and allowed to stand for a day is the best medicine in rendering the powder safe, but there always is the chance that the bullet will stop the oil's progress and prevent it from reaching the powder.

The next step is to remove the breech plug which closes the bore at the rear. Usually these are odd in shape and you

Miller's reaming fixture is driven electrically, the long
threaded rod running parallel to base is the lead screw.

will have to make or modify a wrench to remove the plug.
Tapping the wrench with a hammer, exerting snap pressure,
adding penetrating oil to the plug threads and a little strong
language helps in getting the stubborn plugs out.

Once in a while, a plug will simply refuse to budge. In
this case, heat is the only answer, which presents a problem
if the barrel is loaded. Secure the barrel firmly in a heavy
vise and, with a hand propane torch, heat the breech plug
hot enough that you cannot hold your finger against it, but
no hotter. Pour cold water on the breech plug to rapidly
cool it, then try the wrench.

The heat expands the metal and the cold water contracts
it rapidly to break the rust seal. This usually solves the
problem, but if the plug still will not budge, it will be
necessary to carefully heat the outside of the barrel at the
rear to the same temperature. Pour a little cold water
directly on the breech plug and try the wrench, while the
barrel is hot and expanded and the breech plug is contracted. This will do the trick, but be careful not to get the
barrel red hot and fire the load.

Once the breech plug is out, remove the load, if one is
present, and scrub the bore with a good solvent and a stiff,
close-fitting brass bore brush. Hot soapy water will help
dissolve old powder residue.

If the bore is still dark after all of your scrubbing, rein-
stall the breech plug hand tight and pour a mixture of ten
percent nitric acid down the bore until it is completely
filled. Allow this to stand for two minutes, pour it out,
remove the breech plug and flood the bore and breech plug
with clean running water to remove the acid. It is surprising
how much crud and rust the acid will remove without

damaging the bore. One or two applications of the acid
solution will usually provide a clean bright bore.

The rifling now can be inspected and, if still sharp, the
rifle can be rebuilt with no more work on the bore. Before
you make the final decision, take a close look at the rifling
at the muzzle. Dirty ramrods carrying sand and powder
residue can wear the rifling at the muzzle badly. This will
destroy the accuracy even if the rest of the bore is sharp. If
this is the case or the rifling is worn and pitted, it will be
necessary to rebore and rerifle the barrel.

The remains of the old rifling must be removed completely as the first step in rerifling. Roy Miller uses one of
the oldest, yet one of the most efficient methods available.
This is the armory reamer which is nothing more than a
long square section of tool steel, sharp on one edge and
backed with a length of hardwood. The hardwood strip
increases the reamer diameter and presses the edge of the
reamer against the sides of the bore to make the reamer cut.

After the first cutting pass, a slip of paper is placed
between the wood and the square of steel to increase the
diameter of the reamer assembly and make it take the next
cut. You can machine these armory reamers from tool steel,
but an old, worn square hand file will do the same job
after the file teeth are ground off and the sides honed to
razor sharpness with a good slip stone. The original taper of
the rebuilt file guides the reamer.

There are two ways to ream the bore: the push stroke
and the pull stroke. If the pull stroke is used, the reamer is
silver soldered to a solid rod with the small and tapered end
of the reamer toward the rod. The bore is oiled lightly and
the reamer pulled through, as it is rotated. The bore behind

With barrel securely positioned in the holding
fixture, the square armory reamer enters the barrel.
The pan underneath catches oil used during rifling.

the reamer after it passes provides ample room for the chips. The disadvantage of the pull stroke is that the rod size must be smaller than the existing bore size. The push stroke uses a hollow rod with the heavier back end of the reamer fitted to it and holes drilled in the hollow rod just behind the reamer. Oil under pressure flows through the hollow rod and out the holes, pushing the chips away from the reamer's cutting edge.

Miller uses the push stroke with an old oil pump from an aircraft engine providing the pressure and catches the used oil in a pan underneath the barrel. The metal chips settle to the bottom of the pan and the excess oil flows out an overflow pipe at the end of the pan, then through a filter to be reused again. The reamer and the hollow rod are rotated at around 400 rpms as the barrel is held securely in a special fixture that can slide back and forth on the machine's bed. The barrel is fed forward against the reamer by a lead screw passing through the barrel holding fixture and the system works identically to that of a regular lathe. An engagement lever on the side, hooked to a split nut on the barrel holding fixture, allows the barrel's forward movement to be halted by disengaging the split nut from the lead screw if any trouble is encountered during the reaming.

The slow feed and the moderate speed allows the reamer to produce a clean and slightly burnished finish in the bore. After the original rifling has been completely removed and all pits are eliminated, the operator can stop the reaming and begin the rifling operation as muzzleloaders are not limited to exact bore or caliber specifications. In fact, if

you want a .391 caliber rifle, all that is required is to make a bullet mold of the same caliber. Usually however, the calibers are .32, .36, .40, .45 and on up to the big .70 caliber and even larger in some cases. A lead slug pushed through the new clean bore and miked will provide the land diameter measurement and allow the operator to decide if additional passes with the reamer are necessary to reach a desired caliber.

With the bore reaming finished, the barrel is removed from the reaming fixture and installed in the rifling fixture. The barrel goes through the hollow headstock spindle and is centered at both of its ends by adjusting four screws that are located at each end of the spindle. The screws bear against the barrel and serve as the chuck to hold the barrel secure during the rifling. The number of grooves to be cut is decided and the indexing plate at the rear of the headstock assembly is set for the first cut. By selecting the correct series of holes in the index plate, any desired number of grooves can be cut in the barrel. In use, the first index hole is selected, a groove cut and the plate rotated into position to the next selected index hole and locked in place for the second cut. This is repeated until all of the grooves have been cut.

The pitch or twist of the rifling is specified as one complete turn of the bullet in a certain number of inches. There are quite a few different ways to achieve the spiral twist, but one of the simplest was invented by a gunsmith named Howard Schley and is usually referred to as "cam bar rifling."

A long bar is attached at one of its ends by a bolt on the rifling machine base at the headstock. The other end is supported by another bar affixed to the tail end of the rifling machine at a right angle to the machine. The loose end of the cam bar can be moved on the fixed right angle bar to create any angle. However, it is locked at one selected angle during the rifling operation. Attached to the cam bar by rollers on one of its ends is another bar to which is bolted a flatrack gear that can slide back and forth across the carriage of the rifling machine. A pinion gear, mounted on the carriage with its teeth engaged in the rack gear, is attached to a shaft supported in bearings. The shaft is drilled and tapped at its front end to accept the threaded rear of the rifling rod. Sliding the rack gear back and forth under the pinion gear causes the pinion gear to rotate which, in turn, rotates the rifling rod.

During the rifling operation the carriage, with its pinion gear's teeth engaged in the rack gear, is pulled away from the barrel toward the rear of the machine. The cam bar, being angled away from the rifling machine, pulls the attached rack gear from under the pinion gear and outward toward the extended cam bar. This causes the pinion gear to rotate at a steady rate as the carriage moves toward the rear of the machine and away from the barrel. The rifling rod and the cutter, being attached to the pinion gear shaft, is rotated and pulled through the bore at a constant rate thereby producing the spiral rifling cut and forming the groove.

By increasing the angle of the cam bar away from the rifling machine, the rack gear is moved faster as the carriage and attached rifling rod is pulled toward the rear which in turn increases the pitch of the rifling. Decreasing the angle of the cam bar will decrease the pitch of the rifling, as the rack gear is moved less as the carriage and rifle rod move toward the rear. If a gain twist is desired, all that is necessary is to replace the straight cam bar with a curved cam bar.

The rifling head itself is a simple affair consisting only of

Carriage assembly of rifling machine showing rack and pinion gears. Note the rollers that are attached to cam bar and hand hold top bar.

a section of rod slightly less in diamater than the bore with a cutter bit on one side and a strip of hardwood on the opposite side. The wood increases the rifling head diameter and presses the cutter bit against the walls of the bore. To make a rifling cut, a slip of paper is placed between the wood and the rifling head, thereby increasing the overall diameter and causing the cutter to bite into the metal and cut the groove as the rifling head is pulled through the bore. The width of the groove is determined by the width of the cutter bit. The depth of the groove is increased by the addition of other slips of paper between the wood and the rifling head. Roy Miller prefers brown wheat paper, but substitutes common cigarette paper when the former is not available. A thin coat of glue keeps the additional slips of paper together.

In actual operation, the first cut is made through the barrel and the rifling head allowed to exit from the barrel. The wood and paper shim is removed and a cloth patch soaked in light cutting oil is placed on the front end of the rifling head and is pushed back through the bore. This cleans the bore of all metal chips and positions the rifling rod and the cutter assembly for the next pass. The index plate is rotated and locked in place which, in turn, rotates and aligns the barrel for the next groove. The wood and the paper shim are repositioned in the rifling head and the cut is made to produce the second groove. This is repeated until all of the selected grooves have had one pass with the wood and one paper shim.

A second paper shim is added and all grooves receive the second and deepening cut. This is continued with additional paper shims added until full groove depth is achieved. The barrel is then removed from the fixture, lapped and is ready to be placed back on the rifle.

The boring and rifling of an average barrel consumes around four hours on Roy's equipment. It is by no means a modern tape-fed automatic rifling machine, but it does produce first class barrels capable of good accuracy. Harry Pope, the famous barrelmaker, used an old converted lathe worth less than $200 to produce barrels that were master-pieces, proving that the man and not necessarily the equipment determines quality. — *Ralph T. Walker*

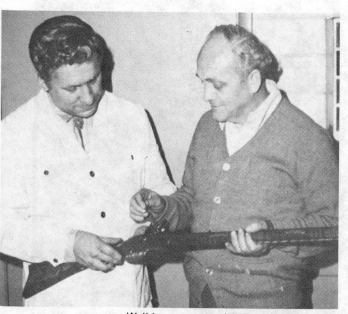

Well known gunsmith Ralph Walker (left) examines one of Miller's custom-built muzzleloaders, as he explains lock work.

CHAPTER 23

CARE, CLEANING & BLACK POWDER

If Cleanliness Is Next To Godliness, Muzzleloaders Should Create Believers!

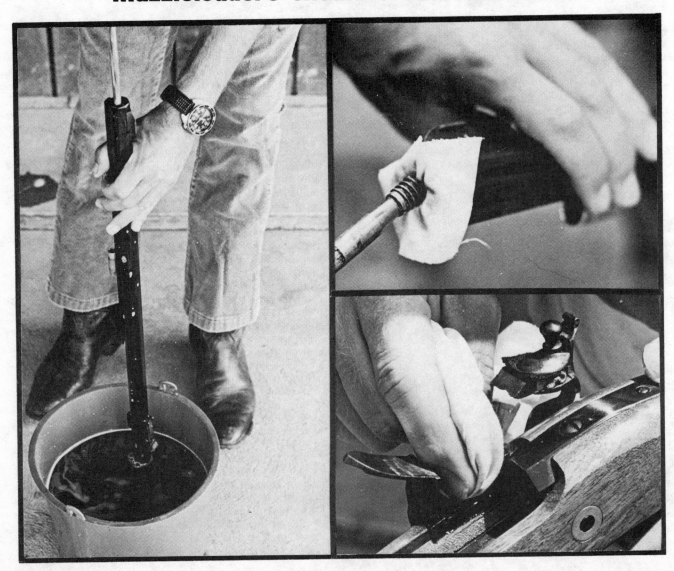

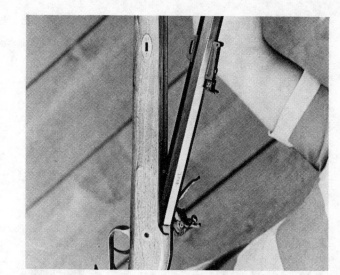

With wedge out, barrel can be lifted free of the stock to disengage the hooked tang at rear of breech

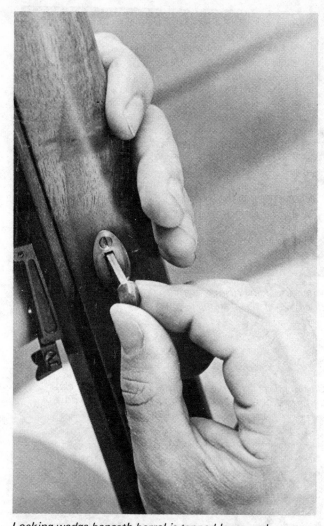

Locking wedge beneath barrel is tapped loose and withdrawn as preliminary in disassembling certain designs, so as to protect woodwork during cleaning.

HERE AND THERE in this book we have touched upon the subject of cleaning and caring for the different forms of black powder rifles, revolvers and shotguns. However, little has been written to give an in-depth description of the cleaning procedures that will keep your favorite charcoal burner in top condition for years to come.

As a starter, let's take a look at black powder, itself. As you know, black powder is extremely corrosive and the reasons behind this are simple.

Corrosion of metal is actually an oxidation process, the hydrogen molecules of the metal's surface combining with the oxygen. This dehydrogenation commonly appears in the form of hydrated ferric oxide, or in plain English, good ol' red rust. When left unchecked for any length of time, this surface rusting action penetrates deeper and deeper into the metal.

Black powder presently being manufactured consists of approximately 11.85 percent sulphur, 13.51 percent carbon and 74.64 percent saltpeter, the latter being the propellant's corrosive ingredient. More properly designated potassium nitrate, saltpeter provides the oxygen needed to enable the confined powder to burn, or better yet, ignite and burn fast enough to cause propelling pressures.

Chemically, potassium nitrate — KNO_3 — is made up of three atoms of oxygen for each atom of potassium and nitrogen. Roger Bacon and earlier chemists seeking the discovery of an explosive mixture found potassium nitrate in the form of cyrstalline salt that had resulted from nitrification of the chemicals in arable soil.

Loaded and fired in a muzzleloading gun, black powder leaves a considerable amount of residue inside the barrel and chamber area. Although the majority of the potassium nitrate is consumed during the burning of the powder charge, there is always an extremely small amount left clinging to the barrel walls. Remembering that potassium nitrate is actually a salt and that salt attracts moisture, visualize the condition of a muzzleloader's bore, if left uncleaned for several weeks, months, or even a year.

Too often a fine reproduction as well as beautiful old original guns are subjected to such treatment from thoughtless owners too lazy to take a few minutes to clean such guns after a day of shooting. It makes little difference if the gun was fired once or a hundred times; the result will be the same, unless time is taken to clean the gun before putting it away, possibly a totally ruined bore.

It's not unusual to get carried away during a shooting session and realize suddenly that you've overstayed your visit. Upon your arrival back at the homestead, you find yourself in a spot: To please the little lady and rush into the shower for that dinner date or to thoroughly clean that pet benchrester.

With the rapidly growing number of new moisture displacing lubricants and special black powder solvents available today, luckily incidents like this can be avoided.

Bucheimer's black powder solvent and Black-Solve are only two of the rapidly growing lines of special black powder solvents that now are available. When presented with the decision of either taking valuable time to clean the bore on a black powder gun or wait until a more convenient time, it now is a quick chore to spray a corrosion-preventing coat of the new solvents into the dirty bore. With the solvent preventing the oxidation process from taking place, cleaning can now be put off for as much as a week. One thing is certain, however, and that is the necessity of cleaning out the gummy residue before the next firing session.

A number of cleaning solvents, including the previously mentioned two, make some of the cleaning easier and less

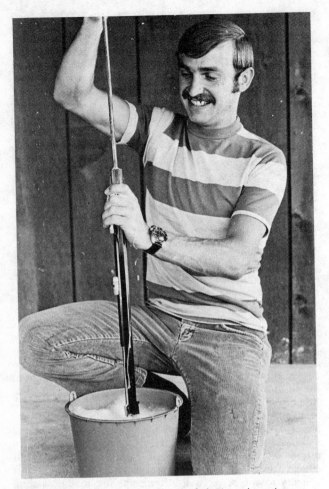

When design permits, breech end of the barrel can be dunked into the bucket of hot, soapy water and rod pumps the solution in and out through the nipple.

Water-displacing rust-preventive compound can be sprayed over the cleaning patches in the final stages.

Cleaning jags usually are furnished with the gun, can be turned onto end of ramrod to pull patch up, down.

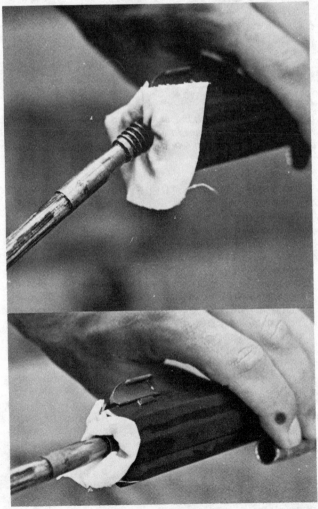

messy, but when used in confined areas, they occasionally leave a strong odor and give off some eye-stinging fumes. For this reason, the majority of today's black powder shooters not having an open, well aired place to clean their guns prefer to use a simple solution of hot soapy water.

When mixing this solution, the hotter the water the better it will clean. The soap — although some shooters prefer one particular brand over the other — can be of the general dish washing variety found at any super market. If lots of suds are your thing, squirt into an empty plastic pail a fairly generous amount of detergent, then fill with the desired amount of hot water.

Of all the muzzleloading rifles I have shot, the easiest to clean is the Thompson/Center Hawken. The hooked breech system on this particular gun allows the barrel to be completely removed within the matter of a few seconds. A wedge through the forearm on this rifle's half-stock also travels through a rectangular slotted loop located on the bottom flat of the octagon barrel. By tapping this wedge to the right, it disengages the loop and frees the barrel from the stock.

The breech plug on the Thompson/Center rifle is in the form of an upward swept hook. This hook fits into a recess located on the barrel tang; with the forward portion of the barrel free from the stock it can be removed by lifting it from the rest of the rifle and allowing the hook to disengage from this recess.

Completely removed from the stock and lock work, the barrel now can be submerged into the soapy water solution. A cleaning method I find quite effective is to place the vent hole end of the barrel into the bucket of water, place a cleaning patch on the ramrod cleaning jag and start pumping. As the ramrod and patch are drawn toward the muzzle, it causes a vacuum which, in turn, causes a fresh supply of hot soapy water to be drawn in through the submerged vent hole. After a few pumps, I find it easy to draw the solution the entire length of the barrel, for a fresh barrel full of cleaning solution with each pump. This system of cleaning hooked breech guns is very effective and results in about as clean a barrel as can be obtained.

Unfortunately, not all rifles and muskets have the hooked breech and cleaning is a little more difficult. Even without a barrel that is removed easily like the Hawken's, there still are easy ways to clean the majority of the muzzleloading rifles and shotguns without having to remove the barrel at all.

If you have lots of time and plenty of cleaning patches, the solvents will do an excellent job of removing powder fouling from not overly dirty bores. For really dirty and built up bores, however, the hot soapy water solution is hard to beat.

A simple but effective way of cleaning the barrels on percussion caplock rifles is to slip a piece of neoprene surgical tubing over the nipple, then drop the other end into a bucket of the soapy water solution. By pumping the ramrod in the same manner as mentioned earlier, the solution will be drawn through the tubing and into the barrel.

Of course, the tubing should form a tight fit to prevent possible leakage of the soap and water onto the stock. Although a small amount of the soapy solution that I commonly use has yet to have any effect on the stock's finish — for the short period of time it is on the wood — there is a possibility that a few of the detergents available could ruin that beautiful high-gloss shine, so be careful not to slosh any out of the muzzle.

Now and then the pumping of the dry bore won't cause enough vacuum to draw the soapy water through the tubing. If you've ever had to use a water pump, you should be familiar with the term priming the pump, which is what you'll have to do to get the water flowing from the bucket and into the barrel. To prime the barrel, for the sake of terming this step, pour a small amount of the water into the muzzle before inserting the cleaning rod and patch, which could also be dipped into the solution first. It is a good practice to place a piece of absorbent cloth around the muzzle to prevent water from running back down onto the stock.

Scrubbing with soap and water should be followed by a thorough rinsing with clean, hot water. This removes the soap film and the surface of the metal dries quickly. As soon as the barrel is dry it should receive a thin coat of moisture displacing oil, such as WD-40 or G96 Gun Treatment. As an extra precaution against rust in the bore, I

Bucheimer's Black Powder Solvent can be sprayed down the bore as a hasty means of temporary protection or after a full course of cleaning for long-term protection.

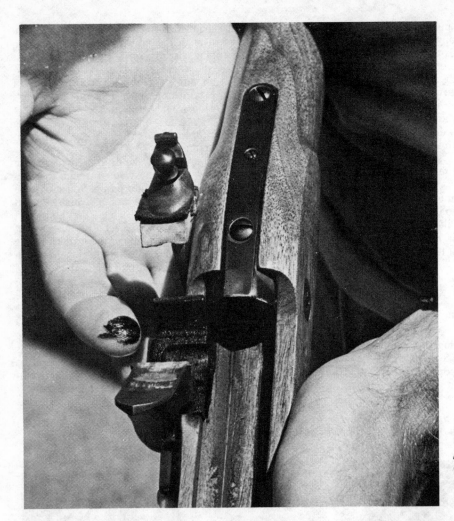

Flintlocks can build up heavy fouling deposits in the priming pan, requiring thorough cleaning and maintenance in this area for protection.

usually follow the drying with a patch soaked in Hoppe's No. 9 solvent run the entire length of the barrel several times. This is followed by several dry patches, then yet another patch sprayed with one of the super lubricant/rust-preventers, such as WD-40.

With the exception of a few late 1700 and early 1800 duellers, few single-shot pistols employed the hook breech. For the most part, these pistols having a caplock can be cleaned in the same basic manner as rifles and shotguns with conventional breech plug. As with the rifles produced by Thompson/Center, however, the firm also uses the hooked breech on their Patriot pistol. The short nine-inch-barrel on this pistol can be totally submerged in a bucket of water, making for easy cleaning.

Unless the barrels can be removed from flintlock rifles, shotguns and pistols, the cleaning of these is a little more time consuming. One of the best methods is to place the bucket of soapy solution near the muzzle, dip the patched cleaning jag into it, then make several complete up and down strokes through the barrel. The patch then is dipped into soapy water again and the process repeated; it may be necessary to change patches after several repetitions to make certain that the bore is getting cleaned thoroughly.

When using a water solution to clean flintlock guns, care should be taken to make sure that some of this water doesn't slosh out of the flash pan's vent hole and onto the stock. It is possible that even the slightest amount of moisture seeping between the metal and wood could result in the bottom of the barrel or the inside of the lock work rusting unnoticed.

Undoubtedly some shooters prefer one particular oil or grease over another, but for the most part, today's scientifically developed gun oils and lubes are just about equally suited for any cleaning and preserving needs. Once a favorite of the black powder shooting crowd of quite a few years ago, sperm oil still is available from several muzzle-loading accessory distributors and gunsmithing houses. Brownell's of Montezuma, Iowa, is just one source from which sperm oil is readily available. When using this natural preservative rendered flesh-up from the sperm whale, it is a good practice to place the oil in the refrigerator overnight to allow the fats to harden; the pure oil then can be poured off and this is what should be used.

Kept clean and free of moisture, metal parts on a muzzleloading rifle, musket, pistol or shotgun will last indefinitely. Wood, on the other hand, will deteriorate rather quickly — at least much faster than the metal — if not well cared for. Oil seepage from the barrel and lock work is one problem that causes discolored and damaged stocks. I never apply more oil than is necessary to coat the metal surfaces in question. Excess oil won't be absorbed by the metal and can only take one other course, running into crevices that usually lead to one area or another of the wooden stock.

Even stocks need an occasional cleaning; the powder fouling that commonly occurs around the nipple or flash pan vent must be wiped off continually or eventually it will ruin the finish in that area of the stock and could possibly soak into the wood and discolor it. Using a dry lather, a mild soap and very little water, the stock can be easily cleaned with the aid of a soft cloth and a soft bristled brush for hard to reach angles and checkering. Wiped clean, a little paste wax and gentle buffing will result in a beautiful luster.

Of all the black powder guns, cap and ball revolvers win the title of being the easiest to clean and care for. Almost all of the replicas and reproduction revolvers presently being sold are generally of two designs, either following the pattern of the open frame Colt or the solid frame Remington. Both of these guns are easily broken down to allow thorough cleaning of each and every part.

To dismantle the Colt, a wedge located just forward of the cylinder is tapped to the left, the hammer is placed at half-cock and the cylinder is rotated until the loading lever comes in contact with the metal separating two of the chambers. By applying pressure on the lever the barrel assembly will disengage the remainder of the percussion revolver. With this removed, the cylinder freely slips off of the cylinder pin or arbor; for general cleaning, this is as far as you should have to break the gun down.

The solid-framed Remington-designed revolvers are almost equally as easy to dismantle. Dropping the loading lever down to where it lies at about a forty-five-degree angle from the barrel, the cylinder pin can be pulled forward. The loading lever is then placed back to its original position and by placing the hammer at half-cock the cylinder should rotate out of the encircling frame.

Of the two types of revolvers, I still find the Colt-patterned guns the easiest to clean. The majority of this cleaning is done to the barrel and cylinder; the frame and grips usually can be wiped clean with a soft cloth and a little oil applied to the metal should be adequate. The barrel and cylinder, however, require a much more thorough cleaning to remove the powder residue left from firing.

The feature that I like best about the Colt-type revolver is the barrel being separate from the frame. This allows the barrel to be scrubbed from the chamber end. Again hot soapy water is about as good as anything for cleaning out residue left from an afternoon's shooting session, but occasionally a really dirty barrel may require a little more. Recently Armite Laboratories of Los Angeles, California, introduced an amazing new bore cleaning agent known as Gun-Soap. My first impression of the product upon opening the glass jar-type container was that it reminded me of lime jelly, if there is such a thing.

The barrel on a Navy Arms' Colt Navy replica that I picked up for little or nothing looked as if it hadn't been cleaned, since it was purchased by its neglectful owner several years earlier. It was almost impossible to make out the rifling because of the built-up powder foulings.

Dismantling the .36 caliber revolver I soaked the cylinder and barrel in a hot soapy water solution for twenty or thirty minutes. Using a wire brush and the Gun-Soap,

Bucheimer's Black Powder Solvent is sprayed liberally over the pan and frizzen as preliminary to cleaning.

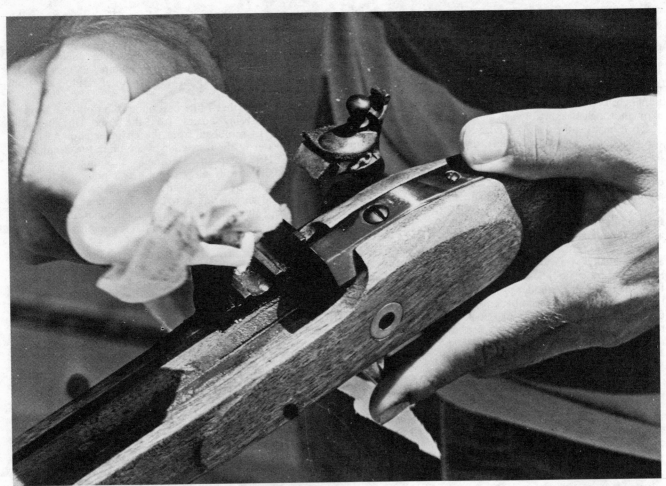

Cleaning rags, as well as old toothbrushes, can be used in removing solvent-loosened fouling residue in pan.

With cleaning completed, breech hook is re-inserted under the tang and wedge is replaced to reassemble gun.

along with a little elbow grease, the bore soon was returned to nearly new condition. Although I haven't tried the new cleaning solvent on the barrels of any of my muzzleloading rifles, I personally believe that it would do wonders for a rifle that has become heavily fouled.

The nipples of a percussion revolver usually are one of the little areas that consume a large amount of time when being cleaned. A fast and simple remedy for this is to use an old toothbrush to scrub out residue accumulated in the numerous machined grooves surrounding the nipples.

Again, all cleaning with a detergent and water solution should be followed by a good rinsing in hot and clear water. As an extra precaution to preventing rust, I often find it a good idea to place the washed revolver parts in a warmed oven — 250 degrees or so — to assure that all of the water is completely dried. With Colt-type revolvers this usually consists of just the barrel assembly and the cylinder. On Remington reproductions, however, it is advisable to first remove the wooden grips before placing the rest of the gun into the hot oven; removing the grips before the entire cleaning job is even more advisable.

Reasoning behind the removal of the Remington design revolver's grips before cleaning is to allow the barrel to be scrubbed with water without damaging the finish on the wood. Unlike the Colt replicas, the barrels on these pistols do not separate from the frame. Instead, they must be scrubbed from the muzzle end and, if completely submerged, the internal parts will have to be lubricated after each cleaning. With the removal of the grips, however, the majority of the internal parts can be reached with a pen oiler by the simple removal of the trigger guard.

Never reassemble any gun that has been cleaned in water until each and every part has been oiled or, as is the case with the cylinder pins on a cap and ball revolver, greased.

It's not uncommon to run into an occasional shooter who is experiencing all sorts of trouble in cocking a cap and ball revolver. Part of the time this can be attributed to the lack of enough clearance between the chamber mouth and the breech of the barrel or the lack of lubrication — grease — on the arbor or cylinder pin. There are all sorts of fancy special purpose greases that will work nicely, but one that I find to be just as suitable and much cheaper is regular automotive grease.

Muzzleloaders have a way of mellowing with age, especially if they are well taken care of and cleaned regularly. Remember, it's nearly impossible to over-clean a black powder gun, but one that isn't cleaned properly is just as bad off as one that isn't cleaned at all. — *Toby Bridges*

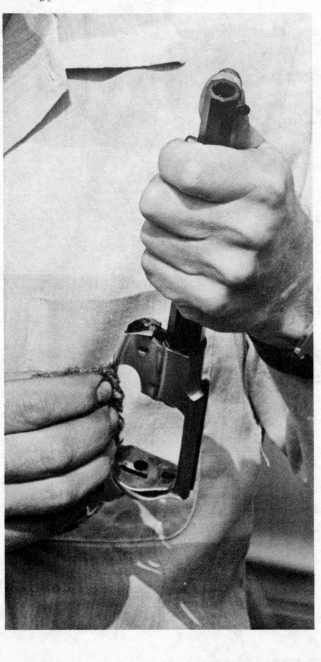

Since guns of the Remington pattern are not readily capable of separating barrel and frame, care must be taken, as discussed here, to prevent damage to the lockwork from water or fouling.

CHAPTER 24

THE LORE OF LEAD

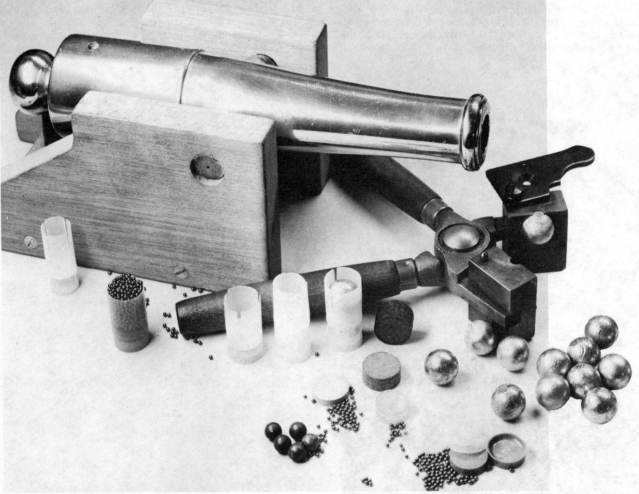

Lyman mould for .672'' round balls, together with 12-gauge plastic wad assemblies is used in firing this antique bronze cannon with bore of that size.

Facts And Figures On A Metal Without Which Shooting Might Have Been Delayed For Centuries!

Although round balls and Minie projectiles can be bought in most of the common sizes, apparatus to make them yourself is neither overly expensive nor difficult to use with highly satisfactory results.

Let us pause briefly to give thanks for the existence of lead. For that humble metallic element has simplified the gunner's problems down through the centuries since the invention of firearms; aiding the shooting arts to an extent that few appreciate properly.

There's an old folk saying to the gist that, "you never miss the water till the well runs dry." In much the same manner, you start recognizing the many useful virtues of lead right about at the time you begin trying to find an adequate substitute for it. This has become quite evident in certain areas of waterfowling, due to the fact that lead shotgun pellets remain on hard bottoms beneath shallow water to be ingested by the bottom-feeding species of ducks. This, in turn, causes the loss of serious quantities of the birds, due to lead poisoning.

The best replacement for lead shot that has been found to date has consisted of pellets formed from soft iron or steel. Sadly, it's far from satisfactory. The steel is so much harder that it tends to be rough on the bores of shotguns and it's quite a bit lighter than lead, volume for volume, so that pellets of the same diameter won't travel as far or retain their velocity as well. In order to get comparable performance, steel pellets must be of larger diameter and that automatically decrees that you can't get as many pellets into the same amount of space and this, in turn, cuts down seriously on your chances of making an effective hit.

This discussion has little concern with steel shot as a replacement for lead but it is mentioned by way of pointing out the admirable virtues of that heavy gray metal. What are these virtues? It is available in generous quantities and at relatively modest cost. It is heavy and dense, that is, it has a high specific gravity – of which, more later. It is easy to form into desired shapes since it has a low melting point. It is comparatively soft, which makes it adapt easily to the shape of the lands and grooves of a rifled barrel, without danger of damaging the rifling. Being soft, it has consider-

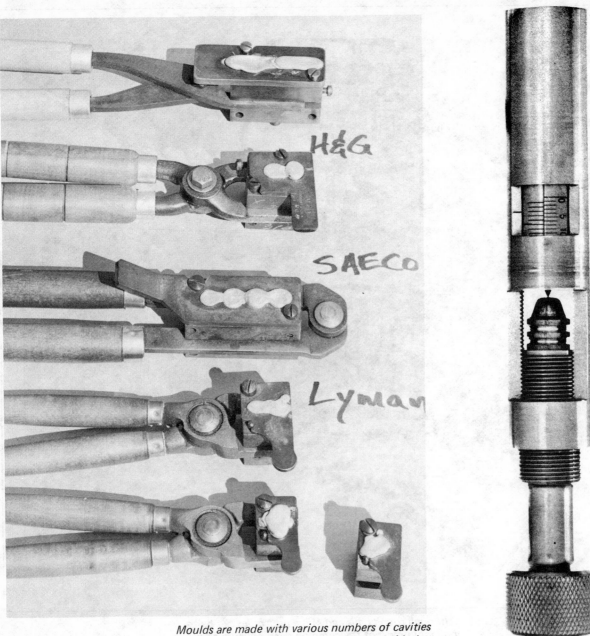

Moulds are made with various numbers of cavities to expedite production. Three lower moulds, by Lyman, have 1, 2, and 4 cavities. Saeco also has a hardness tester for measuring this in samples.

able capability for upsetting — flattening — at the time of impact so as to increase its striking effectiveness.

Lead has been known and used since ancient times. Unlike copper, it is rarely if ever found in the native state as a fairly pure metal. However, lead ores and the technique for smelting them have been a part of mankind's technology for over two thousand years.

The old Romans were well acquainted with lead, calling it by the name of plumbum, from which stems the modern chemist's symbol for that element, Pb. Likewise, this is the root-word for other terms such as plumbing — in which lead was and still is used extensively — plumb bob and so on.

Specific gravity is the term used to denote the comparative weight of a given volume of a material in relation to an equal volume of water. In the example of lead, it's about 11.37 times as heavy as an equal volume of water. To fairly precise specs, that makes a single cubic inch of lead scale out at 0.4105 pounds or 2873.5 grains, since there are 7000

grains in one avoirdupois pound. To establish comfortable familiarity with the avoirdupois weight system, it can be noted that is the same one in which your bathroom scale is graduated.

If you have a good supply of pencils and scratch paper, plus patience and curiosity, you can work out the weight for a round lead ball of any given diameter with the information given here. The final bit of data — if your third-grade arithmetic is getting rusty — is that you determine the volume of a sphere by multiplying the diameter cubed times .5236. To take an easy example, a caliber .50 round ball would be .5 x .5 x .5= .125; this, times .5236 gives us .06545 cubic inch as the volume. Since lead weighs 2873.5 grains per cubic inch: 2873.5 x .06545 = 188.070575 grains as the probable, approximate weight for the caliber .50 round ball.

Admittedly, predicting the weight to a millionth of a grain is a bit more precision than that for which most of us

NAME OF ELEMENT	CHEMICAL SYMBOL	SPECIFIC GRAVITY	MELTING POINT °F	°C
Aluminum	Al	2.70	1218	660
Antimony	Sb	6.62	1168	630.5
Arsenic	As	5.72	1550	817
Barium	Ba	3.5	1550	817
Bismuth	Bi	9.8	522	271.3
Cadmium	Cd	8.65	321	610
Copper	Cu	8.96	1981	1083
Gallium	Ga	5.91	86	30
Gold	Au	19.3	1945	1063
Iron	Fe	7.86	2774	1536
Lead	Pb	11.4	622	327.4
Mercury	Hg	13.58	-38.4	-39.5
Osmium	Os	22.6	4892	2700
Silver	Ag	10.53	1762	961
Tin	Sn	7.30	450	232
Zinc	Zn	7.14	786	420

NOTE: Some of the entries in this chart are obviously unsuited for use in bullets, but they were included as being of possible interest. For example, if osmium were cheap and plentiful, with a lower melting point, it would make a wonderful bullet!

This photo of a Lyman mould illustrates principle of such devices. Sprue cutter has just been driven over and solidified ball is ready to be tapped out.

might feel a burning need, but it's handy to have the basic information available, where you can find it when needed.

In actual practice, the textbook figures often don't work out quite that closely. For one thing, you can encounter a rather broad band of disparity as to the exact specific gravity of lead in the first place. The quoted figure of 11.37 as the specific gravity, along with 0.4105 pounds as the weight of one cubic inch of lead, is taken from an excellent work entitled Complete Guide to Handloading, by the late Philip B. Sharpe. My high school chemistry textbook, circa 1936, pegs the specific gravity of lead at 11.24 times the weight of water. A periodic chart of the atoms, appearing in The Random House Dictionary of the English Language, offers the figure of 11.4 as its entry for the sweepstakes.

I once quizzed a friend who works for the Bureau of Standards, in Washington, D.C., as to his explanation for such apparent paradoxes, pointing out that you can find about the same number of figures for the specific gravity and melting point as the number of reference works you consult. He looked harried for a moment, shrugged and said, "The heck of it is, every time you try to work it out, you come up with a slightly different answer."

I rather doubt if the Bureau of Standards would care to consider that an official pronouncement, but I offer it as a sort of pre-explanation if you find that other reference sources do not agree with the figures quoted here.

As metals go, lead is a friendly sort of soul, happily entering into partnership with numerous other elements to

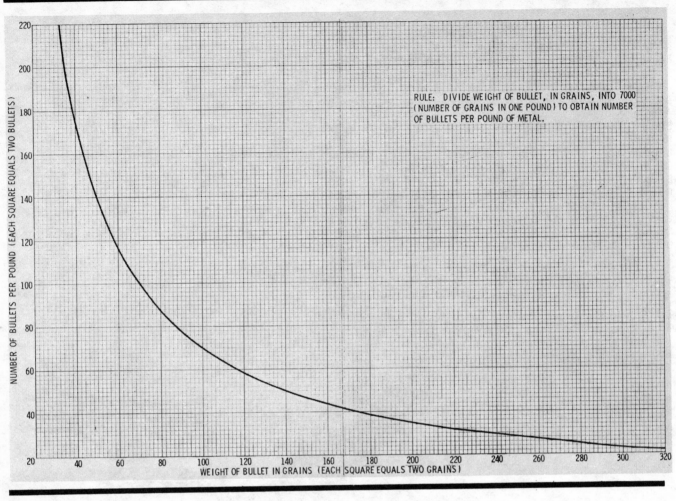

The chart shows axes labeled:
NUMBER OF BULLETS PER POUND (EACH SQUARE EQUALS TWO BULLETS)
WEIGHT OF BULLET IN GRAINS (EACH SQUARE EQUALS TWO GRAINS)

RULE: DIVIDE WEIGHT OF BULLET, IN GRAINS, INTO 7000 (NUMBER OF GRAINS IN ONE POUND) TO OBTAIN NUMBER OF BULLETS PER POUND OF METAL.

This handy chart tells how many bullets of a given weight one can cast from a pound of lead or alloy.

form compounds. It is most cordial toward oxygen and it will oxidize rapidly upon exposure to air, regardless of temperature. As it turns out, this dull, gray coating of lead oxide is extremely durable and resistant to the effects of weather and climate. It would not be too far off the mark of characterize lead as "the self-painting metal." Iron, as all of us are ruefully aware, oxidizes into the familiar red coating of rust, but this loosens and falls away, exposing fresh interior metal to further oxidizing so that, after a time, there's nothing left but rust. It's this durable trait of lead that has preserved century-old musket balls and Minie projectiles so they can be turned up in an amazing state of preservation in sites such as Civil War battlefields. Likewise, it's the source of the duck-poisoning problem previously mentioned.

We have noted that lead melts easily; the approximate melting point being 621 degrees on the Fahrenheit scale or 327 degrees Centigrade. Most combustible materials will burn at a flame temperature which exceeds the melting point of lead by a comfortable margin, qualifying that useful metal as one of the most convenient of all casting materials.

Lead, as we've noted, combines chemically with several other elements. Likewise, it mixes physically with most of the other metals having melting points in the same thermal neighborhood. Tin and antimony are the two metals most

frequently used in producing alloys with lead, although bismuth, cadmium and zinc will combine if you give them a chance.

Practically any metal — offhand, I can think of no exception — when alloyed with lead, will result in a mixture that is somewhat harder than the pure lead was in the first place. Properly mixed lead alloys can serve useful purposes when working with the more modern and sophisticated firearms designed for use with smokeless (nitro) powders. However, it is the general consensus that the most pure and soft grade of lead that you can get will give you the best performance out of the beloved old black powder muzzleloaders and their modern-made counterparts to which the book at hand is dedicated.

Which brings up the question: What are the sources for pure, soft lead, suitable for producing muzzleloader projectiles? One obvious approach, though far from the most economical, is to go to a plumber's shop and buy as many pounds of pig lead as you need. Depending upon current prices, as well as the good tradesman's generosity or lack of it, virgin pig lead can span a cost range from around thirty to sixty cents per pound.

In earlier years, lead pipes were used widely in domestic plumbing. Sadly, this has been changing with the shift to the use of galvanized iron, copper and — more recently — plastic pipe. At one time, most plumbing shops had a pile

Long a landmark at Bridgeport, Connecticut, this 167-foot tower at the Remington Arms plant is used in making shot in the various sizes, as described later in the text.

of salvaged lead pipe somewhere about the place and many of them would sell you any reasonable quantity at well below the going price of virgin metal: i.e., fresh from the mines and refineries. Plumbers continue to use lead for joining sections of cast iron soil pipe: They pack the joint with oakum fibers, pour molten lead into it and beat around the joint with a hammer and caulking iron to assure a watertight seal.

Some shops will melt down scrap pipe to obtain further supplies of soft lead for pouring joints, but most prefer to buy virgin pig lead, due to the rising hourly scale of the trade, which tends to absorb any saving of money via the salvage operation.

So you still may be able to find plumbers who rip the occasional batch of lead pipe out of older houses in the process of replacing plumbing systems and they may be willing to sell it to you for about the same price as they'd get from the local scrap dealer. Once it gets into the hands of the scrap dealer, it seems to be gone. At least, I've yet to find one who would part with this sort of treasure at any realistic price level.

Scrap lead pipe may be found joined together in the form of various Ys and Ts by means of plumber's wiping solder. This is an alloy consisting of about 67 percent lead and 33 percent tin. Since you don't want tin in your muzzleloader mixture, it's best to cut the wiped joints off

and set them aside before melting down the sections of plain pipe. Don't throw the joints away, as they can be used in casting bullets for smokeless powder loads. If you have no use for them, they can be swapped for soft lead from a shooting buddy who casts for the more newfangled ordnance!

Lead pipe will average about the same degree of purity as commercial pig lead: approximately 99.6 percent lead, with the remainder consisting of insignificant quantities of zinc, silver, arsenic, antimony, tin or even a trifle of gold. However, these impurities do not harden the lead to any serious extent and they can be disregarded. Most of the other metals turn up amid the lead ore in varying quantities and are separated at the refinery to the extent that it may be necessary and/or commercially economical to do so.

So the unwritten law among bullet casters is, "always be kind to plumbers," because you never know when they might provide you with needed raw material at friendly prices ranging clear down to free, which is the friendliest price of all! Much the same observation applies to telephone company lineman, who can be valuable sources of scrap telephone cable sheathing.

The common estimate of purity on cable sheathing is around 98.5 percent, which still is quite sufficiently pure for the purposes of black powder aficionados. However, the solder used in joining sections of cable sheathing contains

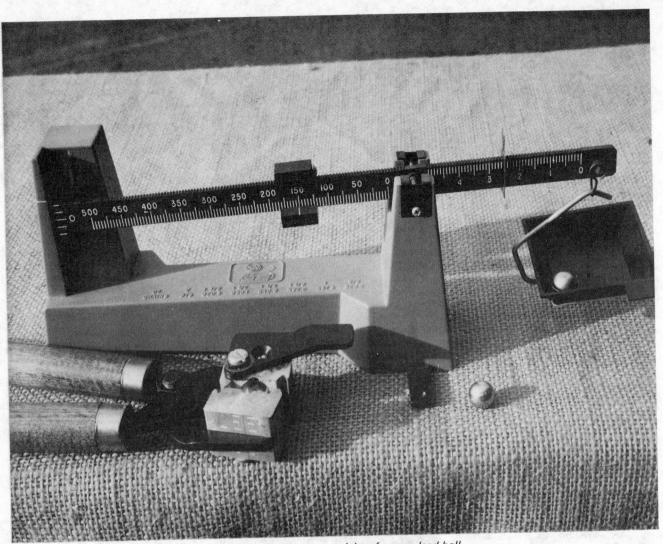

*If you know the exact weight of a pure lead ball
from a given mould, another ball from the same
mould, of unknown alloy can be weighed as test.*

some insidious and obnoxious ingredient which, if it gets into your melting pot, even in small amounts, makes it all but mandatory to consign the entire batch of metal for use in such non-critical applications as gluing weights or boat anchors. Whatever the stuff is, it makes the mixture pour with the consistency of corn meal mush, even at quite high temperatures. So you quickly learn to clip and trim away all of the cable sheathing solder and put it aside for careful disposal where it won't get mixed in with the choicer metals.

Lead pipe, cable sheathing and commerical pig lead are the primary sources of metal sufficiently soft for the purposes under present discussion. Should you gain access to large amounts of jacketed bullets, such as from the fall-out area of a range, these can be smelted down and the jackets skimmed away as they float to the surface and the resulting cleaned metal will be suitably soft and pure. It's not a practical source unless low-cost labor is available. Nor are the unjacketed lead bullets found on most civilian target ranges of much use for making soft lead bullets, since most of them will have been hardened through the addition of gosh-knows-what by the previous caster for use in smokeless powder loads.

Battery plates contain a considerable quantity of antimony, up to eleven percent or so; moreover, they can

have little pockets of trapped acid which can erupt with explosive violence when you go to smelt them down.

Wheel weights vary widely as to content, typically around 90 percent lead; most of the rest is antimony and a bit of tin may have gotten into some of them. There is no practical way for the individual to refine this metal back into reasonably pure lead. Much the same applies to the various alloys used in the printing trades.

One further category of available metal must be mentioned: scrap metal of unknown composition, meltable and more or less lead-like in appearance. Such finds can and do turn up in every conceivable form and the question is one of determining if the metal is sufficiently soft and pure for use in projectiles for muzzleloaders.

Happily enough, almost everyone possesses a testing device which can yield a valid clue as to whether it's soft lead or not; it's known as a thumbnail. Put on a little pressure and try to scribe a line in a smooth area of the metal being tested. If your nail can leave a mark of detectable depth, exposing the beautiful, silvery glint of unoxidized lead, then it's a fairly safe bet that the metal does not contain enough impurities to disqualify it for your purposes.

One further quick and simple test is easy to carry out. Some time when you happen to luck onto a really super-

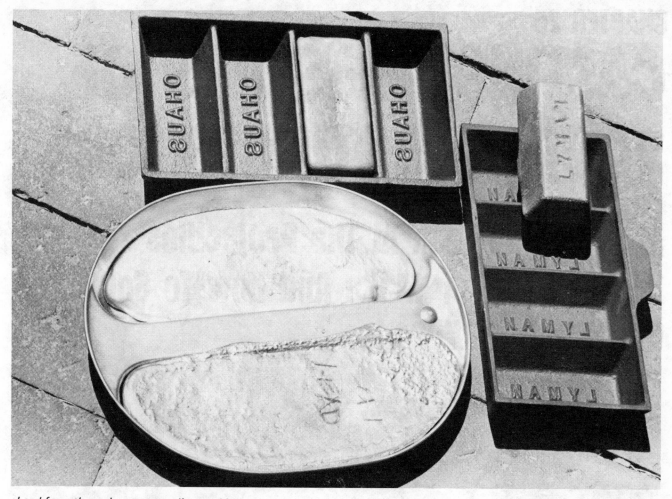

Lead from the various sources discussed here can be melted down, cleaned and cast into pigs by means of ingot moulds or old messkit top. Below: Thumbnail test is a quick and reliable means of determining degree of metal softness.

grade batch of pure lead, so luxuriously soft that you can almost spread it on bread with a table knife, try to cast up one perfectly filled sample out of each of your moulds. Set these samples aside, or weigh them carefully on an accurate powder scale and record the weight for each mould where the data will not get lost — which is no minor feat, in itself! Then, as you acquire hunks of metal of dubious parentage or analytical content, it becomes a simple operation to cast up a sample from one of the moulds you've pre-checked with the dead-soft lead. When you get a ball or bullet that's filled out as completely as was the original test specimen, toss the new sample on the pan of your scales and compare its weight to that of the one known to have been pure lead.

Since all of the metals apt to be present in lead as impurities have specific gravities well below that of lead, the less pure alloys will produce samples having identical volume but perceptibly lighter weights. The evaluation procedure just described will not indicate whether it's tin, antimony or what-have-you that's present, but it does provide a useful yardstick as to the amount of impurities on a percentile basis. If your test sample weighs within a few grains of a pure lead casting out of the same mould, it's an excellent bet that it's pure within any fairly charitable definition of the word. However, you can expect to be astonished at the weight-loss possible because of impurities. This can run to ten percent or more, although anything that tests much more than three percent weight-loss probably will not pass your initial thumbnail test. – *Dean A. Grennell*

CHAPTER 25

CASTING THE STARS OF YOUR SHOOTING SHOW

A Thoughtful Look At The Projectiles You Can Buy Or Make And How To Sort Out Which Is Which!

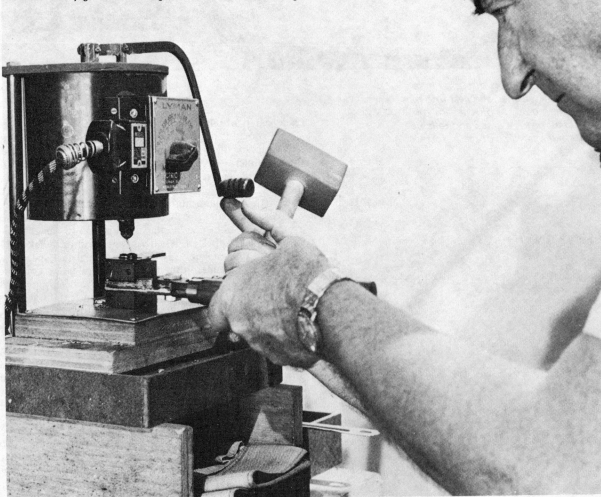

As discussed in the text, this moulder would be well advised to wear safety glasses and long sleeved shirt while casting.

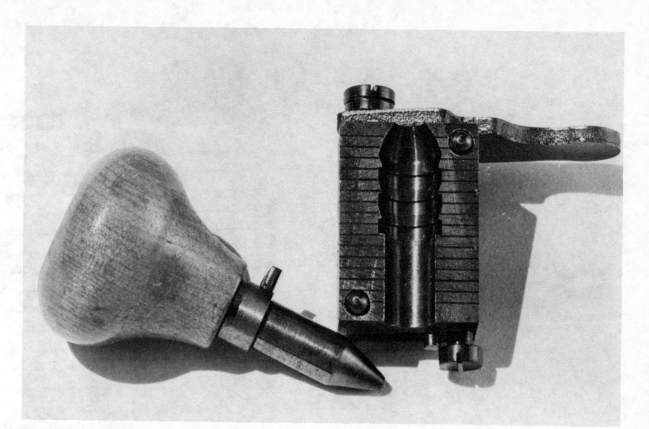

Moulds for Minie balls require the separate base cavity forming punch, which makes them more expensive to produce and prevents furnishing as multi-cavity types.

Lᴇᴛ ᴜѕ ѕᴛᴀʀᴛ by considering a few basic safety precautions before we begin discussing operations concerned with the melting and casting of lead. It is sound good judgment to form the habit of wearing eye protection — such as safety glasses or a face shield — when working with melted lead. Dress sensibly, which means long-sleeved shirts, if temperatures make this bearable, with the minimum area of unprotected hide being exposed to the hazards of spills and spatters.

Lead has certain toxic properties, as do some of the other metals with which it may be mixed. It is well to wash your hands thoroughly after handling lead and before eating, with appropriate cautions about how you handle cigarettes, cigars, et al., when working with lead, either in the molton or solidified state. Melted lead gives off sufficient aerial contaminants to make the provision of adequate ventilation necessary if exposure is frequent and/or extended. Zinc and cadmium, when melted or vaporized, are much more toxic than lead in this respect. Dust-fine particles of lead are suspended in the air after firing, so that ventilation can be required for indoor ranges, as conditions may indicate.

It is particularly important to isolate any lead-melting activities, such as casting, cleaning, et al., from any of those flammable materials employed in shooting such as powder, primers, caps and the like. A tiny spatter of molten lead, falling into an open container of black powder spells instant catastrophe and this is worth avoiding at almost any cost!

In bringing up such gloomy topics, I do not mean to discourage you from exploring the interesting and rewarding field of bullet casting but, rather, to help assure that you will enjoy this absorbing pastime without falling prey to its occasional hazards. All it really takes is a moderate ration of common sense.

For example: On a night long ago, common sense should have kept me from filling a large old frying pan nearly to the brim with melted-down hunks of lead pipe, which I was cleaning up and pouring into pig moulds for future use. Certainly, common sense should have blown the whistle when I went to pick it up by its use-worn wooden handle which, under the strain of about forty-odd pounds, slipped on its shank and abruptly decanted quite a bit of the lead over the top of the gas range, onto the linoleum of the floor, with a goodly dollop of the fiery stuff ending up inside the loose-fitting bedroom slippers I happened to be wearing (common sense, we were talking about: remember?). This discolored patch of the linoleum reminded me of my folly for as long as we lived in that house, as did my long-suffering better half!

For the record, an old frying pan on the kitchen stove works well enough — if you can live with the gamy odors arising from reclaimed plumbing pipes — but the secret is to clamp down tightly with a large pair of Vise-Grip pliers on the edge of the pan opposite the handle before attempting to lift and pour from your jury-rigged smelting pot.

As noted in the foregoing discussion, almost any fuel produces flame temperatures high enough to top the required 621 degrees F, with some to spare. However, you

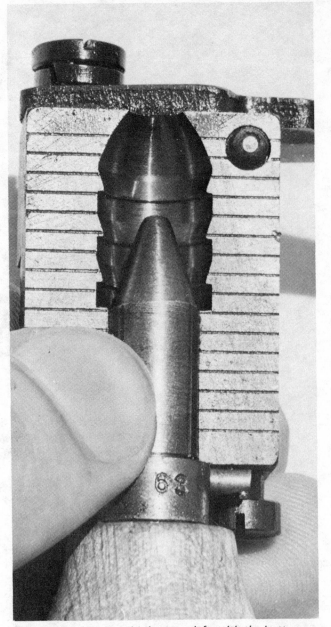

Lyman moulds are identified by a design number, first three digits of which indicate diameter. The 672 is serial for the day's production assuring that the two halves both match.

This is half of the mould shown at left, with the bottom punch held in place to show how it forms the base cavity.

could hold a ten-pound pot of lead over a cigarette lighter all day and nothing would happen. Your heat source must generate enough BTUs of thermal energy to offset heat lost from the metal by means of radiation, convection and conduction or you'll never raise it beyond the melting point.

I've used blowtorches, camp stoves, kitchen ranges powered by wood, gas and electricity, plus assorted gas and electric hotplates for melting down lead, with varying degrees of success and satisfaction. The handy little propane torches, such as Pratt & Lambert or Bernz-O-Matic, can be used to good advantage during the initial melting phase of the operation to hasten the lead into a liquid state.

If you've started out with several lumps, pigs or odd-shaped pieces of lead in a clean pot, it will take a long while before it starts to melt. This is because the lead only touches the metal of the pot at a few small points. Once the metal has melted, it is in contact over a much larger area

and the rate of heat transfer is much more rapid and efficient. For this reason, it's best to start with small amounts of lead until you get a shallow layer of molten metal across the bottom, after which you can feed in the larger pieces.

Try to leave your melting pot with a small layer of metal at the bottom, so that things will go more quickly the next time you fire up for a session. Any excess can be ladled out and poured into pig moulds for future use, leaving a half-inch or so in the pot.

Several suppliers offer handy little pig moulds, well made of cast iron. These turn out a pig shaped like an oblong, truncated pyramid, about three inches long, 1½ inches wide and three-quarter inches thick, weighing a pound or a bit over. If desired, the four-trough mould can be filled brim-full, producing an ingot that weighs around six pounds, which can be broken up into the four small

This is the Lyman mould designed for producing 12-gauge slugs for use in shotguns, including muzzleloading designs.

Ohaus Minie mould, design number 58-275-M turns out a caliber .58 projectile which weighs 275 grains in soft lead.

pieces at your convenience.

You may find that one-pound pigs are a bit small for volume production. I did and made the happy discovery that the top half of an old GI messkit makes the greatest pig mould of all time. Usually made of stainless steel, it's durable and lead won't stick to its shiny surface. Depending upon how deeply you fill the messkit top, it yields two kidney-shaped pigs weighing upward of six pounds apiece or, if poured full, it solidifies into an oval blob that can be broken into two sizeable chunks with the aid of a small hatchet and a chopping block. The messkit pigs are just the right size for feeding into the top of those small electric melting pots which represent the pinnacle of going first class, so far as the bullet caster is concerned.

Several firms have produced electric lead melting pots over the years and some of these continue in business: Lyman and SAECO being two noteworthy examples. At the lower end of the price range, there are utility pots, open at the top for feeding and ladling, with their temperature being regulated by the slightly more primitive technique of plugging or unplugging the cord, as necessary.

A notch higher up the melting pot peck-order of luxury, we find the open-topped pot with an adjustable, thermo-statically controlled heating element which will cut in and out to maintain any pre-set temperature from about 550 to 800 degrees F. You still have to dip the lead out of the top with a ladle but it maintains a uniform temperature at the chosen point and that is extremely helpful in producing the best possible bullets.

Whether you're melting your metal in an electric, open-topped pot or an old skillet, you quickly develop a prac-ticed roll of the wrist that backs the lower surface of your ladle across the dull, gray skim of oxidized metal on the surface so as to dip from the pure, coin-bright supply of metal beneath.

After the metal has melted, drop in a small piece of beeswax, about the size of your smallest fingernail, and stir the metal to flux it. This causes the metal to combine into a uniform mixture and brings dross and impurities to the surface where they can be skimmed off and discarded. An old spoon works well for this purpose. After that point, don't try to remove the thin film of new oxide that forms immediately as the bright metal is exposed. Leave the film alone to protect the rest of the metal from the air and, thereby, cut down on oxidation.

It should be noted that the beeswax or other material used as a flux may catch fire and flare up above the melted metal. It depends upon whether or not the metal tempera-ture exceeds the wax's flash point. Bear this possibility in mind and take care not to have flammable material in the area within three or four feet from the top of your melting pot. If it doesn't flare up, it will smoke furiously.

The slickest deals of all are those electrically operated, thermostatically controlled melting pots with a lever on the side to open and close a small valve on the bottom. When open, molten metal is delivered through an outlet nozzle

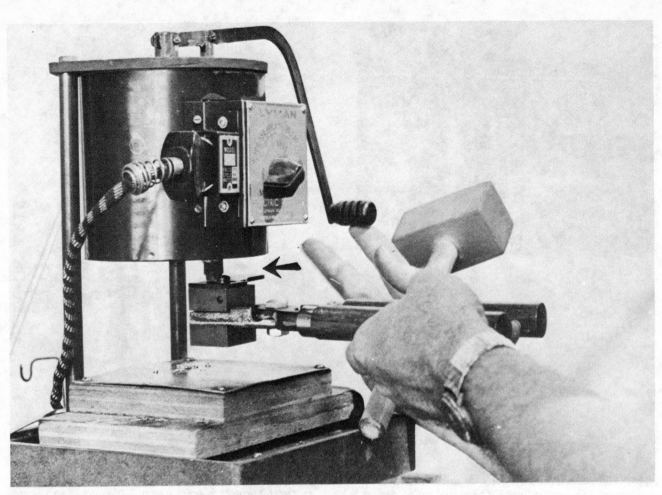

Photos above and below illustrate the two different techniques discussed for casting with bottom-delivery melting pots. Above, sprue cutter is held in contact with spout to provide a slight amount of pressure; below, lead drops through air to flow in.

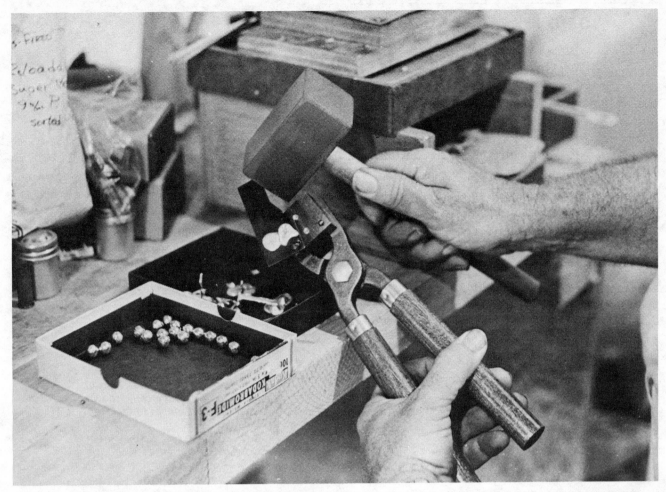

A non-marring mallet is used to knock the sprue cutter over and the sprue is dropped into a separate box for return to pot.

having a tapered outer surface. This moves the lead from pot to mould without contacting the air and reduces oxidation loss to a minimum. Likewise, the rigs are extremely convenient to use.

Here, you have a choice between holding the tapered opening on the sprue-cutter of the mould against the conical delivery nozzle, thereby delivering the metal into the mould at a small head of pressure; or you can hold the mould an inch or less beneath the spout and "air-pour" instead of using the "pressure-pour" technique. Neither method is necessarily best for all purposes and it may take a little experimenting to find which to use for the given mould or design.

The Lyman or Ohaus dipper, with its front hood and tapered snout, permits the pressure-pouring approach in much the same manner. You fill your ladle, hold the mould on the side with your left hand, position the snout in the hole of the sprue-cutter and rock the assembly upright to pour in the metal. It works perceptibly better than air-pouring in several instances.

Form the habit of either mounding up the metal on top of the sprue-cutter slightly — if air-pouring — or leaving the spout in contact for a few seconds, if pressure-pouring. This tends to bypass the formation of air pockets in the upper part of the ball or bullet which might otherwise be caused by shrinkage of the metal as it cools.

Lead, in the soft and pure state that's best for muzzle-loader projectiles, is something less than the caster's dream metal, it must be conceded. In fact, it tends to be a trial to

the patience and a challenge to the perserverance. Even if you crank up the temperature to around the 700-mark or so — unless otherwise stated, all temperatures in this discussion are Fahrenheit — it's often hard to fill the mould smoothly and avoid little wrinkles in the finished casting. This poses a minor problem in the case of round balls, but it's worse when casting hollow-based projectiles such as Minie balls.

The first thing to do is to remove any rust-preventive oils that may have been applied to the mould at the factory or at the close of the previous casting session. Most moulds are made of iron or steel alloys which seem to rust if you look at them or even so much as think about them. Accordingly, an effective rust-preventing coating is mandatory. One of the best materials I've found is Micro-Mist. This comes in a pressurized spray can and it's easy to apply to the mould, after it cools and prior to storing it away from the next session. Micro-Lube, Incorporated, (8505 Directors Row, Dallas, Texas 75247) also make a companion product called Micro-Solv which offers a handy and effective means of flushing away any coating of oil, grease or similar rust-preventing compounds, leaving the surface of the mould interior clean and ready to do the best casting of which it is capable.

Most moulds will not cast smoothly until they have been heated up to a considerable extent. Normally, they'll reach this point after some six or a dozen fillings, depending upon the size of the cavity, the temperature of the molten metal and such factors. The heating process can be hastened by

SHOT				BUCK SHOT		
NUMBER	DIAM. IN INCHES	APPROX. PELLETS IN 1 OZ.		NUMBER	DIAM. IN INCHES	APPROX. PELLETS IN 1 LB.
DUST	.04	4565				
12	.05	2385		4	.24	340
11	.06	1380				
10	.07	870		3	.25	300
9	.08	585				
8	.09	410				
7½	.095	350		1	.30	175
7	.10	290				
6	.11	225				
5	.12	170		0	.32	145
4	.13	135				
2	.15	90				
AIR RIFLE	.175	55		00	.33	130
BB	.18	50				

The chart at left, giving specifications on the various sizes of shot, is from Remington Arms Company, shown at actual size, and applies to their shot production. Specs may vary with the other manufacturers. Below: After casting, it's important to sort out the defective castings such as these. They can be returned to the pot with sprues.

careful use of a propane torch flame on the interior surfaces of the opened-apart mould blocks. Likewise, this helps to burn away any remaining trace of oil or solvent. If pre-heating the blocks in this manner, take precautions to keep the flame moving so as to heat the blocks evenly, preventing them from warping.

When using one of the electric pots, it may be practical to place the mould on top of the pot, with its blocks over the lead supply, as the pot comes up to temperature and melts the metal. This can be helpful in preheating – if you take care that the mould does not fall into the hot metal.

With moulds such as those for Minie balls, a propane torch or similar flame can be applied carefully to the metal of the lower punch which forms the base cavity of the bullet, helping to eliminate wrinkles and gaps in the skirt of the completed casting.

Make it a practice to drop the sprue and the balls or bullets – even if imperfect – into some sort of shallow cardboard box or similar container and, as necessary, pour the scrap back into the pot from the box. Do not drop the bullet from the mould directly back into the molten metal, since this is apt to cause spattered drops of metal to adhere to the exposed inner faces of the blocks. These would prevent the necessary tight closing of the block halves and would cause unsightly fins around the bullet at the juncture of the blocks.

In addition to guarding against corrosion, the iron, brass, aluminum or other material used in making bullet mould blocks must be handled gently to prevent damage. Never use the tip of a screwdriver, ice pick, scratch awl or similar device to jab the bullet free from the blocks as this will quickly ruin the relatively soft metal from which the mould is made. On extended production runs, make it a firm habit to check the holding screws which fasten the blocks to the handles or tongs; do this every one hundred bullets.

Selection of the proper size of ball or diameter of Minie bullet is discussed elsewhere in this book. The following listing is intended to assist the reader in choosing which of the several manufacturer's moulds he may wish to purchase. (Addresses appear in the directory section at the rear of the book.)

Ohaus Scale Corporation offers a catalog of their shooting products, free upon request. Casting items include:

Single cavity mould blocks, plain	$10.00
Single cavity mould blocks, Minie, etc.	14.00
Double cavity blocks (plain only)	13.50
Four cavity blocks (plain only)	21.95
Universal mould handles (fit all of above)	4.95
Lead pot, cast iron, holds ten pounds	2.50
Lead dipper, snouted	2.00
Ingot mould, four pig	2.00
Mould mallet, wood	2.49

Since Minie designs require the separate base stem which forms the cavity, they are priced higher, as noted and are available only in the single cavity blocks. Ohaus Minie designs include:

No. 45250M	.445" dia.	250-grain weight
No. 58275M	.575	275
No. 58400M	.575	400
No. 58500M	.575	500

Ohaus round ball moulds are available in single, double and four cavity blocks, except for those marked with an asterisk (*), which are available only in single cavity:

NUMBER	DIAMETER	WEIGHT
311R	.311"	59 grains
323R	.323	63
350R	.350	70
375R	.375	79
378R	.378	82
380R	.380	84
395R	.395	92
424R	.424	115
433R	.433	123
440R	.440	127
445R	.445	138
451R	.451	139
454R	.454	142
457R	.457	145
470R	.470	158
490R	.490	176
495R	.495	181
562R*	.562	264
662R*	.662	405

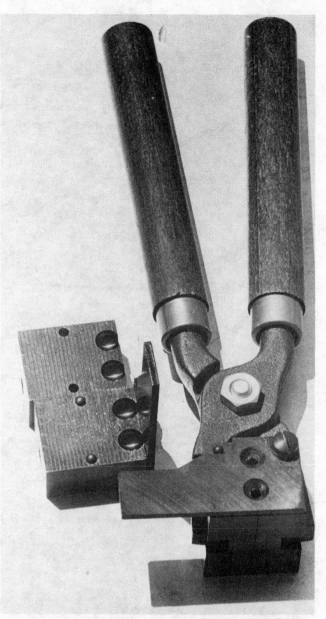

Since round ball moulds have no bottom punches, as do the Minie designs, they can be made for producing more than one ball at a filling, such as this Ohaus double-cavity mould.

SAECO Reloading, Incorporated, offers a catalog of their shooting products, free upon request. Items of special interest to the shooter of muzzleloaders include:

Lead hardness tester; No. 420001: $28.50.

Model 24 melting furnace, thermostatically controlled, bottom valve, 110-115-volt, 1000-watt, 650-850 Fahrenheit, 11 lbs. cap., with four-pig mould; No. 240001: $44.50.

Model 24 furnace, 220-volt; No. 240002: $48.50.

Model 32 utility furnace, thermostatically controlled, 650-850 Fahrenheit, 110-115-volt, 1000-watt, top-dipping, with four-pig mould; No. 320001: $36.50.

Model 32 furnace, 220-volt; No. 320002: $40.50.

Model 31 utility furnace, top-dipping, no thermostat, otherwise, same as Model 32, 110-115-volt; No. 310001: $24.50.

Model 31 furnace, 220-volt; No. 310002: $28.50.

Extra ingot mould, four-pig; No. 230001: $2.00.

The Shiloh IV mould for round balls, shown assembled above and taken apart below, has an ingenious design which permits production of four at a filling and is treated for non-rusting.

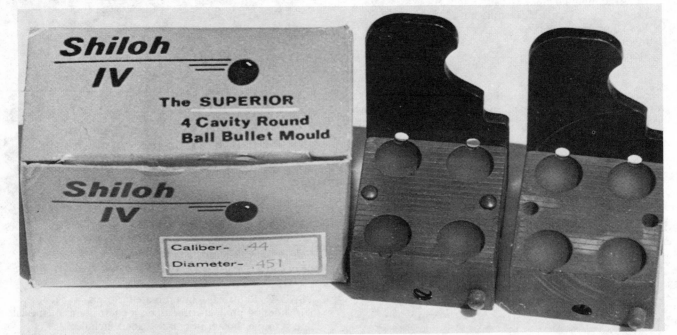

It may be noted that SAECO has plans for adding a series of round-ball designs and, possibly, Minie balls to their present line of bullet moulds. An inquiry to the firm, at the address given, will bring information as to the current status of availability.

Lee Precision Manufacturing offers a catalog of their shooting products, free upon request. Items of special interest to the shooter of muzzleloaders include:

Single cavity bullet moulds, complete with handle and aluminum blocks, diameters of .296, .308, .311, .319, .323, .336, .350, .375, .378, .380, .390, .395, .424, .433, .440, .445, .451, .454, .457, .470, .490 and .495-inch. $8.98

Mould blocks only	6.98
Handles only	3.50
Drawn steel lead pot, 4-lbs cap.	1.48
Pouring ladle	1.48

As this book was going to press, Lee Precision was planning a series of Minie designs, but final details were not available for inclusion here. Information supplied on request from the manufacturer.

Shiloh IV offers an illustrated brochure describing their round ball bullet moulds and allied accessories, free upon request. Their mould blocks feature a novel design in which two cavities are cut on the top of the blocks and two more are cut on the bottom, giving a capacity of four balls with each filling. Mould pliers (handles) are available from Shiloh

IV at $5.25, although the blocks can be used with Lyman double-cavity mould handles, if these are available. A moulder's hammer, of novel design, is offered at $4.95, intended for striking the sprue-cutter with the face or dislodging the balls with a pointed, non-marring spike on the opposite end.

Shiloh IV blocks are offered in diameters of .320, .350, .375, .380, .424, .440, .445, .451, .454, .457, .490, .498, .562 and .575-inch. They are especially treated to produce a surface which does not require solvent, oil or cleaning fluid, either before or after use. The suggested retail price of the Shiloh IV blocks is available by writing to the manufacturer.

Lyman Gun Sight Corporation offers a complete catalog of their shooting products, free upon request. Items of interest to the shooter of muzzleloaders include:

Lyman Mould Master bullet casting furnace, complete with four-pig ingot mould, capacity of 11 lbs., 115-volts, 1000-watt heating element, calibrated thermostatic control from 450-859 degrees Fahrenheit, controling temperature of metal within 20 degrees Fahrenheit, lever-operated bottom discharge spout | $52.75

As above, with mould guide	58.50
Add for optional 220-volt wiring, if desired	11.00
Mould guide, positions mould below spout	8.00
Lead pot, capacity 8 lbs	2.50
Lead dipper, snouted delivery nozzle	2.50
Four-pig ingot mould	2.50
Single cavity mould handles	4.50
Double cavity mould handles	4.50
Four cavity mould handles	6.00
Single cavity blocks (round ball, etc.)	10.00
Single cavity blocks (Minie balls, hollow base, etc.)	14.00
Double cavity blocks (round ball, no Minies)	13.50
Four cavity blocks, as above	22.00

Eleven designs presently are listed in the Lyman catalog for Minie moulds, with a twelfth said to be under development for use in the caliber .50 Thompson/Center Hawken replica rifle. For information on the last, contact the Lyman firm.

Diameters available in Lyman round ball moulds include the following: .235, .244, .300, .308, .311, .313, .319, .323, .330, .340, .345, .350, .358, .360, .370, .375, .378, .380, .389, .395, .400, .410, .420, .424, .429, .433, .437, .440, .445, .451, .454, .457, .465, .470, .490, .495, .498, .500, .526, .535, .550, .560, .562, .575, .648, .662, .672, .678, .690, .715 and .735-inch.

Diameters available currently in Minie balls, with weights as noted, include: .445 (250 grains); .533 (410); .557 (475); .575 (400); .575 (460); .575 (505); .575 (315); .577 (570); .580 (520); .580 (535) and .685 (730).

Dixie Gun Works, Incoporated, offers a 362-page catalog at $2.00 per copy, devoted to muzzleloading shooting supplies, which include certain proprietary lines of bullet moulds, some of which have metal handles, integral with the blocks and shaped similar to those of tin snips. These do not have a sprue-cutter, requiring that the sprue be trimmed off after cooling. They can be furnished in almost any conventional diameter in increments of .001-inch but the catalog notes that delivery is slow and recommends consideration of other makes of moulds that they stock, such as Lyman.

Herter's, Incorporated, offers a 653-page catalog of their items for shooters and others, the price being $1.00 per copy. Their listing of round ball and Minie moulds is quite similar to that of the Lyman line, with single cavity plain blocks at $8.59 plus $3.89 for the handles; $11.97 for

Micro-Mist can be used to prevent rust or corrosion between casting sessions and Micro-Solv removes the coating quickly.

single cavity hollow base blocks such as those for Minies; double cavity blocks (no hollow base designs available) are $11.59 and double cavity handles are $3.89.

Before discussing the technique of bullet and ball production, let's review the steps covered previously. Pure, soft lead is obtained and, if necessary, cleaned of its non-metallic impurities by stirring, fluxing and skimming. As possible and practical, it is made up in sizeable batches so that a considerable quantity will be of uniform softness and specific gravity, thus assuring consistent performance out of the gun. After mixing and cleaning, it is cast into pigs of convenient size for future use. Such pigs can be marked — using a scratch awl, or by an established code such as Roman numerals stamped with a small cold chisel — as to its content or properties.

Pig lead is melted in a suitable pot or furnace — even a small pot over a wood campfire or fireplace will serve, as countless pioneers could testify — and brought to a temperature of about 700 degrees F. Lacking thermostatic controls for the purpose, this temperature will have been reached when lead poured into the mould will begin producing satisfactory castings.

The molten lead is poured into the top of the mould, through the hole in the sprue-cutter, if the mould is so provided. A small surplus is mounded over the opening, or the nozzle is kept in contact with the cutter plate so as to

produce a slight head of pressure during the few seconds required for the lead to solidify within the mould.

After the metal hardens, the sprue cutter is driven over by means of a few judicious whacks of a mallet made of non-marring material, so as not to damage the mould. A hardwood stick of appropriate size works well, as does a wooden or plastic mallet. For many years, I used an old screwdriver with a plastic handle until an apprentice caster allowed the plastic to droop into a pan of hot lead and the plastic vanished amid some spectacular pyrotechnics. My present pet mallet has a block of polyurethane plastic on a wooden handle; the head material is resilient, non-marring, yet fantastically tough. You can drive finishing nails into wood without leaving a mark on the plastic, yet it won't damage a mould in the course of producing bullets by the thousands.

The trimmed sprue is dropped into a separate catch-box for later return to the pot, along with any sub-standard balls or bullets. A small pair of pliers on the bench is convenient for handling hot castings. I keep an old pair of welder's gloves in the storage compartment of the base I built for my Lyman Mould Master furnace, along with the stirring stick, an old tablespoon for skimming off impurities and a 3/16-inch screwdriver for tightening or changing blocks.

Most bottom-delivery pots, such as the Lyman, SAECO or Herter's, have more room between the base and the spout than you really need. Lyman makes a mould guide that clamps to the upright columns, being adjustable to position the mould precisely under the spout. The trouble is, this gets in the way when you're working with the moulds having a base stem on a wooden handle, such as those for the Minie balls. I fastened a couple of slabs of three-quarter-inch scrap plywood together to slide under the spout as a rest when working with those moulds which have no base punch and handle. Spilled lead stuck to the wood, so I covered the top with a piece of sheet aluminum, to which lead won't adhere. It removes in a jiffy for casting with hollow base mould designs and, after a good many years of extended use, I still consider it the most practical accessory for this purpose.

After the trimming of the sprue — an operation not to be confused with William Shakespeare's play of nearly the same name! — the mould is moved over the catch-box for the finished bullets and the handles are spread apart to separate the two halves of the mould block. Often, the ball or bullet will drop out freely at this point. If it remains in one half or the other, a few careful taps on the side of the tongs, ahead of the pivot pin, should dislodge the bullet to drop into the box.

Since the balls or bullets are quite hot when they come from the mould and, as a result, soft and vulnerable to damage, it pays to drop them onto a fairly yielding surface. I use a shallow cardboard box — the ones for sheet film or photo paper are perfect for this — and, if necessary, I cut a sheet of one-quarter-inch corrugated cardboard to put across the bottom of the box. From time to time, I raise

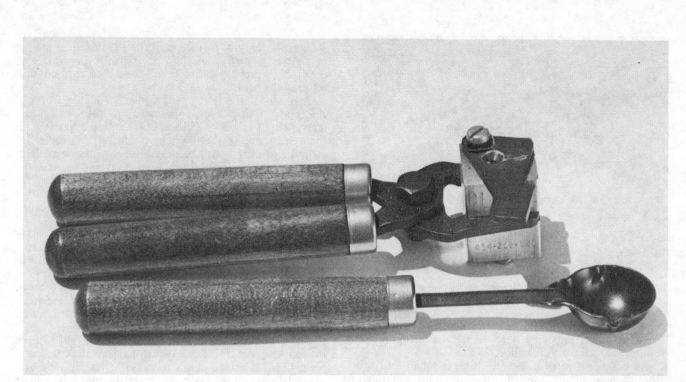

Lee moulds, here with same firm's dipper, feature blocks of aluminum which heat up quickly and resist rust and corrosion.

the near edge of the tray to let the cooler castings roll to the front end, so that the fresh ones won't land on top of earlier production to the damage of both. An old towel, shop rag or piece of scrap carpet can be used as a landing pad for the bullets, if preferred.

As the catch box fills up with balls or bullets, they can be poured — with appropriate care — into some other container for further processing, so as to make room for more new castings in the box. Then, when you feel ready for a break in the routine, you can address yourself to inspection of the cooled batch, tossing all of the imperfect specimens back into the sprue box for re-melting. Unless your standards as to accuracy are pretty carefree, it pays to be rather critical and ruthless in scanning the output, rejecting any that are wrinkled or not completely filled out, since metal and casting time are less expensive than the risk of a shot missed because of imperfect bullets.

A powder scale can be used to good effect as a means of inspection. Adjust the weight poises so that it will balance the beam on center with typical balls or bullets. You may have to weigh a dozen or so to establish the typical average weight. After that, any bullet that doesn't lift the end of the pointer should be rejected for the obvious reason that it has wrinkles, rounded corners or a concealed air pocket. The last defect is impossible to detect by any other method.

Lyman makes a series of slug moulds for all of the popular shotgun gauges. These are closely similar in design to the moulds for Minie balls. The blocks are single cavity, but are made to fit the Lyman double cavity handles. At one time, they offered a set of male and female dies for swaging the rifling grooves onto the sides of slugs from these moulds. However, extensive testing turned up the surprising fact that the rifling marks on the side of the shotgun slugs made scant difference in their accuracy in comparison to slugs fired as they came from the mould, without the rifling marks.

It turns out that the reason a shotgun slug flies nose-foremost is not due to any spin imparted by passage of the

rifled slug up the barrel or through the air; rather, it's stabilized by the fact that the center of its weight is up near the nose, with the lighter skirts at the rear of the slug serving much the same function as the vanes on an aerial bomb, the fletching on an arrow or the feathers on a badminton bird.

Since most muzzleloading shotguns have straight bores, unchoked at the muzzle, a Lyman slug mould of the appropriate gauge may well prove a useful accessory to broaden the versatility of the tradition-soaked smoothbore. You can expect to expend some time and effort in tracking down the most accurate powder charge, but that can be a fair percentage of the fun.

As with other muzzleloader projectiles, dead-soft, pure lead is the best material for casting the shotgun slugs and you may find it something of a challenge to produce perfect specimens of these consistently, since they're a bit more stubborn and cantankerous to use than the Minie moulds — and those are tough enough! However, it can

Aligning grooves for Lee blocks can be seen here.

Shiloh IV mould blocks can be used on Lyman handles intended for their double cavity blocks. Note the double sprue cutters and two boxes for good balls, sprues and scrap.

make an interesting project to tackle and the potential rewards are well worth the effort.

As has been noted elsewhere, firing a round lead ball from a smoothbore musket produces some amazingly random groups, measurable in feet rather than inches. In high probability, this is due to the fact that the ball, in whizzing up the bore, rubs harder on one side than the other and, as a result, picks up a considerably amount of rotation in some direction other than in line with the axis of the bore. As it emerges from the muzzle, let's assume for purposes of discussion that it's spinning in a horizontal plane, clockwise, as viewed from above. This means that the left side is traveling faster in relation to the passing air than is the right side. This uneven distribution of air resistance will tend to make the ball curve to the right, in the direction of least resistance. It's the same basic principle that makes it possible for a baseball pitcher to throw a curve ball. And, next shot, it may spin and veer in the opposite direction, vertically, up, down or in any of an infinite number of diagonals. Hence, the morning-glory configuration of the groups delivered by such arms.

However, there is a solution to this problem of obtaining fair accuracy with round balls out of smoothbore barrels, provided they happen to be dimensioned in diameters close to those of the more popular shotgun gauges. The answer lies in putting the round ball down into one of the plastic wad assemblies, as supplied for reloading conventional shotshells. The thin but tough plastic sleeves at the front of such wads, intended to protect the charge of shot as it goes up the barrel, likewise protects a round ball and, at the same time, keeps it from picking up any significant amount of crosswise spinning motion.

As a result, it becomes possible to maintain some reasonable semblance of accuracy with round balls. The potential will vary with the given gun, of course, but keeping hits in an eight-inch circle at fifty yards is not uncommon and it may prove possible to better that by a bit.

There is one question that rolls out of the mail bag and onto the desks of shooting editors with dependable regularity: "How can I make my own shot?" Alas, it's an inquiry that does not admit of a simple and practical answer. True, you can produce your own buckshot, moulding the pellets one at a time in the mould of the proper diameter. As for the smaller sizes, you may recall the passage in Mark Twain's book, A Connecticut Yankee in King Arthur's Court, in which the hero — transported from the late

Nineteenth Century to the era of chivalry, hit upon the use of shot as a perfect medium of exchange, impossible to counterfeit since he had built and controlled the only shot tower in the land.

A photo of the shot tower at the Remington works in Bridgeport, Connecticut, appeared a few pages earlier and it's typical of such installations. Lead is hoisted to the work room at the top of the tower by means of elevators and is melted and mixed with such additives as may be desired. Usually, a small percentage of arsenic is mixed to make the shot harder, less apt to lose its spherical shape from the stresses of going up the gun barrel. Such hardened shot is termed chilled shot, the unhardened version being called drop shot.

The size of shot being produced is controlled by using one of several screens or grilles through which the molten lead or alloy is poured. These break the metal down into droplets of approximately the desired size and the lead — still in a molten state — makes the long drop down through the open center of the tower. In some instances, a current of air is directed upward through the tower by means of blowers to hasten the cooling process.

The melted lead, being unsupported in free fall, assumes the shape of least resistance, which happens to be that of a perfect sphere, retaining this form as it cools and solidifies. You might expect it to take the shape of a conventionalized teardrop, pointed at the rear, but it doesn't — for which we may feel suitable gratitude. As a matter of fact, high speed photos of raindrops show that they, too, fall as spheres.

The lead, now solidified into round pellets, falls into a shallow pool of water at the base of the tower and is scooped out and dried. It then is sorted as to size by passing it through a series of screens having openings of the proper diameters. Naturally, there is some variation as to size in the given batch, so that small amounts of the next few numerical sizes larger and smaller than the desired production will be obtained.

Even so, not all of the pellets will be suitably perfect in symmetrical roundness. Again, the process of separating the oddballs from the perfect specimens is surprisingly simple. The pellets, sorted as to size, are trickled onto a flat inclined plate and allowed to roll along for a bit. The misshapen pellets do not roll as fast as the round ones and, after a bit, they come to a gap in the plate. Pellets traveling at or above a certain speed will hurdle the gap and continue on down the incline to the room where they are put through the final operations prior to shipment. The slower ones drop through the gap and are sent back to the top of the tower for re-melting and another try at making the team.

The pellets which passed their finals are tumbled in graphite to polish and coat them with a friction-reducing outer layer, after which they are bagged up for sale or sent along to the shell loading rooms of the factory.

The accompanying chart specifies the nominal particulars on the various sizes of shot, as quoted from data furnished by Remington. However, it should be noted that actual production can vary from these specs to a substantial extent, particularly among different manufacturers. As an example, elsewhere in this book, we've detailed the use of Lawrence brand, No. 1 buckshot in the modern replica of the Colt Navy Model of 1851, noting that its diameter miked out to .400-inch, quite closely, with average weights of 87-90 grains apiece. That would be about 78-80 pellets per pound. You'll note on the chart that No. 1 buckshot is listed at a diameter of .300-inch, running about 175 to the pound. Obviously, a pellet of No. 1 Lawrence buckshot is considerably bigger and heavier than the same size as made

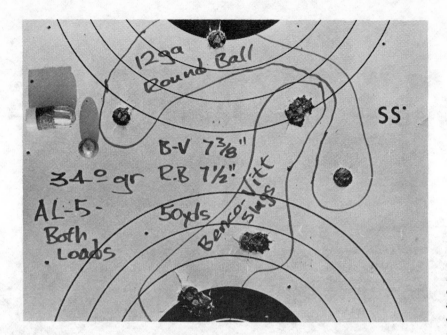

Round lead balls in 12-gauge Alcan Flite-Max wads, as at lower left, are capable of reasonable accuracy in smoothbores, equaling groups from a factory-made slug at 50-yards. Below: This No. 4 shot is plated.

by Remington.

The foregoing is intended, hopefully, to forestall a blizzard of puzzled inquiries from readers and to suggest that it would not be a good idea to order a hundredweight or so of any given size of buckshot for use in your muzzleloader until you have verified that its diameter is acceptably close to your requirements.

Even though few shooting enthusiasts would find it practical to build their own shot tower, you can lift a leaf from the manufacturer's production techniques by tumbling your own cast round balls to polish them smooth and erase some of the irregularity of the sprues. There are several tumblers on the market, priced to fit the hobbyist's purse, intended for such applications as polishing rocks and gems, bullets, cartridge cases and the like.

You may wish to add a small quantity of graphite in the microfine, colloidal grade, or molybdenum disulphide (sold under various trade names such as Moly-Kote) in order to provide a friction-resisting coating. Lacking a tumbler, you can coat them by swirling small amounts about in the bottom of an empty oatmeal carton, together with a little graphite or moly powder. Many find that this helps to prevent bore leading or abrasion of the round balls when they are fired unpatched, as in muzzleloading revolvers.

One further technique for pellet production should be noted, predating the invention of the shot tower — an event, Mark Twain to the contrary, that actually occurred long after the time of King Arthur! — namely, the cutting up of sheet lead, first into strips and then into cubes or small squares. This can be done quite rapidly if you happen to have access to a squaring shear, as commonly used in sheet metal shops. It should go without saying that the pattern of dispersion of such square-cornered pellets is both broad and abrupt. However, you may wish to file the possibility away for future employment in a shooting situation where you'd want the widest possible pattern at short ranges. – *Dean A. Grennell*

YESTERDAY'S TECHNIQUES

CHAPTER 26
FOR TODAY'S SHOOTING

The Oldtimers Learned A Thing Or Two About Rapid Loading Before There Was A Rapid Loader!

IT IS THE relatively rare shooter who is fortunate enough to own a collection of original muzzleloading rifles or shotguns that are in prime working order. And even when an individual does possess such valued memorabilia, flintlock or percussion, chances are slim he would cotton to the thought of putting his valuable collection to use in the field. For most collectors, the risk of irreparable damage is simply too worrisome a matter.

While all of what I have stated is certainly true of probably ninety-eight percent of today's rare gun owners, it is, however, not true of all. Not when it's a fact that several of us here in the East have spent some portion of our past three hunting seasons in the enjoyable company of one Dick Weller. This is a man who has spent over twenty years researching, collecting and shooting a number of the world's finest examples of original muzzleloading rifles and shotguns.

Now, before anyone begins thinking negatively regarding the wisdom of Dick Weller's actions, let me point out that he is a highly knowledgeable ordnance expert, a professional in the handling of modern military and combat-type firearms. He also serves as consultant in the matter of identifying and choosing rare muzzleloading pieces for several of the country's most famous collections. Each antique firearm that he actually shoots has been checked and re-checked for reliability by one of the most respected names in this field.

There having been times, when upon watching him dash off through the brush carrying one of his near-mint Brown Besses at Chinese port, I have felt a shudder of apprehension. I'm happy to report that to this day he had yet to booger one of his cherished pieces and each season has collected the exact species of big game which he had set out to take.

His .77 caliber Long Land Bess (First Model) last season accounted for a bull moose, in a near instantaneous one-shot kill, along with a legal assortment of whitetail dropped in exactly the same manner.

When you add to these trophies such items as Canada geese, ducks and grouse, downed while shouldering one of his English fowling pieces (an item whipped up by William Clark around 1795) or Brown Besses, you begin to suspect you are in the presences of someone magically displaced from a bygone age.

This resourceful gentleman has complete faith in the reliability/performance of the guns he prefers to take afield. He has, through experience, reached a point of familiarity where he never doubts his piece will fire, even when hunting during the worst weather. Nor does he doubt for an instant that the majority of his muzzleloaders will shoot tighter groups than a good many modern center-fire rifles carried by today's hunters.

As a fair judge of talents, I'll be the first to admit

Hunting guide Arlie Day inspects black bear taken with replica .58 caliber Buffalo Hunter. Dick Weller (opposite page) with a fine bull moose he shot with original Brown Bess musket.

Arlie Day takes aim and fires at black bear
reaching for an apple in an old grown over
orchard. The .58 caliber Buffalo Hunter is
a good choice when hunting in brush country.

nothing of Weller's preparations, target or hunting techniques, or his practiced, in-the-field performance are the result of anything but painstaking care of details, coupled with a longtime love and usage.

Whether it be a matter of luck or pocketbook I'm not certain, but I, like so many others, have had to go about my black powder hunting armed with various replica guns that suited the situation. There has been a .58 caliber Buffalo Hunter, percussion, from Navy Arms; a .45 caliber flintlock Minuteman from Numrich Arms, along with a modest assortment of other replicas of famous old coal burners. Each year, since becoming interested in black powder, I've become somewhat more adept in their field use and actually have managed to collect a few fair heads of my own.

The big difference is that I've never really been all that assured as to the kind of performance I'd give on a specific day. Would the rifle fire when I needed it? Would I respond with the required precision, if I must reload and make a follow-up shot? The answer is simple: Probably not, if I

didn't progress further than the basic ABCs of black powder shooting. Basing your scores on nothing more than essentials simply isn't enough, when you move off to the boondocks, placing all your faith in a favorite flintlock, no matter how mechanically sound it may be. In itself, it simply isn't enough to make a consistent scorer.

To sum up, it wasn't long before I noted that Dick Weller leaves nothing to chance, nor is there ever a time when he goes afield ill prepared. Most all of his preparations and techniques have long been available to those who are widely read. Particularly if they occasionally browse old-time and contemporary manuals.

At this point, I'm sure some of you are wondering what Weller is doing that has made me stand up, as a black powder hunter, and take notice. I can only give one answer — I am smart enough to spot a "pro" when I see one in action and smart enough to realize that the techniques he has been practicing, I should have been practicing all along.

Several months ago, I began looking over his shoulder

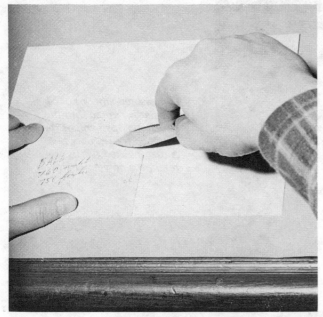

To make paper ball cartridges, the first step is to cut a predetermined size of paper (above). The template for this is basically the same as used several hundred years ago. Using a dowel with a concave end (right), ball is rolled in paper.

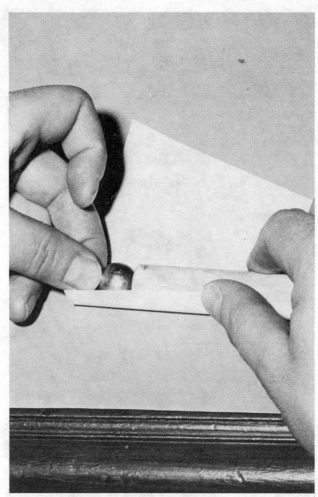

With the paper nose of the cartridge tied, a second tie (left) is made directly behind the ball. The projectile end of the paper cartridge is then dipped into the melted lube mixture. These homemade concoctions are made from a wide variety of ingredients.

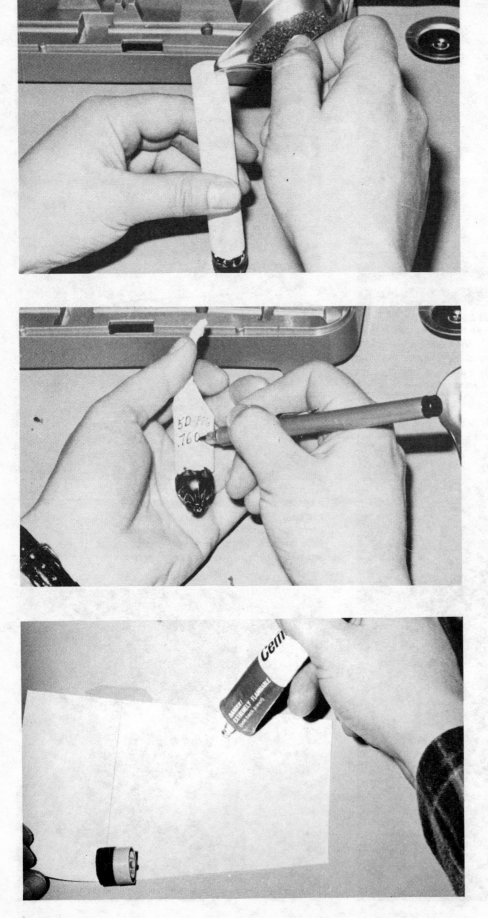

A measured amount of black powder is poured into the remaining open end of the paper cartridge tube, this is then twisted tightly to retain the powder charge.

Completed, the paper tube receives distinctive ink marking to make sure that cartridge is not mistaken for different caliber gun.

To load shot cartridges, a commercial shotshell wad is glued to a premeasured point on the square piece of paper. The upper edge is then glued also, the paper is then rolled into a tube for powder and shot.

whenever he was making preparations for a shooting or hunting session. While looking over that shoulder I decided it might not be a bad idea to do my looking through a camera, and make a few notes to keep the facts clearer for the future.

Here then is the Weller brand of thinking and doing, on a number of subjects relating to shooting and hunting with muzzleloaders. What I have learned from him has helped me to become more proficient at a sport which so many are now finding to be both enjoyable and challenging.

(1.) The first important step of preparation concerns itself with the need for truly exact grades of powder. Straight out-of-the-can powders, unfortunately, are neither uniform nor clean. The three compartment box, each having its own screen for sifting, works as follows: when powder such as FFg is dropped, any Fg in the batch will lie on No. 16; FFg goes through No. 16 and lies on No. 26 of second tray, finally FFFg goes through No. 24 and lies on No. 34 mesh of third compartment. This last compartment also will show some trace of FFFFg.

Notes — Do your powder dropping out of doors on a breezy day, holding the powder can a good two feet above

the first screen. This allows a breeze to blow away most of the powder dust that is present in every batch.

(2.) During an actual hunt, when the need for a reasonably fast second shot is sometimes a necessity, there is good reason for believing that a technique is required whereby the pressured hunter can reload rapidly, without having to pull out every accoutrement in his bag.

The answer is to prepare paper cartridges, an innovation having its beginnings as early in the history of firearms as pre-1600. The first paper cartridges contained only the powder measure, but it wasn't much later that the packets were prepared with both bullet and powder in one neat package. Long prior to the American Revolution the armies of both England and France were carrying these fast-loading cartridges.

Note — It should be remembered that loads must vary according to bore diameter, heaviness of construction in a specific firearm, original quality and present conditions.

Preparation Of Ball Cartridges — Cut out paper in accordance with a predetermined size, based on a template cut to the same form as originally made in this country during Colonial times of the Revolutionary War.

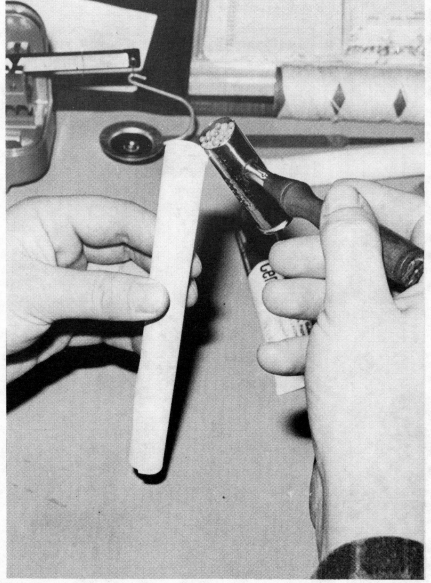

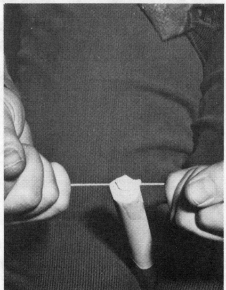

A measured amount of shot (left) is poured over the wad. The shot end of the cartridge (above) is tied.

The ball is placed at the end of a wooden dowel (hollowed at one end to position the ball). The dowel and ball are rolled in paper, as shown in photos, and rolled until one edge comes around and underneath dowel and ball. Remaining exposed paper is glued prior to completing rolling of balance of paper around dowel and ball.

Now take a length of string and tie front end of ball, trimming the string close; a second piece of string is used to tie the cartridge between the ball and end of the dowel. Withdraw the dowel, leaving the ball tied inside of the paper tube.

You now are ready to take a dozen or so of these ball-loaded tubes to a pot in which you have heated a mixture of half beeswax and half Crisco, or half Crisco and a commercial lubricant such as available from Lyman (American Colonials originally used beeswax and tallow). Using a paint brush, or by dipping, coat area covering ball with lubricant, which then will dry upon contact with the air.

You may now return to your loading area and begin filling each tube with sifted powder (FFg), 5 drams in the case of Weller's Brown Bess (.760). Powder charges can be either bulk measured or weighed. Finally, firmly twist the paper tail closed, then mark cartridge with proper loading data.

Preparation Of Shot Cartridges — Glue a commercial wad to a premeasured point, as illustrated, (front of wad

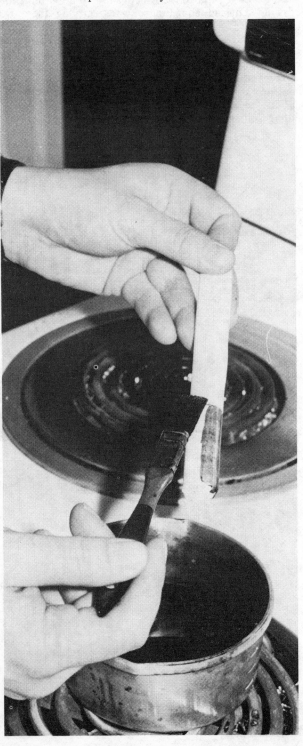

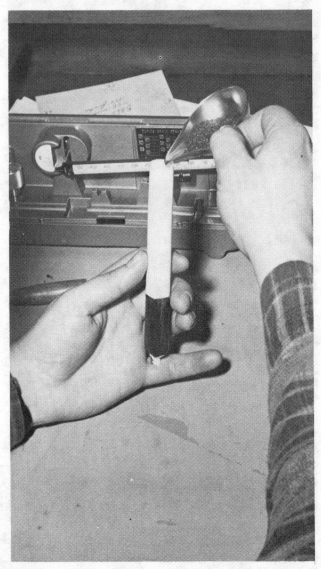

The melted lubricant is applied to the shot portion of the cartridge (left) with a small paint brush. The powder charge is then poured into the open end (below), then twisted shut.

Weller (above) swings his original Brown Bess flintlock muzzleloader into a ready position. Below, he bites paper from powder end of cartridge as he prepares to reload.

Using paper cartridge, as described in text, Weller fires one of his original flintlock muskets, smoke belches from both priming pan and the end of the antique gun's barrel.

With a clean barrel, the first shot may be loaded with ball close to gun's actual bore diameter. Black powder residue makes it necessary to load succeeding shots with smaller diameter ball, paper is the patching.

Seating the round ball in a clean barrel is a simple operation, but unless smaller size ball is used when hunting, second and third shots are difficult to seat, due to fouling in bore.

Weller (right) primes the powder pan with FFFg black powder. With cartridge loaded in gun and the pan primed, the musket is ready to fire.

2¼ inches from the left-hand edge of cut paper). Paper is glued ahead of wad, then rolled with paper to form a tube. Let dry. Shot charge is poured in front end of tube; in cases where larger sizes of shot (such as buckshot or number 2s are to be used) they are padded with cream of wheat or corn meal (alternating wheat, shot, wheat, shot). This alleviates "backing up" of the shot upon itself, which, in turn, reduces deformation.

You are now ready for lubrication. Using the same mixture as prepared for ball cartridges, apply it from back of wadding to front of cartridge. You are now ready to load back end of cartridge with measured powder charge. Finally, twist tail closed, then mark with proper loading data. For musket or fowling pieces (smoothbores) remember to use a wad of the next smaller size, e.g., a 10-bore (.775) uses a 12-gauge wad; a 16-gauge uses a 20-gauge wad.

Loading In The Field — I will first assume that the muzzleloader you are to use is spotlessly clean inside and out, and the bore free of oil. Consistent reliability is possible only when each component of your equipment is kept in perfect order.

Ball Cartridge — First bite off the twisted tip of paper. Pour powder into barrel. Now reverse cartridge in hand and place greased ball section in barrel. At the second string tear paper off, flush. You are now ready to ram greased paper and ball down the barrel, seating firmly against powder. The final step requires that you prime the pan (in case of a flintlock) or a percussion cap (in case of percussion-type muzzleloaders).

Shooting the Brown Bess, using 5 drams of sifted FFg and a .760 ball (weighing 658 grains) I chronographed Weller's loads at 1106 fps. Little wonder even the mighty moose considers this to be potent medicine.

Under hunting conditions, where a second shot will be required, a number of experienced individuals will have their second cartridge loaded with a smaller size ball (.750) so that reloading can be accomplished all the faster. The cartridge is loaded, powder end first, and not reversed.

If you incorporate these field methods into your hunting procedure, most especially the use of prepared paper cartridges, it is guaranteed that you will function faster as a shooter, find yourself using more precisely measured loads, and relaxing far more easily when the thought of a second shot is facing you in some tangled alder patch or when hard-pressured among the deadfalls.

Most hunters new to black powder shooting, and especially those who have accepted the ultimate challenge of going afield with the flintlock, have experienced the horror of taking careful aim at what might well be a potential trophy, pulling the trigger, then finding that they have no ignition. Such happenings I have found simply do not happen with experienced black powder shooters. The care they take with each step practically guarantees that misfires

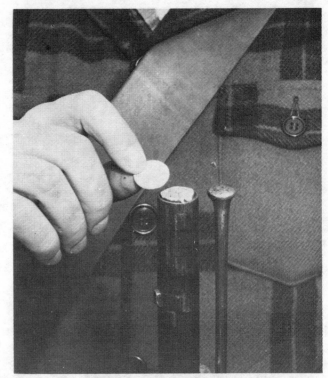

At left Weller inserts the paper shot cartridge. The tied end is then cut off to expose lead shot. A cardboard wad (above) is then placed over the shot and the whole charge is rammed down barrel.

When not using pre-made paper cartridges, some shooters carry premeasured powder charges is an assortment of containers. This one is a cut off shotgun shell with a cork serving as a stopper.

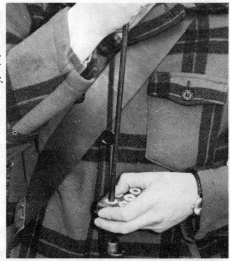

To aid in quick reloading, Weller uses a loading block with pre-patched lead balls.

Flintlock protector keeps powder in pan dry (left). Weller (below) with goose taken at thirty yards with William Clark fowling piece.

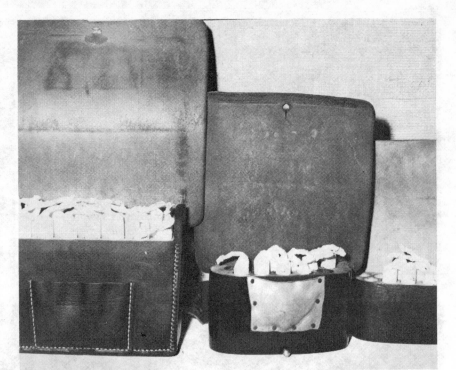

The sprue is removed from cast lead ball with a file (above), prepared cartridges are carried in leather cartridge boxes in photo at right. Bob Zwirz fires Navy Arms' .58 caliber Buffalo Hunter replica (below), this rifle is available in smoothbore also.

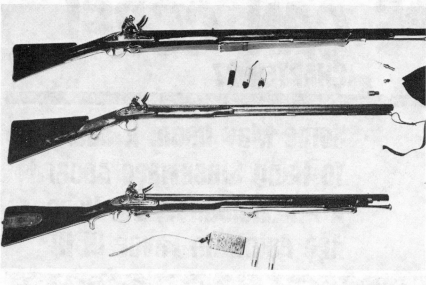

Three of Weller's hunting flintlocks, from top to bottom they are: Third Model Brown Bess; a 10 gauge fowling piece; and an original Baker rifle in .625 caliber, made by John Brown.

Special care must be taken when firing fine old original muzzleloaders. Weller (below) carefully cleans his English fowling piece, giving special attention to areas where powder foulings build up.

will not occur.

However, such assists as lock covers, for hunting in foul weather, are part and parcel of the accoutrements of knowledgeable hunters like Weller. Made like a small hat for a gnome, this type of deer skin cover, called a "cow's knee," fits completely over the area of the lock: being well greased it turns even heavy rain.

Weller has been using a homemade cover, based upon a Colonial design, featuring a strap with button hole, so that it can be fastened to a button on his shirt or jacket. When game is sighted, all he need do is start the muzzleloader to this shoulder. The cover comes away clean, leaving it attached to his jacket so that, as an added dividend, it will not be lost underfoot. A device of this sort is just as necessary for the hunter using percussion, as for the flintlock aficionados.

Though I know it marks me as a lesser-sophisticate, on a number of occasions I've chosen a percussion rifle for hunting bear, whitetail and mule deer. My favorite, so far, has been the Navy Arms Buffalo Hunter in .58 caliber. Loaded with the rapid loading 505-grain, lubricated soft lead Minie, it has proved deadly on every species of big game that I've so far hunted.

This past season, after I had taken bear and deer with this highly accurate muzzleloader in Canada and New England, I tracked along while one of my old-time hunting cohorts, Arlie Day, borrowed it, learned to use it competently, then quietly went about collecting himself a black bear. It was his first hunt with black powder and he performed so smoothly, he dropped his bear with a one-shot, near instantaneous kill. He too has now joined the fast growing group of sportsmen who are finding new enjoyment and challenge with one or another of today's shooting replicas.

I would strongly suggest serious shooters join the National Muzzle Loading Rifle Association, P. O. Box 67, Friendship, Indiana 47021.

Whether you begin furthering your knowledge of reading from volumes as old as "Pickerings Manual," or prefer to peruse more recently prepared and printed guides, it is a good bet that everyone can profit from time so spent.

Speaking for myself, when I'm not peering over Dick Weller's shoulder, I'm sure to be caught up in some interesting volume dealing with this never uninteresting area of shooting. In fact, I've been going to bed each night, reading and re-reading Von Steuben's letters to the troops! — *Bob Zwirz*

A SCOPE CAN COPE!

CHAPTER 27

Some May Deem It Sacrilege To Hang Glassware Aboard A Muzzleloader, But Here Are Points In Favor Of It!

Prodigious output of smoke, fumes and high-velocity
particles dictate scope mounting well forward, as here.

THERE ARE TWO schools of thought that seem to form
in regard to the collecting and use of the artifacts from the
past and this most definitely includes the field of muzzleloading firearms.

There are the purists, the traditionalists, who avow that
if it was good enough for their more remote ancestors, it
shall be equally good for them, for ever and ever, world
without end, amen.

The opposing school of contention may point out that,
if this philosophy were to be carried to its natural limits,
then all progress should have been suspended by morato-
rium as of the day that first pithecanthropus erectus picked
up a hunk of granite with which to whap a sabertooth
atwixt the eyes. If we're to accept the thesis that weapon
improvements are a no-no, they contend, then we should
draw the line at binding a stick to the rock with lengths of
vine so as to make an axe out of it!

The furor waxes thick and furious when it reaches areas
such as the use of optical — telescopic — sights in conjunction with black powder antiques and replicas. Those pre-
occupied with the sacredness of tradition say that Dan'l
Boone didn't use a scope on his trusty flintlock so, by jing,
they aren't going to use one, either. Their opposing counterparts respond by yelling "heil," right in the furor's face
and deck out their coal-burning artillery with modern
scopes, callous as to the unesthetic effect of the resulting
anachronism. "It's renegade, but it's right," is their rallying
cry!

Actually, as it turns out, telescopic sights for firearms
are not really all that disgustingly newfangled. They have

been materializing upon the shooting scene in some sort of
primitive and rudimentary form since some time well prior
to the War Between the States. Again, as is the case so often
in such matters, the earliest origins of optical sights are
cloaked in the foggy mists of misinformation and controversy. It is impossible to assert with positive confidence
that, for example, the scope sight was invented on Tuesday
morning, the 10th of May, 1757, by one Alois Weilbacher
in the picturesque village of Braunfogel, high in the Swiss
Alps. It just as well could have been some other time, some
other place, some other guy; in fact, it is superlatively
probable!

This much can be hypothecated with reasonable confidence and plausibility: From all of the data which has been
handed down to the present day on the personality traits of
Dan'l Boone, Davy Crockett, Jim Bridger, et al., it seems
likely to at least sixteen decimal places that, had scope
sights been available in their day, they would have had
them mounted atop their rifles and would have used them
with immense satisfaction.

Which may — or, again, may not — settle the matter of
whether or not such sights are moral and ethical. What
remains to be established is the question, are they or are
they not practical?

And, as the old lady said when she kissed the cow, that's
something else again. The crux of the problem stems from
the vast, thick clouds of smoke, fumes and miscellaneous
murk which go a-boiling about the immediate adjacency
when a shot is set off in most designs of flintlock or percussion firearms. What happens when these cubic yards of

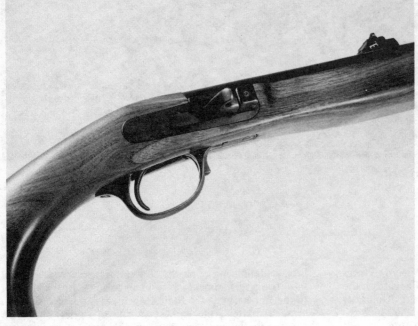

Rear-mounted scope on the rifle above will entail serious problems with deposits of powder residues on its lens. The Esopus Pacer .45 rifle at left has an enclosed cap, nipple and straight-line hammer, making it well adapted for addition of scope sight.

crud and corruption condense across the exquisitely polished surfaces of a scope lens?

That's quite correct: The scope becomes more or less opaque in short order and a scope with opaque lenses is just about as useful and practical as the addition of the sunshine vitamin to rat poison.

In fact, the design of the breechwork may be such that small hot particles of powder residue and/or priming compound are impacted against the glass surface with sufficient force to leave pockmarks in it which defy your most tender solicitude in cleaning up the lens for another try. It is quite possible that you have had an unwary hand in the wrong place at such a time, in which case, you're thoroughly familiar with this particular problem.

However, scope sights do offer some notable advantages to the shooter, especially to those shooters whose eyes are not getting a bit younger with the passage of the decades. Trying to achieve a simultaneous focus upon rear sight, front blade and target can be a real challenge under ideal circumstances. But if you're reaching that stage of life where your eyes are fine but your arms are just too short, the rear sight tends to become nothing but a hazy blur, offering no more than token assistance in aiming.

Here, a scope can be a friend in need. The actual magnification of the target image is of no more than secondary importance. What counts is the fact that the crosshairs and the point at which you're aiming are all incorporated into the same plane of focus and you're working with just one sharp picture. Even if your eyes have wandered off into some non-standard focal length of their own choosing, the objective lens of the scope usually can be adjusted to compensate for the aberration. It's almost as handy as having your auto's windshield ground to your optical prescription, though it may croggle your friends if they grab up your rifle for a hasty shot.

There are certain black powder rifle designs that are much better suited to the installation of scopes than are most of the rest. These are the ones in which the fuss and commotion of ignition is not in close proximity to the logical mounting place for the scope, i.e., atop the barrel and near the breech end of it. Typical examples of such designs would include the Hopkins & Allen rifles, with their hammer located underneath the barrel and driven by a trigger guard which doubles as a mainspring. Then, there's the Esopus Pacer .45 rifle, with its hammer and cap nipple located in a recess in the receiver on the side of the action

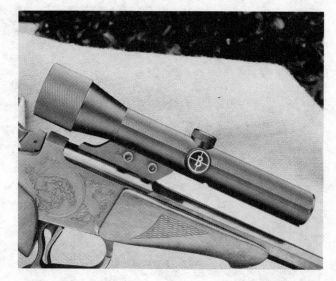

Here are three modern scope sights that are well suited for mounting some distance forward on the barrel. Above left, the M8-2X by Leupold-Stevens; top right, the Bushnell Phantom in 1.3X – also available in 2.6X – and, at right, the 1.5X Puma scope by Thompson/Center.

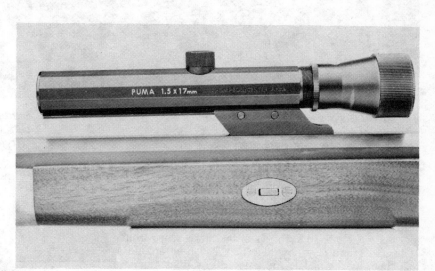

above the trigger and well out of the way of a scope. The break-action Harrington & Richardson Huntsman rifles, with their cap nipples tucked away in the area that would be the chamber of a breechloader, are adaptable for scoping in much the same way.

Those who essayed — with varying degrees of success and satisfaction to mount a scope on the more common, top-ignition rifle designs usually took the hopeful step toward a solution to their lens-fogging problems by locating the scope well forward on the barrel, several inches away from the nipple or flash-pan. This was more or less helpful, depending upon the smoke-spewing traits of the given rifle. However, it presented another problem in that most scopes are designed to provide an eye relief of not much over three inches between the aiming eye and the rear or objective lens of the scope.

If you back off farther than that distance, the image, as seen through the scope, shrinks down into a tiny area in the center of the glass, hardly more than a half-inch across and it becomes a time-consuming challenge to find the target by squinting through the optics.

There have been accessory eyepieces, by means of which the eye relief of a conventional scope could be extended to permit their use when mounted well forward along the barrel. Such devices have not proved overly popular with the buying public and, as a result, have not remained on the market in general supply for very long.

One reason that most shooters are disinclined to attempt modification of standard scopes for purposes of increasing the eye relief is that there are several scopes that are designed expressly to provide a longer eye relief. These have been appearing on the market in increasing variety in the last ten years or so.

Many such scopes were developed initially for use on handguns, with eye relief on the order of eighteen or twenty inches. One of the earliest to appear was a small unit made in Germany, known as the Nickel scope. Small and light in weight, it had no provision for internal adjustments as to elevation or windage, relying upon adjustments in the mount for these. The field of view was quite narrow and there was but little magnification of the image, but the crosshairs of the reticle were seen by the aiming eye as being in the same plane of focus as the target and this was acclaimed as quite helpful by many shooters.

One aspect of scoping handguns should be noted, however, and that's the way they seem to accentuate your

The late Al Goerg was a tireless pioneer and advocate of scope sights for muzzleloaders and handguns, here with a predatory seal.

Hunting the steep slopes of Waimea Canyon, on Kauai Island, Goerg regretted the lack of carrying strap on H&A's Heritage Model rifle.

amount of wavering and wobbling across the target when fired from unsupported or offhand positions. Actually, you don't waver much more with a scope than without one, but the oscillations are a lot more apparent than when aiming with iron — open — sights.

I first encountered examples of the Nickel scope around 1948 and cannot say how long they had been around at that time. By the middle and latter '50s, various American scope makers were adding models with extended eye relief to their lines. Redfield had their "FrontIER" line — the last three letters stood for "Intermediate Eye Relief" — Leupold had their fine little M8-2X unit and Bushnell began importing their Phantom pistol scopes in 1958.

These designs were intended for use at about an arm's length distance from the eye and ingenious shooters began mounting them on various problem rifles, as well as upon the handguns for which they had nominally been designed. Such impromptu grafting projects included the old, lever-action Model 94 Winchester carbine — heretofore impractical for scoping by reason of its top-ejection of spent cases — and any number of muzzleloading rifles, plus a few front-feeder handgun designs.

One of the most intrepid, indefatigable and innovative workers in the field of scoping guns that had never been fitted with such sighting systems before was the late Al Goerg — lost in a plane crash while hunting Alaska in the fall of 1965. During that era, Goerg scoped air rifles, innumerable types of handguns, muzzleloading rifles and stopped barely short of slingshots; he might have gotten around to those, had fate been more kindly.

By conducting the initial installations — often jury-rigged with vast ingenuity — and then working the bugs out of the setup, going on to prove the practicality of the

Goerg had left the hooded iron front sight in place on the H&A and its scope was mounted to permit use of open sights if emergency were to rise.

With grouping capability on the order of six minutes of angle, Goerg felt a bit undergunned for the vast reaches of Waimea Canyon, but he vindicated his choice, as usual!

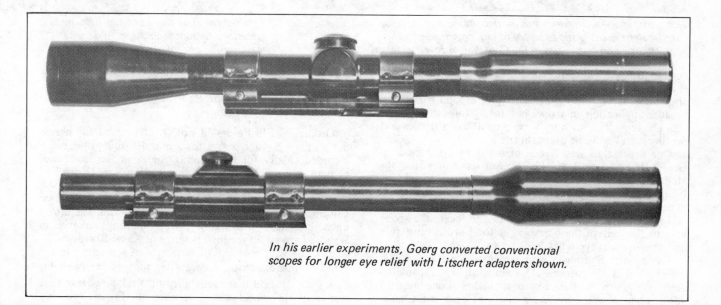

In his earlier experiments, Goerg converted conventional scopes for longer eye relief with Litschert adapters shown.

Not a true scope sight, since this particular one lacks lenses, tubular sight is authentic example of equipment used by sharpshooters on both sides in the Civil War. A few had lenses.

Limited reach of black powder rifle made it necessary to approach game by patient stalking and climbing of steep slopes.

combination via successful hunting in the field, followed by enthusiastic accounts of the entire procedure in the firearms press, Goerg did a great deal toward popularizing the broader application of scopes in hunting and target shooting. The impact of his work upon present-day attitudes and practices can hardly be over-estimated.

One such safari was typical of the many conducted by Goerg. He had mounted a J2.5 Weaver scope on a Heritage Model Hopkins & Allen — the modern replica as sold by Numrich — using a pair of Weaver number 39 bases and the same firm's top scope mount. Due to the underhammer design of the H&A, he had been able to locate the scope well to the rear of the barrel, so as to afford comfortable and conventional eye relief.

Preliminary sighting-in and target tests with the rifle indicated that its patched .45 round ball was capable of delivering groups on the order of six inches at one hundred yards, when powered by 70 grains of FFFg powder. Chang-

ing to FFg granulation opened up the groups to around twenty inches at the same distance and, oddly enough, shifting back to FFFFg powder focused things right back to the six-inch diameter again.

Ordinarily FFFFg would not be considered for use as the primary powder charge for a muzzleloading rifle, being intended chiefly for the priming charge in flintlocks and, perhaps, for the smallest handguns. However, Goerg had not contented himself with sallying forth to strafe some rockchucks in his native Pacific Northwest with the new lash-up. Instead, he had flown to Hawaii and was intent upon bagging a goat on a private hunting preserve in Waimea Canyon, in the high country of Kauai Island.

Arriving with a supply of powder that was sparse to the verge of non-existence, Goerg attempted to replenish his flask, only to find that availability of black powder in that corner of the world was close unto nil. Frantic scouring

From about fifty yards, the Heritage Model fired its .45 ball with more than ample force for a one-shot kill.

dispersion would have held more optimistic hopes of success. His hunting companions, residents of the area, were armed with modern rifles in the .270 Winchester class and tended to look in askance at Goerg's unlikely choice.

The lay of the land was vertical, or nearly so, to a predominant extent, requiring long interludes of hand-and-foot climbing. This prompted the reflection that the absence of a sling or carrying strap consituted something of a major handicap, equally as much a problem as the comparative limitations of the rifle as to range and grouping ability.

However, while midway up a precipitous slope, Goerg paused and, after a bit, one goat showed a cautious exposure of head. While debating the odds in favor of landing a hit on the tiny area presented, a second goat appeared, almost completely exposed to view and at a distance the hunter estimated at fifty yards.

Holding the top of the post reticle well up on the goat's shoulder, Goerg squeezed off his one and only round — since reloading procedures would have been even slower than usual on his precarious perch — and, as the blue smoke billowed and eddied about him, he knew he had scored by the sound of the goat, rolling bonelessly down the rocky canyon wall.

The .45 ball had struck precisely at the point of aim, on the shoulder and had penetrated completely through the goat, exiting on the far side for a clean and instantaneous kill. All that remained was to dress down the carcass and pack the hindquarters and backstraps back to camp in a plastic sack which had been carried in Goerg's pack against just such a moment of need.

Upon his return, after displaying the proof of his success Goerg felt gratified and somewhat vindicated to observe that the rest of the hunting party had come to regard his primitive artillery with respect that was considerably different from their good-natured chaffing of the same morning. It was, he felt, one more small victory in his one-man campaign to win recognition and appreciation for the rifles of an earlier and simpler day — and for the concept of employing telescopic sights in conjunction with them.

One of the simplest and most satisfactory avenues for assembling a scoped muzzleloader takes the form of the Thompson/Center Hawken replicas. Available in a choice of .45 or .50 barrels, with option of percussion or flintlock ignition, it is an easy operation to replace the open, adjustable rear sights furnished on these rifles with one of the Thompson/Center Puma scopes, offered by the firm for use on their single-shot breechloader pistols which feature interchangeable barrels in a wide assortment of calibers.

Installation is but a matter of tapping out a roll pin and removing the factory rear sight after loosening a couple of screws that fasten it to the barrel. The mount for the Puma scope screws into place on the barrel, using the same holes as the open iron rear sight, putting the rear surface of the lens a good five and one-half inches away from the nipple or priming pan.

Magnification of the Puma's optical system is 1.3X and the eye relief is just right to afford a comfortable sighting picture when mounted on the Hawken. All that remains is to convince yourself that the practical aspect of the installation outweighs any disturbing effect it may have upon your innate sense of the fitness of things and your own visualization of the proper image of the muzzleloader shooter and huntsman.

Once your own misgivings are reconciled, it should not prove unduly difficult to still the jeers of your contemporaries by the same method Goerg used with repeated success, namely by bringing home the bacon and flashing it in their faces. *– Dean A. Grennell*

turned up the one lone can of FFFFg and, after determining that the Hopkins & Allen could perform capably with the stuff, the remaining quantity was husbanded carefully for employment in the actual hunt.

Goerg noted, in writing up the ensuing adventures, that the open expanses of terrain suggested that he would have been better advised to bring one of the flattest-shooting modern magnum rifles in place of his faintly diffident black powder replica. His H&A had a cone of fire spanning some six minutes of angle when, it appeared, one-twelfth of that

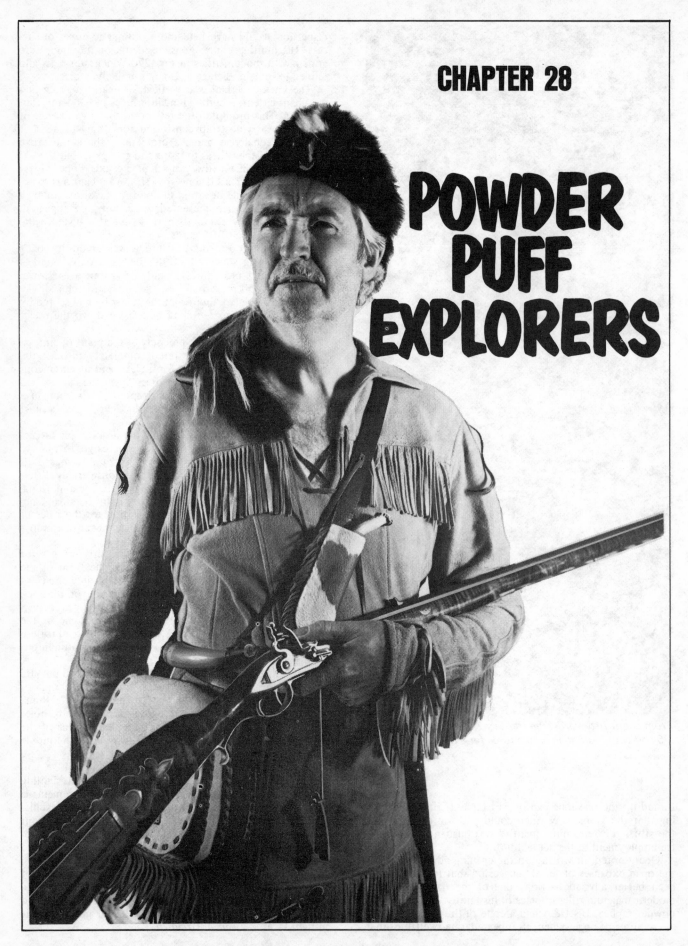

CHAPTER 28

POWDER PUFF EXPLORERS

R.O. Ackerman

A Whole New Scouting Program Devoted To Muzzleloading Marksmanship Brings The Sport Into The Public Eye!

THE MUZZLELOADING SPORTS have received the biggest boost they have had in many years. As only a handful of people had advance notice of this, the story should be of interest to everyone who shoots black powder, and who hopes to continue doing so in the face of bitter opposition. After many bad breaks, we can use a good one!

It all began in mid-fall of 1971, when I was contacted by our good friend, Turner Kirkland. The well known Tennessee dealer always has been in the forefront in promotion of this wholesome sport, so it was appropriate that the first news came from him.

Kirkland asked if I could lend a hand to the Boy Scouts of America, who were planning to incorporate muzzleloading and related skills into their new training program. This was on the national level and naturally BSA executives wanted some technical guidance in inaugurating such an ambitious project.

Rest assured, before another sun rose behind the Sandia Mountains of Albuquerque, these great people had a volunteer! "Willing" would be the understatement of the year..."stuttering with excitement" would be more accurate!

In the months which have followed, this enthusiasm had increased steadily among all the people associated with the program. Many careful planning sessions have culminated in a brand new concept in the advanced training of Explorer Scouts and scout leaders.

Villa Philmonte was given, completely furnished, to the BSA by Waite Phillips. One of the many interesting displays is a rare silver beaver pelt.

Of several scouting activities which include the use of muzzleloaders, by far the most intriguing has been named "The Rocky Mountain Fur Trappers Company." This was started in the 1972 training season at the huge, 214-square mile Philmont Scout Ranch and Explorer Base near Cimarron, New Mexico. In the years ahead, similar programs doubtless will spread to other scout training centers across the nation. Not only will these young people be introduced to the challenge of muzzleloading, but they will absorb a great deal of meaningful history and gain a personal insight into our priceless heritage. They incidentally will learn a degree of self-reliance which no other training could surpass.

To properly understand why Philmont Scout Ranch is the one logical place to launch such specialized training, it is necessary to know what Philmont is. As it is little publicized outside of scouting circles, the visitor always is amazed at its many facets of interest.

As one enters Philmont Ranch from the direction of Cimarron, a good road extends for miles past administration buildings, classrooms, tent cities, horse barns and a modern library and museum building. This houses important collections of pioneer and Indian artifacts, plus the world's largest collection of the drawings and paintings by Ernest Thompson Seton, famed artist and naturalist who was one of the founders of the Boy Scouts of America.

On this main road, one also passes the magnificent former home of the late Waite Phillips, the Tulsa oilman. Phillips donated his sprawling mountain ranch to the Boy Scouts of America, including his beautifully furnished mansion. There are conducted tours of the great house for visitors. Total expanse of Philmont is now 137,493 acres.

This main road abounds in western history. It is part of the original Santa Fe Trail and, in places, deep covered wagon wheel ruts still can be traced. You may see the large Philmont buffalo herd along the way and antelope grazing beside the ranch's beef cattle.

The terrain becomes wilder and more mountainous. A 9,000-foot peak, the Tooth of Time, was once a landmark for the covered wagon trains that followed this famous

The Tooth of Time towers 9000 feet above the plains, once was landmark for westbound pioneers.

Straining to resist the downward drag of massive .50 T/C Hawken flintlock, scout Norman Tyler fights "flinter's flinch" for a try at elusive bull.

trail. Shortly before it divides into many smaller paths leading up into the Sangre de Cristos, the road passes the homes of Kit Carson and of Lucien Maxwell, whose Maxwell Land Grant was three times the size of Rhode Island.

Yes, this is the big country. A youth quickly absorbs the historic flavor of it, especially as the traditional stamping grounds of famed mountainmen-trappers like Carson, Maxwell and others of their rugged breed.

There could not be a more appropriate area for a program that teaches Explorer Scouts muzzleloading and all other skills of these old mountainmen. The Rocky Mountain Fur Trappers Company is designed for the self-reliant type of youth who has done all of the conventional things which scouting offers and is now ready for a greater challenge.

The RMFTC is based at Clear Creek, the most remote of all of the ranch's many little camps. It is high in this part of the Rocky Mountain chain...the Sangre de Cristo range, meaning Blood of Christ, was actually a favorite beaver trapping area for mountainmen in the early 1800s. You can be sure that an almost inaccessible spot like Clear Creek would have been chosen by the original trapper-explorers,

perhaps by Kit Carson himself. They were a breed of loners who liked their privacy above all else, except at the annual rendezvous when they traded their bundles of plews for supplies and one big rip-roaring blast...then rode out to do it all over again!

Clear Creek was chosen carefully, to inaugurate a scouting program which is expected to be tremendously popular among a long list of optional activities. These include gold panning, mountain climbing, survival techniques, lumbering and a host of others appropriate to the area. Out of them all, it is encouraging to see the number of young men who are including Clear Creek in their choice of an itinerary. As the size of each party coming through must be limited due to the personal nature of the instruction, let's hope they can all be accommodated.

The instructor group at Clear Creek also was selected carefully. I know them all, and they are tops. There's quiet Bill Reilley, who hunted with his flintlock back in Pennsylvania's wooded hills, and Luther Jones, to whom "store-bought" buckskins is a cuss-word. The others are of the same caliber and they are doing a man's job. These men will live the mountainman's austere life for months, to pass on their skills to all who wish to learn them.

Granite monument marks location of the original
Santa Fe Trail which covered several miles across
the land now made available to BSA for training use.

Anyone heading for this camp may choose to take some preliminary instruction before leaving the main training center. This could include throwing a diamond hitch on a pack burro (taught by a leathery wrangler). Other subjects may be handled by scouters, Park Service personnel, forest rangers or even Air Force Academy cadets. A number of these cadets serve as summer instructors to the scouts, as this augments their own training in leadership.

Arriving at Clear Creek, the explorers enter a different life. Instructors are authentically garbed in buckskins or homespun hunting shirts and leggings. There are no can openers, no transistor radios. The food is the fare of the mountainmen: trout, game, venison jerky stew, parched corn, pemmican; it is good and appetites are tremendous in that mountain air.

Every student learns to load and fire a percussion rifle, a flinter or both, as both were used in the mountainman era. He learns to clean a muzzleloader and care for it. He may be shown such things as replacing a mainspring in the wilds. By the evening campfire, each student will cast rifle balls for the next day's shooting.

Trapping, tanning small hides, curing jerky, throwing the knife and tomahawk, building a trapper's lean-to with a Green River knife...every related skill dear to the heart of the muzzleloader will be a part of the Clear Creek experience. But most emphasis will be upon the use of the rag-nosed rifle, and we hope every scouter who becomes part of the RMFTC will look up his nearest black powder club upon his return home!

This will make it a lasting experience for him and it will swell the ranks of voting sportsmen materially as each season produces thousands of new enthusiasts. These men of today and of tomorrow will be less apathetic about preserving their rights and their national heritage than some of the former crop seem to be.

Points to consider: About 15,000 scouts and 1,500 leaders come through Philmont's camping department each season. The training center gets another 5,000 professional leaders each year. Another bonus is that Philmont is open to all scouting type organizations, worldwide. Men, women and children come there from Nigeria, Israel, England, Jamaica and countless other countries. It has a universal reputation among scouters. The Japanese particularly love

Scouts soon learn that a gun needn't be brand-new to pack a wicked wallop! This gallon can, filled with water was exploded by a lead .58 Hawken ball.

Great emphasis is placed upon the importance of following approved safety precautions at Philmont.

Philmont.

As this is written, the response to RMFTC is already terrific, in many dialects. This might be the turning point that could put some additional anti-gunners out to pasture in the years ahead.

Equally terrific has been the generous support given by manufacturers and dealers, in donating muzzleloaders and accessories to get this project started.

Turner Kirkland of Dixie Gun Works led off with nearly a thousand dollars worth of equipment — rifles and pistols, flint and percussion, with all moulds and accessories. His catalog is becoming the latest Boy Scout Handbook.

Then Dale Edwards of Indian Ridge Traders sent a bunch of his Green River knives — modern made, but by the same company who supplied them to the original mountainmen! A converted Green River owned by Kit Carson is on display in the Carson home and museum here.

The Mowrey folks in Texas donated a fine rifle and shotgun to help the program. Others keep coming in, until I have lost exact track of what they are receiving.

Also demonstrated at Philmont, and tried by a large group of instructors, were examples of arms by the other major manufacturers. The Lee Paul .58 custom-made Hawken, Navy Arms flinter, Esopus double rifle, Thompson-Center Hawken, Replica Arms shotgun and M1862 revolver and the new Ruger percussion revolver, among others, were enthusiastically received. Related items such as the new Miami-Whitewater hunting pouch, Free'n'kleen's Kit in a Kan black powder solvent and the new Ohaus line of round ball moulds were chosen for the demonstrations.

We were careful to expose these young people only to top quality equipment, as some of the cheapies could have turned them off.

We can expect this Boy Scout muzzleloading program to expand rapidly, as it contains all of the desirable ingredients: A challenging sport, an element of competition, a wide variety of approaches and different facets, an outstanding opportunity for ingenious personal craftsmanship — and a close tie-in with tradition and United States history.

I am proud to be even a small part of it! — *R. O. Ackerman*

TWO CENTURIES OF BLACK POWDER

CHAPTER 29

Muzzleloading benchrest rifle used in test was fitted with Tower lock above. Reverse side is shown in photo at right.

What Happens With Muzzleloaders Had Been Theoretical, Until 7000 Frames Per Second Told The Story!

Cameraman Elmer Herman looks through Fastex camera while Warren Barnes sights down rifle barrel; mirrors reflect firing sequence to camera.

MY OLD MAN started my shooting education the summer I was eight years old. "Safety" was older and well along in his training and my other brother, Jack, was only a few months old. Of course I remember the gun; it was the most beautiful rifle ever built. At least I thought so. As a matter of fact it was a beauty...a Marlin 1897 take-down .22 with a twenty-four inch octagon barrel and three folding Marble sights.

The peep sight on the tang folded down so the leaf sight on the barrel could be used. The front sight had an ivory bead in the open position or when the bead was down, a pin head on a post with a protecting ring was up. I have owned hundreds of fine guns since that wonderful summer

of 1908 but none any better than the little Marlin. They still make an octagon barrelled .22 the 39A.

Occasionally, Grandfather Al would drop by to observe our progress. I remember he used to say, "Always be careful, a gun is dangerous without lock, stock or barrel."

I didn't know exactly what he meant; I knew what the barrel and the stock were but that lock bit threw me, but in those days a boy of eight didn't horse around with or ask dumb questions of grandfathers. I think he was misquoting, but I didn't know that then. The old boy was sharp and spry for his seventy-odd years and he could take that .22 rifle and "make it sing," so I had great respect for him.

The locks on most modern guns are not a definite thing

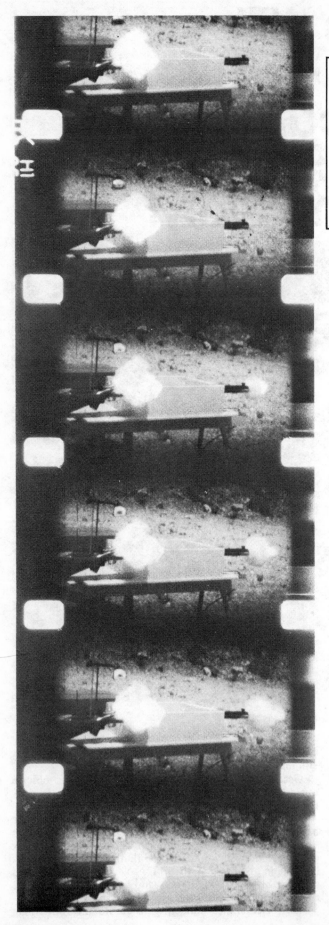

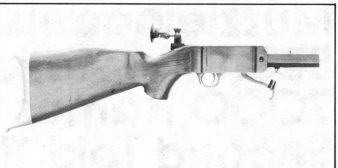

Direct path of flash from percussion cap to powder in chamber makes this Wiechold-Range-King one of best caplock designs. Below, Furst's operation at work, shot from flintlock has just broken the front mirror; replaced after each shot.

Sequence at left demonstrates the speed of camera being used. In frame one the powder in flash pan has ignited, but there is no evidence of the shot leaving the flintlock's muzzle until frame three.

you can take out as a unit and study as you can the locks of a muzzleloader. In fact, I didn't pay much attention to locks until the muzzleloading phase of target shooting bit me about twenty years ago. Then locks became definite, important things. I never have collected muzzleloaders as a hobby. I bought a gun because I wanted a shooter, a good target gun; so I bought and tested many guns and either kept them or traded or sold them off, in the process of getting my equipment together.

Sometimes it was impossible to find an antique to meet my specs; then I would have one made. At times it would be a new gun from the ground up or maybe all new except for the lock which might be a venerable item of more than 100 years. In any event, I would end up with a fine target gun that will permit somebody to enjoy this hobby one hundred or more years from now when many of the current crop of prize antiques no longer will be serviceable.

The ideal situation for me would be to have one gun with which to fire all matches. It certainly would simplify things and make the whole hobby more fun for me. I am close to such an ideal condition, with Buttercup, my free-

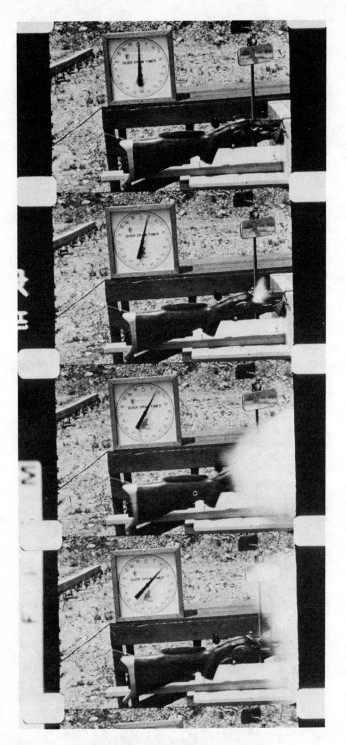

Taken at 24 frames per second, clip above shows the hammer falling with clock reading .01 seconds in frame one. At .04 seconds in frame two, the pan is ignited, gun has fired in frame three, the clock reading .085 seconds. Fair estimate of firing time author judges to be from .055 to .075 seconds.

style, flintlock, fifteen-pound rifle.

In discussing the ignition time of flintlock versus caplock guns with the experts, opinions varied so, and my own "eyeball" observations only added to my confusion. So I felt it necessary to make a careful study of the subject. Having spent four years in Hollywood in the late twenties making feature length moving pictures and since my son Bill, in addition to being an avid target shooter, makes his living as a professional photographer, we decided to make a movie test of the two types of locks for our own information.

It all started out as a simple experiment, using one Bolex 16mm camera. This unit operates at a normal speed of twenty-four frames per second; the film can be speeded up to sixty-four frames per second which slows down the action two and two-thirds times slower than normal. I thought this would do the job but sixty-four fps were not fast enough to find out what we wanted to know.

Bill did some recruiting and we finally made the test with three view cameras, two Bolex movie cameras and one Wollensack Fastax camera complete with cameraman Warren Barnes, who was experienced not only with the camera but with the accompanying electronic gear. We had a Quick Draw Timer and Jim Quinn covered the whole production with his 35mm color slide camera. The three movie cameras used color film, the still cameras black and white. All cameras photographed each firing. The Fastax camera used a special color film that is kept refrigerated. We ran thirteen of these one hundred-foot good reels of 16mm film through the Fastax that day and only got two good ones. Luckily one was of a flintlock shot and the other a caplock shot. Our troubles are of no interest to this account. The quality of our high speed shots were disappointing to me but Bill and Warren assured me it was better than most high speed stuff. It certainly gave us the information we sought.

When choosing the guns to be tested, we deliberately selected the fastest or what we believed (and still do) to be the fastest firing caplock rifle: A Weichold Range-King with an understriking action. The short hammer fall, and short, straight path for the ignition-fire to follow, may be seen in one of the illustrations. The flintlock rifle selected belonged to Vaughn Wiley and was completely modern made except for the Tower lock which was one of the late Elmer Herman's best. The lock shows its age but it was in perfect mechanical condition. Elmer tuned-up both guns and was in charge of the loading and firing operations. To be sure the gun was fired, when the Fastax camera was going at full speed, the trigger was pulled by a solenoid actuated from the programming device under the Fastax operator's control.

The gun was loaded and mounted in the cradle, the mirrors were aligned, the gun was primed and the solenoid was plugged into the control panel or programming device; now the Fastax cameraman was in charge of the whole deal. He checked to make sure the range was clear (we almost got Quinn twice), gave the Bolex cameramen a five-second countdown; then started the cameras at minus-three and at "blast," he hit the start button. A lot of things happened all at once. The film started through the camera and after .43 seconds it had built up to a speed of over 6,000 frames per second and the trigger was pulled. The hammer fell, striking the frizzen and the powder in the pan ignited. The film was now going at the rate of 7,000 frames per second as the gun fired. All this took place in the space of one second.

The high speed camera so extended the time of firing that it permitted us to see and study wonders the eye alone could never catch. What a pleasure it would be to show this

The series of shots at the left show the bullet actually breaking the mirror. Camera has already recorded shot.

picture to a man like Joseph Manton of England or LePage of France who were masters in advancing the perfection of the flintlock action in the late 1700s. I wonder what interpretations they would put on what they would see? The findings of this experiment showed that the caplock fired (time taken from the start of the hammer fall to first sighting of fire at the muzzle) in .022 second (twenty-two thousandths of one second). The flintlock fired in .055 second.

Even though this caplock rifle fired 2½ times faster than the flintlock rifle, I think the firing time of a conventional caplock rifle, with lock in the side of the gun and the hammer falling down on a nipple, exploding a cap, whose fire must travel around a ninety-degree angle to get into the powder chamber, would slow down almost to the .055 second speed of this Tower lock.

The way the flintlock guns have been winning open matches over caplock guns in recent years leads me to believe they may be more accurate than we have been giving them credit for and possibly for reasons we don't even suspect.

This first hi-speed movie investigation of ours, like most movie productions, exceeded the budget several times. Even so, we are starting to plan for the "second round" with improved backgrounds at the lock and muzzle, larger mirrors, two clocks in every shot and several other refinements which will make the picture worthwhile for showing at club meetings, etc., especially after dialog and sound have been dubbed in.

My biggest disappointment with this hi-speed movie was the fact that one could not see the bullet coming out the muzzle from the side view. The only view of the bullet is the one the mirrors give you from the front as the bullet smashes into the front mirror and powders it.

We are studying flintlock actions and their performance, overall life of the piece of flint itself, sharpening interval as well as potential improvements in the handling of the flintlock target rifle and maximum results possible. Concurrently with the study of the flintlock phases, such items as speed of twist, depth of rifling and the strange phenomenon of the difference of the quality of the explosion in the chamber of a caplock rifle as opposed to a flintlock rifle are being considered. — *Bob Furst*

The Fastex cameras were manually started four or five seconds
before the actual shot. In frame one the camera is going as
the solenoid automatically pulls the flintlock's trigger.

CHAPTER 30 OUT OF THE PAST, INTO THE FUTURE

Departing From Duplicated Oldies, Here Are Glimpses Of Things To Come!

WITH THE GROWING interest in black powder shooting by the gun-oriented, new means of developing that interest are on the drawing boards around the country. We already have mentioned Bill Ruger's departure from the cartridge magnum handgun field to come up with a black powder six-shooter, as well as Colt's return to the past to reintroduce one of their early cap and ball models.

But the developments have not stopped here. Instead of updating old models, some firms are taking a long look at the potential and now are introducing new and revolutionary designs that tend to cure many of the problems of the more ancient arms.

Two of these firms are Rocky Mountain Arms Corporation of Salt Lake City, Utah, and Esopus Gun Works. The latter is a division of Port Ewen Products, Incorporated, in upstate New York.

Except for the ramrod, there is little in the appearance of the Esopus Pacer .45 to mark it one of the muzzleloader type.

But the better mousetraps being built by RMAC aren't for our four-legged, furry friends. They're for the coonskin cap crowd that get their kicks out of drilling holes in a piece of paper with a lead ball propelled by black powder.

RMAC has three new black powder rifles on the market in .22, .36 and .44 calibers. These rifles are not a reproduction of anything, but completely new designs from butt plate to muzzle. And instead of loading from the muzzle,

all these are breechloaders that use a simple turret to hold the powder, ball and cap. The advantage of breech loading was recognized by early black powder gunsmiths, but a reliable system was not developed until the late 1800s. But by then smokeless powder had stolen the thunder from the ramrodders.

Richard J. (Dick) Casull, designer and inventor of the turret rifles and other firearms, decided that breechloading

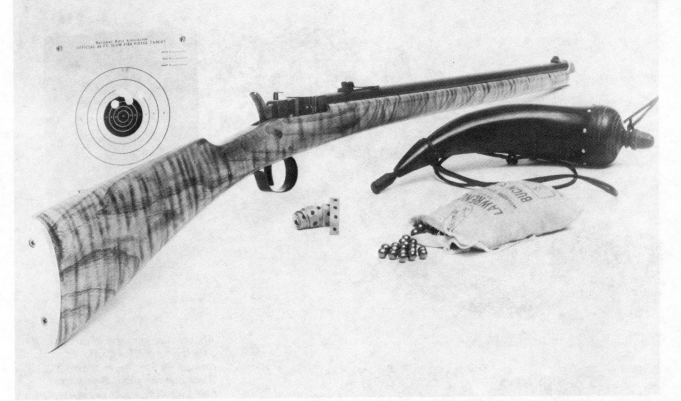

Rocky Mountain Arms' unique breechloading black powder rifle features safety, low purchasing and operating cost with accuracy in three calibers.

was an inexpensive way to get more people back into shooting black powder. Other advantages of his turret rifles are the inherent safety and speed of loading and firing. They all use standard pure lead buckshot and "cap gun" percussion caps in the firing system.

In addition to the new turret system, all the rifles have a unique reducing cone in the barrel breech that gives the lead ball a cylindrical shape for better ballistics. This, combined with machine cut rifling, makes the rifles extremely accurate at fifty yards, with an effective range about a hundred yards. The reducing cone also insures a more effective gas seal. No other black powder rifles on the market today have all these modern features.

In spite of their all-new design, these rifles have all the lines and flavor of the original Kentucky and Plains rifles. The .36 and .44 calibers have full length stocks, hand-worked from rich woods. The .22 is available with a resinous fiber or wood half-stock.

One of the prime objectives of their inventor, Dick Casull, and Rocky Mountain Arms was to offer black powder buffs an opportunity to own and shoot rifles that didn't require a second mortgage. Price for the .22 with resinous fiber stock is $37.50, ($49.50 with wood stock). The .36 or .44 caliber with full Mannlicher stock goes for $99.50, although current prices are subject to change as with most things these days.

But the best part of it all is the low cost of shooting. The .22 caliber costs about $1 to fire 250 shots, compared with an average cost of eighty-five cents for a box of fifty .22 long rifle shells. It uses ordinary No. 3 buckshot. The .36 and .44 calibers use No. 1 buckshot and .45 caliber lead balls respectively, and are correspondingly economical to fire. The percussion caps are ordinary Fourth of July cap gun

Inventor Dick Casull checks milling operation on turret for RMAC's new breechloading b.p. rifle.

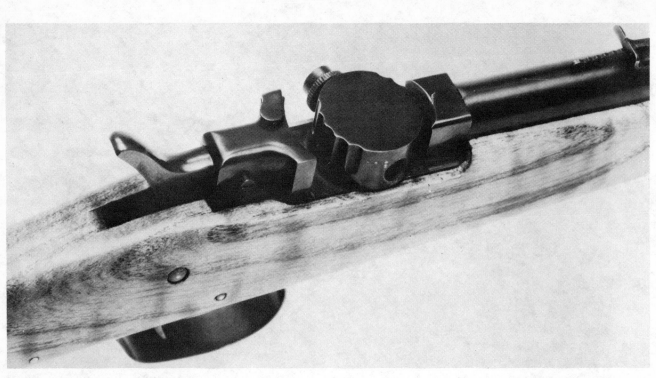

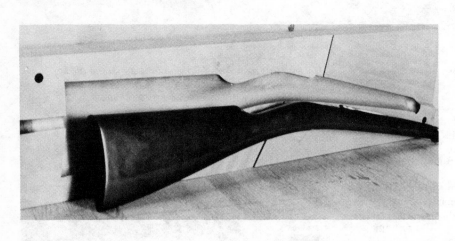

Above: A closer view of breech details on the RMAC rifle. It's rotated for loading, as shown. Black powder and ball go into hole on turret, paper cap goes under nipple cover. Turret then rotates into line with barrel for firing. Left: RMAC .22 rifle is available with resinous fiber moulded stock or optional wood.

variety, giant size, costing about a dime for two hundred or more. These simple igniters are very positive in action.

The simple turret system is identical in principle on all three rifles. The turret is held in line with the bore by a strong spring latch. The latch is released and the turret turned to expose the powder and ball chamber on one side and the nipple with cap cover on the other. A loose powder charge is poured and a lead ball seated in the chamber by hand until it is flush with the chamber opening. Then a simple paper cap is inserted in the nipple cover, which also serves as a gas seal when it is replaced. The turret then is rotated back in line with the bore and the rifle is ready to fire. The whole operation takes just a few seconds. Extra nipple covers are available for preloading with paper caps to further reduce the loading time.

RMAC's simple turret system presents many advantages. The rifles cannot be overloaded, since the chamber has a fixed powder capacity. As the ball is larger than the bore, it cannot be loaded from the muzzle. Powder charges have been calculated to give the best accuracy at velocities higher than standard .22 shells. This is aided by the swaging

chamber that reduces the ball to a cylinder and forms a tight seal with the bore.

Another feature of these rifles is the flat-faced hammer with a positive action safety. The guns will not fire when the lock latch is depressed and the hammer at half-cock.

The simplicity of the turret and action make these rifles extremely easy to clean and maintain. There are only five moving parts and the rifles can be easily disassembled for the traditional hot soapy water treatment. However, the new black powder solvents now available make frequent disassembly unnecessary. Watts Water, one such solvent, is also marketed by Rocky Mountain Arms.

Barrels are turned from 4140 chrome-moly steel. They are bored, reamed and finished with precision, machine cut rifling (button rifling on the .22). The receiver block, turret, hammer and trigger mechanism are machined from high strength steel. A deep bluing is used for extra protection and lasting beauty. The wood to metal fits are exact.

All three rifles are designed to be soft shooters, as far as recoil is concerned. The .44 slug is powered by 45 grains of FFg, for a muzzle velocity of about 1360 feet per second

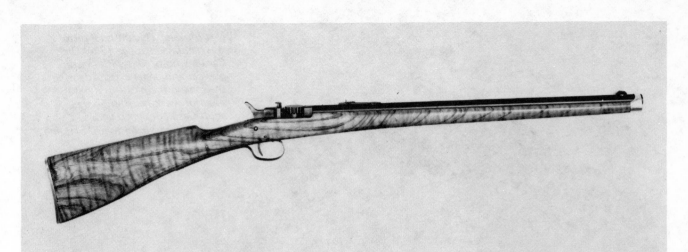

Attractively figured wood of the A36 RMAC rifle, above, sets off the sleek lines of its stock. The A44 version, below, is of adequate size for hunting deer.

and a recoil about like the mild-mannered old .25-20. The .36 caliber takes 30 grains of FFg, with 6 grains in the .22. The characteristics and cost of these black powder beauties should make them ideal for the entire family.

Dick Casull, gunsmith and inventor of the rifles, holds a doctorate from the school of hard knocks. He made his first pistol at the age of 12, and since has learned by doing, not sitting in a classroom. Along the way he has gained expertise in stock inletting, tool and die making, heat treating and metallurgy, barrel making, and barrel ballistics. He is the inventor of the .454 Casull magnum single action revolver, called the world's most powerful handgun.

The recent renewed interest in the black powder rifles inspired Casull to rethink the entire problem. Most shooters had to depend on the ancient guns themselves, dug out of attics and barns. Or they had to lay out a sum for new black powder rifles imported from abroad.

His answer was to design an entirely new black powder rifle, using modern materials and methods. The answer turned out to be a quality, low cost black powder rifle that is economical to fire; one that even a youngster can handle with safety, while learning the basic functions of a rifle and how it fires.

Designing a line of new black powder rifles is a tremendous challenge and accomplishment. So is manufacturing and getting them out to the public. Charles W. Taggart, founder and president of Rocky Mountain Arms Corporation, immediately saw their potential and made Casull director of research and development for RMAC. Taggart is a Salt Lake City businessman with interests in publishing, land development, manufacturing and diversified international investments.

Taggart found an entire arms plant for the manufacture of the new black powder rifles. The plant was disassembled and brought to Salt Lake City, where production of the rifles now is under way. Taggart and Casull both have wide ranging interests, plus a blend of inventive and business genius. In addition to the black powder rifles, RMAC is manufacturing the Casull .454 revolver, a miniature five-shot .22, precision barrels and a gun rest for large frame revolvers. A variety of related firearms products now are in pre-production testing.

Specifications of the new black powder rifles:

A44 Black Powder Breech Loading Rifle: Single-shot; Length, 46 inches; Length of pull, 13½ inches; Barrel length, 28 inches; Muzzle velocity, 1360 fps; Muzzle energy, 700 foot/pounds; Twist, 1 in 30; Weight 6 pounds, 6 ounces; .45 caliber ball/45-50 grains of FFg.

A36 Black Powder Breech Loading Rifle: Single-shot; Length, 39½ inches; Length of pull, 13½ inches; Barrel

Not for sale! This unusual pistol was handmade at age 12 by Dick Casull, who fired it with blasting powder and paper caps. Adapting the same principles — but with superior workmanship! — the adult Casull designed and is in charge of producing the RMAC line.

Novel squeeze-down principle of the RMAC rifle obtains remarkable velocity and accuracy with a comparatively small powder charge and lead balls.

Flat faced hammers of the RMAC rifle have a half cock notch for added safety. They cannot be fired from this position, even if turret is in firing line.

length, 22½ inches; Muzzle velocity, 1406 fps; Muzzle energy, 305 foot/pounds; Twist, 1 in 30; Weight, 5 pounds, 4 ounces; No. 1 buck shot/23 grains of FFg.

A22 Black Powder Breech Loading Rifle: Single-shot; Length, 35¼ inches; Length of pull, 13-1/8 inches; Barrel length, 20 inches; Muzzle velocity, 1340 fps; Muzzle energy, 99 foot/pounds; Twist, 1 in 16; Weight, 2 pounds, 15 ounces; No. 4 buck shot/7 grains of FFg.

At the other end of the country, the principals behind Port Ewen/Esopus Gun Works, John Waters and Al Pace, have lined up the executive talent necessary for the development and efficiency of a specialized gun manufacturing operation. In this department is Werner Vogel, who has spent many years in this field and is accomplished as an authority on black powder shooting and hunting, as well as firearms in general.

At present there are two muzzleloading guns in production at the Esopus plant. Each is as unlike the other as Calvin Coolidge differs from Ann Margaret. One of these guns is a swivel-breech double rifle in .45 caliber, perfectly suited for many hunting situations. In the cosmetic sense, this gun bears the Traditional Look, though that is where similarity ends. This swivel-breech is unique in a number of important ways, not the least of them relating to its internal design.

The second gun is a different cup of tea. Its only

similarity to any other muzzleloader is that it is loaded from the front. To date its design board designation has been MLI-.45 Cal., but we've just learned that it will, for-ever-more, be dubbed "The Pacer."

The Esopus two-shot over and under turn-barrel style rifle is produced on the most advanced industrial equipment you are likely to find in this type of operation. As stated, it is to be available in .45 caliber. Other calibers will be added, but not during 1972. The barrels of the two-shot measure twenty-eight inches and are tooled from high grade ordnance steel. This break with tradition was deemed important, since the customary "soft iron" simply does not offer the wear resistance or safety inherent in modern high grade ordnance steel.

Barrels for the new RMAC rifles are bored, reamed and finished with machine-cut rifling, being turned from No. 4140 chrome-moly steel and then blued.

The barrels are slow drilled to better guarantee a distortion-free barrel which does not require straightening. While at the plant, it was noted that Werner Vogel and his team do not use button or swage rifling. Instead, their barrels utilize eight grooves, cut with a single point tool to a depth of .007 inch. This is what Vogel has found to be most efficient for such a rifle, though it is not always what you may find in some current imports as well as many domestically produced. The twist for the two-shot barrels is one right turn in fifty-six inches — just the ticket for round balls, the short picket or the hollow-base conical Minie balls.

Looking further to the business of physical characteristics, the rifle measures exactly forty-four inches overall and allows a pull of 13¾ inches from the center of the curved butt plate to the trigger. The weight of the test over/under was precisely 8½ pounds. Density of wood can affect this, of course, by several ounces.

The Esopus gun features 7030 ordnance brass for all decorative furniture. This not only is handsome but corrosion-resistant. The stock and the forend panels are turned from American black walnut. A number of stocks examined at the New York State plant showed an interesting dark-grained wood that tends to impart a richness to the overall products.

Each of the two barrels has its own silver blade front sight, plus an open notch rear sight. Simple, traditional and

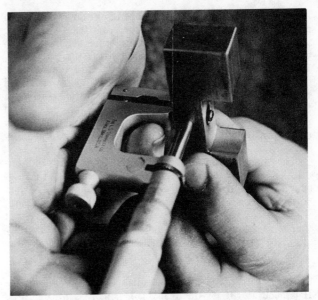

Each part of the RMAC black powder rifles is held to highly exacting working tolerances during the manufacturing process; this is turret holding block.

adequately effective for all normal hunting conditions, as well as for serious practice sessions on paper targets, they are dovetailed so that adjustment can be accomplished readily. During our test sessions with this swivel-breech, we found that, at fifty yards, there was a slight spread of approximately 1-1/8 inch between the groups fired from each of the two barrels. A few moments spent with a leather mallet, coupled to a few test rounds, corrected this to a point where both barrels now fired to the same point of impact.

Firing three shots from each barrel, at the fifty-yard mark, it was possible to produce one exceptional target that measured 1-3/8 inches for the total six shots from my benchrest. Other groups, though not as tight as this, were good enough to be classified as well above average for the combination of muzzleloader/open sights.

This particular satisfactory target was fired while using 70 grains of DuPont FFg, a .455 round ball and a fairly thin pillow ticking patch. Thin, unbleached muslin or broadcloth could have substituted just as well. Since the gun would be fired almost immediately after each loading, a greased patch was not deemed a necessity. Instead, saliva — a good old-fashioned spit patch — was substituted as the lubricant. The percussion caps used during these sessions were Remington's No. 11 as recommended both by experience and the gun's maker.

For those who would prefer to use a hollow-base Minie sans patching material, for greater speed of loading while on a hunt, I can recommend Lyman's 445599 mould. I have found this Minie performs best with from 50 to 53 grains of FFg.

On the subject of accuracy, this rifle or any other muzzleloader performs best when the bore is clean. My own rule of thumb calls for removal of fouling after every six rounds. In fact, many black powder match shooters insist on wiping out their muzzles with a damp patch following each round.

When it comes to operation of the Esopus swivel-breech, the barrel locking system is foolproof and positive. There is no manual latch with which to fumble and the barrel can be rotated in either direction, depending on whims and physical preferences of each shooter. All it takes after firing the first barrel is that the shooter bring the hammer to half-cock, then impart a quick wrist-twist to the barrels.

From the offhand stance, we have found that it takes just about four or five seconds to get off two well aimed shots. It is not necessary for the shooter's thumb to leave the hammer between shots and his hand on the forend panels is pre-positioned to make the necessary twist. Each barrel has its own drum and nipple, which position themselves to be fired by the same hammer and lock combo.

The barrels can be pivoted clockwise or counter-clockwise, with strong, spring-loaded ball bearings guaranteeing positive and correct barrel alignment. When correct alignment is reached, an audible click can be heard.

The lockwork of this swivel-breech is conventional, but that is as far as it goes. In the Esopus gun it is centrally mounted and has only two moving parts, allowing for the design of exceptionally large, strong components.

The new Esopus offering is not another replica or just one more of dozens of average-quality black powder guns. It is accurate, it is American made and it is priced to be within reach of most all serious shooters and hunters at $139.50.

What we have in the Pacer is a muzzleloading rifle of completely new design. As previously stated, its only similarity to any other muzzleloader is that it loads from the front end and uses black powder. The decision to venture this break from antiquity has enabled them to produce a rifle of mechanical simplicity and excellence. This model embodies softer cosmetic features, plus

handling and shooting qualities that are something near impossible when working with a copy of what was done 150 or more years ago.

Chances are that you will immediately be struck by its completely modern, contemporary feel not to even mention its streamlined pistol grip stock, beaver-tail forend, natural pointing, and modern sights. It is almost impossible to tell the Pacer from that up-to-date, high-power rifle. Built-in balance makes pointing it "on target," practically instinctive.

Rugged, reliable simplicity is the keynote of the RMAC design, plus safety, accuracy and economy.

An end mill puts the finishing touches on the turret used in the RMAC breechloading black powder rifle.

The MLI-.45 caliber rifle or Pacer will, for the time being, be available only in .45 caliber, still the most popular muzzleloader bore around the country.

The barrel measures exactly twenty-six inches and is round, tapered and what might be described best as of medium weight. Overall weight of the rifle is about six pounds, light enough for an easy day afield, yet offering enough heft to provide a steady hold.

The Pacer has good, clean lines, graceful contours and a handsome appearance. Add to this the rifle's gold square blade front sight, open speed shooters-type rear and you have a thoroughly modern approach. The rear sight, by the way, is fully adjustable for both windage and elevation. And if perchance a wise old head among hunters cottoned to the idea of installing a favorite low power, low profile scope, (or a receiver sight) just for that extra-added optical assist, chances are that no one would arch an eyebrow.

Close scrutiny, plus a screwdriver, enabled us to find out that here indeed is a black powder rifle with a totally new mechanism. As an example of their concept, the safety goes on whenever the hammer is cocked, solidly locking the sliding hammer in place and it can't jar off or be knocked off by a blow against the unit. There is no fumbling with any half-cock notch — it's automatic and it's sure. Actually, there is no way to cap the nipple and leave the safety off.

The Pacer, unlike most all previous muzzleloaders, boasts a relatively fast lock time. Remember, there is no old-style swinging hammer. Instead, it is all straight line forward motion — both short and snappy. You'll also quickly note that nothing protrudes anywhere near the shooter's line of sight. The nipple and cap are positioned well forward of the shooter's face and, for that matter, the nipple and cap point directly forward, away from the shooter to guarantee no cap spatter.

Most all shooters are fully aware of the inherent virtues attributed to coil springs. However, a high carbon steel, flat main spring, though more expensive, does a much better job. This is what you will find in the Esopus two-shot — it is a spring and functions as a spring should function.

While visiting with Pace, Waters and Vogel, some time was spent working with proof loads. Needless to say, there were no problems encountered though they represented loadings far in excess of any worthy of some consideration by the shooter.

The ramrod that comes with the Esopus Pacer is made from high tensile aluminum alloy. It is virtually unbreakable and unbendable and is not affected by either boiling water or known cleaning solutions. The rod also is threaded to accept all standard cleaning aids.

This newest of the Esopus muzzleloaders brings us a fully modernized concept in which every part has a func-tion and every contour is designed that way for sound reasons. What it added up to is a first class functional mechanism that delivers reliability and ease in handling. Suggested retail for the Pacer will be $79.50.

The final terms among the line-up of those we checked out while visiting the Port Ewen/Esopus group included a new idea in an in-line capper, working on the gravity feed principle. It is made from heavy gauge brass and features only one moving part, a sliding weighted lever which facilitates pushing the caps along their track. Though it handles various size percussion caps, we had opportunity of testing it only while using the Remington No. 11s. If memory serves correctly, it held twenty-seven of these caps. At $3.95 per copy it is a worthwhile accessory for black powder/percussion aficionados.

Esopus may market a complete accessory kit for the fraternity. It probably will include a flask, capper, mould, patch lube, cleaning solvent, black powder instruction manual and just about anything else of importance to the new shooter. — *Bob Zwirz/Jack Lewis*

Inventor/designer Casull feels that inbuilt advantages of the RMAC rifle will be of great aid in further popularizing black powder branch of the shooting sports in the years ahead.

BLACK POWDER DIRECTORY

ANTIQUE ARMS DEALERS

Robert Abels, P.O. Box 428, Hopewell Junction, NY 12533 (Catalog $1.00)

Ed Agramonte, Inc., 41 Riverdale Ave., Yonkers, NY 10701

F. Banne man Sons, Inc., Box 126, L.I., Blue Point, N.Y. 1 715

Wm. Boggs, 1243 Grandview Ave., Columbus, Ohio 43212

Ellwood Epps Sporting Goods, 80 King St., Clinton, Ont., Canada

Farris Muzzle Guns, 1610 Gallia St., Portsmouth, Ohio 45662

A. A. Fidd, Diamond Pt. Rd., Diamond Pt., N.Y. 12824

N. Flayderman & Co., Squash Hollow, New Milford, Conn. 06776

Fulmer's Antique Firearms, Detroit Lakes, Minn. 56501

Herb Glass, Bullville, N.Y. 10915

Gold Rush Guns, P.O. Box 33, Afton, Va. 22920

Gold Rush Guns Shop II, 2211 Clement St., San Francisco, Cal. 94121

Goodman's for Guns, 1101 Olive St., St. Louis, Mo. 63101

Griffin's Guns & Antiques, R.R. 4, Peterboro, Ont., Canada

The Gun Shop, 6497 Pearl Rd., Cleveland, O. 44130

Heritage Firearms Co., 27 Danbury Rd., Rte. 7, Wilton, Conn 06897

Holbrook Arms Museum, 12953 Biscayne Blvd., N. Miami, Fla. 33161

Ed Howe, 2 Main, Coopers Mills, Me. 04341

Jackson Arms, 6209 Hillcrest Ave., Dallas, Tex. 75205

Jerry's Gun Shop, 9220 Ogden Ave., Brookfield, Ill. 60513

Lever Arms Serv. Ltd., 771 Dunsmuir St., Vancouver 1, B.C., Canada

Wm. M. Locke, 3607 Ault Pk. Rd., Cincinnati, O. 45208

John J. Malloy, Briar Ridge Rd., Danbury, Conn. 06810

Charles W. Moore, R.D. 2, Schenevus, N.Y. 12155

Museum of Historical Arms, 1038 Alton Rd., Miami Beach, Fla. 33139

National Gun Traders, Inc., 225 S.W. 22nd Ave., Miami, Fla. 33135

New Orleans Arms Co., Inc., 240 Chartres St., New Orleans, La. 70130

Old West Gun Room, 3509 Carlson Blvd., El Cerrito, Cal. 94530 (write for list)

Pioneer Guns, 5228 Montgomery, Norwood, O. 45212

Powell & Clements Sporting Arms, 210 E. 6th St., Cincinnati, O. 45202

Glode M. Requa, Box 35, Monsey, N.Y. 10952

Martin B. Retting Inc., 11029 Washington, Culver City, Calif. 90230

Ridge Guncraft, Inc., 234 N. Tulane Ave., Oak Ridge, Tenn. 37830

S.G. Intl., P.O. Box 702, Hermosa Beach, CA. 90254

Safari Outfitters Lt., Rte. 7, Ridgefield, CT 06877

San Francisco Gun Exch., 74 Fourth, San Francisco, Calif. 94103

Santa Ana Gunroom, P.O. Box 1777, Santa Ana, Calif. 92702

Ward & Van Valkenburg, 402-30th Ave. No., Fargo, N. Dak. 58102

M. C. Wiest, 234 N. Tulane Ave., Oak Ridge, Tenn. 37830

Yeck Antique Firearms, 579 Tecumseh, Dundee, Mich. 48131

GUNS & GUN PARTS, REPLICA AND ANTIQUE

Antique Gun Parts, Inc., 569 So. Braddock Ave., Pittsburgh, Pa. 15221 (ML)

Armoury Inc., Rte. 25, New Preston, Conn. 06777

Artistic Arms, Inc., Box 23, Hoagland, IN 46745 (Sharps-Borchardt replica)

Bannerman, F., Box 126, Blue Point, Long Island, N.Y. 11715

Shelley Braverman, Athens, N.Y. 12015 (obsolete parts)

Carter Gun Works, 2211 Jefferson Pk. Ave., Charlottesville, Va. 22903

Cornwall Bridge Gun Shop, Cornwall Bridge, CT 06754 (parts)

R. MacDonald Champlin, Stanyan Hill, Wentworth, N.H. 03282 (replicas)

David E. Cumberland, 3509 Carlson Blvd., El Cerrito, CA 94530 (Replica Gatling guns)

Darr's Rifle Shop, 2309 Black Rd., Joliet, Ill. 60435 (S.S. items)

Dixie Gun Works, Inc., Hwy 51, South, Union City, Tenn. 38261

Ellwood Epps Sporting Goods, 80 King St., Clinton, Ont., Canada

Kindig's Log Cabin Sport Shop, R.D. 1, P.O. Box 275, Lodi, Ohio 44254

Edw. E. Lucas, 32 Garfield Ave., Old Bridge, N.J. 08857 (45-70)

R. M. Marek, Rt. 1, Box 1-A, Banks Ore. 97106 (cannons)

Numrich Arms Co., West Hurley, N.Y. 12491

Replica Models, Inc., 610 Franklin St., Alexandria, VA 22314

Riflemen's Hdqs., Rt. 3, RD 550-E, Kendallville, IN 46755

S&S Firearms, 88-21 Aubrey Ave., Glendale, N.Y. 11227

Rob. Thompson, 1031-5th Ave., N., Clinton, Ia. 52732 (Win. only)

C. H. Weisz, Box 311, Arlington, Va. 22210

Wescombe, 10549 Wilsey, Tujunga, CA 91042 (Rem. R.B. parts)

MUZZLE LOADING BARRELS OR EQUIPMENT

Luther Adkins, Box 281, Shelbyville, Ind. 47176 (breech plugs)

Armoury, Inc., Rte. 25, New Preston, Conn. 06777

Barney's Cannons, Inc., 61650 Oak Rd., South Bend, IN 46614 (ctlg. $1)

Dan Barr, Rte. 1, Thornville, OH 43076 (hunting bag)

Henry S. Beverage, New Gloucester, Me. 04260 (brass bullet mould)

John Bivins, Jr., 446 So. Main, Winston-Salem, N.C. 27101

Jesse F. Booher, 2751 Ridge Ave., Dayton, Ohio 45414

G. S. Bunch, 7735 Garrison, Hyattsville, Md. 20784 (flask repair)

Pat Burke, 3339 Farnsworth Rd., Lapeer, Mich. 48446 (capper)

Challanger Mfg. Co., 118 Pearl St., Mt. Vernon, NY 10550 (Hopkins & Allen)

Caution Tool Co., Scout Rd., Southbury, CT 06488

Cherry Corners Gun Shop, Rte. 1, 8010 Lafayette Rd., Lodi, Ohio 44254

Cornwall Bridge Gun Shop, Cornwall Bridge, CT 06745

Earl T. Cureton, Rte. 6, 7017 Pine Grove Rd., Knoxville, Tenn. 37914 (powder horns)

John N. Dangelzer, 3056 Frontier Pl. N.E., Albuquerque, N. Mex. 87106 (powder flasks)

Ted Fellowes, 9245 16th Ave. S.W., Seattle, Wash. 98106

Firearms Imp. & Exp. Corp., 2470 N.W. 21st St., Miami, Fla. 33142

Golden Age Arms Co., 657 High St., Worthington, Ohio 43085 (ctlg. $1)

A. R. Goode, R.D. 1, Box 84, Thurmont, MD 21788

Green River Forge, 4326 120th Ave. S.E., Bellevue, WA 98006 (Forge-Fire flints)

Virgil W. Hartley, 1602 S. Hunter Rd., Indianapolis, IN 46239 (ML pouch)

International M. L. Parts Co., 19453 Forrer, Detroit, MI 48235

JJJJ Ranch, Wm. Large, Rte. 1, Ironton, Ohio 45638

Art LeFeuvre, 1003 Hazel Ave., Deerfield, Ill. 60015 (antique gun restoring)

Kindig's Log Cabin Sport Shop, R.D. 1, Box 275, Lodi, OH 44254

Les' Gun Shop (Les Bauska), Box 511, Kalispell, Mont, 59901

Lever Arms Serv. Ltd., 771 Dunsmuir, Vancouver 1, B.C., Canada

J. Lewis Arms Mfg., 3931 Montgomery Rd., Cincinnati, Ohio 45212 (pistol)

McKeown's Guns, R.R. 1, Pekin, IL 61554 (E-Z load rev. stand)

Maryland Gun Exchange Inc., Rt. 40 West, RD 5, Frederick, MD 21701

Maywood Forge, Foley, MN 56329 (cannons)

Jos. W. Mellott, 334 Rockhill Rd., Pittsburgh, Pa. 15243 (barrel blanks)

W. L. Mowrey Gun Works, Inc., Box 711, Olney, Tex. 73674

Muzzle Loaders Supply Co., Rte. 25, New Preston, CT 06777

Numrich Corp., W. Hurley, N.Y. 12491 (powder flasks)

R. Parris & Son, R.D. 5, Box 61, Gettysburg, Pa. 17325 (barrels)

Penna. Rifle Works, 319 E. Main St., Ligonier, Pa. 15658 (ML guns, parts)

Fred Renard, Rte. 1, Symsonia, Ky. 42082 (ML)

H. M. Schoeller, 569 So. Braddock Ave., Pittsburgh, Pa. 15221

Shilo Ind., Inc., 173 Washington Pl., Hasbrouck Heights, NJ 07604 (4-cavity mould)

C. E. Siler, 181 Sandhill School, Asheville, N.C., 28806 (flint locks)

Thos. F. White, 5801 Westchester Ct., Worthington, O. 43085 (powder horn)

Lou Williamson, 129 Stonegate Ct., Bedford, TX 76021

MISCELLANEOUS

Breech Plug Wrench, Swaine Machine, 195 O'Connell, Providence, R.I. 02905

Cannons, South Bend Replicas Inc., 61650 Oak Rd., So. Bend, IN 46614 (ctlg. $1)

Capper, Muzzle-Loading, Pat Burke, 3339 Farnsworth Rd., Lapeer, Mich. 48446

Flat Springs, Alamo Heat Treating Co., Box 55345, Houston, Tex. 77055

Nipple Wrenches, Chopie Mfg. Inc., 531 Copeland Ave., La Crosse, Wis. 54601

Powder Horns, Thos. F. White, 5801 Westchester Ct., Worthington, O. 43085

Powder Storage Magazine, C & M Gunworks, 4201 36th Ave., Moline, IL 61265

Rust Bluing/Browning, L.B. Thompson, 568 E. School Ave., Salem, O. 44460

Salute Cannons, Naval Co., Rt. 611, Doylestown, Pa. 18901

Shooting/Testing Glasses, Clear View Sports Shields, P.O. Box 255, Wethersfield, Conn. 06107

Shooting Glasses, Bausch & Lomb, Inc., 635 St. Paul St., Rochester, NY 14602

Shooting Glasses, Bushnell Optical Corp., 2828 E. Foothill Blvd., Pasadena, CA 91107

Shooting Glasses, M. B. Dinsmore, Box 21, Wyomissing, Pa. 19610

Shooting Glasses, Mitchell's, Box 539, Waynesville, Mo. 65583

Shooting Glasses, Ray-O-Vac, Willson Prods. Div., P.O. Box 622, Reading, PA 19603

RELOADING TOOLS AND ACCESSORIES

Alcan, (See: Smith & Wesson-Fiocchi, Inc.)

Anchor Alloys, Inc., 966 Meeker Ave., Brooklyn, N.Y. 11222 (chilled shot)

H. S. Beverage, New Gloucester, Me. 04260 (brass bullet mould)

Bonanza Sports, Inc., 412 Western Ave., Faribault, Minn. 55021 (powder scales)

C-H Tool & Die Corp., Box L, Owen, Wis. 54460 (scales)

Division Lead Co., 7742 W. 62st Pl., Summit, Ill. 60502

Farmer Bros. Mfg. Co.,1102 Washington St., Eldora, IA 50627 (Lage wads)

Ed Hart, U.S. Rte. 15 Cohocton, NY 14826 (Meyer shotgun slugs)

Herter's Inc., RR1, Waseca, Minn. 56093 (lead pot, moulds)

B. E. Hodgdon, Inc., 7710 W. 50 Hiway, Shawnee Mission, Kans. 66202 (Spit-Ball, Spit-Patch, Powder)

J & G Rifle Ranch, Turner, Mont. 59542 (case tumblers)

Kush Plastics, P.O. Box 366, Palatine, IL 60067 (shotshell wads)

Lee Engineering Box 107, Hartford, Wis. 53027 (dipper-type measures)

Lee Precision Mfg., Route 3, Hartford Wis. 53027 (moulds)

Ljutic Industries, 918 N. 5th Ave., Yakima, Wash. 98902 (shotgun wads)

Lyman Gun Sight Products, Middlefield, Conn. 06455 (moulds)

Murdock Lead Co., Box 5298, Dallas, Tex. 75222

National Lead Co., Box 831, Perth Amboy, N.J. 08861

Ohaus Scale Corp., 29 Hanover Rd., Florham Park, N.J. 07932 (moulds, scales)

Pacific Tool Co., Box 4495, Lincoln, Neb. 68504 (scales)

RCBS, Inc., Box 1919, Oroville, Calif. 95965 (scales)

Redding-Hunter, Inc., 114 Starr Rd., Cortland, N.Y. 13045 (scales)

Rochester Lead Works, Rochester, N.Y. 14608

Ruhr-American Corp., So. East Hwy. 55, Glenwood, Minn. 56334 (moulds, electric pot)

SAECO Rel. Inc., P.O. Box 778, Carpinteria, Calif. 93013 (moulds, melting pots, lead hardness tester)

Shiloh IV, 173 Washington Place, Hasbrouck Heights, N.J. 07604 (moulds)

Smith & Wesson-Fiocchi, Inc., 3640 Seminary Rd., Alton, IL 62002 (Alcan wads)

Webster Scale Mfg. Co., Box 188, Sebring, Fla. 33870

MUZZLELOADING ASSOCIATIONS

(Each includes a magazine with the membership)

National Muzzle Loading Rifle Association, Box 67, Friendship, Indiana 47021. $6.00 a year.

National Rifle Association, 1600 Rhode Island Ave., N.W., Washington, D.C. 20036. $7.50 a year.

Western States Muzzle Loaders Association, 414 E. Grand Ave., El Segundo, California 90245. $4.50 a year.

North-South Skirmish Association. Address inquiry to Chas. M. Hunter, 6214 - 29th Street, N.W., Washington, D.C. 20015.

The American Mountainmen, P.O. Box 259, Lakeside, California 92040. $4.00 a year.

A MUZZLELOADING MARKET SURVEY

The Shooting Enthusiast With Blackpowder In His Bloodstream Never Had It So Good – As A Browse Through These Pages Will Prove!

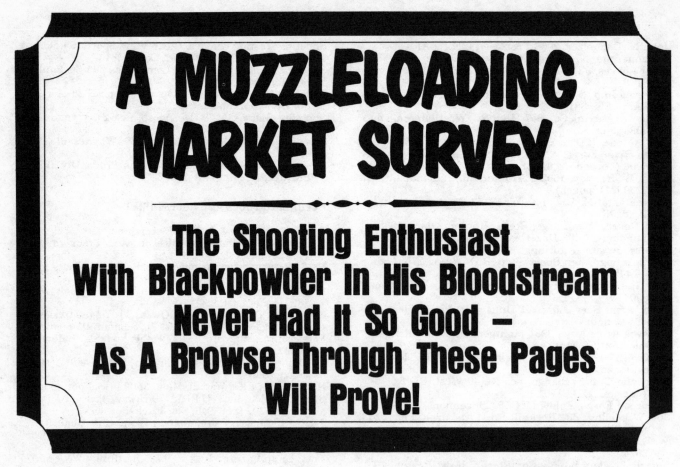

Flintlock Rifles

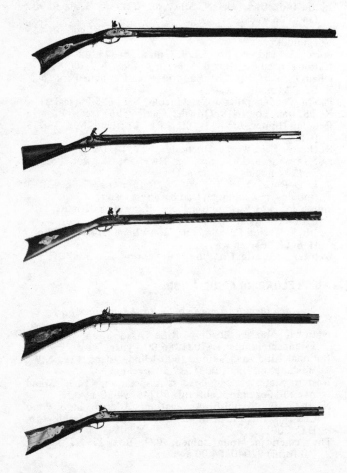

DIXIE DELUXE PENNSYLVANIA RIFLE: A fine reproduction of .45 caliber with a 40-inch rifled barrel measuring 13/16 inch across the flats; standard Kentucky type sights; chestnut-colored straight-grained maple stock with Roman nose butt section; extra wide brass butt plate; inlaid brass patch box; overall length of 55 inches; weighs about 10 pounds. Percussion, **$195.95**; flint, **$199.95.** Engraved model, flint or percussion; **$235.**

DIXIE FIRST MODEL BROWN BESS: A true reproduction of the two hundred-year-old original, Dixie's flintlock Brown Bess sports a .75 caliber, 46-inch smoothbore barrel; hand engraved locks marked Grice 1762, with crown and initials GR underneath; barrel and lock were left bright as on originals; hand finished walnut stock; brass furniture; weighs about 13 pounds. **$275;** bayonets, **$15** extra.

DIXIE STANDARD KENTUCKY RIFLE: Referred to as the Dixie squirrel rifle, in .45 caliber; 40-inch rifled barrel; blade front sight, Kentucky notch type rear; brass trigger guard, thimbles and butt plate; chestnut-colored maple stock; candy-striped cleaning rod with cleaning jag; brass cap box inlaid in stock. **$169.50,** percussion; **$179.95,** flintlock with color case-hardened lock.

NAVY ARMS KENTUCKY RIFLE: Featuring the eye-pleasing rounded lines typical of Kentucky rifles, the rifle is fitted with a .44 caliber, 33½-inch octagon barrel; traditional Kentucky type lock; hardwood stock; polished brass patch box, trigger guard and butt plate; blade front sight, V-notch rear; overall length of gun is 50 inches. **$129.95.**

NUMRICH H&A MINUTEMAN: An exacting replica of the Kentucky long rifle, the Minuteman features a high blue, deep luster rifled octagon barrel; available in .36 or .45 caliber; American maple stock; overall length of 55 inches. **$179.95,** flint or percussion.

NUMRICH MINUTEMAN BRUSH RIFLE: A companion to the famous Minuteman Kentucky long rifle; features either rifled or smoothbore 24-inch barrel in .45 or .50 caliber; hand-rubbed select maple stock with polished brass furniture; color case-hardened lock; flint or percussion; weighs 8 pounds. **$160.**

THOMPSON/CENTER HAWKEN: Similar to the Rocky Mountain rifles of the early 18th century; built for rugged use, button rifled for accuracy; available in .45 or .50 caliber; hooked breech; double set triggers; polished brass trigger guard, patch box and butt plate; American walnut stock; blade front sight, adjustable rear; color case-hardened hammer and lock plate. **$175,** percussion; **$190,** flint.

Percussion Rifles

CENTENNIAL ARMS 1863 ZOUAVE REMINGTON: In .58 caliber, with rifled 33-inch barrel; color case-hardened lock plate and hammer; lock is marked with an eagle; butt plate and other fittings are of brass; blade front sight, 3-notch rear sight in increments of 100, 200 and 300 yards. **$84.50.**

CONNECTICUT VALLEY ARMS KENTUCKY RIFLE: Rifled 34¼-inch octagon barrel; engraved hammer and lock plate; .44 caliber, .451 bore diameter; brass blade Kentucky-type front sight, open dovetail rear; weighs 7 pounds; overall length is 50 inches; walnut stained hardwood stock; brass-tipped ramrod. **$73.50.**

DIXIE HALFSTOCK TARGET RIFLE: Designed for offhand or snap shooting at big game in the field; in .45 caliber, measuring .450 land-to-land; 32-inch rifled barrel; steel trigger guard and butt plate; checkered pistol grip and forearm; weighs 7½ pounds. **$72.50.**

ESOPUS TWO SHOT RIFLE: Over and under turn barrel type rifle; barrel rotates in either direction; .45 caliber rifled 28-inch barrels; hand finished black walnut stock; polished brass furniture; open notch rear sight, silver blade front; weighs 8½ pounds. **$139.50.**

HARRINGTON & RICHARDSON SPRINGFIELD STALKER: Closely resembling the Springfield rifles used during the Civil War, this caplock rifle comes in .45 and .58 caliber; sports a 28 inch barrel; adjustable open rear sights, fixed blade front; brass ramrod with hardwood handle; walnut stock; weighs 8 pounds. **$150.**

MOWREY HAWKIN HALFSTOCK REPLICA: An exact reproduction of the Hawkin rifle; .45, .50 or .54 caliber; 32-inch rifled octagon barrel, blued and polished; blade front sight, adjustable open rear; features brass Hawkin-type butt plate and action housing. **$179.50.**

MOWREY HAWKINS HALFSTOCK REPLICA: An exact reproduction of the Hawkins rifle; .45, .50 or .54 caliber; 32-inch rifled octagon barrel; blade front sight, adjustable open rear; double set triggers; hand finished select maple stock; brass furniture, custom built to individual. **$250.**

NAVY ARMS BUFFALO HUNTER: Resembling a sporterized Zouave muzzleloading rifle, this big .58 caliber gun offers plenty of knock-down power for primitive arms hunts, uses .575 ball or minie; stocked with a checkered walnut half stock; brass patch box; case-hardened hammer and lock plate. **$125.**

NAVY ARMS MODEL 1863 ZOUAVE RIFLE: In .58 caliber, one of the most rugged replicas on the market; walnut stock with polished brass furniture; blued 33-inch rifled barrel; color case-hardened lock; weighs about 9½ pounds. **$100.**

NAVY ARMS NEW KENTUCKY RIFLE: Available in both rifle and carbine versions, this new addition to the Navy Arms line of Kentucky rifles features the traditional Roman nose stock. In .44 caliber, the rifle features a 35-inch rifled barrel; a 28-inch rifled barrel in the carbine model; walnut colored hardwood stock; brass furniture. **$130.**

NAVY ARMS REVOLVING CARBINE: Designed originally as a companion to the Army revolver, this replica is a 6-shot, .44 caliber cap and ball repeater. Available in barrel lengths of 16, 18 and 20 inches, octagon barrels are precision rifled; polished brass trigger guard and butt plate; buckhorn rear sight, silver blade front. **$130.**

NUMRICH H&A DEERSTALKER: Designed with the hunter specifically in mind, this big .58 caliber hunting rifle fires a .580 diameter slug; is fitted with a 32-inch rifled octagon barrel; hand-fitted American walnut stock; weighs about 9½ pounds. **$87.95.**

NUMRICH H&A DELUXE BUGGY RIFLE: In the Hopkins & Allen underhammer design, has a 21-inch rifled octagon barrel; hooded front sight, full adjustable open rear; walnut stock; all metal parts blued; available in .36 or .45 caliber. **$84.95.**

NUMRICH HALFSTOCK PLAINS RIFLE: A favorite among hunters for its accuracy and light weight, the half stock rifle features a rifled or smoothbore 32-inch barrel in .45 or .50 caliber; hand finished maple stock with brass furniture; weighs 10 pounds. **$174,** flint or percussion.

NUMRICH H&A HERITAGE MODEL: Based on the underhammer designs of the 1830s, trouble-free design ensures positive ignition; available in .36 and .45 caliber; fitted with a 32-inch rifled barrel with non-glaring matted flat top; hooded front sight, Kentucky open type rear and Hopkins & Allen aperture long range sight; weighs about 8½ pounds, varying with the density of the walnut stock. **$99.95.**

NUMRICH H&A OFFHAND DELUXE: Combining all the qualities of the Deluxe Heritage Model into a more economically priced rifle, Hopkins & Allen offers this deluxe offhand rifle. The underhammer rifle features an American walnut stock; octagon 32-inch rifled barrel in .36 or .45 caliber. **$87.95.**

NUMRICH H&A OVER/UNDER RIFLE: Offers two quick shots for those hunting moments when just one shot won't do. The swivel breech rifle features 28-inch rifled barrels of .45 caliber; American walnut stock with crescent butt plate; overall length of 43 inches; weighs about 8½ pounds. **$139.95.**

NUMRICH H&A '71 TARGET MODEL: Designed for the target shooter, underhammer gun features a full 32-inch rifled octagon bull barrel without forearm and ramrod ferrules, making it an ideal benchrest gun; available in .45 or .50 caliber; fitted with 3 aperture rear target tang sight; American walnut stock; overall length of 49 inches; weighs about 11 pounds. **$84.95.**

REPLICA ARMS BERDAN RIFLE: A reproduction of the Wesson rifle; double set triggers; .45 caliber 25-inch rifled octagon barrel; hardwood stock; brass blade front sight, adjustable open rear; brass trigger guard, cap box and butt plate; lock mechanism set in metal housing; weighs 9 pounds, 8 ounces. **$99.95.**

REPLICA ARMS PLAINSMAN: A reproduction of the Cecil Brooks rifle; walnut halfstock; .38 and .45 caliber; 37-inch rifled octagon barrel; blade front sight, adjustable open rear; polished brass trigger guard, patch box, butt plate; Roman nose shaping of comb; double set triggers; weighs 7 pounds. **$229.95;** deluxe engraved model, **$299.95.**

ROCKY MOUNTAIN ARMS A22: A completely different design of black powder rifle featuring a unique swivel breech; .22 caliber, using No. 4 ball and 7 grains of FFFg; barrel swaging develops velocities to 1340 feet per second; 20-inch rifled round barrel; overall length 35¼ inches; one-piece hardwood stock; weighs 2 pounds, 15 ounces. **$49.50.**

ROCKY MOUNTAIN ARMS A36: Swivel breech for speedy loading; 22½-inch rifled barrel; .36 caliber, using No. 1 ball and 23 grains of FFFg to develop muzzle velocity of 1406 feet per second; full length hardwood stock; overall length is 39½ inches; weighs 5 pounds, 4 ounces. **$99.50.**

ROCKY MOUNTAIN ARMS A44: Quick reloading big bore hunting rifle; .44 caliber, using .45 ball with 50 grains of FFFg to develop muzzle velocities up to 1360 feet per second; 28-inch rifled barrel; full length stock; blade front sight, adjustable open rear; overall length is 46 inches; weighs 6 pounds, 6 ounces. **$99.50.**

TINGLE MODEL 1962 TARGET RIFLE: Available in .360, .450 and .500 caliber; 32-inch rifled octagon barrel, 1 turn in 52 inches; adjustable double set triggers; fixed blade front sight, windage and elevation adjustable rear; lacquered walnut stock; blued barrel, lock and trigger; polished brass trigger guard and butt plate; weighs 10 pounds; overall length is 48 inches. **$139.95.**

Shotguns

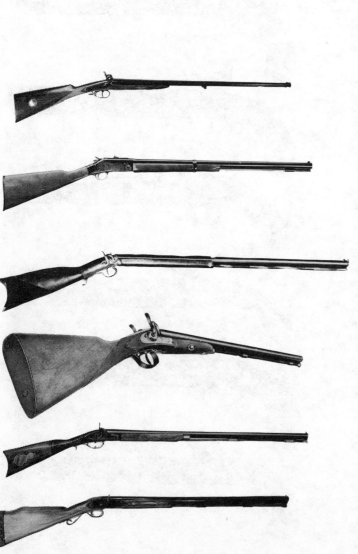

DIXIE DOUBLE BARREL SHOTGUN: A good black powder hunting shotgun made from original parts in Belgium; proof tested; 32-inch blued barrels of approximately 20-gauge; steel furniture; brass cap box; back and front action locks. **$99.50.**

HARRINGTON & RICHARDSON HUNTSMAN: A modern design muzzleloader featuring an enclosed percussion cap for all-weather dependability. Available in .45, .58 caliber and 12-gauge; barrel length is 28 inches; fully adjustable open sights; color case-hardened frame; walnut finished hardwood stock; solid brass ramrod with hardwood handle. **$59.95.**

MOWREY 12-GAUGE SHOTGUN: Following along the lines of the firm's Allen & Thurber replica rifles is this 12-gauge muzzleloading shotgun; two-piece maple stock; candy-striped ramrod; brass trigger guard, action housing and butt plate; maple stock; weighs 7½ pounds; 48 inches overall. **$139.50.**

NAVY ARMS DOUBLE BARREL SHOTGUN: Designed with styling similar to that of early English and French doubles, with rabbit ear sidelocks; 30-inch browned barrels choked improved cylinder and modified; weighs about 6¼ pounds; hand-checkered walnut stock with hand-rubbed oil finish; overall length of gun is 45 inches. **$125.**

NUMRICH H&A MUZZLELOADING SHOTGUN: To an ever growing line of black powder guns, Hopkins & Allen adds their new lightweight single-barrel shotgun. Available with 28-inch modified choke barrel only, the gun weighs in at 6 pounds and features a honey toned maple stock with brass furniture. **$119.50.**

TINGLE SINGLE BARREL SHOTGUN: Features a mule ear side hammer lock; 12 gauge; 30-inch barrel, straight bore with no choke; blued metal finish; lacquered walnut stock; iron trigger guard; rubber recoil pad; weighs 5 pounds. **$99.75.**

Flintlock Pistols

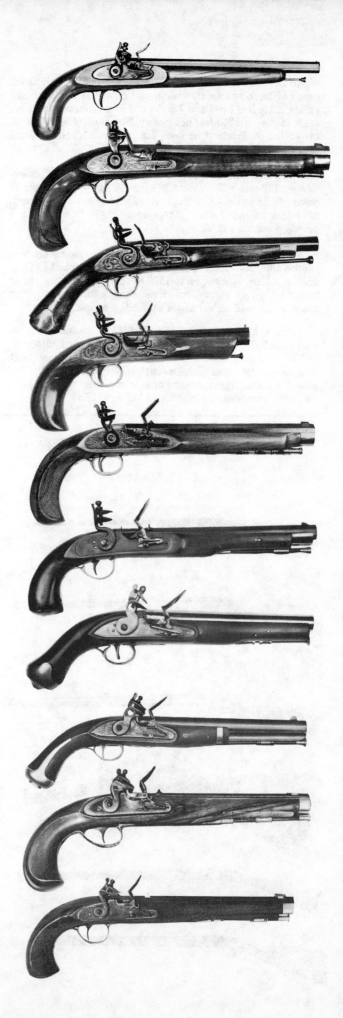

CENTURY ARMS FLINTLOCK DUELLER: Big bored .50 caliber pistol; blued 11-inch octagon barrel; walnut finished hardwood stock; steel furniture; bead front sight, V-notch rear. **$26.50.**

CENTURY ARMS DELUXE KENTUCKY FLINTLOCK: .44 caliber; 9-inch rifled octagon barrel; engraved hammer and lock plate; checkered, hand finished hardwood stock; fixed blade front sight, notch rear; polished brass furniture. **$54.95.**

CONNECTICUT VALLEY ARMS TOWER PISTOL: Reproduction of the Horse Pistol used by the British in the Revolutionary period; engraved lock plate and hammer; smoothbore 8-inch round barrel; weighs 40 ounces; polished brass furniture; high gloss walnut stock; overall length is 14 inches; steel ramrod. **$44.95.**

CONNECTICUT VALLEY ARMS ENGLISH BELT PISTOL: Engraved, case-hardened lock plate and hammer; .44 caliber, .451 bore; 6¼-inch rifled octagon barrel; weighs 29 ounces; dark, high gloss walnut stock; hardened frizzen; bead front sight, dovetail blade rear; steel ramrod. **$33.95.**

CONNECTICUT VALLEY ARMS KENTUCKY FLINTLOCK PISTOL: Rifled 10-inch octagon barrel; .44 caliber, .451 bore diameter; checkered hardwood stock; brass Kentucky type blade front sight, dovetail rear; overall length is 15½ inches; weighs 41 ounces; engraved lock and hammer. **$55.95.**

DIXIE FLINT PISTOL: An authentically designed Kentucky pistol replica, with Kentucky type rifling in a 9-inch barrel of .40 caliber; barrel is fitted with Kentucky type sights; stock is maple stained to take on the appearance of dark cherry; thimbles, trigger guard and eagle head type butt plate are made of polished brass. **$89.95**, flint or percussion.

DIXIE TOWER FLINT PISTOL: Often referred to as the pirate pistol, has a 9½-inch barrel; hardened frizzen and especially adjusted springs to give lock better spark; bore diameter of .670 inch, handling .650 mould balls. **$28.95.**

NAVY ARMS 1806 HARPER'S FERRY PISTOL: An exact reproduction of the first U.S. government-made flint pistols, the Navy Arms replica sports a 10-inch rifled .56 caliber barrel, browned as was the original; the case-hardened lock is stamped Harper's Ferry 1807 at rear of plate, with a spread eagle and U.S. stampings near the center; overall length is 16 inches; oil-finished walnut stock; brass furniture. **$89.95.**

NAVY ARMS KENTUCKY PISTOL: An exact duplicate of an original Kentucky pistol; measures 15½ inches overall; equipped with a 10½-inch blued ordnance steel barrel of .44 caliber, designed for patched .430 ball; color case-hardened lock, engraved around plate and hammer; polished brass furniture; oil-finished walnut stock. **$89.95.**

REPLICA ARMS 1830 KENTUCKY FLINTLOCK: Hardwood stock; case-hardened hammer and lock plate; brass blade front sight, notched brass rear; brass trigger guard; .44 caliber. **$72.50.**

Percussion Pistols

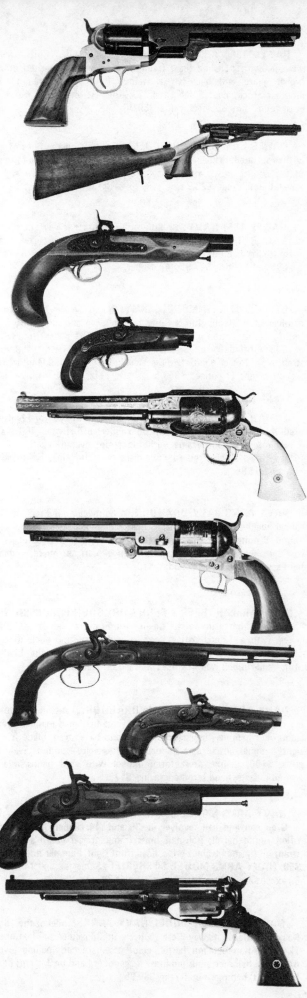

CENTENNIAL ARMS BRASS NAVY: A fine reproduction of the famous .36 caliber Navy Colt; features a polished brass frame, trigger guard and backstrap; octagon 6-inch barrel; walnut one-piece grips; made in Italy, fully proof tested, **$31.95**; .44 caliber, **$34.50.**

CENTENNIAL ARMS NEW MODEL ARMY: An exact replica of the 1860 Colt New Model Army in .44 caliber, features a full fluted cylinder; fitted with an 8-inch round rifled barrel; walnut grips; case-hardened steel frame; brass trigger guard; fitted for butt stock featuring brass butt plate and yoke. **$64,** gun alone; stock is **$34.95.**

CENTURY ARMS ENGRAVED POCKET PISTOL: Scroll engraved lock plate and ornately figured hammer; .40 caliber; blued octagon barrel; polished brass trigger guard; oil-finished hardwood stock. **$29.50.**

CENTURY ARMS PHILADELPHIA DERRINGER: Resembling the pistol used by John Booth to assassinate President Lincoln; .41 caliber; 3½-inch blued round barrel; engraved lock plate and hammer; checkered hardwood stock; has a polished brass trigger guard. **$24.50.**

CONNECTICUT VALLEY ARMS ENGRAVED NEW MODEL ARMY: Reproduction; .44 caliber; high tempered steel frame; polished brass trigger guard; 8-inch rifled octagon barrel; blade front sight, hammer notch rear; ivory grips; scroll engraved frame, cylinder, barrel and loading lever. Engraved model shown, **$99.95**; standard model with walnut grips, **$69.95.**

COLT 1851 NAVY: A reproduction of an original instead of a replica, the Colt Navy is a hefty 40-ounce cap and ball revolver of .36 caliber featuring a 7½-inch barrel; bead type front sight, hammer notch rear; knurled hammer spur; American walnut grips; color case-hardened frame, loading lever and hammer; silver plated trigger and backstrap. **$150**; cased Ulysses S. Grant and Robert E. Lee Commemoratives, **$250.**

DIXIE DUELING PISTOL: A fine reproduction of the type of pistol used for dueling during the 1840 era, the 9-inch smoothbore barrel varies in caliber from .44 to .50; checkered maple stock; front action lock; handles round ball or shot. **$59.95.**

DIXIE PHILADELPHIA DERRINGER: Based on the original designs of Henry Deringer, this big bore .41 caliber replica features a 3½-inch barrel; walnut stock; blued lock; polished brass trigger guard. **$22.50**

DIXIE SPANISH PERCUSSION PISTOL: An inexpensive but dependable import from Spain, .40 caliber; 9-inch smoothbore barrel, handling .395 balls or birdshot; checkered grip; steel fittings and ramrod. **$19.95.**

HAWES 1858 NEW ARMY REMINGTON: Predecessor to the modern single action revolver; .44 or .36 caliber; blued case-hardened steel frame; blued steel back strap; polished brass trigger guard; walnut finish grips. **$69.95.**

HAWES 1860 ARMY: Replica of the .44 caliber Colt Army; available with polished brass frame or steel frame; polished brass trigger guard and back strap; walnut finish grips; pre-cut for shoulder stock; overall length of 13½ inches; weighs 44 ounces. Brass frame, **$59.95;** steel frame, **$69.95.**

HAWES EL CABALLERO DUELLER: Built on the lines of an authentic duelling piece; .41 caliber; octagon barrel; engraved lock plate; walnut finish stock; steel trigger guard; bead front sight; dovetail notch rear. **$23.95.**

HAWES 1851 NAVY: Brightly polished brass trigger guard and back strap; .44 or .36 caliber; rifled 7½-inch octagon barrel; bead front sight, hammer notch rear; walnut grips; weighs 44 ounces. **$44.95,** .36 caliber; **$47.95,** .44 caliber.

LYMAN .44 NEW MODEL ARMY: Based on the 1858 Army revolver of E. Remington & Sons, Lyman's cap and ball Army is a faithful reproduction of .44 caliber, utilizing .451 balls; fitted with an 8-inch rifled barrel; high-tempered steel frame, with solid top strap; brass trigger guard; two-piece walnut grips; overall length 13½ inches; weighs 41 ounces. **$96.95.**

LYMAN .36 NEW MODEL NAVY: Design of type of revolver used during the Civil War era; .36 caliber, utilizing a .380 ball; 7½-inch barrel; solid frame with top strap; overall length of 13 inches; brass trigger guard; two-piece walnut grips; weighs 41 ounces. **$94.95.**

NAVY ARMS BABY DRAGOON: A lightweight and rugged .31 caliber revolver; available with a rifled 3 or 6-inch barrel; weighs 1 pound, 9 ounces with 6-inch barrel; overall length with 3-inch barrel is 7½ inches; polished brass back strap and trigger guard; Indian fight scene engraved on cylinder. **$70.**

NAVY ARMS HARPER'S FERRY DRAGOON PERCUSSION: A big .58 caliber, true holster pistol with an overall length of 18½ inches, with a 12-inch rifled barrel; blued barrel and back strap; color case-hardened lock plate and hammer; leaf rear sight, blade front; hand-rubbed walnut stock; polished brass furniture. **$95.**

NAVY ARMS 2nd MODEL .44 DRAGOON: A distinctive looking revolver with roll engraved cylinder; case-hardened loading lever, frame and hammer; brass trigger guard and back strap; blade front sight, hammer notch rear; 7½-inch barrel; weighs 4 pounds; walnut grips. **$100;** deluxe presentation model with gold bands inlaid around muzzle, hand scroll engraving, **$175.**

NAVY ARMS MODEL 60: Replica of the Confederate Griswold & Grier cap and ball revolver in .36 and .44 caliber; has 7¼-inch rifled round barrel; polished brass frame, trigger guard and back strap; oil finished walnut grips; bead front sight, hammer notch rear. **$50. NAVY ARMS MODEL 60 SHERIFF:** Same as standard Model 60 except available with a 5-inch barrel. **$50.**

NAVY ARMS NEW MODEL NAVY YANK: Model of the 1851 Navy that blazed its way West, replica is in .36 caliber and features a 7½-inch rifled octagon barrel; color case-hardened loading lever, frame and hammer; polished brass trigger guard and back strap; bead front sight, hammer notch rear. **$89.95.**

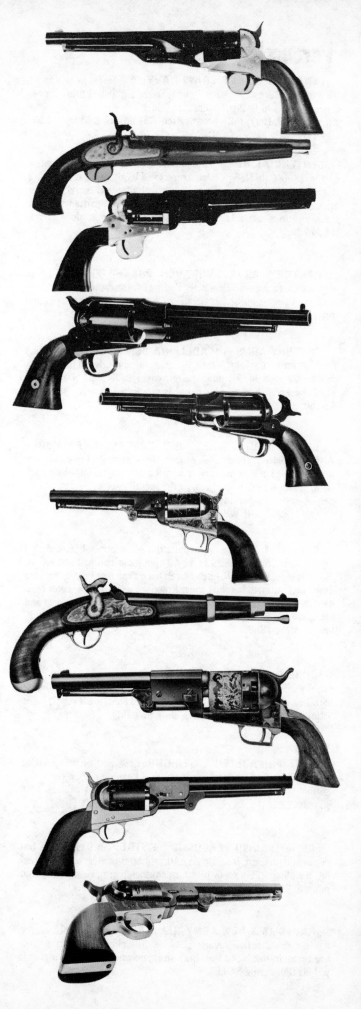

NAVY ARMS THIRD MODEL DRAGOON: This big .44 caliber six-shooter features color case-hardened loading lever and frame; blued 7½-inch barrel; polished brass trigger guard and back strap; weighs about 4 pounds. **$100** or **$175** for engraved presentation model.

NUMRICH H&A BOOT PISTOL: Available in .36 or .45 caliber, the simplicity of design provides shooter with years of trouble-free performance. Barrel length is 6 inches; overall length 13 inches; sculptured walnut target grip; target trigger. **$39.95.**

REPLICA ARMS 1860 ARMY: Engraved cylinder; .44 caliber, for use with .451 ball; 8-inch rifled round barrel; fixed blade front sight, hammer notch rear; case-hardened frame, loading lever and hammer; iron back strap; polished brass trigger guard; one-piece walnut grip; available with round, fluted or semi-fluted cylinder; weighs 3 pounds, 8 ounces. **$89.95.**

REPLICA ARMS 1850 KENTUCKY PISTOL: Hand-finished hardwood stock; .44 caliber, for use with .424 diameter ball; brass blade front sight, notched brass rear; case-hardened hammer and lock plate; polished brass trigger guard and rod ferrules; weighs 3 pounds. **$72.50.**

REPLICA ARMS 1862 POLICE MODEL: Last pistol to be produced in Colt's black powder era, this replica is available in .36 caliber with 4½, 5½ or 6½-inch barrel; frame, loading lever and hammer are color case-hardened; brass trigger guard and back strap; bead front sight, hammer notch rear; one-piece walnut grips; one-half fluted and rebated cylinder. **$89.95.**

REPLICA ARMS SINGLE-SHOT TARGET PISTOL: In .44 caliber; 9-inch rifled octagon barrel; both sides of frame are engraved with pioneer scenes; brass back strap and trigger guard; one-piece walnut grips; case-hardened hammer; adjustable rear sight for windage and elevation. **$64.95.**

REPLICA ARMS 1847 WALKER: One of the first Colt cap and ball revolvers to have a safety notch on the hammer, the original saw use with Captain Walker's mounted cavalry. The replica is an exact reproduction of .44 caliber; fitted with a round 9-inch rifled barrel; case-hardened frame, loading lever and hammer; iron back strap; brass trigger guard; weight around 4 pounds, 9 ounces. **$115.**

RUGER OLD ARMY: The black powder version of the firm's Blackhawk pistol; .44 caliber; 7½-inch barrel; solid steel constructed frame with top strap; ramp blade front sight, adjustable target rear; stainless steel nipples; walnut grips; blue finish; weighs 46 ounces. **$100.**

THOMPSON/CENTER PATRIOT PISTOL: Inspired by early gallery and dueling type firearms; .45 caliber; 9¼-inch rifled barrel; overall length of 16 inches; coil spring lock; hooked breech system; target sights; double set triggers; American walnut stock; brass furniture. **$112.**

TINGLE SINGLE-SHOT TARGET PISTOL: A choice of serious target shooters, the .40 caliber pistol is available with a 8, 9, 10 or 12-inch rifled octagon barrel measuring a true .400-inch from land to land; fitted with hand-filling lacquered walnut grips; adjustable rear sight, fixed blade front; blued finish; weighs 33 ounces with 8-inch barrel. **$64.95.**

A BASIC GLOSSARY FOR BLACKPOWDER GUNNERS

If Some Of The Terms Sound Confusing, Here Are Some Helpful Definitions!

ACID ETCHING: *A process of marking gun barrels that was common to the early 1800s. The metal surface first was coated with wax; the initials or name then was scribed through the thin layer of wax, until the metal that would bear the markings was exposed. A minute amount of acid then was applied to the etched lines and this would discolor the exposed metal. The process was not permanent and was abandoned for the most part in the search for a better way to mark gun barrels.*

AMPCO NIPPLE: *A modern design percussion nipple made of Beryllium, an alloy that resembles brass but is much harder and more resistant to erosion of the flashhole. AMPCO nipples feature an extremely small flashhole at the bottom; this results in a hotter flame, as the fire concentrates to pass through the tiny opening. The hotter ignition flame, in turn, ignites the powder more readily in the breech, giving a more spontaneous shot than with ordinary nipple designs.*

APERTURE SIGHT: *Often referred to as a peep sight, because it requires the shooters to visually center the front sight in the center of a small round hole in the rear sight while aiming. This arrangement makes it one of the most accurate metallic sights.*

APPLEWOOD: *Occasionally used in the making of gunstocks. The fine grain of this wood resists warpage and a rifle so stocked maintains its zero. Applewood is one of the easiest to work with, rounding and shaping nicely; also, inlays are installed easily in a stock made of this wood.*

ARQUEBUS: *An early term for matchlock shoulder guns. The term originated from the German word of Hakenbuchse, meaning hook gun. The French equivalent to hook, or Haken, is arque. The German Buchse, or gun, became a suffix to be tacked onto the end of the French word and, by the turn of the 16th Century, all such guns were know as arquebuses.*

BACK ACTION LOCK: *A later type of percussion lock. A true side-lock, this type of lock features a mainspring that is to the rear of the tumbler and hammer.*

BALL: *Spherical lead projectile used most commonly in the majority of the muzzleloading rifles and nearly all black powder pistols and cap and ball revolvers. In many cases a certain size of buckshot works well in such guns of a caliber of the same size; the shot then becomes a ball, being loaded one at a time.*

BALL SCREW: *Resembling a wood screw, this attachment threads into the end of the ramrod and is used for removing the ball from an unfired loaded round. The threaded point of the ball screw digs into the soft lead of the ball and grips it firmly enough so that it can be pulled from its seating and through the length of the barrel.*

BALTIC LOCK: *Crude and early version of the flintlock. Guns fitted with this type of lock appeared around 1600. Design soon was replaced with advanced versions of the flintlock.*

BAYONET: *A metal knife-like blade — occasionally doubling as a knife — made to be attached to the muzzle of a shoulder arm and used in hand-to-hand combat.*

BAND SPRING: *The spring attached to barrel bands on a musket to hold them securely in place. To remove these bands, the band springs are depressed and the bands slip off.*

BAR ACTION: *The more common of the side locks; the mainspring of this lock is in front of the tumbler and hammer.*

BARREL: *The round, octagonal, et al., metal tube through and from which the ball, bullet or buckshot emerges upon being fired.*

BARREL KEY: *The wedge-shaped flat key that holds the barrel assembly to the forestock on many half-stock rifles and shotguns.*

BARREL PIN: *On most early full-stock rifles these were used to fasten the barrel to the long fore-stock.*

BELTED ROUND BALL: *A special design lead ball that was purposely cast with a raised belt of lead around its circumference. Belted round balls were mechanically started into the muzzles of deep two groove rifled bores found on many of the British rifles. The belted ring acted as a gas seal, at the same time being guided through the length of the barrel by the rifling groove on the bullet caused by the mechanical starter. The result was a bullet that was somewhat faster and more accurate than the standard patched ball.*

BENCH RIFLE: *A heavy muzzleloading target rifle especially designed and built for firing from a benchrest with the shooter seated.*

BLACK POWDER: *A mixture of potassium nitrate, charcoal and sulphur. Combined, these ingredients form the standard propellant for muzzleloading guns.*

BLUNDERBUSS: Arms of this type were used most commonly aboard ships to repel boarders during Naval conflicts. The blunderbuss featured a flared muzzle that probably was just as frightening to anyone unfortunate enough to view it from that angle as it was deadly. Although it is doubtful that such a flared muzzle did actually spread the shot any considerable amount over a gun with just a straight cylinder choke, it was nonetheless a deadly close range gun.

BOOT: A water resistant leather cover that fits over the flash pan of a flintlock rifle. The shield sheds rain and helps keep the priming powder in the pan dry during inclement weather.

BORE: The drilling or hole through which the bullet or load of shot travels the length of the barrel.

BORE BUILD-UP: Continuous firing of a black powder rifle, pistol or shotgun will result in a build-up of powder foulings in the barrel. For regular target practice, lining of sights or just plinking, this is cleaned out usually after a dozen or so shots with a few swipes with solvents and a jag threaded into the ramrod. Serious competitors, however, often wipe the barrels of their guns after every shot.

BOX LOCK: The hammer on this type of lock is fastened on the inside and projects above it.

BREECH: The rear end of a muzzleloader's barrel; the area immediately in front of the loaded round.

BREECH PLUG: The threaded plug that is screwed into the breech end of a muzzleloader's barrel. This forms a gas tight seal and is actually the rear or bottom of the chamber; the barrel tang usually is attached to the breech plug.

BREECH (CHAMBER) PRESSURE: As the loaded charge of powder is ignited and rapidly burns it results in trapped pressures as this pushes the projectile up the barrel. The pressure caused by these gases is known as the breech pressure and is measured in pounds per square inch — psi.

BROWN BESS: Smoothbore flintlock musket used by the British forces during the Revolutionary War. The long barrel and approximately .75 caliber made it fairly accurate and a hard-hitting military arm.

BROWNING: Predating bluing, browning is the result of an oxidation process. It is probably the result of some long ago gun owner unknowingly storing his gun in a damp or extremely humid spot and not remembering where it was until the bright metal had turned brownish red from rust. If treated properly, browning results in a beautiful barrel finish.

BUCKSHOT: Large spherical shot commonly used for big game hunting, combat and riot control. Shot ranging in sizes from .240 to .380 is occasionally used for loading muzzleloading rifles and pistols.

BUGGY RIFLE: Sometimes appearing in the form of a long barreled single shot pistol; many short barreled, lightweight rifles were commonly carried for protection, hunting small game and target shooting during the second half of the 1800s. These were known as buggy rifles and were usually of around .36 caliber, though there were many sawn off military rifled muskets of around .58 caliber used for this purpose also.

BULLET: It is a common practice to refer to an entire cartridge as the bullet. Actually the bullet is just the lead projectile that is fired from the assembled cartridge.

BULLET MOULD: Usually made from a soft iron, bullet moulds are

nothing more than two pieces of metal that have hollow cavities into which molten lead is poured; when sufficiently cooled and the lead hardened, a bullet is formed.

BUTT PLATE: The plate that is fitted to the rear of the butt stock and fits into the shoulder as the gun is being fired. These can be made of metal, bone, horn, plastic or just about anything that suits the gun owner's fancy.

CALIBER: Diameter of the bore of a firearm, most commonly expressed in thousandths of an inch, although some are in millimeters.

CANNELURE: A shallow groove that encircles the circumference of a conical bullet. This serves as a grease groove and affords both the bore and the bullet some lubrication.

CAP BOX: Usually appearing as a hinged compartment on the butt stock of a rifle or shotgun, the cap box is exactly as the name suggests: a place to carry caps. It may, however, be located in places other than the butt stock and in some pistols is in the butt of the grip. The term also was used to describe a small leather belt pouch used during the Civil War for carrying musket caps.

CAPLOCK: A term often used to describe a percussion lock.

CARBINE: A shortened rifle; although usually not as accurate as rifles with longer barrels, the carbine is easier to manuever when hunting or shooting in brushy areas.

CAST-ON: Shaping of a gunstock that aligns the barrel of a gun to the left of what is considered normal alignment. This aids in sighting and shooting for the southpaw. When the alignment is in the other direction — to the right — for aiding a right handed shooter, it is termed, "cast-off."

CHAMBER: Although not commonly found in muzzleloaders in the true sense, a chamber is the unrifled portion of a barrel that holds the loaded round.

CHARGER: A term used to describe anything — flask, horn, dipper, et al. — that measures out one exact charge of powder.

CHERRY: A steel burr that has cutting edges running its vertical circumference or length, of an exact size. These are used to cut the cavities of bullet moulds. An old practice was to clamp a cherry between two pieces of soft iron or any other suitable metal in a vise. The elongated shank connected to the cherry was turned in the direction of the cutting edges until they had cut away enough metal for the cherry to turn freely. The vise then was tightened further and the process repeated until a cavity the exact proportion of the cherry had been formed.

CHOKE: The varying constrictions of shotgun barrels that determine the type of pattern the gun will throw. The tighter the constriction, usually the tighter the pattern. Some muzzleloading rifles also feature a slight choking at or near the muzzle that improves the gun's accuracy.

COACH PISTOL: An inaccurate pistol of the 1700s that was carried for protection while traveling. These were nearly always smoothbores — accounting for the lack of accuracy — and small enough to be concealed easily.

COCK: A term once used to describe the hammer of the early locks, today it is used to describe the action of drawing back the hammer.

COMB: The raised line of the butt stock that runs to the rear of the wrist; the area of the stock that the cheek comes into contact with when a rifle or shotgun is being aimed and fired.

COMBUSTIBLE CARTRIDGE: *Muzzleloading cartridge that contains the powder and projectile rolled in a paper casing. This paper is nitrated and the entire unit is loaded into the gun, the paper being completely combustible.*

CONE: *An early term for a percussion nipple.*

CORNED POWDER: *An early attempt to form black powder into grains, powder of this type was crude and grain sizes were inconsistent.*

CORROSION: *The worst enemy of muzzleloading guns; the deterioration of metal parts through chemical reaction or oxidation.*

CULOT: *An expanding wedge made of iron that was originally used in the hollow base of the Minie bullet. This wedge was abandoned by American shooters.*

CURLY MAPLE: *Early gunsmiths favored this wood for stocking Kentucky and Pennsylvania rifles. The best wood comes from trees that have grown to maturity in hard and rocky soil; this results in a fine grained dense wood. The popularity of this wood is still seen in today's black powder rifles.*

C-SHAPED SERPENTINE: *An early matchlock, as the term implies, a lock of this type was fitted with a C-shaped cock, which ignited the primed flash pan by being struck rearward mechanically.*

CYLINDER: *The revolving multi-chambers of a percussion revolver; these commonly had six chambers, but those with five are not uncommon.*

CYLINDER BORE: *The unrestricted bore of a shotgun, having no choking at all; improved cylinder barrels have been choked slightly to improve patterns.*

DAMASCUS BARRELS: *Early barrels formed by welding together strips of various steels. These were wrapped and hammer forged around a mandrel that was the same diameter as the intended finished bore — in the case of smoothbore or shotgun barrels — or on the smaller side if the finished barrels were to be rifled.*

DAG: *An early English term used to describe any massive, heavy and powerful pistol. Its origin is unknown.*

DETENT: *A fly added to the tumbler when a set trigger is installed. This cams the sear nose to some extent during firing by missing the half-cock notch.*

DERRINGER: *A short barreled pocket pistol of a general type and not particularly a gun made by Henry Deringer. The word, however, is now used to describe the type of small handgun; born through public recognition of a Deringer-built pistol used in the assassination of President Lincoln; the second 'r' was added to differentiate the two.*

DISC PRIMER: *During the transitional period appeared a Sharps rifle that self-primed itself for each shot. The rifle's hammer action caused a tiny magazine to place a disc-like primer over the nipple for each shot.*

DOG LOCK: *The manually operated hammer catch on many early snaphaunce and crude flintlocks.*

DOGHEAD: *The spring loaded arm found on wheellocks to hold the pyrite against the rotating wheel.*

DOUBLE ACTION: *The process of cocking the hammer, rotating the cylinder and firing the round with one single movement of the trigger to the rear; a double action revolver also can be cocked and fired manually single action.*

DOUBLE-NECK HAMMER: *Reinforced hammers found on many later flintlock rifles, especially on military rifles that were built for hard use.*

DOUBLE RIFLE: *A popular side-by-side rifle that was used mainly for big game hunting in Africa and India.*

DRIVELL: *An early term for a ramrod.*

DUELLING PISTOL: *Usually a single-shot percussion or flintlock pistol of superb quality — Manton, Purdey, etc. Aristocrats, being as they were, often found it necessary to defend one's honor by placing a well aimed bullet into their oponent. Unfortunately the procedure was outlawed!*

ESCUTCHEON: *The metal inlay through which the barrel key is inserted. This is reinforced for obvious reasons.*

FALSE MUZZLE: *Used to improve accuracy by preventing possible damage to the bullet, this device is placed on the muzzle of the finer target rifles as the bullet is started into the muzzle; this helps prevent possible damage to the crown of the muzzle also.*

FENCE: *Also known as the flash guard, this small projection located on the rear of a flintlock's flash pan diverts the flash of the igniting priming powder from the shooter's eyes; today's flintlock fancier would be wise to wear a pair of good shooting glasses in case the sparks and flame happen to by-pass the diversion.*

FINIAL: *The decorative ending lines of an inlayed patch box, trigger guard strap or most any other pieces of furniture; these ornate touches are usually what make truely one-of-a-kind guns..*

FLASH: *As the hammer on a flintlock strikes the hardened frizzen it results in a minute portion of molten metal falling into the priming powder located in the flash pan. This ignites the powder and the result is an audible and visible flash that can cause the shooter to flinch.*

FLASH PAN: *Rifles and pistols that rely on the sparking of flint against steel for ignition have a small pan located below the frizzen or striking arm. A fine granulation of black powder — FFFFg — is placed in the pan; this serves as a primer for the main charge that is located in the chamber which is ignited by the flame that shoots down the flashhole leading from the flash pan.*

FLINTLOCK: *The principal arm used during the late Seventeenth and Eighteenth Centuries; the first appeared in France around the end of the first quarter of the Seventeenth Century. It was the principal lock until the introduction of the percussion lock.*

FORESIGHT: *English term meaning front sight.*

FORE-STOCK: *Also known as the forearm and forend, the wooden area of a one piece stock or the wooden section of a two piece stock that lies under the barrel.*

FORSYTH LOCK: *The first successful percussion lock, designed and built by Reverend Alexander Forsyth, an amateur chemist from Scotland. Forsyth obtained a patent for his invention in April, 1807, and the following year went into the commercial production of this lock — this actual manufacturing being supervised by his assistant, James Purdey.*

FOWLING PIECE: *This was an early term used to describe a gun that was intended for use with a load of shot instead of a single solid projectile. With the exception of the type of shot used, these were loaded practically the same as today's reproduction muzzleloading shotguns. Early shot had been small cubes chopped from a strip of lead, not the well formed spherical shape known today.*

FRENCH LOCK: *The earliest successful flintlock; this type of lock first appeared around Paris sometime about the end of the first quarter of the Seventeenth Century.*

FRIZZEN: *The hardened steel surface which the flint strikes to ignite the primed flashpan of a flintlock. Occasionally this may be referred to as the pan cover, steel, battery or by a similar term.*

FRIZZEN SPRING: *An external spring that controls the position of the frizzen, sometimes applying pressure on the frizzen to make better contact with the flint when the trigger is pulled.*

FULMINATE OF MERCURY: *An explosive priming charge used in the making of percussion caps. The discovery of fulminate of mercury — announced on March 13, 1800 — led to the invention of the percussion cap around 1820. Other detonating agents, such as fulminate of gold and silver, had been around since the 1600s, but had no practical use.*

FURNITURE: *The metal trim found on muzzleloaders, usually made of brass or German silver; this trim is usually decorative and adds to the overall appearance of the gun.*

FUSIL: *A late 1600 military flintlock; this gun resembled a kind of French woodcock gun and is the reason why the English cavaliers referred to them as fusils or fusees — a French term meaning any non-military sporting gun.*

GAIN TWIST: *Rifling of a bore that increases in the number of turns as it progresses toward the muzzle.*

GAUGE: *The size of a shotgun bore. This is determined by the number of spherical lead balls of the bore's diameter it takes to weigh exactly one pound. For example; a 20-gauge cylinder bore would weigh out twenty lead balls to the pound; the same with 16 gauge and 12 gauge, the number of lead balls to the pound equalling the bore size. This term also is used to describe various types of measuring devices.*

GERMAN RING TARGET: *A popular match ring target of the mid to late 1800s. This type of paper target was used extensively during the formal shooting matches of the Schuetzen era of the 1880s.*

GERMAN SILVER: *Another name used to describe nickel silver. An alloy of copper, zinc and nickel, its silver white appearance makes it ideal for furniture on muzzleloaders.*

GLOBE SIGHT: *A fine front sight blade with an extremely small bead. This delicate sight is almost always shaded in a cylindrical tube.*

GOOSE-NECK HAMMER: *The type of hammer found on many beautiful early flint and percussion sporting arms. Unlike the thick and heavy hammers found on military arms, these hammers were slender in proportion and graceful in design.*

GROOVES: *The spiral channels cut in the rifling of a bore, the raised portions are known as the lands or flats. The lands and grooves of a rifle's bore make the bullet rotate during flight and are instrumental in a gun's accuracy.*

GROUP: *The consistent placement of bullets into any distinguish-able area on the target, not necessarily the point of aim. These are desirably in close proximity of one another and hopefully measure in diameter under that magic minute of angle mark. If the shots are placed tightly in one area, the sights can be adjusted to place them at the point of aim.*

GUNFLINT: *High quality flint shaped with a forward chisel edge, used for firing a flintlock.*

HAIR TRIGGER: *The extremely light trigger pull of the front trigger on a set trigger mechanism. These usually are adjustable and many can be adjusted to the point that they will release at the slightest amount of pressure.*

HALF-COCK: *A safety position of the hammer on rifles and pistols; the half-cock position of revolvers allow the cylinder to be freely rotated for easier loading.*

HALF-STOCK RIFLE: *A term occasionally used to depict the mountain and plains rifles used by early westward traveling settlers or adventurers. These were built to withstand rugged use and the graceful lines of the Pennsylvania and Kentucky long rifles weren't usually found on these guns; this was also the gun of the famed mountain man.*

HAMMER: *The arm that strikes the detonating device on percussion and cartridge guns or the arm that contains the flint on flintlock guns. This part was known as the cock on earlier wheellock guns.*

HAMMER SPUR: *The contoured protrusion found on the hammer of cartridge and percussion guns; on flintlocks, this appeared in the form of a part of the jaw that held the flint.*

HAND: *The part of a revolver's working mechanism that protrudes through the rear inside of the frame and turns the cylinder as the hammer is cocked or the trigger pulled on double action revolvers.*

HAND CANNON: *The earliest form of a small arm; first used during the mid-1400s, although its origin is unknown and the exact date it was first introduced remains a mystery to historians. Nearly every force in Europe was using one form or another of this type of armament by the turn of the Sixteenth Century. Resembling a metal tube, the cannoneer ignited the loaded round by placing a touch to the exposed flashhole, which was extremely hard on the finger tips!*

HANDGUN: *Originally this term was used to describe all guns that were held by hand, later to depict only pistols and revolvers.*

HANG-FIRE: *A dangerous situation, a hang-fire actually is what appears to be a misfire but discharges after a short delay. Perhaps more common with flintlocks than percussion locks, it's good practice to keep the muzzle pointed downrange should an apparent misfire occur. Never place your face near the muzzle in case of such a situation, the delayed ignition could cause serious injury to you or anyone else unlucky enough to be in front of the muzzle.*

HEEL: *The rear top corner of the buttstock, the portion of the stock that is in conjunction with the top of the butt plate.*

HORSE PISTOL: *An early pistol used by horsemen; the large and chiefly military pistol was most often carried in a pommel holster.*

IGNITION: *The method used to fire the main charge in the breech; a number of different means have been used or tried in the past, among which are the slow match, wheellock pyrites, flintlock, percussion cap.*

INCISE: *To cut the surface of a stock to a certain depth in preparation to relief carving, inlaying, et al.*

INLAYS: *The decorative touches added to the stock of many rifles, these may either be of different woods, metal, ivory or just about anything the stock makers chooses to use. These are finished flush with the surface of the stock; such inlays are the little extras that make a gun one-of-a-kind.*

INLETTING: *The precise removal of wood from the stock in preparation for the fitting of a lock, barrel or other parts that come into contact with the wood's surface and demand some removal.*

JAG: *An accessory that fits into the end of the ramrod to aid in cleaning the barrel; this is usually in the form of a buttonlike device that has serrated edges to grip the cleaning patch.*

KENTUCKY RIFLE: *A term mistakenly used in reference to the numerous long rifles, many of which were manufactured in other armsmaking states, such as Pennsylvania or North Carolina. Such rifles are traditionally long flintlocks that saw much use in the settling of what is now the state of Kentucky, in which armsmaking never reached the level as that found in several other states.*

KNAPPER: *A professional craftsman who chips out gunflints. This work is nearly all done with the aid of handtools, with perhaps the only mechanized help occuring during the mining of the flint. Today the only remaining professional knappers operate in the village of Brandon, England.*

LAP: *The process of smoothing out rough areas of a bore. This is most commonly done with the use of a lead bit or mandrel and various abrasive materials, such as diamond paste.*

LINEN: *This cloth material, woven from flax fibers, is one of the best patching materials.*

LOADING BLOCK: *A wooden block that has been drilled with holes for carrying pre-patched balls. To use, the hole in the block is aligned with the muzzle and with the use of a short starter the ball is seated into the muzzle. When carried hunting, a loading block saves a lot of time when loading succeeding shots and makes packing the round balls less tedious when it comes time to dig one out for loading.*

LOADING LEVER: *The lever that is attached underneath the barrel on the majority of the cap and ball revolvers, used to seat the balls over the charge of powder in the chambers.*

LOCK PLATE: *The metal base for the mechanism of a conventional muzzleloader's lock; all screws, pins, etc., are usually mounted to this.*

LOCK SCREW: *The screw that runs laterally through the stock to hold the lock in place.*

LONG RIFLE: *Acutally the only true term that should be used to describe the type of rifle most common to this country during the period from the mid 1700s to the end of the second quarter of the Eighteenth Century. Many people erroneously refer to this type of rifle as a Kentucky Rifle, even though that same type could have been produced in Pennsylvania or North Carolina.*

MAGAZINE CAPPER: *A device used to dispense percussion caps directly onto the nipple. These are commonly spring-loaded and hold a quantity of percussion caps; the spring keeps the cap in line for jam free feeding. To use, the percussion cap that is extending or appearing in the exit hole of the capper is placed over the nipple and a slight tug frees it from the capper. Such devices are most commonly used for loading cap and ball revolvers, eliminates fumbling for caps in pockets or removing them from the tin.*

MAINSPRING: *A heavy spring that controls the fall of the hammer.*

Early springs were commonly of the flat leaf type, later and improved springs appeared in the form of a V, some of today's modern black powder rifles utilize even superior coil springs.

MATCHCORD: *Another term for the burning match of early matchlock guns.*

MATCHLOCK: *The earliest form of mechanical lock; first matchlocks required shooter to lever match into touchhole, later versions mechanically struck match into primed flash pan.*

METALLIC SIGHTS: *Any open, hooded or tube sight that does not rely on the magnification of the target through the use of precision-ground glass lenses.*

MINIE BALL OR BULLET: *Developed into its present state by Captain C. E. Minie of France in 1848, the Minie is an aerodynamically stable cylindrical ogive bullet with a hollow base. This bullet is easily seated in the dirtiest of bores, usually requiring very little effort. When fired, the expanding gases of the rapidly burning powder in turn expands the hollow base of the Minie into the rifling. Immortalized as the "minny ball" during the Civil War, the Minie-designed bullet made quick reloading in battle possible.*

MISFIRE: *A state when the round loaded in the chamber fails to fire as the primer — powder in flash pan or percussion cap on the nipple — ignites. It is also possible to have a misfire as a direct cause of the primer not igniting.*

MRT: *Mid Range Trajectory; the curved flight of a bullet as measured halfway between the muzzle and the target or game.*

MIQUELET: *Forerunner of the true flintlock, this type of lock followed the Dutch snaphaunce lock. The main improvement over the miquelet and the snaphaunce was that it featured a frizzen and pan cover that was combined into a single part; mainspring on this type of lock was located on the outside of the lock plate.*

MULE EAR LOCK: *Percussion lock that features a flat side hammer that pivots horizontally.*

MUSKET: *The long full stocked shoulder guns used by early military force. These were commonly smoothbore, those that featured rifled bores are referred to as rifled muskets. The soldier that carried one of these as his principle means of armament was known as a musketeer. A shortened carbine version of this type of arm is a musketoon.*

MUZZLE: *The end of the barrel opposite the breech; the point where the bullet, shot load, projectile leaves the barrel.*

MUZZLE ENERGY: *The amount of force exerted by the projectile as it leaves the muzzle; this is expressed in foot/pounds.*

MUZZLELOADER: *Gun loaded through the muzzle with an enclosed breech. To load, the powder is dropped in first, followed by the projectile, shot or ball, the lock is then primed and the gun is ready to fire. Commonly used to describe nearly all black powder guns that rely on percussion or flint ignition, although cap and ball revolvers aren't actually loaded through the muzzle.*

MUZZLE VELOCITY: *Speed of the projectile as it leaves the muzzle; usually measured in feet per second.*

NIPPLE: *On muzzleloading percussion guns, the small metal cone that the percussion cap is fitted to; flame from exploding cap is passed through hollow cavity of the nipple to the main charge of powder loaded in the chamber.*

NIPPLE WRENCH: *A tool used for replacing or removing nipple* from percussion type guns. Nipples come in a variety of sizes and so do nipple wrenches.

OCTAGONAL BARREL: *An eight sided barrel commonly found on many of the early muzzleloading rifles and a number of pistols and revolvers; once just as common as the round barrel.*

OGIVE: *The radius of the curve of a bullet nose, commonly expressed in calibers.*

OPEN SIGHTS: *Metallic sights that usually appear in the form of adjustable or fixed V-notch rear and fixed blade front sight.*

PATCH BOX: *An inlaid lidded box that is found on some of the muzzleloading rifles, although an assortment of accessories now find their way into these, they were originally intended for carrying greased patches or tallow for lubricating patching material.*

PATCH CUTTER: *A circular cutter used for pre-cutting patches; this is placed with the cutting edge down on a piece of suitable material and rapped with a mallet, resulting in a perfectly circular patch. Often confused with a patch knife, which is a bladed instrument used to trim excess patch material from around the ball as it is being seated into the muzzle.*

PATCHING: *Cloth used to form a gas tight seal around the round ball loaded into a muzzleloading rifle or single-shot pistol; this also improves accuracy by engaging the rifling and causing the ball to rotate better as it leaves the muzzle and while in flight.*

PATINA: *As a gun ages the stock takes on a mellow yellowish tint, this is patina. Too often the nimrod gun enthusiast tries feverishly to remove this and give the gun that new look; as with fine furniture, this is a mistake.*

PATTERN: *The spread of the pellets from a shotgun's barrel. The choke of a gun is best established by the percentage of pellets placed inside a thirty inch circle from a distance of forty yards.*

PEPPERBOX: *A small repeating pistol of the mid 1800s, so named since its usual multi-barrel appearance resembles a pepper shaker, or pepperbox.*

PERCUSSION CAP: *Small metallic cup containing a minute charge of fulminate of mercury; when placed on a nipple, the striking of the hammer causes the fulminating charge to explode which in turn ignites the powder in the chamber or breech.*

PICKET BULLET: *An early conical bullet used in this country; the base of this bullet was the only area that was of bore size, tapering toward the nose, care had to be taken in loading to ensure that bullet was seated straight. Such loading problems are the reason that the bullet never became as popular as the Minie.*

PILL LOCK: *An early type of percussion lock; a small globule of fulminate was used in place of the percussion cap — which wasn't around when this lock first came out.*

PIN-FIRE: *An early cartridge; casing had small hole near the head of the brass, a percussion-type cap was inserted into this, followed by a small pin. The cartridge was loaded into the chamber, the pin and chamber walls holding the cap in place. The hammer struck the pin which ignited the percussion cap when fired.*

PISTOL: *A small, usually concealable and short-barreled handgun, generally not a term used to describe a revolver. Some sources claim that the term originated from the Italian gunmaking center of Pistoia, others claim the word was derived from a short Bohemian handgun known as the pist'ala; actually its origin remains unknown.*

POCKET PISTOL: *A general term used to depict nearly any small pistol or revolver that can be easily concealed. Certain short barreled pistols that are actually pocket pistols became known as derringers after the assassination of President Lincoln with a Henry Deringer-made pocket pistol.*

POWDER FLASK: *Carrying container for powder, commonly made of metal having characteristics of copper and brass, but occasionally made from stag horn or like materials. Powder flasks usually have some type of charger mounted on top.*

POWDER MEASURE: *A graduated measuring device that can be adjusted to measure out different grain loads, the weights of which are usually shown on scale form.*

POWDER TESTER: *Also known as an eprouvett. A device for measuring the comparative strength of powders. The ignition of the powder registers on some sort of needle or gauge — there were various types — and depending on the strength of powder being tested, the needle or whatever was used to measure the burning force would register. As a rule such devices weren't very reliable.*

PRICKER OR VENT PICK: *A piece of fine wire used to clear the vent of a nipple or flashhole, on a flintlock, of foulings or obstructions.*

PYRITES: *Commonly known as fool's gold, this material actually is iron pyrite; when struck against a hardened steel surface it results in sparks. Early wheellocks and later early versions of the flintlock relied upon this principle for ignition.*

QUEEN ANNE PISTOL: *A screw barrel breechloading style flintlock pistol commonly found in England during the early 1700s; pistols of this design lacked forends.*

RAMROD: *Usually made of wood, although brass and steel ones aren't uncommon. A rod that is used to seat the ball over the powder charge in muzzleloading rifles. Ramrods are commonly carried under the barrel, held by ramrod pipes or thimbles.*

REVOLVER: *A multi-shot handgun, using a revolving cylinder to align the chambers with the barrel.*

REVOLVING RIFLE: *The perfection of the cap and ball revolvers and the noticeable need for a repeating rifle resulted in a combination of the two, a revolving rifle. This gun sported nearly the same mechanism as the revolver, but had a longer barrel and rifle-like butt stock. Remington and Colt were the chief producers of these during the mid 1800s.*

RIFLED MUSKET: *Occasionally a thin barreled musket was produced that featured a rifled bore. Erroneously these sometimes are referred to as rifles when actually they are rifled muskets; rifles have much thicker barrel walls.*

SALTPETER: *Potassium nitrate, used in the production of black powder.*

SCHNABEL: *Often misspelled and commonly referred to as a nose cap; the metal cap found on the front of most muzzleloading rifle forearms, especially on guns featuring a full stock.*

SCREW BARREL PISTOL: *A breechloading black powder pistol that required the barrel to be unthreaded from its specially designed breech plug in order for it to be loaded. Pistols of this design were most common during the first half of the Eighteenth Century.*

SEAR: *The lock part — usually in the form of a notch — that is* engaged by the tumbler and hammer until it is released by exerting pressure on the trigger.

SELF-COCKING REVOLVER: *A forerunner to the first true double action revolvers; this type of revolver was developed by London gunmaker Robert Adams during the early 1850s. Unlike the true double action, it had no provision for manually cocking the hammer back, but instead relied upon trigger action to work the hammer and rotate the cylinder.*

SERPENTINE POWDER: *The crude first black powders, since corning powder into grains was discovered later, this first powder appeared in the form of meal.*

SET TRIGGER: *A double trigger mechanism in which the rear trigger is first pulled to set up the front trigger so that it can be released with a very slight amount of pressure. This type of trigger usually is found on target rifles and occasionally on the finer hunting rifles.*

SHOT: *Small spherical balls commonly used in a shotgun load; these range in size from .33 inch diameter — 00 buck — to .04 inch diameter — dust shot. Occasionally the larger shot may be used to load smaller bore rifles and pistols, but in general use shot is loaded in given quantities — the smaller the shot, the increase in the number of projectiles — in shotguns.*

SHOT POUCH: *A container, most often made of leather, used for carrying shot.*

SHORT STARTER: *A short, five to six-inch rod fitted with a round or flat palm fitting handle used for starting patched balls down the muzzle of rifles and some pistols.*

SKIN CARTRIDGE: *An advanced combustible cartridge; propellant is encased in nitrated animal intestine. This cartridge was introduced by Captain John Hayes in 1856.*

SLUG GUN: *Term used to denote an extremely heavy barreled match gun; slug gun shooters may spend as much as ten to fifteen minutes to load their guns, meticulously checking and rechecking every loading step.*

SNAPHAUNCE: *Early forerunner to the flintlock; frizzen and flash pan cover were two separate parts.*

SPANNER: *Key or wrench like device used to cock or span a wheellock.*

SPERM OIL: *The oil extracted from the flesh of the sperm whale. Among its many uses it once was a favorite gun lube.*

STEEL: *The hardened surface of the frizzen that causes spark when struck by the flint on a flintlock; on some early locks it was a strip of hardened metal that was attached to the pan cover to cause the spark for igniting the primed flash pan.*

STRAIGHT BARREL: *A barrel on which the outside diameter remains the same its entire length; barrels that gradually decreased in outside diameter to the muzzle are known as tapered barrels; barrels that taper toward the middle then return to the original diameter at the muzzle are known as tapered and flared barrels.*

SUPERIMPOSED ROUNDS: *Among the first repeating smallarms appeared ingeneously designed guns that featured two or more locks located at intervals along the rear area of the barrel. These then were loaded one round on top of another, the powder charge of each shot coinciding with the lock that was to fire that round, the lead ball*

sealing the flame of the first round from igniting the one directly behind it — hopefully. Care surely had to be taken not to fire the last round first! Such guns appeared as early as the Sixteenth Century.

SWAGING: *The precision sizing of a conical bullet to bring it to an exact size; done with the aid of precision tools.*

TANG: *Most often an extension from the breech plug, the tang is the retainer for the long screw that runs vertically through the stock, holding the breech portion of the barrel securely in place. The screw that holds this in place is known as the tang screw, which commonly fastens to the trigger assembly and helps hold it in place also.*

TANG SIGHT: *A rear sight aperture that attaches to the barrel tang; commonly a folding type that allows the usage of regular open sights.*

TAPE PRIMER: *A strip or roll of paper tape that has small charges of fulminating powders attached to it; designed for use with specially modified rifles during the Civil War.*

TENON: *The metal loop or flat piece of metal that extends from the bottom of the barrel which engages the barrel key or pin that holds the barrel to the stock.*

THIMBLE: *The metal ferrules located along the ramrod channel or under the barrel for storing and carrying the ramrod.*

TOE: *The rear bottom point of the butt stock; the area of the stock located at the bottom of the butt plate. Occasionally a rifle will have a metal plate running along the bottom of the butt stock. This is the toe plate; most commonly found on Kentucky type-rifles.*

TOMPION: *Plug used to prevent dust and moisture from getting into a muzzleloader's barrel during storage.*

TOP JAW: *The upper area of a flintlock's hammer that holds the flint; the screw that forms the vise that holds the flint is the top jaw screw.*

TOW: *Unspun flax, an early patching material for shotguns and often used as cleaning patches for rifles; coarse fibers made it undesirable for patching round balls in rifles or pistols.*

TOWER LOCK: *The type of flintlock found on the Brown Bess; locks are usually stamped with a crown and the initials GR on the area of the lock plate that is located in front of the hammer and the date of manufacture and the word Tower to the rear of it. Locks of this type were being installed first on Brown Bess muskets at the turn of the Eighteenth Century; occasionally a lock of this type is found on various muskets and fowling pieces.*

TOUCHHOLE: *The vent hole leading from the pan of a flintlock to the powder charge in the chamber; originally used to describe the vent hole on hand cannons which required the cannoneer to ignite the round by placing or touching a burning stick, hot coal, etc. to this vent.*

TUBE LOCK: *An early percussion type lock; to fire, a small copper tube five-eighths inch in length and a sixteenth inch in diameter — filled with percussion powder — was inserted into the vent hole. All but about an eighth of the tube went into the hole, the remainder rested on a small anvil shaped piece of metal. The hammer striking this would ignite the powder inside the tube, which in turn ignited the charge in the chamber.*

TUMBLER: *The central piece of a conventional lock that turns with the hammer; contains the half-cock and full-cock notches as well as the detent if the lock has one.*

UNDER HAMMER STRIKER: *A percussion type lock that features the hammer underneath; as on some of the modern made under hammer muzzleloaders, the trigger guard doubles as the spring to power the striking of the hammer.*

UNDER RIB: *The metal rib running beneath the barrel on a half stock rifle; supports the thimbles for the ramrod.*

VENT: *The small hole on muzzleloaders through which the priming flame reaches and ignites the main charge.*

VERNIER SIGHT: *A precision rear aperture commonly found on target rifles of the 1800s.*

V-SPRING: *Flat V-shaped spring used in locks; stronger and more durable than the flat single leaf spring.*

WAD CUTTER: *Nearly identical to a patch cutter, a small handtool featuring a circular cutting edge. By placing this edge onto wadding material and hitting the handle with a mallet, a perfect circular wad is punched out. This tool also can be used to cut patches for small rifles.*

WHEELLOCK: *The lock that made the first pistols practical; ignition relies upon the sparks created by the iron pyrites held in the cock coming into contact with the serrated edge of a rotating wheel. The first wheellocks were introduced during the first quarter of the Sixteenth Century.*

WINDAGE: *A term used to describe any lateral adjustment made to the rear sight.*

WIPING ROD: *A separate rod used to wipe the bore clean of powder fouling between shots.*

WORM: *A corkscrew type device used to remove a cleaning patch stuck in the bore of a muzzleloading rifle or removal of a shotgun wad; screws into the threaded tip of a cleaning rod.*

WRIST: *The small of the stock; the portion of the stock that forms the grip.*

"....let your gun be your constant companion on your walks...
this gives exercise to the body and independence to the mind...
no free man shall ever be debarred the use of arms...."

Thomas Jefferson